Azores

the Bradt Travel Guide

David Sayers

edition
3

www.bradtguides.com

Bradt Travel Guides Ltd, UK
The Globe Pequot Press Inc, USA

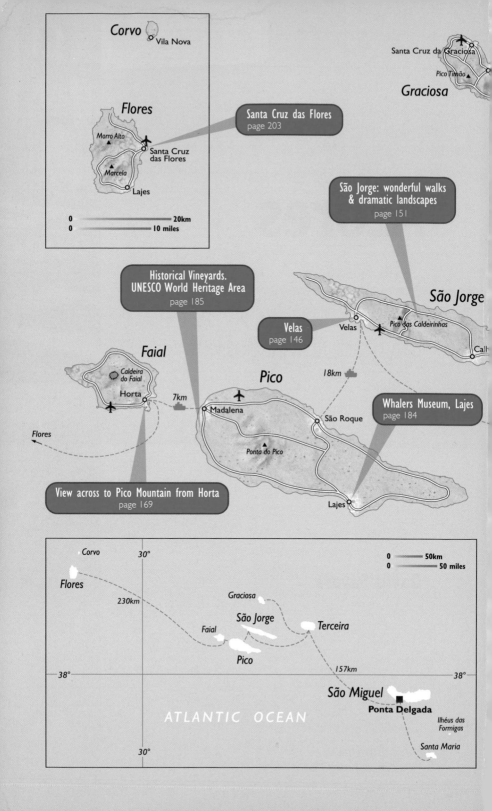

Corvo

Vila Nova

Flores

Morro Alto

Marcela

Santa Cruz
das Flores

Lajes

0 ——————— 20km
0 ——————— 10 miles

Santa Cruz da Graciosa

Pico Timão

Graciosa

Santa Cruz das Flores
page 203

São Jorge: wonderful walks
& dramatic landscapes
page 151

Historical Vineyards.
UNESCO World Heritage Area
page 185

Velas
page 146

Velas

São Jorge

Pico das Caldeirinhas

Call

Faial

Caldeira
do Faial

Horta

Pico

18km

Flores

7km

Madalena

São Roque

Whalers Museum, Lajes
page 184

Ponta do Pico

Lajes

View across to Pico Mountain from Horta
page 169

Corvo

30°

Flores

230km

Graciosa

São Jorge

Terceira

0 ——————— 50km
0 ——————— 50 miles

Faial

Pico

38°

157km

38°

São Miguel

Ponta Delgada

Ilhéus das
Formigas

ATLANTIC OCEAN

Santa Maria

30°

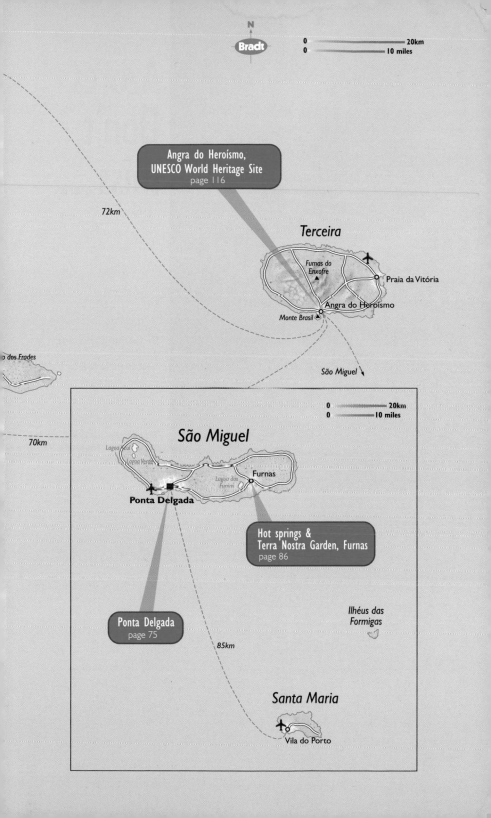

N

Bradt

0 ————————— 20km
0 ————————— 10 miles

**Angra do Heroísmo,
UNESCO World Heritage Site**
page 116

72km

Terceira

*Fumas do
Enxofre*

Praia da Vitória

Angra do Heroísmo

Monte Brasil

o dos Frades

São Miguel

70km

Lagoa Azul
Lagoa Verde

São Miguel

*Lagoa das
Furnas*

Furnas

Ponta Delgada

0 ————————— 20km
0 ————————— 10 miles

**Hot springs &
Terra Nostra Garden, Furnas**
page 86

*Ilhéus das
Formigas*

Ponta Delgada
page 75

85km

Santa Maria

Vila do Porto

Azores
Don't
miss...

Beautiful parks and gardens
Terra Nostra Garden, São Miguel
(DS) page 68

The ever-changing view from Faial towards Pico Mountain
(LS) page 177

Walks and dramatic landscapes
Capelinhos, Faial
(MB) page 174

Whale and dolphin watching
Sperm whale
Physeter macrocephalus
(LS) page 53

Flora
Cannas
Canna x generalis
Porto Formosa, São Miguel
(DS) page 10

top   **Traditional village life, near Lajes, southeast Pico** (MB)

centre **Village near Horta, eastern Faial** (MB)

left   **Harvesting grapes below Lagoa das Furnas, São Miguel** (RC)

top **Vila Franca do Campo, São Miguel** (TB) page 87

right **Ox cart, Santa Maria** (DS)

top South African candelabra aloe, *Aloe arborescens*, Faial (DS) page 238

above left Thyme, *Thymus caespititius*, and heath, *Daboecia azorica*, endemic wildflowers on the higher slopes of Pico (DS) pages 235 and 232

above right The endemic *Azorina vidalii*, Corvo (DS) page 234

below Roadside flowers near Povoação, São Miguel (DS)

top left **New Zealand Christmas tree or pohutukawa** *Metrosideros excelsa* (DS) page 238

top right **Cannas,** *Canna x generalis,* **and waterfalls of Fajãziinha, west coast of Flores** (RC)

centre **Tropical rhododendron, Terra Nostra Garden, Furnas, São Miguel** (DS)

below left **Banksia** *Banksia integrifolia* (DS)

below right **Pineapple in flower, São Miguel** (DS) page 81

top **Pilot whale**
Globicephala macrorhynchus
(LS) page 14

centre **Common dolphin**
Delphinus delphis
(LS) page 14

left **Canoa racing, Faial**
(LS) page 186

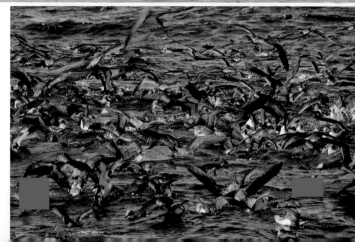

top   **Spotted dolphin**
    Stenella frontalis
    (LS) page 14

centre   **Bottle-nosed dolphin**
    Tursiops truncates
    (LS) page 14

right   **Shearwaters**
    Calonectris diomedea
    (LS) page 12

above **Sete Cidades, seen from Vista do Rei, São Miguel** (MB) page 89

left **Volcanic landscape, São Jorge** (MB)

top Caldeirinhas to Norte Grande, São Jorge (walk 4) (MB) page 154

centre Looking towards Ribeira Grande, Flores (RC)

right Volcanically active hot springs, near Lagoa das Furnas, São Miguel (RC) page 86

top left   **Town Hall, Ponta Delgada, São Miguel** (DS) page 78

top right   **Roofs in Corvo's only settlement, Vila Nova do Corvo** (DS) page 221

below   **Church of Nossa Senhora da Puricação, Santo Espírito, Santa Maria** (DS) page 104

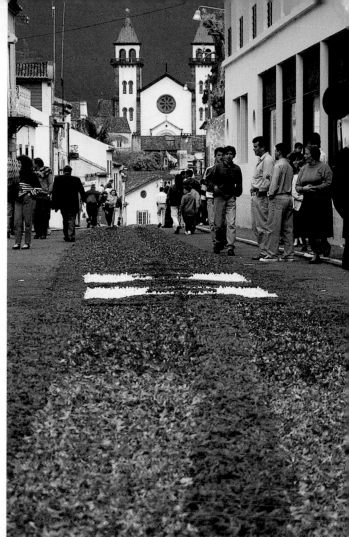

above **São Lourenço Bay, Santa Maria** (DS) page 104

below **Fishing boats, Biscoitis, Terceira** (DS) page 123

Author/Illustrator

After qualifying as a botanical horticulturist from the Royal Botanic Garden, Kew, **David Sayers** spent three years studying plants and habitats in Asia and Australasia then joined Durham University to develop their new botanic garden based on plant geography. A degree in social sciences with the newly founded Open University and then business school led to a second career in social policy and corporate planning. Annual holidays were spent leading adventure/botanical holidays for Thomas Cook and other companies and then for 24 years he ran David Sayers Travel, arranging botanical travel worldwide. Offering the Azores in 1984, he led the first ever tour group to climb Pico and to visit São Jorge, Flores and Corvo. The Azores are always a favourite destination and David Sayers now arranges custom-made holidays there through Andrew Brock Travel (✆ *01572 821330*).

ILLUSTRATOR

Hedvika Fraser comes from Prague and has lived in Britain for the past 30 years. A physicist by training, she now works as a technical translator in five languages. A childhood fascination with orchids led to painting them in watercolour, and the charm of the Azores led her to the line drawings illustrating this guide.

DEDICATION

To the workmen who painstakingly maintain and replant the roadside verges, hedgerows and viewpoints and thus make the islands so attractive and floriferous.

Reprinted August 2007, August 2008, July 2009
Third edition October 2006 First published 2001

Bradt Travel Guides Ltd
23 High Street, Chalfont St Peter, Bucks SL9 9QE, England; www.bradtguides.com
Published in the USA by The Globe Pequot Press Inc, 246 Goose Lane,
PO Box 480, Guilford, Connecticut 06475-0480

A catalogue record for this book is available from the British Library
ISBN-10: 1 84162 156 0   ISBN-13: 978 1 84162 156 2

Photographs *Text* Malorie Martine-Remy Bader (MB), Tony Botelho (TB), Ruth Croome (RC), David Sayers (DS), Lisa Steiner/Whale Watch Azores (LS)
Front cover Pico Volcano seen from Ponta de Espalamaca, Faial (Günter Gräfenhain/Fototeca 9x12)
Title page Town Hall, Ponta Delgada (DS), Festa Sr dos Enfermos, Furnas (DS), Village near Horta (MB)
Back cover Sperm whale, *Physeter macrocephalus* (LS)

Illustrations Hedvika Fraser
Maps Alan Whitaker

Typeset from the author's disc by Wakewing
Printed and bound in Italy by Legoprint SpA, Trento

Acknowledgements

First and foremost my thanks go to Albano Cymbron of the Melo Travel Agency who originally introduced me to his Atlantic sanctuary and with whom many days were spent pioneering trails to provide the first walking holidays in the islands; without this good friend the Azores would have remained just another happy travel memory. Time passes, and it is with huge pleasure that I find myself indebted to his daughter, Catarina Cymbron, who now runs the agency and unstintingly comes to my aid at vital moments.

For original contributions to this guide and for their time and interest I am hugely indebted to: Isabel Soares de Albergaria from São Miguel who wrote the pages on art and architecture and thus revealed some of the treasures that might otherwise have remained hidden, to António Pedroso from São Jorge for providing many cultural anecdotes, and Monique Cymbron from São Miguel for her Azorean kitchen.

Vital practical support came from the Azores airline SATA and the Azores Regional Directorate of Tourism in Horta for whose assistance I am most grateful.

Anyone visiting the islands for however short a time will inevitably have acknowledgements to the Azoreans for their kindness. My list is long and those not mentioned I hope will forgive me, but I would like especially to record my thanks for the continuing help and prompt replies to my emails from Sandra Dart of the Regional Tourism Office in Faial, and Mario Rego and Eva Goulart respectively of the tourism offices on Terceira and Pico. John and Jane Cockshott of www.diving-azores.com on São Miguel provided much stimulating discussion on matters marine, although they failed to persuade a convinced landlubber to take a try-dive, and to Carlos Paulus for further input. For numerous comments on the text in general, I am most grateful to Chris Beer. It was a joy to experience Luis Silva's enthusiasm and commitment to developing and managing walking trails in conjunction with the Povoação Municipality on São Miguel and a privilege to hear from him some of the fascinating local social/environmental history he is recording before it is shortly lost forever from memory. Pierluigi Bragaglia's love of his adopted island of Flores shows with his every email and his knowledge of all the Atlantic Islands curbs unwise assumptions. As many visitors discover, a good taxi driver soon becomes a friend and mentor for their Azorean stay and I am especially indebted to the continued guidance of José de Fontes Sousa on Santa Maria and Eldar Espinola on Graciosa.

Beyond the Azores, I am most grateful to Peter Alfrey from the UK for his remarkable accounts of autumn birdwatching in the western isles, and to the many readers of earlier editions of this guide who have so generously taken the trouble to write in with feedback. Finally, and most importantly, my thanks go to my wife Hedvika Fraser for her considerable general support and for her copious illustrations.

Contents

FEEDBACK REQUEST

Although much has remained the same for many years, within this sameness changes do occur and often only come to light from first-hand experience. The Azoreans' natural modesty and the blessed lack of 'spin' often means interesting developments for the visitor go unannounced. It is easy never to know about them, especially such things as youth hostels or campsites. The condition of footpaths is another and very important topic that is difficult to monitor.

If, upon your return home from the islands, you can find time to send a postcard or longer note with any updates or corrections to the information I have provided, it would be greatly appreciated and very helpful for the next edition. Government officers and elected members responsible for tourism are also pleased to have your feedback and I should be delighted to be able to send them a composite report based on your comments. In this way we might all contribute to what I hope will be an acceptable way forward for tourism in the Azores.

Happy travelling!
David Sayers

Bradt Travel Guides Ltd
23 High Street, Chalfont St Peter, Bucks SL9 9QE, England
☎ 01753 893444; f 01753 892333; e info@bradtguides.com
www.bradtguides.com

Introduction

It is perhaps strange to think there is a cluster of nine small islands, isolated but thriving, lying between Lisbon and New York and surrounded by the great Atlantic Ocean.

Very much part of Europe and members of the European Community, they have many of the accoutrements of modern life: the latest fashion trainers, cars, second homes, and the very latest communications technology connecting home computers with the internet.

Yet few people are aware of their existence and many of those who are hold an image of dry, sun-baked volcanic islands like Lanzarote in the Canaries. And they almost always assume they belong to Spain.

The Azores are Europe's best-kept secret: verdant, tranquil, diverse, exquisitely beautiful, always welcoming. Further south and close to the African coast lies Madeira, Portugal's more familiar Atlantic island; sunnier and with less rain and cloud but considerably more developed for tourism, and famous for its well-promoted flowers and gardens. It was going to Madeira that aroused my curiosity about those other far-off islands; a flight from Funchal took me to Ponta Delgada, and back to an ambience that possibly could have been found in Madeira half a century ago. One needs to take the Azores at their own speed. Fight it, and you will be frustrated; relax along with it and you will return a different person. Old World courtesy prevails, a reminder of the many tiny niceties of life that have been sacrificed to the exigencies of faster lifestyles.

Since they were first settled in the 15th century, each island has developed at a different speed, depending upon the quality of its harbour, terrain, crops, and its distance from the others. Today this is reflected in their diversity, each island offering the visitor its own individual character that makes the Azores such a varied entity.

All the islands are green, the flowers are mostly sophisticated and subtle, the gardens are steeped in history and, like the flowers, are more cerebral than flamboyant. While some main towns have their roads and traffic, just a short distance away men ride horses to their pastures and pony carts filled with milk churns clatter over cobbles. Flashing neon lights are rare, streets are narrow, shops modest and in keeping with the streetscape, coffee bars are numerous while nightclubs are few. The islands reflect their turbulent geological past and offer rural landscapes enhanced by rocky or precipitous coasts surrounded by an often travel-brochure-blue sea. Religious and secular festivals riot through the calendar and touch the lives of every island and islander. There are sailing regattas, golf tournaments, big-game fishing tournaments, cycle races, car rallies and other events that come as rather a surprise and largely leave the non-enthusiasts in happy oblivion. There is so much to explore, so much to experience; these islands should be savoured like a rare wine.

Part One

GENERAL INFORMATION

Islands São Miguel, Santa Maria, Terceira, Graciosa, São Jorge, Faial, Pico, Flores, Corvo

Location In the Atlantic Ocean, approximately 1,500km from Lisbon and 3,900km from the east coast of North America

Size Nine islands varying from $17km^2$ (Corvo) to $746km^2$ (São Miguel), spread across some 600km of ocean

Climate Temperate, maritime climate with agreeable temperatures ranging from 13–14°C in Jan/Feb to 22–23°C in Jul/Aug. Rain throughout the year; light cloud common.

Status Autonomous region of Portugal

Population 242,600

Economy Major earners are beef, dairy products, fishing and tourism

Language Portuguese

Religion Roman Catholic

Currency Euro

Rate of exchange £1 = €1.50, US$1 = €0.80 (September 2006)

Time GMT −1; 4 hours later than US Eastern Standard Time

Electricity 220 volts

International telephone code +351

Flag Blue and white block colour. At the centre is a goshawk, with nine golden stars. In the left corner is the national coat of arms.

Coat of arms The shield is silver, with a red border, and includes a goshawk and 9 golden stars.

National anthem 'Hino da Regiã Autónoma dos Açores'

Patron Saint Santo Amaro

Motto 'Antes morrer livres que em paz sujeitos' ('Rather die than subject in peace')

Public holidays See page 51

I

Background Information

LOCATION

The nine islands of the Azores – the European Union's remotest outpost – are spread over some 600km of ocean (the Economic Free Zone is about 940km^2) and are located roughly 1,500km or two hours' flying time from Lisbon and about 3,900km or five hours from the east coast of North America. Running along a southeast to northwest axis they lie on either side of the line of latitude that links Lisbon with New York, and are between latitudes 36–39°N and longitudes 25–31°W. The total population is approximately 242,600.

The islands separate conveniently into three groups: the Eastern Group of São Miguel and Santa Maria; the Central Group of Terceira, Graciosa, São Jorge, Pico and Faial; and the Western Group of Flores and Corvo. The islands closest to each other are Pico and Faial at just 6km apart.

ORIGIN AND INVASIONS

GEOLOGICAL ORIGIN The archipelago is formed from the upper sections of volcanoes. In mid Atlantic on the ocean bed, tectonic plates are pulling apart. The gap between them is filled by molten volcanic material that rises from the Earth's mantle and continuously forms new oceanic crust. This extrusion wells up and forms an enormous underwater mountain chain or mid ocean ridge, and the sea floor spreads. The Mid-Atlantic ridge runs from the Arctic to the Antarctic, meeting on its way the Indian Ocean ridge off the southern tip of Africa. Along its length lie Iceland, the largest landmass created from oceanic crust, the Azores, Ascension and Tristan da Cunha islands. Mid-ocean ridges occur beneath all our major oceans, and only in exceptional cases are there so many eruptions that they build up to appear above sea level and form islands. In the Azores, giant linear ridges have been created, conspicuously Pico and São Jorge, and these are among the largest such volcanic ridges actively forming anywhere on our planet. With the ocean floor roughly between 1,000m and 3,000m below sea level, it is fun to try and imagine the landscape that would confront the traveller if the Atlantic Ocean could be emptied.

The situation is more complicated because, near the Azores, three plates meet in a T-shaped triple junction. The North American, African and Eurasian plates meet at a point between the western and central groups of islands, between Flores and Faial. Flores and Corvo are on the North American plate. The Mid-Atlantic Ridge forms two legs of the 'T' and the other islands are alongside a spreading centre called the Terceira Rift, formed about 36 million years ago. It is not certain on which plates, African or Eurasian, the remaining islands belong or whether some might be on an Azorean microplate.

The seismic tremors felt in the islands are mostly caused by magma flowing up the cracks left in the Earth's crust as the plates separate. At times these tremors,

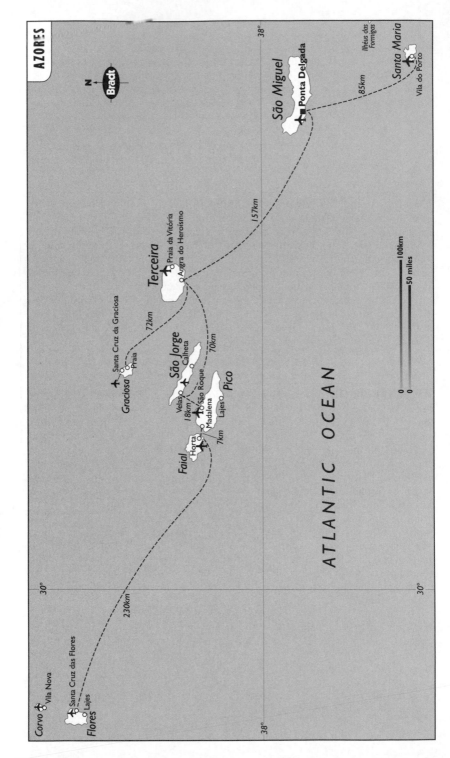

AZORES

Bradt

N

ATLANTIC OCEAN

Corvo
Vila Nova
Santa Cruz das Flores
Flores
Lajes

230km

Graciosa
Santa Cruz da Graciosa
Praia

72km

São Jorge
Calheta
Velas
18km
São Roque
Madalena
Lajes
Pico
7km
Faial
Horta

70km

Terceira
Praia da Vitória
Angra do Heroísmo

157km

São Miguel
Ponta Delgada

38°

85km

Ilhéus das
Formigas

Santa Maria
Vila do Porto

30°

30°

38°

0   100km
0   50 miles

4

measuring less than 5.0 on the Richter scale, will occur with surprising frequency. Six of the islands have all been subject to eruptions and earthquakes within recent historical times, but the remaining three, Santa Maria, Flores and Corvo, are now considered inactive.

Of the central and eastern islands Santa Maria was the first to rise above the sea some five million years ago but changes in sea level and tectonic activity caused it to submerge. A million years later, the Formigas islets and what is now the eastern end of São Miguel rose above the sea and Santa Maria reappeared. It was during this period of submergence that the island acquired its marine fossils, the only island to have them. The oldest part of São Miguel is around Pico da Vara in the east; at the far western end Sete Cidades began around 290,000 years ago, at the same time as Água de Pau started out from the ocean bed. Thus São Miguel was once two islands, only becoming united when the Picos region north of what is now Ponta Delgada began a long series of eruptions starting 5,000 years ago. Terceira, Graciosa, São Jorge and Faial are all younger than a million years, Pico being the youngest at a mere 300,000 years. The two western isles, Flores and Corvo, lie on the western flanks of the Mid-Atlantic Ridge; the oldest rocks on Flores date to around 600,000 years ago.

In 1811, about a mile off the coast of São Miguel opposite Ferreira, a new island appeared. One hundred metres tall and about 1.5km long, it took about a month to create. The British frigate *Sabrina* was in the area and her captain, Captain Tillard, landed on the still steaming island, planted a Union Jack, named the island 'Sabrina' and claimed it as British territory! Unfortunately for his credibility, when the next surveyors arrived, there was no trace of the island; in just four months the sea had washed it away and all that remains now is a bank 40m below the sea. Most recently, in 1957, an eruption began just off the west coast of Faial that added a further 2km^2 of land to that island.

In this region much more frequent activity occurs under the ocean's surface on the seabed than is seen on the surface of the islands. Constantly, seamounts rise and fall, and new lava pressure ridges are formed. Recently there was a submarine eruption 10km west of Terceira on a small area known as the 'Serreta High'. It began in 1998, initially in three different areas, later spreading to six. Surface signs are plumes of smoke coming from floating lava debris as it cools. The basalt magma is rich in gases that are trapped inside, creating 'balloons' which float upwards towards the ocean's surface. As they rise the gases inside expand and cause the 'balloons' to explode. The debris floats on the surface for about 15 minutes and sinks when seawater enters as it cools. When great volumes of gas rise to the surface the sea becomes pale green, and it is very dangerous for boats, since they could easily sink. This surface evidence is not continuous, and its absence reflects quieter periods of submarine activity. The earliest eruptions detected were at around 400m below sea level, and the magma subsequently has risen to 180m.

THE FIRST INVADERS Oceanic islands such as the Azores differ from continental islands in that they are usually basaltic volcanoes, distant from the mainland and surrounded by vast oceans. They have to gain their flora and fauna by invasion, unlike continental islands that are close to geologically diverse landmasses to which they were once attached. The flora and fauna of an oceanic island is therefore distinct because it is made up of those organisms that can cross oceans. This barrier filters out many potential colonists so that the Azores lack certain groups, such as mammals (excluding bats), that are important on the mainland.

Not only has half the Atlantic Ocean to be crossed to reach the Azores from the nearest land, but on arrival landfall is extremely tough, on a new, raw, volcanic island presenting hardened flows of lava or desert-like ash. How tough a challenge it is to colonise new ash deposits can be seen at Capelhinos on Faial. This area was engulfed and enlarged by an eruption in 1957. When you stand by the remains of the old lighthouse, and the wind drives sharp volcanic sand into your face with stinging force, look at the few plants that are establishing. There is *Arundo donax*, planted and artificially aided by humans, and the human-sponsored evening primrose. Left entirely to nature, colonisation takes a long time.

Winds and sea brought life to the Azores. Ocean currents transport marine organisms and shoreline animals to scavenge and survive upon what the sea washes ashore, along with others such as land crabs that have a marine larval stage. Travelling on prevailing winds and also the jet stream came spores of ferns, algae, fungi, lichens and mosses, seeds and microscopic animals, even spiders and other insects. All lightweight and adapted to wind dispersal, they landed on the Azores, even falling to earth in raindrops. Ground-nesting seabirds deposited their guano, providing further food for scavenging invertebrates and micro-organisms while rain slowly washed out minerals from the lava, all helping to create a very fertile soil. Currents, prevailing winds and distance from land masses all influence which organisms will become established on an island, and where they, or their ancestors, came from. Land birds that have wandered or been blown off course by storms will bring seeds, either in their stomachs or attached to their bodies. For the early colonists, survival would have been a harsh process, but it needed only some to succeed.

Slowly these first organisms changed the bare habitat by contributing organic matter to form soil. By retaining moisture, and modifying light, temperature and exposure, they enabled later arrivals to establish, thus slowly creating a more hospitable environment which in turn would allow further colonists to establish. They had to be adaptable, able to adjust to climatic variations and different food sources, and to survive both competition from other species and many other challenges in a new habitat. Variation in some species may have allowed them to adapt better to the conditions, thus leading over time to new species and subspecies. Today, there are 59 endemic plant species in the Azores, unique to the islands and found nowhere else in the world.

The Azores, along with the other archipelagos of Madeira, the Salvages, the Canaries and the Cape Verdes, comprise the region known as Macaronesia. The most characteristic vegetation is the dense evergreen forest, or laurisilva. It is a representative relic of the evergreen forests that grew in late Tertiary times (around 2.75 million years ago) in what is now southern Europe and northwest Africa. Possibly because of the Azores' oceanic climate, these forests escaped the extremes of climate changes and thus survived while elsewhere it became extinct.

Colonisation and evolution never cease. New plants will arrive – see *Two bullies*, page 11 – and others will be eliminated due to changing circumstances. Islands are living laboratories where the processes of dispersal, immigration, establishment, adaptation and extinction can all be studied. These are just some of the reasons why areas need to be protected from human depredation so that they may be there for future generations of students and provide an account of the changes going on around us.

THE SECOND WAVE: HUMANS The islands were pristine until the 15th century; there were no indigenous peoples, and no-one had ever settled there. They were known to exist, for in the Medici Atlas of 1351 the seven islands of the central and eastern groups are shown. Less than a century later the Portuguese 'Age of Discoveries' began and they made the first recorded landfalls on Madeira (c1419), the Azores (c1427), Cape Verdes (1456–60), St Helena and Ascension (1501–02) and Tristan da Cunha (c1506). Bartolomeu Dias rounded the Cape of Good Hope in 1488 and thus opened access to the Indian Ocean, and Pedro Álvares Cabral landed in Brazil in 1500, to say nothing of the numerous inland expeditions in Africa and elsewhere. It is not known for certain who discovered the islands for the Portuguese, nor the exact dates; numerous stories abound from which to take your choice. One I rather like which caps the debate is that a caravel came upon them by chance when sailing homewards from the west coast of Africa using the trade winds. Another is that Prince Henry ordered one Gonçalo Velho Cabral to sail westwards to find the islands he thought must exist. Cabral found only the Formigas rocks, the Ants, and went back home, getting a low mark from the Sagres Management School. Sent out again the following year, and sailing 15 miles distant from the Ants, a much better prospect came into view. Since it was 15 August, the Feast of the Assumption, he called the island Santa Maria and was later appointed governor. São Miguel was supposedly discovered when an escaped slave clambered up a hill and saw a much larger island in the distance; this was settled in 1444. By chance some unknown mariners spotted a third island, and with a stroke of originality called it Terceira, 'Third Island'. Another version is that Prince Henry sent out caravels, date unknown, to find the islands and they discovered five, later named Santa Maria, São Miguel, Terceira, Faial and Pico. Most popular accounts give Diogo de Silves the credit for finding the first island, Santa Maria, in 1427. In 1439 Alfonso V sanctioned Henry to settle seven islands, so they must have been discovered before that year. Flores and Corvo were certainly added last. The usual practice was followed when discovering islands; cattle, goats and pigs were landed to provide future food, and also very likely to begin the tremendous task of penetrating the dense vegetation. Settlers came from mainland Portugal, particularly the Algarve and Alentejo, and from Madeira. Portugal's population was only 1.5 million, so Henry encouraged immigration from Flanders and for a time the Azores were known as the Flemish Islands because so many settled there.

The first settlers faced an enormous task and probably used fire to begin to clear the vegetation. On some of the islands this would have revealed a very stony soil, and especially on Pico it must have been heartbreaking. Huge neatly piled stacks of stones metres square and 2m tall remain testimony to this tenacity and determination, as do the numerous stone walls. With such an inhospitable coastline, wherever it was possible to land must have dictated the location of those first settlements. Looking at them today, some still appear daunting, often at the foot of steep cliffs or ravines. Farming slowly spread across the islands as the vegetation was cleared and by the next century there was a surplus of production for export: wheat for the Portuguese garrison in north Africa, sugar and woad for dyeing to Flanders. Each island grew more of the crops that best suited its climate and terrain.

From the early days of subsistence agriculture and the development of the first cash crops these have changed through the centuries as fortune has favoured wine on Pico, or oranges on São Miguel, then tea and pineapples, tobacco, chicory, sugar beet, even a hectare or two of African marigolds (the dried petals were exported for hen feed to make them lay eggs with dark yellow yolks).

Now, more than ever before, all the islands produce grass, their most important crop, and milk and beef are the most important farm enterprises. In the mid 1980s there were about 10,000 dairy farmers with an average herd size of seven cows; change has come, but still there are many small herds. The main dairy products are cheese, butter and milk powder, with the surplus exported to mainland Portugal and the USA. Beef is on the increase, both for home consumption and for export. Fishing, especially tuna, has also played an important role in the economy with several fleets and canning factories. However, with rapidly diminishing fish stocks this now faces a very uncertain future.

The Azores, although so distant from the Portuguese mainland, nevertheless have often played an important part in Portuguese history. They contributed to the

THE AZOREAN COW

Luis Silva

In the 15th century, when the islands were first settled, one of the first things that was done was to introduce many Portuguese domestic animals. Of these the cow was extremely important because she not only provided milk and meat but was also a hard-working animal around the farm, for ploughing, carting, etc. Some of the distinct cattle breeds that were imported from Portugal include *Alentejana, Mirandesa, Minhota* and *Algarvia*. There is also historical suggestion that some cows were imported from Flanders but there is no information on specific breeds. Importation would have continued until the numbers reached a reproductive level that was self-sustaining, and then probably stopped. The following five centuries of cross-breeding between the original breeds imported from Portugal and Flanders evolved into a distinct breed known today as Ramo Grande. This Ramo Grande breed dominated on most of the islands. Then, in the 1950s, Friesians were imported from England and later on from the USA and soon after that an artificial insemination programme was set up on Terceira and São Miguel. By the 1980s there were quite a few importations of dairy heifers (Holsteins) and beef breeds (Limousin, Charolais and Fleckview) from Germany, England, Holland, France and Canada. A small number of Jersey heifers have since been added plus Jersey embryo transfers. Consequently, and in a very short time, the Azorean breed became almost extinct.

Fortunately, in the area of Ramo Grande on Terceira, a group of farmers continued to maintain small herds of these animals. Today there is increasing interest in the conservation of this Azorean genetic heritage, and in its potential for producing beef; its specific characteristics have been defined and all individuals are now registered. At present, the genetic line in the Azores is mostly Holsteins for dairy and Limousin and Charolais for beef. Just recently, the Azores University through its agricultural sciences department has concluded from a study of various dairy breeds that Jerseys would be the most suitable for the region. Hopefully, the Azorean Ramo Grande will survive the effects of globalisation and someday might even contribute its distinctive characters to future breeding.

conquest, defence and supply of the Portuguese strongholds on the north African coast, caravels stopped in the Azores on their return from India, they supported the ships sailing to the Americas, and they strongly resisted Spanish domination between 1580 and 1640. Two centuries later the islands featured in the Liberals' struggle with the Absolutists; two presidents in the First Republic came from the Azores and, most recently, the islands provided important bases for the Allies in the two world wars, and in the Gulf War.

THE WEATHER

For small islands the weather, especially when in the middle of a large ocean, is all-important. For the busy city worker, as everywhere, the weather impacts little on a daily basis, and for the visitor rain is but a passing nuisance. However, for farmers even a relatively short dry period causes problems because the volcanic soils are very quick-draining, while a rough sea means the coastal fisherman cannot go out, there is no income for them and no fresh fish for the villages. The Azores have a maritime climate, which is equable throughout the year with an average temperature of 13–22°C. Sea temperatures range from 15–23°C. The annual rainfall increases westwards and ranges from 700mm in Ponta Delgada on São Miguel to 1,600mm in Santa Cruz on Flores. Like everywhere else in the world, the local weather patterns have changed and what was always seen as a good holiday period can now be very wet, while other times never previously viewed with much favour can be truly glorious. Now the weather is a gamble, a game that has to be seen as part of the fun of an Azorean holiday, and for residents just another challenge.

HOW THE WEATHER WORKS Of the few things generally known about the Azores, the 'Azores High' probably tops the list. This is an area of high pressure or anticyclone that is semi-permanent.

Very simply, warm moist air rises over the tropics leading to low pressure there; this warm moist air then moves north towards the sub-tropical latitudes and cools. It then descends, increasing the pressure over sub-tropical latitudes, at the same time becoming drier and resulting in largely clear skies. This tropical/sub-tropical circulation on average varies little in position; in summer it is more northerly, in winter and spring more southerly, usually lying to the south or southwest of the archipelago. This high pressure belt is part of the global circulatory system and is called the Hadley cell. In the north Atlantic it is centred close to the Azores for most of the time, hence the 'Azores High'. The reason it is centred there is because the Azores lie roughly midway between the influence of the African and American continents. Land masses distort the process and strong summer heating at these latitudes can cause, for example, low pressure in the northern summer over southeast Asia and India and bring monsoon rains. Surface layers of the ocean do not heat up in the same way as the land does, and therefore allow the high pressure belt to persist.

Sometimes the 'Azores High' extends northeast towards the British Isles, especially when they have a good summer. In winter it can sometimes recede southwards, if the jet stream is also further south. Occasionally it disappears altogether to be replaced by low pressure whilst often, at the same time, high pressure dominates northern Europe giving cold weather in winter and hot, often eventually thundery weather in summer.

In the Azores the weather is influenced by the strength and location of this high, particularly in summer. A strong high gives pleasant, warm weather with little wind. A weak high gives weather that is changeable and wet, and you can tell when a depression is coming by a sudden drop in the barometer and a southerly wind, veering from southwest to northwest. A low approaches with steadily lowering and thickening cloud. The wind increases, bringing heavier cloud and rain showers, and then often torrential rain by which time all sight of any nearby island has vanished. Then comes a break, the wind changes direction, and blustery, blue skies return. Finally, it all calms down, and the high reasserts. This drama might sometimes be over within a few hours and, if you are on land with a good vantage point, it can be fun to watch the rain squalls skating across the ocean. Winds come from the west, travelling eastwards, and this is reflected in the higher rainfall of the Western Group. In early summer, winds are mainly from the southwest and by July and August are predominantly northeasterly, gentle and with frequent calms. By September they return to the southwest and become gradually stronger. Occasionally bad storms hit the islands, but mostly they follow a narrow path. As you drive round the islands from time to time you will see cryptomeria trees snapped off like broken toothpicks.

Another major climate influence on the Azores are the ocean currents, especially those originating from the Gulf Stream. This is a movement of warm water of equatorial and tropical origin into the colder northern waters of the Atlantic. West of the Azores, the Gulf Stream splits into two main branches, the North Atlantic Current that passes north of the islands, and the Azores Current passing to the south. This Gulf Stream gives the Azores their warm temperate climate.

A further complication is the North Atlantic Oscillation (NAO), a northern equivalent of El Niño, which concerns atmospheric circulation.

NATURAL HISTORY

Although so many visitors come to the Azores because of the islands' natural environment, nature reserves with information centres, wardens and controlled access with marked paths are unknown. Many of the remaining patches of native vegetation are now in protected zones and you might just see notices to this effect. The vegetation of the islands, particularly on Pico, Terceira and São Miguel, is interesting not only because it represents communities that were once widespread in parts of Europe millions of years ago, but also because very few aspects of its ecology and biology have been studied and the opportunities for simple observation and research are considerable. There is a desire to know what is happening in amongst the evergreens. Many stretches of coastal cliff are protected zones, mostly for seabirds; again you might see the signs. The marine environment is similarly protected. Few geological sites are protected, however, and here the lack of interpretation for visitors is doubly frustrating because the Azores must be one of the most fascinating areas for vulcanology in Europe.

THE VEGETATION The dense evergreen forest that once covered much of the islands has long been cleared for agriculture and settlement. Visually the quite extensive plantations of the exotic conifer *Cryptomeria japonica* now add considerably to the aesthetics of the Azorean landscape since tree cover within the lifetime of elderly islanders has been very considerably less than it is today. Planted to reduce erosion, lessen water loss and provide shelter for cattle and produce timber, these plantations are a substantial if sometimes controversial plus. Emigration has left many previously cultivated areas abandoned, to be invaded by a mix of native *Myrica faya*, *Erica azorica* and introduced and subsequently naturalised *Pittosporum undulatum* and, encouragingly, some other native species such as the endemic *Picconia azorica*. There is a tremendous battle raging, because *Myrica faya* is light demanding, and must fight with the pittosporum for survival.

The native vegetation remains in a number of isolated areas. Evergreen forest is found as remnant forest or as individual species surviving in hedgerows above the 500m contour. The quite different coastal region of steep cliffs, of lava flows, agricultural land and seashore have their own mix of native, endemic and introduced exotic species.

The Azores archipelago has a total of 850 or more plant species, most of which have been introduced by humans. Of the total, some 300 are native, and of these possibly 60 species are endemic, found nowhere else in the world but in the Azores. Of the 11 species of native trees, eight are endemic to the Azores, and two others are found elsewhere only in Madeira. Dominant species of the forest include *Ilex perado* ssp. *azorica*, *Juniperus brevifolia*, *Erica azorica* and *Laurus azorica*. Growing in the mountains at altitudes where the hillsides are often embraced by cloud, such vegetation is called cloudforest; often the trunks and branches are adorned with epiphytic ferns, while bryophytes (mosses and liverworts) can be exuberant, sometimes even thriving on the leaves as epiphylls.

The largest area remaining of undisturbed forest is on Terceira, on the Caldeira da Santa Bárbara and a small area between Juncal, Pico Alto and Serra do Labaçal, not the easiest to access for the relaxed naturalist on holiday. The forests of the Caldeira da Santa Bárbara at over 800m are often cloud-covered and are largely dominated by *Juniperus brevifolia* although all the Azores tree species can be found in gullies and other places. Areas of natural grassland are to be seen inside the caldera and endemic grasses such as *Festuca jubata* and *Holcus rigidus* are to be found growing with endemic herbaceous species such as *Tolpis azorica*.

São Miguel's only remaining area of natural forest can at least be easily seen! It is to be found at the eastern end of the island, and covers about 600ha on Pico da Vara.

Pico has the most accessible of all native forest, although little remains and that in small patches, often where the ground is badly tumbled with small boulder-sized lava and has therefore escaped the predations of farmer and cattle. There are patches of *Viburnum tinus* ssp. *subcordatum*, *Euphorbia stygiana*, *Ilex perado*, *Vaccinium cylindraceum*, *Frangula azorica*, *Hedera helix* ssp. *canariensis*, *Juniperus brevifolia* and its green-branched parasite *Arceuthobium azoricum* and occasionally, in the loose gravel at the edge of the asphalt road, *Thymus caespititius*.

The coastal flora has been badly disturbed by numerous developments and in places by the escape and spread of garden ornamentals such as the several members of the succulent *Aizoaceae*. However, while some of the species are endangered, none is on the verge of extinction and all are to be found, often in places where one least expects them, and in the most inhospitable sites. All the islands have suitable habitats. Characteristic species include the endemic grass *Festuca petraea* and the rush *Juncus acutus*. Widely located but found in small concentrations by the coast is one of the most handsome of all Azorean endemics, the perennial slightly shrubby *Azorina vidalii*.

(See also *Appendix 2, Flora*, for an aid to identifying plants you are likely to see.)

Two bullies Amid all the excitement of introducing new plants into the show gardens of São Miguel came two very gardenworthy species, two species that have more than outlived their mid-19th-century patrons. From the middle altitudes of the Himalayas came the Kahili ginger, *Hedychium gardnerianum*, a handsome plant about 1.5m tall with beautiful, sweetly scented, terminal spikes of orange-yellow spidery flowers. Away from its native habitat it found itself in the Azores in a permanently moist climate, with nothing to limit its growth. It has become a superbly aggressive invader; it can adapt to various Azorean habitats; it is a strongly competitive plant; cut it down and it can quickly recover; it produces abundant efficiently dispersed seeds; can easily reproduce vegetatively; and once established it dominates the site for many years. As a consequence it has smothered areas of native vegetation, prevents the re-establishment of desirable species and has invaded large areas of cryptomeria forest – a real pest, and very difficult to eradicate. The second garden delight is *Gunnera tinctoria*, one of the 'giant rhubarbs' from South America. You will see this invading parts of the Furnas Valley and especially the pastures high above; also Lake Fogo, a protected area for flora, and Sete Cidades. Deeply rooted with a strong constitution it covers hectares of pastures; the occasional container-load taken to Holland for sale to garden centres makes little impact.

THE BIRDS Studies have shown that the Azores are one of the least attractive birdwatching destinations in terms of numbers of birds that might be seen and the cost per bird seen! Almost without exception there are no full species in the Azores that cannot be seen closer to, or on, continental Europe. However, for the independent birdwatching traveller, there are some 150 species recorded for the islands plus 35 breeding species; of these breeding species ten are endemic subspecies and one is an endemic species. Of the total number of species, 45 have a regular presence in the archipelago, and seven have been introduced. The subspecies present a substantial challenge, even to the experts. In addition, birds which are blown off course when migrating between North and Central America occasionally add exotic interest. Such incidences can be expected to increase as the weather becomes more turbulent with climate change and September to November

2005 proved an especially suitable time following the several hurricanes to hit North America, particularly hurricane Rita. American waders and waterfowl were known but now land birds like wood warblers are being recorded for the first time.

Two regular migrants are the common tern and the black-headed gull. The first arrives in April and stays until October, when the black-headed gull arrives, remaining until spring. The beautiful glaucous gull, *Larus hyperboreus*, can also be seen in winter where it stays in Madalena harbour on Pico. Along the coast where lava has flowed into the sea and shallow pools form, wagtails, rock doves, turnstones, dunlins, little egrets, whimbrels and other waders come to feed. On stacks and, importantly for breeding, small offshore islets where nests are protected from predators, gulls and terns crowd together. There are few sandy beaches in the Azores, but here may be seen Kentish plovers, *Charadius alexandrinus*, although one of the best places to see them is at Santa Maria airport! Steep sea cliffs are important nesting sites for shearwaters; in some places the rocky faces are over 300m high and are made up of layers of lava, scoriae and cinders. It is in the cinder layer where the circular nesting holes may be seen. Cory's shearwater, *Calonectris diomedea*, is quite common on all the islands and during daytime it is possible to see them at sea interacting with dolphins and big fish such as tuna; it is usually absent from mid November to February. Like the shearwater, terns are also regular breeders and the endangered roseate tern, *Sterna dougalii*, mixes in breeding colonies with the common tern *Sterna hirundo*; the latter can often be seen catching and feeding on small fish in the harbours.

Inland there are habitats of fields surrounded by hedges or stone walls, extensive areas of lava where vines are often planted, areas where native erica or myrica predominate or where introduced pittosporum or eucalyptus have invaded, and many areas of planted conifer forest. Above 600m conditions generally are very wet and humid; pockets of native evergreen forest remain, surrounded by cattle pastures. Birds are everywhere, including chaffinches, blackbirds, blackcaps, grey wagtails and canaries.

If you walk quietly through wooded areas you may chance upon the shy and diminutive goldcrest, *Regulus regulus*; there are three subspecies on different islands, distinguished by the colour of their plumage. One of the prettiest birds is the Azores grey wagtail, *Motacilla cinerea particiae*. Often running about on quiet roads or near a water fountain, the wagging tail and bright yellow underparts are unmistakable. It is a paler yellow and has a slightly longer bill than its Madeiran counterpart. The blackbird, *Turdus merula azorensis*, is darker and glossier than the European bird while the female has feathers of a deeper brown, and the chaffinch, *Fringilla coelebs moreleti*, has a different colour and song from that found on the mainland. The sparrow is most frequently seen and was introduced in the 1940s – on one island even the name of the Italian ship that brought the stowaways is known. The starling is the next bird most often seen, particularly at dusk when great flocks of them soar around large Canary Island palms prior to roosting. Incidentally, these palms are sometimes favoured homes for bats. Memorable is the song of the canary, especially in concert with the sound of cowbells. These pleasurable brown-and-yellow birds, *Serinus canaria*, take exception to common sparrows and, since their immigration, have largely moved away from urban areas to the fields and higher places where they flock and serenade the walker.

The Azorean bullfinch, *Pyrrhula murina* (*priôlo* in Portuguese), is the bird that receives all the promotional publicity, and it is rare. Once common, it was shot almost to extinction long ago, mainly by the fruit farmers who also killed chaffinch, canary, blackbird and blackcap because they viewed them as agricultural pests and the government paid compensation on the number of beaks presented. The priôlo can now be seen with much patience in the reserve of Pico da Vara on São Miguel amidst the dense evergreen forest. With a considerably higher profile is the endemic Azorean buzzard that, when misidentified by the early settlers, gave its false name to the islands; *açor* in Portuguese means 'goshawk'. Another explanation suggests that when the first settlers arrived they found the birds so tame they came to hand like goshawks. Anyway, *Buteo buteo rothschildi* has been in the islands for a very considerable time and subjective observation suggests their number has increased over the past few years. They are frequently seen soaring over the countryside, and it is possible to get quite close to them when they perch on telegraph poles or buildings.

WHALES AND OTHER CETACEANS Cetaceans, from the Greek meaning 'sea monster', are members of the order *Cetaceae*, commonly known as whales and dolphins. Altogether there are a little over 80 species worldwide, and off the Azores some 25 species have been sighted. They are mammals, have lungs and nostrils (blowholes), suckle their young and have front flippers evolved from forelegs. Within the Cetaceae are two subgroups, the toothed whales and the baleen whales.

WHALING

Whales have been hunted for a long time, but in early times primitively and in very small numbers. The first known organised commercial whaling was done by the Basques in the Bay of Biscay who, from the 10th century, hunted migrating right whales (*Eubalaena glacialis*) that passed inshore. The whales were spied by lookouts onshore, and they were hunted from land-based small boats. Six hundred years later the right whales had declined in number and the catches were small, so the Basques went cod fishing instead, in the Grand Bank area of Westfoundland, where they discovered large numbers of whales. These they hunted, as did the Dutch, British and Germans. From a larger ship small boats were used to approach the whales and harpoon them. The carcasses were then towed ashore where the blubber was processed for eventual use as lighting oil, lubrication, soap and paint. Within a century the whale numbers declined here as well so that the ships had to search further afield, and the blubber was processed on board. In the early 18th century the American colonists began hunting whales, especially the sperm whale, near their shores. American whalers then spread out to the Caribbean, the Azores and Africa, and later to the Indian and Pacific oceans. Predictably, as each species was hunted down, its numbers declined.

The next major development was the arrival of the explosive harpoon and the motorised whale catcher in around 1870. By the beginning of the 20th century the very large whale numbers in Antarctica could be exploited through the development of efficient factory boats. At first this was done by British and Norwegian whalers, then German and Japanese; British Arctic whaling stopped in 1912. In the 1930s annual catches were over 40,000 whales. However, whaling continued remorselessly and some species were driven almost to extinction while stocks of others were seriously depleted; the Washington Convention of 1946 was an attempt to regulate whaling. As the century continued the numbers allowed to be caught were reduced substantially, but economic and other factors caused nations finally to abandon whaling: a combination of declining stocks, falling prices and availability of substitutes. The International Whaling Commission in 1982 agreed zero commercial quotas, but Norway and Japan continue under the guise of research. Ironically, it now seems Norwegian whales could be toxic to humans, and pressure groups in Japan are objecting to their import on the grounds that they have enough problems with their own whales.

The former have teeth and a single blowhole while the latter have, instead of teeth, a horny baleen or plate descending from the upper jaw and paired blowholes. This difference is important when feeding; the toothed whales eat larger prey such as cephalopods and fish and the baleen whales use their comb-like plates to filter very small fish and the shrimp-like krill. Many of these filter-feeding whales often undertake long migrations because they need warm waters for the growth and development of their young, but they also need the food resources that concentrate in colder waters.

The mid-Atlantic location of the steep-sided volcanic islands of the Azores causes great upswellings of cold water currents from the ocean depths which meet the warm waters of the Gulf Stream, producing nutrient-rich waters. The species most readily identified with the Azores is the sperm whale or cachalote (*Physeter macrocephalus*), the largest of all toothed whales. Other toothed whales frequently seen during the main season are Cuvier's beaked whale (*Ziphius caviostris*), northern bottlenose whale (*Hyperodon ampullatus*), short-finned pilot whale (*Globicephala macrorhynchus*) and Sowerby's beaked whale (*Mesoplodon bidens*).

Dolphins seen regularly are common Atlantic (*Delphinus delphis*), bottlenose (*Tursiops truncates*), Risso's (*Grampus griseus*), Atlantic spotted (*Stenella frontalis*) and striped (*Stenella coeruleoalba*). Since 2001 observations of baleen or great whales have increased, during early April to late June. Species include fin (*Balaenoptera musculus*), sei (*Balaenoptera borealis*), humpback (*Megeptera novaeangliae*) and the blue whale (*Balaenoptera musculus*), thought to be the largest animal ever to have lived on Earth.

SOCIAL TOPICS

POPULATION A few years ago the total population of the Azores was around 242,600 and, demographically unlike most of the rest of Europe, there is a higher proportion of young people. Islanders who emigrated are returning in retirement, and some who find themselves as parents return because they feel the Azores offers their children a safer and better quality of life.

For centuries emigration has played a major part in the life of the islands. In the early days heavy taxation was an incentive and later the passing whalers were often a temptation, sometimes fatal. At times emigration was prohibited, and the dangerous journey in a small boat to meet with a passing vessel could end in disaster. During the beginning of the 19th century the economy was depressed by the devastation caused by the Napoleonic Wars and, in the case of young men, the wish to avoid military service was stimulus enough. Crop failures through disease such as the loss of the grape vines on Pico prompted mass emigration. Hawaii,

ISLAND SIZE AND APPROXIMATE POPULATION				
	Length (km)	Breadth (km)	Surface area (km²)	Population
São Miguel	65	14	746	130,000
Pico	42	15	447	15,000
Terceira	29	17.5	382	58,000
São Jorge	56	8	246	10,000
Faial	21	14	173	15,000
Flores	17	12.5	143	4,000
Santa Maria	17	9.5	97	6,000
Graciosa	12.5	8.5	61	5,000
Corvo	6.5	4	17	400

needing workers for the sugar fields, recruited in Madeira and São Miguel; by 1888, in just ten years, more than 11,000 Azoreans had crossed half the world, including rounding Cape Horn. Other natural disasters like earthquakes and eruptions drove islanders away after their homes and fields had been destroyed, even up until the 1980s. As a result there are large populations of Azoreans in Canada, the USA, Brazil and many elsewhere.

GOVERNMENT Initially, except for a period during the Spanish occupation, the Azores had no central government, and it was not until 1766 that a governor and captain-general for the whole group were appointed by the Marquis of Pombal. In 1832 a new constitution was agreed and in 1895 the islands were allowed limited autonomous administration.

In 1976 the Azores became an autonomous region with its own government of Regional Assembly and Executive. The Executive or Regional Government is responsible politically to the Regional Legislative Assembly. The Region elects five deputies to the National Parliament in Lisbon. The Regional Parliament has 51 deputies elected every four years and meets in Horta. The president of the Azores, whose official residence is in Ponta Delgada, is the leader of the party with the greatest number of elected deputies. There are nine regional secretaries, each in charge of a department, eg: Finance and Planning, Tourism and Environment. The secretariats, or ministries, are based in Ponta Delgada, Angra do Heroísma and Horta. Each island is divided into district councils, from six on São Miguel to just one on each of the smallest islands, which are in turn divided into parishes. The islands' autonomy includes responsibility for their economy. Education, health, the army, police and judiciary are controlled directly by the national government in Lisbon. The Portuguese government is represented by the Minister of the Republic who maintains residency in Angra do Heroísma, Terceira. The Azores has one MEP.

ECONOMY Since 1976 island infrastructure has been given priority with new airports, harbours and telecommunication systems completed. Now the principal problem is economic, and investment in the expanding fishing industry is but one of the alternatives being sought to reduce the dependency upon cattle breeding. However, despite that according to WWF literature the Azores are one of only two European areas with a sustainable fishery, stocks are getting low and are erratic and tourism is increasingly seen as the key new growth area.

The Azores, or at least Ponta Delgada, have changed hugely in the past few years with new industrial/commercial estates on the outskirts and many new shops in the town. Everywhere in the islands one sees the European Union flag on a hoarding announcing funds for some new development, from further new port facilities to a tiny family enterprise for rural tourism. Objectives of the Autonomous Regional Government are to reduce bureaucracy, privatise, and open the economy to foreign investment. Publicly owned companies have been sold or are in the process of being sold, and membership of the EU and adoption of the euro are seen to be essential to inward investment and future prosperity. Unemployment is at an all-time low, new jobs have been created in new sectors, agricultural productivity has increased, and so has tourism. The economically active population is about 100,000.

Tourism is a significant growth area and high-quality development is seen as the way forward with priority given to the towns and new initiatives in rural areas. Inter-island transport services have improved with more flights and a summer ferry service, new hotels have opened in Ponta Delgada, Angra and Horta and other towns, but there remains a great need to attract visitors during the low season. Direct charter flights through the winter from Scandinavia to São Miguel are proving successful, but generate little benefit to the other islands. The Azores are a small market and are located in the middle of the Atlantic and to reduce this barrier to investment air fares and port taxes have been reduced and fibre optic cable now links all the islands, improving communications at lower costs.

LANGUAGE Portuguese is both the national and native language, but there are strong regional dialects and vocabulary that often mother-tongue Portuguese speakers from the mainland find difficult to understand. Natives of each island can be quickly recognised by fellow Azoreans, and even from which part of an island they come. Try learning Portuguese from tapes before you travel; you may get by in Lisbon, but stay in Furnas on São Miguel and you will be in difficulty. While in Furnas learn some new vocabulary and then try the words out in Ponta Delgada. Pronounce them in every different way you can imagine, and finally you are taught another new word for the same thing. Generally, of course, you will get by, but it is mostly in smaller cafés that it is useful to speak Portuguese, and in villages to ask the way. Some taxi drivers are fluent in English; many know enough to get by, but many speak only Portuguese. In the towns very many people speak English, it is a standard subject in school, and there are numerous Azoreans who have worked abroad. There are English-language television channels as well, CNN, BBC World, and films. Some French is spoken in Faial and Flores.

RELIGION The Azores have been Catholic from their first settlement. The rare Protestant churches were built much later, for example in Ponta Delgada on São Miguel in the 19th century, primarily in response to the mainly English merchants who came to live in the islands to manage the orange trade. Although very much a minority, there was also a strong Jewish presence from the early days with some originating from north Africa. The Catholic parish priests were very influential, and the religious orders, especially the Franciscans, built many convents and churches and organised the first schools. In modern times it is the older parishioners who mostly make up church congregations, although young people still make up the numbers on festival days.

ART AND ARCHITECTURE

SECULAR, RELIGIOUS AND MILITARY ARCHITECTURE
With thanks to Isabel Soares de Albergaria
Architecture in the Azores is an offshoot of the designs known in continental Portugal, sharing the simplicity of form common to the Mediterranean. It does, however, have its own characteristics. The most obvious are the easy integration of the buildings in the landscape and the structure of the settlements in which streets tend to converge in small irregular squares where stand the most imposing buildings, the church and town hall. Until very recently most houses were modest in size and appearance and had distinctive features: they were built of stone, with a characteristic contrast between whitewash and black basalt.

Vernacular architecture, less affected by variations in style and the dictates of fashion, perhaps best reflects the Azoreans' relationship with their island environment. Their isolation, the simple agrarian way of life and the use of naturally available materials have led to very simple, almost rudimentary designs for both houses and utilitarian buildings such as barns, cowsheds and mills. These together with the small shrines and chapels have, through the centuries, gradually developed their own style and form leading to regional characteristics.

As you go around the different islands variations emerge: Santa Maria has white houses with coloured bars marking the shapes and windows and Algarve-style prismatic chimneys, whilst on Pico, houses are black with no plaster on the walls and balconies running along the upper floors are accessed via outside staircases. On Terceira a long house is common, with its row of windows and doors with the kitchen at one end indicated by the presence of the broad chimneys called *de mãos postas* ('with joined hands'). On São Miguel low window–door–window-style houses are more frequent, similar to those in the Alentejo or, in some areas, houses with their gable end directly on the street. Variations can also be seen in the generally very simple decorative elements, focused around the windows and doors: mouldings of curved lines; the *aventais* (aprons) of the windows outlined in black; the characteristic staircase eye-windows decorated with geometric motifs, possibly Arabic in influence; or the windows with wrought-iron balconies, with a more cultivated influence. Another very common element, especially in the islands of the central group, is the bands of basalt that cut vertically and horizontally across the façades, as a form of proof against earthquakes.

It is not possible to talk about popular Azorean architecture without mentioning one of the most peculiar and unique aspects of its heritage: the *impérios* (small chapels) of the Holy Spirit. Linked to an age-old religion, which existed in the Azores from the times of their earliest settlement, the *impérios* are fundamental to the ritual practices of this extraordinary cult that on the mainland disappeared long ago. Here again variations can be seen between the various islands, but the most famous are the *impérios* on Terceira, immediately recognisable for their festive appearance, bright colours and designs, and triangular pediment.

On approaching any Azorean village from the sea, the most prominent feature is always the more or less imposing façade of a church. The most notable in this respect is the view of Horta on Faial, with the façades of the parish church, the Convent of São Francisco and the beautiful façade of the Carmelite monastery dominating the group of houses and 'gazing out to sea'. Hills near the villages are often topped by little pilgrimage chapels; of the many that are to be found scattered through the islands is the group of chapels and pilgrimage houses of Nossa Senhora da Ajuda above the small town of Santa Cruz da Graciosa, among which is also what is perhaps the best example of a fortified church with huge buttresses, decorative battlements and ribbed vaults inside.

In spite of limited resources, religious art in the Azores always had the benefit of fine talents and this enabled the islands to keep up with the artistic developments of mainland Portugal. The initial period, characterised by Gothic-Manueline architecture which lasted until the mid 16th century, is represented by almost all the surviving early parish churches of the main towns; for example the parish churches of São Sebastião in Ponta Delgada and of São Sebastião on Terceira. Then followed a long period of Portuguese classicism, known as *estilo chão* (plain architecture) because of its bare, austere and purely functional style exemplified by the Cathedral of Angra, and the Parish Church of Santa Cruz on Graciosa. The majority of monastic buildings in the Azores belong to this group, in spite of the decorative alterations many of them underwent during the Baroque period of which examples include Nossa Senhora da Graça in Ponta Delgada and São Boaventura in Santa Cruz on Flores.

The religious way of life with its ritual of offerings, processions and pilgrimages had its origins in the mendicant orders established in the early Middle Ages in continental Europe. Monks came to the Azores during the early phase of settlement (15th century), the Franciscans being the most prominent; their monasteries soon sprang up in every town and city. Later on the Jesuits joined them. Soon after the papal approval, in 1540, the Company of Jesus promoted the building of great and elaborate colleges for the whole Portuguese Empire, including the islands. By royal initiative, the Colégio da Ascenção in Angra (the present Palácio dos Capitães-

Generais) was founded in 1570, then the Colégio de Ponta Delgada, dedicated to All Saints (1591) and only much later, in 1680, the Colégio de São Francisco Xavier in Horta (today the seat of the parish church, municipal hall, treasury and museum). The present churches of Angra and Ponta Delgada are not, however, the original ones, there being various reconstructions and additions in later years.

Baroque architecture is well represented on the islands, particularly on São Miguel. It was dominant throughout the 18th and early 19th centuries, and is characterised by exuberant sculptural and decorative forms. Monastery churches entirely rebuilt or substantially altered (for example the Monastery dos Frades in Lagoa, São Miguel; Santo André, c1744; Esperança, 1740–86 and Conceição (Carmo), c1754, Ponta Delgada; São Gonçalo, Angra, 1730–50) use black basalt in capricious curves, highly indented mouldings, twisted columns, garlands and medallions, which form the new decorative language. The reconstruction of the Parish Church of São Pedro de Ponta Delgada (1737–42) was developed on an octagonal plan, original for the period, and the idea was repeated in the Parish Church of Fajã de Baixo. The Church of Santo Espírito, on the island of Santa Maria (18th century), is another example of originality, this time with the application of a dense and compact decoration, which is reminiscent of South American Baroque. Private chapels were often associated with the construction of Baroque manor houses such as St Catarina in Ponta Delgada; also of the 18th century were extravagant Baroque *misericórdias*, institutions for the poor offering medical care, food and other charitable benefits.

Because of their strategic location between Europe and the New World the Azores were important for shipping, especially the returning treasure ships, but the islands were constantly threatened by corsairs. During the reign of D Manuel I (Manuel the Fortunate) early in the 16th century, a series of fortifications were begun 3km apart around the coast, with São Miguel, Terceira and Flores the most fortified. Construction was inspired by Renaissance technology and supervised by Italian military engineers and examples are São Bras in Ponta Delgada and Santa Cruz in Horta. In Angra on Terceira the castle of São Filipe, later renamed São João Baptista, was built during Philippine sovereignty (1580–1640), again as part of a general defence plan; construction was supervised by the Portuguese military engineer João de Vilhena and the Italian fortification specialist Tiburzio Spanochi, and was only completed after the Restoration. Practically impregnable, the castle benefited from the natural situation of Monte Brasil and included, on the landward side of the isthmus, a defensive platform with bulwarks and powerful curtain walls with deep moats. By this device the forces loyal to the Spanish crown were able to resist for long months after the King of Portugal took power.

Surprisingly few vestiges of this vast military effort are left to us. This is probably due to two factors. First, the quality of the constructions varied since often, with an attack imminent, the work was organised by the town hall and executed by the population using the materials and technology immediately to hand. Second, advances in warfare made many buildings obsolete, so that they were abandoned and left to the mercy of the elements and vandalism. Only more recently has the historical and architectural value of this heritage been recognised and efforts are slowly being made to save it from total ruin.

PAINTING AND DECORATIVE ARTS Most paintings, carvings, glazed tiles, furniture and gold artefacts in the Azores come from studios abroad following commissions made in a religious context. Only in a few cases the artist or school, those who commissioned the item and the iconographic association are known to us. On the whole, however, the quality of the work is comparable to the rest of Portugal with the obvious exception of the royal court.

As with the architecture, genuinely Gothic artefacts are extremely rare. One of them is the triptych of the Virgin Mary in the Church of Dos Anjos (on Santa Maria), a portable altarpiece that according to tradition belonged to Christopher Columbus, on which Gothic designs can be distinguished. Another example is the murals of the Church of São Sebastião on Terceira.

Later 16th-century Flemish art is much more visible in the archipelago, both in works imported from the workshops of Antwerp, Brussels and Mechelen, and in works of local artists who succumbed to a veritable passion for the Flemish style. This fashion spread throughout the Portuguese territory, largely because of the privileged relationship Iberia had with this northern European region in the 15th and 16th centuries. In the Azores the Flemish influence was exercised directly by Flemish settlers and through a significant trade in woad and urzela, two dye plants used in the textile industry.

Imported Flemish art includes numerous small sculptures such as the *Virgin and Child* (Horta Museum), *St Sebastian tied to a dry tree trunk* (Ponta Delgada Museum), or the larger sculpture *Our Lady of the Miracles* in the Church of Vila Nova do Corvo, all from Mechelen. More elaborate and emotionally charged is the *Crucifixion and Saint Mary Magdalen* (Horta Museum), a delicate work that must have come from the hands of a Brussels artist around 1520. Another theatrical composition is the *Christ being taken down from the Cross*, probably also from the 15th century, now exhibited in the Church of the Altares on Terceira. A moving group presents the scene of *Our Lady, St John and the Holy Women*, with Roman soldiers and citizens; at the bottom you can see skulls, the bones of Adam and some souls from purgatory. Probably also of Flemish influence, but from the first half of the 17th century, is the magnificent sculpture of *Our Lady of the Tears* (Church of São Pedro, Ponta Delgada), a powerfully modelled work of great expressiveness.

Amongst paintings, the triptych of *Saint Andrew* (Church of Nossa Senhora da Estrela, Ribeira Grande), that came from the chapel of the same name, is a 16th-century work whose Flemish affiliation is obvious in the drawing and sculptural appearance of the figures, the warm colours and delicate play of light on the background landscape, made in perspective. Although more archaic, the Flemish influence is visible also in the magnificent triptych of the *Adoration of the Magi* (Angra Museum) and in the painting of *Saint Ursula and the Eleven Thousand Virgins*, commissioned by the Jesuits of Angra perhaps in the late 16th century, in which a mannerist style is already evident.

The 16th-century purely Portuguese painting also achieved very high standards. Some exceptionally good works of this period can be seen in the Azores, including the polyptych in the Church of Santa Cruz da Graciosa depicting scenes from the Passion of Christ and the Legend of Vera Cruz, and showing all the signs of the late Renaissance pathos that characterises this work. In the Carlos Machado Museum in Ponta Delgada there are two paintings from the Coimbra studio of Manuel Vicente and Vicente Gil, with Gothic-style features, as well as the polyptych of the *Holy Martyrs of Lisbon*, by an anonymous artist but from a major Lisbon studio, closer to the Italian Renaissance style.

The Counter-Reformation movement, the setting up of the Inquisition in Portugal (1547) and Catholic orthodoxy dictated by the Council of Trent (1545–63) dealt a serious blow to artistic expression; painting became increasingly conventional. Altarpieces developed a tendency for compositional repetition and the command of anatomical detail became somewhat precarious. In spite of that there were still some worthwhile works of art, linked to the Italian or Spanish school. These include *Our Lady with Angel Musicians*, commissioned by Ponta Delgada Jesuits from Vasco Pereira for the Church of Ponta Delgada (now in the Carlos Machado Museum) and produced in Seville in 1604, and a set of mannerist paintings by Francisco Álvares in the sacristy of the Church of São Pedro (Ponta Delgada). Outstanding is the group of eight paintings representing the infancy of Christ, painted by an anonymous artist for the Church of São Gonçalo in Angra; it is already linked to the early Baroque and shows a clear Italian influence. Simultaneously with the imposition of artistic conventionality ran the taste for luxury and ostentation in religious rituals; this led to churches being covered in gilded carvings, panels of glazed tiles and altars adorned with gold, silver and marble.

Sailing ships arriving from the Orient brought into the Azores new riches; marble figurines of the Good Shepherd in the meditative pose of the Buddha or Virgins in Glory with oriental features and a hieratic pose of which a collection can be seen in the Carlos Machado Museum. Others include Indo-Portuguese counters with inlays of marble and mother-of-pearl (examples in Angra Museum and Palácio de Sant'Ana in Ponta Delgada) and bookcases designed to hold the plainsong books (Ponta Delgada parish church, Angra Cathedral). In the same way Chinese porcelain – pots, vases, plates and platters – sent by the Companhia das Indias from the 17th–19th centuries were also imported as were Hindu tapestries which greatly influenced the designs of glazed tiles. Worthy of special mention in the context of Hindu-Portuguese art originating from the Malabar coast (Goa) and Sri Lanka are the two paintings in the Church of Santa Cruz da Graciosa, depicting São Francisco Xavier and Santo Inácio de Loyola dressed in long robes with golden adornments, brought in during the 17th century.

Portuguese art makes great use of the glazed tiles that bring colour and brightness to architectural space and can be used to depict natural scenes, tell stories in narrative sequences or extend architectural patterns by illusion. There was no local production in the Azores, so the existing tiles are the product of commissions from the mainland where they have been made for centuries.

After the phase of Hispano-Arabic glazed tiles, some 16th-century examples of which are in various Azorean chapels (the most complete comes from Seville and is now in the Casa da Cultura at Ribeira Grande), Portuguese glazed tile-making expanded, patterns diversified and new techniques developed. There are polychrome altar fronts with a symmetrical composition and plant motifs, directly inspired by oriental textiles, which were in former Azorean shrines and chapels. Good examples are in the Carlos Machado Museum; the sets are full of peacocks, vases of flowers and friezes of exotic animals. There is also the pediment of the private chapel of the Chaves, now in the Palácio de Sant'Ana in Ponta Delgada; another is from the chapel of Anjos, on the island of Santa Maria, dating from 1679. Equally abundant are the wall coverings with blue, white and yellow glazed tiles, called *padronagem em tapete*; they repeat stylised plant motifs, applied inside decorative borders. A fine example of these are the 17th- and 18th-century glazed tiles that completely line the beautiful chapel of the Monastery of Caloura (São Miguel). Entirely mannerist are the tiles from the sacristy of the Church of São José de Ponta Delgada, Church of São Roque (São Miguel), chapel of the Almas of the Church of São Francisco de Vila do Porto (Santa Maria) and Church of Conceição de Angra (Terceira).

In the Baroque period glazed tiles reached their zenith in terms of figurative, narrative compositions in blue and white. There are many examples. Among the finest are the panels in the lower choir of the Church of Esperança (Ponta Delgada) by António de Oliveira Bernardes, dated 1712 and relating scenes from the Passion of Christ; and the tiling of the main chapel in the Church of São José (Ponta Delgada) and in the Church of São Francisco in Horta, both illustrate the life of St Francis of Assisi and date from the same period. Also in Horta and worthy of special mention is the set from the parish church (former church of the Jesuit monastery) with scenes relating the life of Santo Inácio de Loyola. In Angra the glazed tiles which line the Church of São Roque (c1725) are worth seeing; in Livramento there is a fine picture depicting the Sermon of St Anthony to the Fishes; and the chapel of the Santíssimo Sacramento in the Church of Nossa Senhora do Monte do Carmo, with an excellent allegorical composition on the Eucharist, is one of the finest works in the archipelago, made in Lisbon around 1740.

The rococo period is represented in the Azores by some top-quality pieces. The return of polychromy, the spread of borders, bands, garlands, shells and other forms of decorative framing of great linear elegance, make the aesthetics of this Baroque period easily identifiable. The little Church of Santa Bárbara das Manadas on the island of São Jorge has one of the finest sets of polychrome glazed tiles with *rocaille* (shell) motifs, as well as a set of locally made carvings and paintings, which make this church a precious example of the alliance between cultivated and naïve art. Other examples of rococo glazed tiles are in São Pedro de Alcântara at Lages do Pico and in the Church of Santa Cruz da Graciosa. In the Piedade chapel in the Church of São José (Ponta Delgada) the rococo glazed tiles are combined with mouldings consisting of gilded carvings on white backgrounds.

Azorean Baroque is not expressed just in richly decorated glazed tiles; the entire church interior is usually full of gilded carvings, paintings and painted wood. The history of carving also goes back a long way but again it peaked in the Baroque period, especially during the reign of King John (D João V) when many shipments of gold came from Brazil enabling the carvings to be gilded. The Renaissance retables (carved and sometimes painted panels behind the altar) are replaced by the Baroque-style ornamentation with twisted columns, fluttering angels, birds pecking at grapes and drawn-back curtains. Examples can be found in almost every church; particularly rich are the carvings in the Church of São Gonçalo, Angra; in the main chapel of the Church of Esperança, Ponta Delgada, which covers the whole vault; in the Parish Church of Horta; and the most imposing of all the Azorean retables, the one in the main chapel of the Church of the Jesuits in Ponta Delgada, already in transition to rococo style.

The range of devotional sculptures is impressive, if not always of great quality. In addition to the gallery of Catholic saints and tutelary figures, the Virgins in Glory are a favourite theme; Horta parish church contains one of the most spectacular examples. Other subjects include the Holy Family, scenes dedicated to the cycle of Christ's Passion, including *pietàs*, and nativities such as in the churches of São Miguel in Vila Franca do Campo and Angústias in Horta.

Throughout this period in which religious art dominated, gold work was associated with liturgical ritual. A vast range of ornaments and precious objects including chalices, salvers, monstrances, incense boats, censers, chandeliers, candlesticks, crucifixes, processional crosses, etc today fills the church treasuries and is still used in worship. Only a few genuinely old pieces have survived the centuries of constant plundering by pirates, for whom churches and monasteries were a particularly rewarding target. The processional cross of the Church das Altares on Terceira is a late Gothic rarity, Flemish-made; also unique is the altar front in wrought silver in the chapel of the Sacramento in Angra Cathedral (17th century), probably Spanish in origin. Much more common, yet having enormous symbolic significance for the Azoreans, are the Crowns of the Holy Spirit in wrought silver, some dating back to the 17th century. In material riches and artistic value, however, nothing surpasses the treasury of Senhor Santo Cristo (Santuário da Esperança, Ponta Delgada). Consisting essentially of five pieces (*Glory, Crown, Sceptre, Cords* and *Reliquary*) that accompany the figure of Ecce Homo, originally designed and made in the 18th century during the reign of João V, it was later enriched with new gifts from the faithful. The *Glory* stands out, a fabulous piece weighing 4,850g; it is made of gold-plated platinum and contains 6,842 precious stones, among them four extremely rare topazes from Brazil. Made in Lisbon by the finest goldsmiths of João V, the *Glory* presents a complete lesson in theology, containing the symbols of the Trinity, Redemption and the Passion of Christ, all executed with wonderful precision and detail.

Progressively moving away from the religious context, the 19th and 20th centuries finally began to place art in the service of a bourgeois public with secular ideas. The initially timid decorative schemes that the Azorean nobility used in their manor houses and town houses (an unusual example dating from the 1940s are the glazed tile panels alluding to the loss of independence and restoration of Portugal, in the Palácio Bettencourt in Angra) gradually expanded and diversified. The new urban and liberal bourgeoisie, grown rich on the orange trade, contracted artists to paint their portraits and indulged in luxurious furniture, porcelain and textiles bought in England or France. Ambitious artists went to Paris to receive a proper academic training; such was the case with Marciano Henriques da Silva (1831–73) and Duarte Maia (1867–1922), the first a romantic, the second a naturalist, with work in the Carlos Machado Museum, Ponta Delgada.

The 20th century began with a new generation of artists who gathered in Paris, the city of light, along with many others seeking inspiration from the artistic avant-garde. Two Azoreans stand out, Domingos Rebelo (1891–1975) and Ernesto Canto da Maia (1890–1981). Rebelo, a painter, caricaturist and ceramicist, followed a path that diverged from the vanguard, focusing all his attention on local reality, on the landscapes, appearances and attitudes of the simple and common people that he perceived as the most authentic aspect of this landscape, and capturing them with the detail of an ethnographer. His most famous work, *Os Emigrantes* (The Emigrants), portrays with contained feeling the drama experienced by thousands of Azoreans obliged to leave the islands in search of a better future (his paintings may be seen in the Palácio da Conceição, Museu Carlos Machado, Arte Contemporânea in Lisbon, Viseu, Caldas da Rainha, Gulbenkian Foundation for Modern Art and in countless private collections).

Sculptor Canto da Maia embraced Parisian life with enthusiasm, showing in his synthetic and graphic style traces of the symbolism and stylised decorativeness of the 1920s and 1930s. Even so, his work reflects the deeper quest of a probing mind, meditating upon the themes of life, death and love. (Examples of his works are to be found in the Museu Carlos Machado, Gulbenkian Foundation, Musée des Années 30, Boulogne, and the Musée Jeu de Paume, Paris, as well as in various public spaces.)

In 1901, Carlos and Amélia, the Portuguese royal couple, officially visited the Azores. Their temporary residence was to be the Palácio de Sant'Ana in Ponta Delgada, and the occasion was a perfect excuse for the most complete decorative renovation that had ever been carried out in a non-religious context. From 1915 to the late 1930s, painters, sculptors, decorators and carvers, both Azorean and from the continent, worked at Sant'Ana. Worth examining are the enormous paintings in the vestibule by Ernesto Condeixa, referring to the royal visit; the frieze in the former armoury; a bas-relief in gilded plaster of Paris by Canto da Maia; and the dining room lined with magnificent carved panelling and furniture entirely made by local artists. There are also extensive glazed-tile pictures made by the painter Jorge Colaço.

In the second half of the 20th century, particularly in the last two decades, Azorean arts blossomed. Art exhibitions and galleries of fine arts have been supported and new art programmes have been initiated. Throughout its history, Azorean art has mirrored movements in Europe, and developed its own style affected by local conditions and materials. In the 21st century the internet adds to the external influences, while artists and photographers pursue contemporary Azorean themes and concerns.

These are many, both religious and secular, and take place on all the islands, mostly during the summer months. They are listed in each island's chapter; some festivals are common to all the islands, while others are island-specific. Some dates are fixed, others change each year, and you should check with the tourist information office. Visitors during the summer months will be very unlucky not to chance upon one during their stay; they are often joyful occasions and the kindness and generosity given to strangers make for happy memories.

The most important festival that is celebrated throughout the archipelago is that of the Holy Ghost (*Espírito Santo*), held six weeks after Easter on the seventh Sunday. It can also be repeated on the following Sunday if enough people have made promises to make the festival, and if emigrants come back to visit in the summer it can again be celebrated. Of 13th-century medieval origin imported from the mainland, it is one of the most traditional, although each island and each village has its own variation. On the chosen day, offerings of bread, meat and wine are distributed among the needy, followed by a procession through the town or village. You may notice small chapels called *impérios* in most of the villages at road junctions or on prominent corners. These are a source of great pride and they form the centrepoint of the *Espírito Santo* festival. This festival is under the direction of a local group of men, a brotherhood, who undertake the care of the *impérios* and the giving of food to the poor, an important feature of *Espírito Santo*. Above the doors of most *impérios* you will find symbols: the crown, the sceptre, the dove and a red banner. The symbols are also to be found on the silver crowns which are worn by the *imperador*, the member of the brotherhood in charge of that day's festivities. Several *imperadors* may be crowned in each village during the festival season and each has the honour of guarding the crown and sceptre on a throne in his home until the next procession. Some of these precious village crowns and sceptres are many hundreds of years old. Fireworks signal the end of the opening church service and the start of a procession from the church to the *império* led by the crowned *imperador*. Music is provided by the local brass marching band, or *filarmonica*. These bands are a major part of village life in the Azores where there are more such groups than in all of Portugal. After the procession a beef-based broth, called *sopas do Espírito Santo*, is served as well as another Azorean food with a strong tradition: *massa sovada*, a slightly sweet bread made in homes by groups of women taking turns during hours of hand-kneading. This festival, brought by the first settlers to the islands in the early 1400s, is seldom seen in Europe today, but is celebrated by communities of Azorean ancestry around the world, especially in the USA, including Hawaii, and in Canada.

Other festivals are for saints' days or for vows made long ago to God. The most colourful is the Festival of Corpus Christi, and the preparation is as interesting as the procession. This takes place in June. Early in the morning many baskets of various small colourful flowers and finely chopped soft branch tips of the conifer *Cryptomeria japonica* are brought in and laid out in geometrical patterns upon the roadway using wooden templates, the colours all kept in separate shapes. The flowers and petals are frequently sprayed with water to keep them fresh and to stop the wind from disturbing the patterns or blowing them away. Sometimes dyed woodshavings are also used. Summer flowers in baskets and pots adorn balconies, and bright bedcovers hanging from windows add further colour. The procession is led by the priest under a pallium escorted by his followers and many small children dressed as angels. Much less formal is the June Festival of São João, marked with picnics at the many barbecue sites throughout the islands. The secular festivals get bigger every year and are celebrated by music, dance, arts, local culture, food stalls

The Festival of the Holy Ghost differs a little from island to island and from village to village and São Jorge celebrates the festival in its own way. Every village that has a church also has a small chapel called an *império*. The festival extends beyond its religious role; it is also a good excuse to have a good time.

The old traditions can still be enjoyed in the village of Rosais; they are centred on the *Carro das bandeiras* – an oxcart carrying a boat constructed from bamboo canes and green leaves and decorated on all sides with paper flowers, with colourful flags waving from long canes on the top. The carts are not just decorative, they have an important role: to bring to the *império* wine, sweet bread, cheese and lupin seeds. The lupin seeds have to be soaked in seawater for three tides, after which they are boiled. The festive food is then served free to all visitors during Saturday. Usually there are two carts and much rivalry exists between the two competing teams of villagers. The ornaments with which the horns of the oxen are decorated are kept strictly secret until the festive day and can never be repeated.

Independent of the religious festival is Mordomia in which anyone in the village can participate, after joining one of many local groups. Donations of corn and other products are made, usually the previous year, and sold, and the proceeds are used to help with the preparation of the festival. The remaining expenses are divided between the members of individual organising groups. Mordomias are organised by most villages on São Jorge, so don't be surprised if you see cars stopped in the middle of the street to be offered some wine and sweet bread. These celebrations take place on the Saturday before the Festival of the Holy Ghost.

The organiser of the religious festival is called the *imperador* and is usually someone who has undertaken the work voluntarily. These types of festivals are increasingly expensive to organise because in some villages, like Beira and Topo, there is a tradition to invite anyone who passes through to eat for free. In the past people did not have cars

and sporting events. Music includes not only folklore, but pop groups from the mainland and Brazil, something not always viewed with enthusiasm by everyone.

TOURADA Á CORDA – BULLFIGHTS ON A ROPE The bulls are not killed and the only blood spilt is that of over-confident humans! Terceira is especially noted for its *tourada á corda*, but other islands also participate.

The organisers have introduced regulations and planned a classification system for the bulls. No more than four bulls are allowed at any one event. Each must be at least three years old, and can appear only once for no more than 30 minutes. Cloaks and similar items are allowed, but anything that could cause injury to the bulls is banned. Action can only take place during daylight, and in the late afternoon/early evening.

The bull is at the end of a long rope that is held by several men to try and keep him under some control. The fun comes in approaching the bull as close as one dares and then outmanoeuvring him while keeping clear of his horns. I vividly recall one year watching on a quayside when the bull really got up speed and chased five boys the length of the quay. Having nowhere else to go, they leapt off the end into the harbour and the bull had so much momentum he could not stop and went in on top of them to a tremendous cheer from the crowd and creating a huge tidal wave. The bull appeared to rather 'enjoy' it, a nice cooling swim to the slipway at the end of a warm afternoon! Terceira and Graciosa both have bullrings, but here the bull is let loose without a rope.

These events have become very popular with over 200 meetings each year. In the past it was not only an entertainment but also an excuse for people from to get about and only local people came for the meal. Now the feast can attract many people from the entire island and it can be crowded. The village of Manadas has its festivities at lunchtime on the Thursday before the Holy Ghost day. Food is served on long tables, sometimes outside in the street. There is a special Holy Spirit soup, wine, *alcatra* sweet bread and sweet rice for dessert.

In Rosais you can also see the *foliões*: two or three men, one or two playing the drums and the other one singing in front of the *império* and walking up and down the square. The singing is improvised, sometimes repeated; it can be about God and the kindness of the Holy Ghost, or it can praise the organisation. The musicians are accompanied by the *cavaleiro*, a young man with two helpers. The *cavaleiro* carries a flag and the helpers bring two huge loaves of bread, called the castles, usually quite hard because they are so big (100cm x 50cm). On Sunday afternoon after the mass and the procession, *foliões* and the *cavaleiro* perform a traditional dance with the bread, to the accompaniment of the drums and the singing. After that there is a merry game for all. The *cavaleiro* comes out of the *império* with a cake or dolls made of sweet bread in his hands, and attempts a dance, to be accosted suddenly by someone trying to steal the cake and run away with it. The helpers must then run behind and try to touch the thief with a rod. If they succeed, the thief has to return the cake; if he escapes, the cake is his. The more people take part, the more fun there is to be had.

In Norte Grande, each evening of that week a big dog-whelk shell is used to call everyone to the *imperador*'s house. The sound carries round the entire village. The *imperador* then invites the guests to sing the rosary at his house where he keeps an altar made specially for this event. It is decorated with candles and flowers and at the top is the crown of the Holy Ghost. The rosary is sung in a way unique to this event. After the rosary, the *imperador* offers sweets and drinks to all comers.

different villages to meet, both socially and for business. Animals could be bought and sold, goods traded or exchanged, youths could demonstrate to the girls their dash and courage with the bulls, there would be refreshment stalls and it was all huge fun. It still is.

HOW IT WAS IN THE PAST

One day on São Jorge I was sitting over a coffee with António Pedroso, an old friend who lives in a beautifully restored town house in Velas. António is an artist, a collector and restorer of antiques, a church organist and much else. He told me that rural children were given responsibility at an early age. A farmer, for example, would give his young son a small calf to look after and when it was ready for market the boy was allowed to keep the money and reinvest it in more calves thus gaining in his early years a good introduction to the economic world. He continued, reminiscing about the time of his own childhood not so many years ago, and I asked him to write it down. Here is what he sent me:

Life on São Jorge island has changed out of all recognition in the last two or three decades. Before the 1970s, there was no mains electricity and no mod-cons. Life was simple and harsh and people had to create their own amusements. Two major events, one many miles away, the other local, changed all that.

First, there was a revolution in Portugal in 1975 and the liberation of Angola from Portuguese rule when hundreds of ex-patriots returned from Angola. Although some spent only a few years there, most did quite well and a handful became quite rich, but in the upheaval all lost everything; on returning home to the Azores via mainland Portugal financial support was granted to them to begin a new life. Many of them re-emigrated to the United States or Canada, but some remained on São Jorge. Abroad they were used to big country ways and big cities like Luanda with busy, aggressive markets, so when they started new businesses in the Azores, they had a considerable effect on the traditionally run local economy. The second event literally shook the island to its roots. A big earthquake in 1980 destroyed a large area of São Jorge and financial aid again came to the island to help with reconstruction. The two events had a profound effect on the life of the locals. And as always, some changes were good and others bad.

All water had to be brought in from outside water pumps; women had to ensure the supply, sometimes helped in the heavy task by the children. Water was transported in pottery jars which the women carried on their heads. In most developed countries, life without electricity is something to be experienced for fun during holidays or something to be read about; only the oldest people remember it as an everyday fact. Those born in the countryside of São Jorge, however, had the luxury of mains electricity as late as 30 years ago. Before then, there were no refrigerators and no television, and people had much more time for each other. There was enough time for everything.

January with its relatively cold weather was the pig-killing season and as such, a time for friends and families to join together. Whole communities participated in the organisation. Preparations started well ahead with cleaning all the required tools and utensils for carving, salting and boiling, including pottery jars in which the meat would be stored, to be used in the coming months. Next, women would concentrate on peeling and chopping a mountain of onions and parsley for various sausages. The men would meanwhile go in search of armfuls of wild heath (*Erica azorica*), needed to burn off pig bristles. On the chosen day, the men would arrive very early, whilst it was still dark, to be received by the owners of the house, and the pig, and offered a little warming refreshment – usually *aguardente* and *biscoito* (sweet bread).

The pig, quite oblivious to its fate, would be released from its pen and charge, squealing happily with the unexpected freedom, up the village street, pursued by equally merrily squealing men. The fatal blow would come suddenly and then all would turn into purposeful activity. All blood would be caught in a pan, to be mixed with green onions and rice for black sausage, *morcelas*. Skin bristles would be burnt off with heath twigs; alternatively, the carcass would be scalded with boiling water and bristles rubbed off with pieces of basalt. The beast would then be opened, the heart and liver taken out to be cooked immediately for communal lunch, and the intestines would be cleaned with copious quantities of lemons and oranges, and used later as tender sausage casings. After thorough cleaning, the pig would be hung from sturdy hooks in a cellar or another cool part of the house, the empty belly secured open with bamboo canes to air, to rest until the following day when it would be cut up for further processing.

After this exhausting effort, a big meal would be served in the evening to the family and friends, and half the village would join later in a masquerade, accompanied by Portuguese guitar playing, singing and dancing. Next day the carcass would be cut up, large portions salted and stored or cooked and stored, small bits of meat and pork fat would be made into another type of sausage, *linguiça*, that would be hung on hooks in a huge chimney and smoked with bacon joints. All traditional Azorean houses had chimneys built for this purpose. Nowadays a pig of a required size can be dispatched by an efficient butcher at any time, fresh cuts simply stored in a refrigerator or freezer and natural (or artificial) casings, all nicely prepared, bought in a slaughterhouse. Much cleaner, much quicker and much less fun.

São Jorge is relatively mountainous and most villages nestle among pastures at the altitude of 400–500m. Low down near the sea are the *fajãs*, flat areas at the foot of the cliffs. Shelter here results in a microclimate favourable to plants; coffee, tropical fruit, figs and grapes can be grown and most local farmers produce their own wine. During February and March, families traditionally used to move to the *fajãs* for a time to take care of the vines, dig the land and plant potatoes. For this purpose there was often a simple second house built in the vicinity, frequently with a small barn attached, just good enough to provide accommodation for the farmer and one or two milking cows. Between the fields in the *fajã* or higher up on the cliffs, quantities of *Pittosporum undulatum* and other evergreens provided a plentiful supply of green leaves that the cows consumed with relish. This being also the carnival season, children had school holidays and could help their parents in the fields. Not all was work, of course; the usual way of enjoying the *Carnaval* day was to play with water of which there is no shortage in the *fajãs*, and if you got soaked, no matter, the weather was much warmer here than higher up in the villages.

September was the time to make wine and to pick up figs and loquat for *aguardente*, and time for moving down again. The families were moving with oxcarts heaped with mattresses (usually made of strong linen stuffed with corn leaves), blankets, pottery and all the other paraphernalia, women and children sitting on top of all that. Every *fajã* had a small chapel and various patron days meant a big festivity with a mass and a procession; on the Saturday before there would be a bullfight in the street. In the evening there would be theatre and folk music. A bullfight in a *fajã* was always a very colourful affair: the highest walls around the street would become crowded with viewers, especially women carrying coloured umbrellas to protect them from the sun, with green vineyards, black basalt stone walls and the blue sea providing an impressionistic backdrop. The bull was the star of the festival, and was never hurt. The same could not always be said about the people; if the bull jumped into someone's garden, a hilarious scene ensued with umbrellas flying, people running or climbing fig trees.

The only industry on the island was and is the cheese production; however, since all cattle including milking cows are kept on pastures all the year round, milk production drops off in winter and there is enough for cheese only between March and October. In the past when milk was not pasteurised, all farmers kept one or two cows in the barn to ensure a supply of fresh milk for the family in winter. Modern islanders simply buy their pasteurised milk at the supermarket and farmers drive to the *fajãs* whenever work needs to be done; only a few old ones still keep the tradition of twice-yearly migration.

October was a traditional cereal harvest season, neighbours helping neighbours and whole families engaged. Ripe corn would be cut in the field, loaded on to oxcarts and brought to barns (*palheiros*) built on each farm usually from basalt blocks; most barns had a ground floor where the wheat or maize was milled, and a first floor where straw and maize ears were stored. In the evening young people would sit together and clean the husk from the cobs, with much singing and teasing of each other, or dreaming of the future, whilst the village elders would sit, doze, or tell stories from the past. Suddenly a girl cries 'A red one!' – she has just found a red grain that entitles her to a kiss from everyone, but with the strict chaperoning of unmarried girls, it is a wonderful opportunity to receive a kiss from the one dear to her heart. No-one can object.

Theatres, folk dances and philharmonic orchestras have always been much enjoyed on the island during the long winter nights in spite of – or perhaps because of – an otherwise hard life. The traditional theatre had no place for women, men usually performing all the roles and, similarly, participation in some folk dances was the preserve of the men. Even now, with the pervasive influence of television, São Jorge maintains 15 orchestras, each with 40 to 60 musicians. Although nobody wants to miss an opportunity to participate in cultural events, it is becoming increasingly

From the writings of early travellers to the Azores it appears that at least until the end of the 16th century only watermills, *moinhos de água*, were present on the islands, and that the windmills were a later innovation. Old long-disused watermills are still abundant and often now hidden beneath the vigorous growth of ginger lilies that also like the humid stream beds. The mills were built either over streams or below specially constructed dams, or were even seasonal, relying upon the heavier winter rains to drive them.

Like so many aspects of the archipelago, individual islands developed their own style of windmills, and there were at least eight different versions, of which four are still extant.

SÃO MIGUEL TYPE These are similar to the so-called 'Dutch' type and are found mainly on São Miguel, Santa Maria and Graciosa, with small differences between those on each island. They have a conical stone-built base with a wooden semi-ovoid rotating roof, and have four cloth-covered sails.

FAIAL TYPE This has a truncated cone-shaped stone base with a substantial timber upper structure called a *casota*, or little house. Access is by a staircase which also acts as a central tail to the *casota*. Originally it should have had a long mast with a pointed tip and eight crossed poles tied by guides and wire fasteners for triangular cloth sails, without bars. Today it is almost always of the square type, or is even replaced by rotors of two or four vanes. This type is to be seen on Faial and Pico.

SÃO JORGE TYPE São Jorge has two types of windmill: the mechanical mill now most commonly seen is a modified form of an earlier mill. This earlier version had four triangular sails made of cloth without lattice work. The later, adapted version has a stone-built conical base upon which is a narrow vertical mill providing an elevated support for the rotor of either two or four blades. This small mill can either rotate or be fixed in which case only the dome rotates. The narrow tail leads either from the body of the mill or its dome, reaching to the ground.

CORVO TYPE Corvo's distinctive type has a low stone base and a squat conical tower, almost always rendered and whitewashed. The tower is built well inside the edges of the base so there is a wide ledge all round. The mast is long and pointed, leans upwards at a low angle and has eight sail poles with guides and fasteners for triangular cloth sails. Internal access is through a door in the tower reached by an external stone stairway rising from the ledge.

difficult to find dedicated players; practice must now be organised so that it does not interfere with television broadcasts of football matches and soap operas.

People on São Jorge worked very hard; men outside, tending the cows in the pastures and working in the fields, while women stayed mainly in the house; one exception was the village of Toledo where men preferred a good sleep and sent their womenfolk to tend the cows! Generally, however, women were busy at home, taking care of the children, looking after the house and processing wool and flax and weaving. Most houses had a loom on which women would make bedcovers and material for clothes, or they would knit socks and pullovers. Dyes for the wool were made from plants; wool would be boiled with the appropriate plant material and sometimes salt for colour fixing. The following were commonly used: *Erica azorica*, green; *Juniperus brevifolia*, reddish-grey; *Rocella tinctoria* (urzela, a lichen), wine red; and onion skins, light-brown. Men in turn would gather suitable cedarwood for homemade galoshes for which women would make the uppers. Straw was used to make hats; this was done especially on Pico, and at the beginning of summer many women from Pico would come selling hats.

On this island of black lava rocks, many women were always seen in black. Religious customs demanded that any widow had to dress in black for the rest of her life. Apart from black clothes, a widow had to wear a black-fringed square shawl and have her head covered by a triangular woollen scarf. After a loss of a parent, black was obligatory for two or three years; the loss of a brother meant black clothes for a year.

Many women therefore spent most of their life in black. The rule was less strict for the men: mourning was expressed by a simple black band on the upper arm, except for Sundays when they all took out their black suits; this was usually the suit made for the wedding and used until the last journey to the cemetery. In the last 20 years young people have adopted the colour black as a fashion statement, and under the American influence, the widows are changing slowly to wearing grey and even some colours, but in the countryside the traditional black persists.

All expenses associated with a wedding and the related festivities were borne by the bride's parents, who provided the dowry including all linen for the new house. The groom's duty was to pay for the house and the rings. Business was a male activity but women held the purse strings, particularly in the countryside. This was not just because the women were house managers but also because they could often read better than men who were sometimes illiterate. Thus women exercised a big influence on the organisation of rural life.

2

Practical Information

The islands are very green and in the middle of the Atlantic. This means the weather is variable, and while at any time there can be a week or more of continuous glorious sunshine and blue skies, it can also be fickle.

You will be welcomed everywhere and find that English is widely spoken; but when you enter a café away from the main centres or seek directions out in the country you might have fun trying to communicate. You will also be very safe, for there is little crime or street violence, although drugs and alcohol are problems locally.

Ferry services and domestic flights keep reasonably well to the timetables except for understandable delays through bad weather – in the case of aircraft this can just be wind affecting certain of the airports. Communications are excellent, the islands and their public facilities are very clean, and standards are high.

The cost of many items is greater than in mainland Portugal but compared with northern Europe prices for the visitor are very reasonable, and the budget traveller can, with care, manage very well. In winter it gets dark about 18.30, in summer about 21.00, and time is Greenwich Mean Time –1.

ATTRACTIONS

The greatest attraction for many is the tranquillity and the lack of pollution: the quiet rural scenes of small houses, the pastures, the grazing cows on a stage of lush green grass and the backdrop of a deep blue sea, farmers on horseback with milk churns hanging from their saddles, the little pony cart clattering along the cobbles with more milk churns, the cattle dogs perched on top. Then the scenery is so lovely and ever changing, from sea to coast and often spectacular cliffs, to pastures or stony vineyards, up into forest and hills of often conical shape until finally a volcano's caldera and other heights lost in cloud. Blue hydrangeas and the Azores may have become a cliché but to see an island seeming as if a fisherman's net with extra large holes had been thrown over it creating a pattern of blue lines and enclosures remains, all the same, a remarkable sight.

Even the largest towns, including the busy capital, Ponta Delgada, have an irresistible allure that urges the visitor to explore them. Many ordinary street buildings have an elegant simplicity with lovely adornments of wrought-iron balconies or perhaps some ornamented basalt carving while grander places may show a more ornate Manueline influence. Small retailers are modest and sometimes do not advertise their presence while often the stock is held in the shop's dark recess so that it is difficult to decide what it is they are selling. The narrow cobbled backstreets, although plagued by cars, have constricted pavements while bigger thoroughfares have grander ones; whatever their size they are made of small squares of black basalt and imported white granite that is used to make designs appropriate to the place: caravels, whaling boats, whales, fish, figures dressed in the no-longer-worn *capote* or cloak, windmills, sheaves of corn – there is no end to the pavior's enterprise. For the foot-weary there are street cafés and good ice creams to enjoy while seated watching island life pass by, or many a quiet church for contemplation.

Certain islands are perfect for exploring by car, and endless hours can be spent discovering rural roads or following up those that do not appear on maps. There are so many tempting places to park the car and just lean on a fence post and enjoy a view or listen to the birds. Should you tire of rural scenery, then comes the satisfying contrast of dropping down to the coast and into a little village; maybe at its centre is the main church, a tiny public garden with its bandstand, and a café, or perhaps you have chanced upon a fishing village with a harbour and nearby natural swimming pools for an ocean swim and a fish restaurant to follow.

Whale watching has become tremendously popular since it first began on Pico years ago and uses the old expertise of the lookouts to spy the cetaceans. It is a truly world-class cetacean hot spot and between 6% and 10% of all known cetacean species can sometimes be seen in a single three-hour trip. Numerous enterprises now offer the experience. Diving offers a range of opportunities, from wrecks to sea cliffs and extraordinary underwater lava formations, and several companies offer their services. Many small fishing boats can be seen, either drawn up on the harbour quays or gently bobbing a short distance offshore, and if you feel tempted there are fishermen registered to take you out to fish for your supper. At the other end of the spectrum, the Azores are renowned internationally for sport- or big-game fishing, especially for blue marlin, and many world-record catches have been made, although of course these are for putting back and not for eating!

Going hand in hand with the tranquillity and clean environment is walking, the finest way to acquire a real feel for the islands. There are short walks and long walks, in the mountains, along the coast, sometimes on narrow trails, at other times on seldom-used farm roads. The views are always changing, and relics of the past are everywhere, from wheel-worn donkey paths hidden beneath the summer's flush of vegetation to abandoned farmhouses and crumbling watermills. Hiking routes are slowly being signposted, but there is still a long way to go before access and waymarking is reliable. Some published walks are short and not linked to transport, and the descriptions can be vague. Winter storms cause landslides, and vegetation is so lush that in a very few weeks paths are concealed. For mountain walks it is best to check with the local tourist information office or your travel agent that the walk is clear before setting out. The impression is given that routes are managed by office-based bureaucrats, and not by a practical ranger or forester on the ground. However, if you are prepared to risk some possible frustration and the need to fall back upon your own sense of direction, you will enjoy many a memorable walk.

For those who prefer, guides are sometimes available through the local travel agencies.

The golf course at Furnas on São Miguel must be one of the world's most intimate and exquisitely beautiful courses, given its mountain setting with sheltering forests and numerous elegant tree ferns. It is little known, but for any golfer who values the environment and surroundings in which he or she plays, this course cannot fail to impress. However, it is not without hidden challenges, for its luxuriant vegetation reflects its relationship with the clouds, and it can be quite entertaining to drive off into a white mist that has suddenly descended and might well instantly clear to give advantage to your opponent. There are two other equally green courses to play, both at much lower altitudes.

THE CLIMATE The Azores have a mild and equable climate surrounded as they are by a huge expanse of sea and influenced by the warm Gulf Stream. This means they are pleasant to be in at any time of the year. The average winter temperature is 13°C, only sometimes dropping to around 4°C at night; frosts occur only above 1,000m. In summer the average is 23°C with a maximum of 27°C. Rain can and does fall in every month, but it is seldom persistent; and one can drive from rain through a world of rainbows into sunshine. There is a saying in the islands that you can have all four seasons in one day and this is amazingly true. If it is raining in the morning, do not despair – there could be clear skies and sunshine by lunchtime. Likewise, the reverse is often true! Ponta Delgada has an annual rainfall of around 700mm; this increases by travelling westwards to almost 1,600mm in Santa Cruz on Flores. Average humidity is around 80–85%, but can go up to 100%. Flowers love it! Many days are still or with a gentle breeze. However, winds can occasionally be strong and this is especially noticeable on exposed mountains.

For swimmers the sea temperatures also vary relatively little and you will often see people bathing off the beaches throughout the winter when the lowest sea temperatures are 15–16°C in February and March. The highest are in August and September with an average of around 22–24°C.

There are small variations between the individual islands, with Santa Maria seen as the sunniest, while the western islands are the wettest. June and July are the warmest months and should have the most stable weather. April and September normally tend to be the most changeable, but all the old patterns are changing, like everywhere else in the world. Every month is a delight in the Azores and even in January we have enjoyed our ritual walker's lunch of local cheese, fresh bread and a bottle of wine, sitting in a field in bright sunshine without jackets or jerseys.

TIMING The time to go depends upon what you want to do. If it is to do with the sea – inter-island ferry travel, whale watching, sailing or fishing – then you need to go in the summer months between mid April and early October. People swim throughout the year, but the popular times for the beaches are again the summer months and into October, but remember the Azores are not beach destinations. Regarding flowers, there will always be something of interest but for the beautiful and spectacular hedgerows you should consider June and July to see them at their best, and for native species May to September is the best time. For walking, the whole year is good, but the rain in winter is usually colder than in summer! In winter you will also have to take extra care in the mountains. In summer there are more eating places open and they keep longer daytime opening hours. During the high season of July and August hotels throughout the islands are usually fully booked and the casual traveller may have considerable difficulty in getting accommodation. The same goes for car rental. In summer it is impossible to rent a car on arrival and advance reservation is essential; similarly for bicycles. Increasingly this is becoming the situation for June and September. In addition to inbound tourists, many Azoreans who emigrated to North America come back to see relatives, while second and third generations return to discover their roots. March and April, still low season, are beautiful months because spring is early in the Azores and by now nature is wide awake; autumn is a much longer season than in northern Europe and October and November have lovely warm days while the golden hues of falling leaves prevail into December. And December is the Christmas festival season when every town from almost the month's beginning is festooned with lights and decorations in a very Azorean way that is so charming and does not hint of commercialism.

Slow down, relax and enjoy yourself.

As the Azores is so little known beyond Portugal and so many visitors arrive at this archipelago with mixed ideas of what to expect, most are surprised to discover how green the islands are. At the same time we are not a place for sun-drenched holidays, entertainment or busy nightlife. Please accept the Azores, its landscape and many interests for what they are and not what you might have expected them to be. If this is your approach right from the start, we are sure the islands will give you a lifetime of happy memories of your visit.

Slow down and adapt to our way of doing things. We do not have the bustling pressures found in other places of Europe; we have our own scale, and things still get done, although they may take a little longer. It is time for you to relax and enjoy yourself.

HOLIDAY ITINERARY Sometimes arrangements are affected by events beyond our control, and planes and ferries are rescheduled or cancelled. Please be flexible about your itinerary, because everything will be solved and we are here to look after you. Do contact your travel agent in the Azores if you have any questions; please don't feel you are left on your own.

MEETING THE AZOREAN LIFE Travel slowly and enjoy our ways of living should our paths cross when out in the countryside or in a café. Even if the Azoreans do not speak your language, they always try to communicate.

SAFETY Everywhere in the Azores you still feel safe from crime. However, like anywhere else, it is wise to always lock your car and take normal care of your valuables. When out walking in the hills, do be careful of the weather; if thick mist suddenly appears it is easy to lose your way, and make sure you have warm clothing.

COMPLAINTS/PROBLEMS If you have any complaints during your stay, please let your tour operator's representative in the Azores or your Azores travel agent know about it immediately, not at the end of your holiday when it may be too late to improve things.

FINALLY Please think of us as your friends, not guides or travel agents, and of yourselves as our guests, not tourists. We shall enjoy having you as much as we hope you will enjoy being with us.

PLANNING AN ITINERARY: WHICH ISLANDS? The speed of the Azores is slow, and slowly is how one should discover them. There are nine islands and if you were to attempt to see them all in one visit to the archipelago you would need several weeks to do them justice. Should you try and visit too many islands in a short period you will end up spending a disproportionate amount of time waiting in airports. If you have just a week, then you might be well advised to concentrate on the largest and most diverse island, São Miguel. If you have more time, maybe combine São Miguel with Faial and Pico with perhaps Terceira as well for your first visit (these islands will easily take up two weeks) and then see other islands on return visits! Various islands suit different means of touring.

If you like to hire a car and take your time exploring then São Miguel, Santa Maria, Terceira, Pico, São Jorge and Flores would make the best choices.

If you prefer to tour by taxi and public bus then much of São Miguel can be accessed by bus. Graciosa is small, there are buses, and distances are so short taxi fares are reasonable. Terceira means the city of Angra for which you do not need a car and adjacent Monte Brasil can also be explored on foot. A half-day taxi tour would provide a glimpse of many of the other highlights. Faial offers Horta and nearby attractions, and a half-day taxi tour will take in the island's main features. Pico can be visited in a day from Horta, with a half-day tour seeing the western sector.

For walking, São Jorge has long been supreme, but São Miguel is fast catching up with its development of trails around Furnas and Povoação. Then comes Flores followed by Pico if you want to climb the mountain. São Miguel is best for gardens and Pico has the most accessible native flora. Birdwatchers should give priority to São Miguel, São Jorge, Pico and especially Flores and Corvo in the autumn, although the old quarry at Praia on Terceira is also excellent for rare waders at this time.

ORGANISED TOURS

The Azores are most popular with the Scandinavians and Germans, after which come the French, Italians and, in 2004, about 6,000 British, and of course there is a very large Portuguese tourist traffic from the mainland, that make up the vast majority of visitors. For years it has been mostly small companies that have offered this destination, but now big tour operators are also doing so. Tour operators in their brochures sell the Azores for their tranquillity, landscapes, and the islands' way of life, and their retailers should know these qualities. Generally, however, the average high street travel agent knows little about the Azores, and it is the poor inbound agents in the islands who find themselves at the receiving end of irate complaints from clients who have just arrived to realise that there is no constantly blazing sun and endless sandy beaches. For those who wish to travel out of the main season or go to different islands from those offered in the standard package, some of the operators will be able to make a bespoke tour programme for you. Tour operators offering the Azores include the following:

UK

Archipelago Azores 1b Museum Sq, Keswick, Cumbria CA12 5DZ; ☏ 01768 775672; e info@azoreschoice.com; www.azoreschoice.com

Biosphere Expeditions Sprat's Water, near Carlton Colville, Broads National Park NR33 8BP; ☏ 0870 446 080; e uk@biosphere-expeditions.org; www.biosphere-expeditions.org. Arranges hands-on conservation projects collecting data on whales, dolphins and turtles.

David Sayers/Andrew Brock Travel 29A Main St, Lyddington, Oakham, Rutland LE15 9LR; ☏ 01572 821330; e ABROCK3650@aol.com

Destination Portugal Madeira Hse, 37 Corn St, Witney, Oxon OX28 6BW; ☏ 01993 773269; e info@destination-portugal.co.uk; www.destination-portugal.co.uk

Explore Worldwide Nelson Hse, 55 Victoria Rd, Farnborough, Hants GU14 7PA; ☏ 01993 773269/01252 319448; e info@exploreworldwide.com; www.exploreworldwide.com

Sunvil Discovery Sunvil Hse, Upper Sq, Old Isleworth,

Middx TW7 7BJ; ☏ 020 8758 4743; www.sunvil.co.uk

Whale Watch Azores 5 Old Parr Cl, Banbury, Oxon OX16 5HY; ☏ 01295 267652; e info@whalewatchazores.com; www.whalewatchazores.com

Belgium

Anders Reizen/Ikaros cvba Refugiestraat 15, 3290 Diest (België); ☏ +32 013 33 40 40; e info@andersreizen.be; www.andersreizen.be

Canada

Sunmed Holidays Inc 5245 Dundas St W, Toronto, Ontario M9B 1A5; ☏ +1 416 234 0774; www.sunmedholidays.com

Denmark

Billetkontoret A/S Ny Kongensgade 18, 1557 København V; ☏ +45 3690 3000; e jesper.schou@billetkontoret.dk; www.billetkontoret.dk

Festival Tours Tarskov Mølle – DK8462 Harlev; ☏ +45 8694 2411; e festivaltours@festivaltours.dk; www.Festivaltours.dk

Svante Rejser Tvendersgade 6, DK-1363 Copenhagen; ☎ +45 3315 2525; e svante@svante.dk; www.svante.dk

Arts et Vie 251 rue de Vaugirard, 75015 Paris; ☎ +33 01 40 43 20 21; e info@artsetvie.com; www.artsetvie.com
Atalante 5 rue du Sommerard, 75005 Paris; ☎ +33 01 55 42 81 00; e paris@atalante.fr; www.atalante.fr
Chamina-Sylva 52 rue de la Victoire, 75455 Paris; e contact@chamina-sylva.com; www.chamina-sylva.com

Bayerisches Pilgerbüro GmbH Dachauer Str 9, 80335 München; ☎ +49 089 545 8110; e bp@pilgerreisen.de; www.pelgerreisen.de
Berge & Meer Touristik GmbH Andréestraße 27, 56578 Rengsdorf; ☎ +49 060 316 2062; e online@berge-meer.de; www.berge-meer.de
Wikinger Reisen Kölner Str 20, 58135 Hagen; ☎ 0 23 31/90 47 42; e mail@wikinger.de; www.wikinger-reisen.de

Tripper Viaggi via Bari 17a, 10144 Torino; ☎ +39 011 8192413; e postmaster@tripperviaggi.com; www.tripperviaggi.com

Intertrek Da Costastraat 39, 2513 RN Den Haag; ☎ +31 070 36 36 416; e info@intertrek.nl
SNP Natuurreizen Groesbeekseweg 181, 6523 NR Nijmegen; ☎ +31 024 3277000; www.snp.nl

Abreu Tours Empire State Bldg, 350 Fifth Av, Suite 2414, New York, NY 10118-2414; ☎ +1 212 869 1840; e portugal@abreu-tours.com; www.abreu-tours.com
Azores Express PO Box 2819, South Main St, Fall River, MA 02721; ☎ +1 800 762 9995; e reservations@azores-express.com; www.azores-express.com
Azores Walks 8 Rideout Ln, Stoughton, MA 02072; ☎ +1 617 549 2452; e admin@azoreswalks.com; www.azoreswalks.com
Easy Rider Tours PO Box 228, Newburyport, MA 01950; ☎ +1 800 488 8332; e info@easyridertours.com; www. easyridertours.com
FreeGate Tourism 585 Stewart Av, Suite 310, Garden City, NY 11530; ☎ +1 516 222 0855; e mail@freegatetours.com; www.freegatetours.com
Portuguese Tours, Inc 22 Smith Pl, PO Box 400, Williston Pk, NY 11596; ☎ (within US): 908 352 6112, (from outside US): +1 516 742 5902; e info@portuguesetours.com; www.portuguesetours.com

LOCAL TRAVEL AGENTS There are many travel agents in the Azores, and in addition to the usual services of car hire, hotel reservations, airport transfers, etc these offer certain other activities.

Melo Agência de Viagens Rua de Sta Luzia 7–11, 9500-114 Ponta Delgada, São Miguel; ☎ 296 205 385; e geral@melo-lda.pt; www.melotravel.com. The first company to offer walking holidays in the Azores, they have self-guided programmes for nature lovers on both São Miguel and São Jorge. They also pioneered cycling holidays and offer an 8-day package. For whale watching daily departures in season are offered from São Miguel, Faial and Pico, and a 7-night package on Pico. Again for individual travellers, 3-, 4-, and 5-island tours are available, together with a tailor-made service.

RRTUR Agência de Viagens, Rua de Castilho 13, 9500-41 Ponta Delgada, São Miguel; ☎ 296 209 350; e Info@rrtur.com; www.rrtur.com. Offers golf packages, whale watching, and tours for one person to small groups on most of the islands.
Teles Agência de Viagens Rua da Sé 138, 9700-191 Angra do Heroísmo, Terceira; e angra@telestravel.com; www.telestravel.com. Offers a variety of packages from 2 to 10 nights to various islands, an 8-night golf package to Terceira and São Miguel, a week whale watching on Pico, and various anti-stress, recuperation and revitalisation health programmes at the Hotel do Caracol on Terceira.

AZORES TOURISM AUTHORITY The Regional Directorate of Tourism for the Azores headquarters is in Horta, on Faial (*Direcção Regional de Turismo, Rua Ernesto Rebelo 14, 9900-112 Horta*). They have branch information offices on all the islands, and publish informative brochures on each island illustrated with excellent photographs together with various other publications. Compiled each year are lists of approved family hotels (*pensão*) and rural accommodation, available upon request by letter or by email (*acoresturismo@mail.telepac.pt; www.drtacores.pt*).

RED TAPE

Portugal with the Azores are full members of the European Union, and nationals of other EU countries do not require a visa.

Should you need consular assistance during your stay these are the contact numbers of those consulates represented in the Azores. Largely these responsibilities are undertaken by private individuals in an honorary capacity without official premises. They can issue emergency passports and contact relatives.

UK Ponta Delgada; ☎ 296 628 175;
e amgm@net.sapo.pt
Brazil São Roque, São Miguel; ☎ 296 381 425
Canada Ponta Delgada; ☎ 296 281 488;
e canadapdl@mail.telelpac.pt
Denmark Ponta Delgada; ☎ 296 284 291
Finland Ponta Delgada; ☎ 296 381 378;
e Fbtavares@mail.telepac.pt
France Ponta Delgada; ☎ 296 284 129;
e santos.antonio@ftm.pt/aesantos@multi.pt
Germany São Vicente Ferreira, São Miguel; ☎ 296 911 133; e dhkonsul-azoren@iol.pt

Italy Ponta Delgada; ☎ 296 284 920
Netherlands Ponta Delgada; ☎ 296 301 800;
e antoniacordeiro@bensaude.pt
Norway Horta, Faial; ☎ 292 200 400/414;
e hrmartins@oma.pt; Ponta Delgada; ☎ 296 205030; e azevedocs@mail.telepac.pt
Republic of Cabo Verde Angra do Heroísma; ☎ 295 332 842
Sweden Vila Franco do Lampo, São Miguel; ☎ 296 582 776
USA Ponta Delgada; ☎ 296 282 216

GETTING THERE AND AWAY

While cruise ships put in at Ponta Delgada and Horta, really the only way to travel to the Azores today is to fly – unless you have access to a private yacht.

From the UK between April and October there is a weekly SATA Internacional (*www.sata.pt*) direct flight from Gatwick to Ponta Delgada on São Miguel. TAP Air Portugal (*www.flytap.com*) has departures throughout the year from Heathrow or Gatwick via Lisbon to Ponta Delgada, and with less frequency from Lisbon to Horta (on Faial), Lajes (Terceira), Santa Maria and Pico. Flights take approximately two hours to Lisbon and another two hours from Lisbon to the Azores.

SATA's flight cost starts at around £280 return. TAP is a little more with the change in Lisbon countered by the advantage you can fly to one island and return from certain others, thus saving you an inter-island flight or two and maybe some hours out of your holiday waiting at airports; you can also break your return journey and spend some nights in Lisbon. There are also flights from Funchal thus enabling you to combine Madeira with the Azores.

From northern Europe there are scheduled or charter flights throughout the year from Sweden, Norway and Denmark and additionally between April and October from Switzerland, Spain, Finland and Germany and doubtless these services will continue to expand.

The USA has scheduled flights between Boston and Ponta Delgada and from May to September charters from Boston and Oakland to Lajes. From Canada throughout the year there are flights from Toronto to Ponta Delgada and between May and September Toronto to Lajes on Terceira.

SATA Air Açores is the Azores-based airline and operates all the inter-island flights. SATA Internacional is a subsidiary company of SATA Air Açores licensed to operate outside the archipelago. Two other companies, also part of the SATA

Dr Jane Wilson-Howarth

Long-haul air travel increases the risk of deep vein thrombosis. Although recent research has suggested that many of us develop clots when immobilised, most resolve without us ever having been aware of them. In certain susceptible individuals, though, large clots form and these can break away and lodge in the lungs. This is dangerous but happens in a tiny minority of passengers.

Studies have shown that flights of over 5½ hours are significant, and that people who take lots of shorter flights over a short space of time form clots. People at highest risk are:

- Those who have had a clot before – unless they are now taking warfarin
- People over 80 years of age
- Anyone who has recently undergone a major operation or surgery for varicose veins
- Someone who has had a hip or knee replacement in the last three months
- Cancer sufferers
- Those who have ever had a stroke
- People with heart disease
- Those with a close blood relative who has had a clot

Those with a slightly increased risk:

- People over 40
- Women who are pregnant or have had a baby in the last couple of weeks
- People taking female hormones or other oestrogen therapy
- Heavy smokers
- Those who have very severe varicose veins
- The very obese
- People who are very tall (over 6ft/1.8m) or short (under 5ft/1.5m)

A deep vein thrombosis (DVT) is a blood clot that forms in the deep leg veins. This is

group, are Azores Express, operating charter flights between the USA and Azores, and SATA Express which runs charters between Canada and the Azores.

✚ HEALTH AND SAFETY

HEALTH All EU nationals visiting the Azores are entitled to the reciprocal arrangements covering medical care and expenses. Dental treatment will mostly have to be paid for. British nationals should have their European Health Insurance Card (EHIC), obtainable by phone (✆ *0845 606 2030*) or online (*www.dh.gov.uk/travellers*), or from the post office and some travel clinics. You should in any case have additional private travel insurance. Pregnant women, travellers with pre-existing illnesses and those travelling with children or going to remote areas may want to identify healthcare facilities prior to departure. However, larger hotels and tour company representatives are usually able to provide addresses for local services. The Foreign and Commonwealth Office can provide details of the nearest relevant embassy or consulate for emergencies.

Hospitals in the Azores are mostly new and equivalent to normal European standards. On certain islands where there are limited services emergency medical cases have to be flown either to Faial or Terceira. Health centres (*centro medico*) provide non-hospital treatment.

Pharmacies are widespread, but you should always take a sufficient supply of prescription drugs to more than last the length of your holiday. When travelling, do not pack them all in your suitcase; always make sure you have enough tablets and very different from irritating but harmless superficial phlebitis. DVT causes swelling and redness of one leg, usually with heat and pain in one calf and sometimes the thigh. A DVT is only dangerous if a clot breaks away and travels to the lungs (pulmonary embolus). Symptoms of a pulmonary embolus (PE) include chest pain that is worse on breathing in deeply, shortness of breath, and sometimes coughing up small amounts of blood. The symptoms commonly start three to ten days after a long flight. Anyone who thinks that they might have a DVT needs to see a doctor immediately who will arrange a scan. Warfarin tablets (to thin the blood) are then taken for at least six months.

PREVENTION OF DVT Several conditions make the problem more likely. Immobility is the key, and factors like reduced oxygen in cabin air and dehydration may also contribute. To reduce the risk of thrombosis on a long journey:

- Exercise before and after the flight
- Keep mobile before and during the flight; move around every couple of hours
- During the flight drink plenty of water or juices
- Avoid taking sleeping pills and excessive tea, coffee and alcohol
- Perform exercises that mimic walking and tense the calf muscles
- Consider wearing flight socks or support stockings (see www.legshealth.com)
- Take a meal of oily fish (mackerel, trout, salmon, sardines, etc) in the 24 hours before departure to reduce blood clotability and thus DVT risk
- The jury is still out on whether it is worth taking an aspirin before flying, but this can be discussed with your GP

If you think you are at increased risk of a clot, ask your doctor if it is safe to travel.

any medical equipment you use regularly in your hand luggage. The pharmacies in larger towns will have a rota for out of business hours opening; if you need anything, ask at your hotel or a police station to see which one is open.

Inoculations should be up to date and include all those you would have in your own country. A yellow fever certificate is required if you are over one year old and are travelling from an 'infected area' (many countries in sub-Saharan Africa and parts of South America). This certificate is not required if you are in transit at Funchal, Porto Santo and Santa Maria.

Other vaccinations are not usually recommended, but hepatitis A may be considered for long-term visitors or for those who cannot take reasonable precautions over food and water. Shellfish can constitute a particular hazard, so if this is a must on your agenda then it is generally advised that you be inoculated against hepatitis A. A single dose of hepatitis A vaccine (eg: Havrix Monodose or Avaxim) provides protection for one year. The vaccine can be boosted after that time to extend coverage to at least 20 years.

Tap water in the hotels is generally safe to drink; on some islands it tastes better than some bottled waters I can think of. However, if you are in any doubt then drink bottled or treated water (boiled or with iodine drops/tablets). Mineral water is widely sold by the bottle, mostly imported from the mainland, but also sourced on São Miguel.

Occasionally bouts of travellers' diarrhoea may occur through infected food and water. However, this is rare in the Azores and is more likely to be from the change in diet, in particular from an increase in oily or spicy foods. The majority of cases settle down over one or two days. You should increase your fluid intake and replace the salts lost, either by taking rehydration sachets such as Electrolade or by drinking Coca-Cola with a pinch of salt. Diarrhoea with blood, and/or slime, and/or a fever is a sign of true infection and you would be advised to seek medical help as soon as possible.

A few cases of leishmaniasis from sand flies and west Nile fever from mosquitoes have been reported from the Azores. The only way these diseases can be avoided is by using a good insect repellent containing DEET (eg: the Repel range).

Rabies is not considered a risk in the Azores, but all bites from animals should be assessed carefully.

Other hazards of travel not preventable by immunisation include sunburn (wear a hat and apply sunblock regularly, especially if going out), accidents, respiratory tract infections and sexually transmitted diseases (including HIV – though this is limited to high-risk groups).

Travel clinics and health information A full list of current travel clinic websites worldwide is available on www.istm.org/. For other journey preparation information, consult www.tripprep.com. Information about various medications may be found on www.emedicine.com/wild/topiclist.htm.

DISABLED TRAVELLERS The Azores is not particularly geared towards travellers with mobility problems, since narrow cobbled streets and a lack of ramped kerbs don't create a wheelchair-friendly environment.

SAFETY The Azores is considered to be very safe and crime is, on the whole, limited to minor thievery in Ponta Delgada. Women should take the same precautions as they would at home even though the Azores are considered safer than the UK.

WHAT TO TAKE

The clothes you take need to correspond with the quickly changing weather so always remember you are in mid Atlantic! In summer generally the temperatures are very comfortable and at sea level it is doubtful if you will need a jersey. In winter, there will be days when you also do not need a jersey, but then for many days at sea level there will be times when you are very pleased to have one, as well as a wind-proof jacket. At all times you will need to be prepared for weather changes, so a raincoat is recommended, although in summer you may find it too warm and prefer to have an umbrella. At times it can be very humid. Many of the streets are still cobbled, so wear sensible shoes; you will be handicapped in high heels or fashion shoes. Generally, townspeople dress smartly casual, and cotton items are popular. In the evening, men will wear ties and jackets in the more expensive hotels and restaurants.

Away from the coast you should always take a jacket or jersey for the mountains, warmer ones in winter. The same applies if you are making any ferry journeys and like to stay on deck. Walkers will need their favoured walking shoes or boots. Waterproofs in the mountains are fine, but at low altitudes many find them too warm and a poncho style may be more comfortable. Always ensure you have sufficient warm clothing if you are going into the mountains. Always take water with you. You might find a whistle useful to keep in touch with straying companions should the clouds descend and kill visibility.

Hotel laundry services are very good, but for same-day service a 50% surcharge is usually levied, and beware of weekends and public holidays. Increasingly, hairdryers are provided in hotel bedrooms, but this should certainly not be relied upon, and in the cheaper hotels there is not always a shaver socket. The electricity supply is 220V, the standard in western Europe, and the plugs are the usual continental European two-pin.

Budget travellers should take a towel as those provided are often thin and very small, and a universal basin plug.

Photographers using a digital SLR camera could usefully take a standard UV filter to minimise glare off the sea – and protect the lens at the same time. In winter the light is wonderfully clear and sharp and there are some dramatic results to be had. For information on photography, see the *Photographic tips* box, page 42.

$ MONEY

Portugal is a member of the European Monetary Union and the currency is the euro. Travellers' cheques are accepted by most banks in the major currencies. Most banks in the main centres have ATMs and this is certainly the fastest way to obtain cash. To withdraw money, insert your card and enter the pin number, select *leventamentos* (withdrawals); select the amount and wait for your card, money and transaction slip. Credit cards, especially Visa, are accepted in hotels and some shops but not in many restaurants nor the smaller cafés/bars.

Banks are generally open weekdays between 08.00 and 15.30.

BUDGET At present most overseas visitors come to the Azores on a pre-purchased package bought from their travel agent so they know roughly what their costs are going to be. This usually includes visits to several islands, good hotels and excursions and can cost around £1,300 upwards for two weeks. Charter flights are going to increase and that widens the opportunity to travel independently. The Azores are not a cheap-flight destination. Having arrived, you will find a wide range of accommodation from the city business hotel to small *pensão* and camping sites. Two islands (São Miguel and Terceira) have youth hostels. São Miguel, Terceira, Faial and Pico which are the islands most visited are more expensive than the others. Using ferries to travel between the islands is cheaper and more fun than flying, but you do need to be prepared for changes in the timetables and these can be complicated. Using buses will be considerably cheaper than taxis, but often they are not very convenient nor always available, as they cater mainly to local people going to and from work.

Hiring general guides is expensive and in the busy summer months they are usually already occupied with pre-booked clients and tour groups. If you need a guide, then the cheapest way is often to contact the local travel agencies who may be able to assemble individual clients to make a small tour group.

Eating in smaller bars/cafés will be cheaper than the tourist restaurants and hotels and lunches can be delicious picnics with island products from the local supermarket or market. In fact restaurant portions are so generous, a light picnic for one meal is often preferable.

Two budget travellers can expect to spend around €90 each per day in the high season. This roughly breaks down into: accommodation (usually includes breakfast) €40; supermarket lunch €7; dinner including wine €18; bus fares, occasional taxi, say a daily average of €25, excluding inter-island travel.

For two travellers who like their comfort and enjoy spending time over dinner, then allow: €110 for accommodation; a light lunch with wine €17; dinner €40 – which adds up to a daily budget of around €170 per person plus excursions by taxi of €100 per day.

Ariadne Van Zandbergen

EQUIPMENT Although with some thought and an eye for composition you can take reasonable photos with a 'point-and-shoot' camera, you need an SLR camera if you are at all serious about photography. Modern SLRs tend to be very clever, with automatic programmes for almost every possible situation, but remember that these programmes are limited in the sense that the camera cannot think, but only make calculations. Every starting amateur photographer should read a photographic manual for beginners and get to grips with such basics as the relationship between aperture and shutter speed.

Always buy the best lens you can afford. The lens determines the quality of your photo more than the camera body. Fixed fast lenses are ideal, but very costly. A zoom lens makes it easier to change composition without changing lenses the whole time. If you carry only one lens, a 28–70mm (digital 17–55mm) or similar zoom should be ideal. For a second lens, a lightweight 80–200mm or 70–300mm (digital 55–200mm) or similar will be excellent for candid shots and varying your composition. Wildlife photography will be very frustrating if you don't have at least a 300mm lens. For a small loss of quality, tele-converters are a cheap and compact way to increase magnification: a 300mm lens with a 1.4x converter becomes 420mm, and with a 2x it becomes 600mm. Note, however, that 1.4x and 2x tele-converters reduce the speed of your lens by 1.4 and 2 stops respectively.

For photography from a vehicle, a solid beanbag, which you can make yourself very cheaply, will be necessary to avoid blurred images, and is more useful than a tripod. A clamp with a tripod head screwed onto it can be attached to the vehicle as well. Modern dedicated flash units are easy to use; aside from the obvious need to flash when you photograph at night, you can improve a lot of photos in difficult 'high contrast' or very dull light with some fill-in flash. It pays to have a proper flash unit as opposed to a built-in camera flash.

DIGITAL/FILM Digital photography is now the preference of most amateur and professional photographers, with the resolution of digital cameras improving the whole time. For ordinary prints a 6 megapixel camera is fine. For better results and the possibility to enlarge images and for professional reproduction, higher resolution is available up to 16 megapixels.

Memory space is important. The number of pictures you can fit on a memory card depends on the quality you choose. Calculate in advance how many pictures you can fit on a card and either take enough cards to last for your trip, or take a storage drive onto which you can download the content. A laptop gives the advantage that you can see your pictures properly at the end of each day and edit and delete rejects, but a storage device is lighter and less bulky. These drives come in different capacities up to 80GB.

Admission to museums throughout the Azores is often free. For those that do make a charge admission is usually no more than €3 per person.

GETTING AROUND

INTER-ISLAND TRAVEL Most visitors coming by air from Europe or North America arrive in Ponta Delgada on São Miguel or Lajes on Terceira, much less often Horta on Faial.

✈ By plane Flights are inevitably subject to the weather, and can be delayed or cancelled. When it happens, it is bad luck and you simply have to be philosophical

Bear in mind that digital camera batteries, computers and other storage devices need charging, so make sure you have all the chargers, cables and converters with you. Most hotels have charging points, but do enquire about this in advance. When camping you might have to rely on charging from the car battery; a spare battery is invaluable.

If you are shooting film, 100 to 200 ISO print film and 50 to 100 ISO slide film are ideal. Low ISO film is slow but fine grained and gives the best colour saturation, but will need more light, so support in the form of a tripod or monopod is important. You can also bring a few 'fast' 400 ISO films for low-light situations where a tripod or flash is no option.

DUST AND HEAT Dust and heat are often a problem. Keep your equipment in a sealed bag, stow films in an airtight container (eg: a small cooler bag) and avoid exposing equipment and film to the sun. Digital cameras are prone to collecting dust particles on the sensor which results in spots on the image. The dirt mostly enters the camera when changing lenses, so be careful when doing this. To some extent photos can be 'cleaned' up afterwards in Photoshop, but this is time-consuming. You can have your camera sensor professionally cleaned, or you can do this yourself with special brushes and swabs made for the purpose, but note that touching the sensor might cause damage and should only be done with the greatest care.

LIGHT The most striking outdoor photographs are often taken during the hour or two of 'golden light' after dawn and before sunset. Shooting in low light may enforce the use of very low shutter speeds, in which case a tripod will be required to avoid camera shake.

With careful handling, side lighting and back lighting can produce stunning effects, especially in soft light and at sunrise or sunset. Generally, however, it is best to shoot with the sun behind you. When photographing animals or people in the harsh midday sun, images taken in light but even shade are likely to be more effective than those taken in direct sunlight or patchy shade, since the latter conditions create too much contrast.

PROTOCOL In some countries, it is unacceptable to photograph local people without permission, and many people will refuse to pose or will ask for a donation. In such circumstances, don't try to sneak photographs as you might get yourself into trouble.

Even the most willing subject will often pose stiffly when a camera is pointed at them; relax them by making a joke, and take a few shots in quick succession to improve the odds of capturing a natural pose.

Ariadne Van Zandbergen is a professional travel and wildlife photographer specialising in Africa. For photo requests, visit www.africaimagelibrary.co.za or contact her on ariadne@hixnet.co.za.

about it and make sure there is a good book to hand. Getting between the islands is not always straightforward, especially in winter, but more flights are being introduced every year, and independent travellers should spend time studying the SATA website (*www.sata.pt*).

Eastern Group There are direct flights between Santa Maria and São Miguel and São Miguel to Terceira, Faial, Pico, São Jorge and Flores.

Western Group Flores has direct flights with Faial, Terceira and São Miguel and Corvo. You must allow spare days around these flights in case of cancellation through bad weather, especially if your visit there is towards the end of your holiday and you have a fixed international flight to catch. Visits to the Western Group are best seen as the main objective of a two-week holiday and can be combined easily with Faial and Pico.

Central Group There are direct flights from Terceira to São Miguel, Faial, Pico, São Jorge, Graciosa and Flores.

The structure of the air fares favours linking São Miguel, Terceira, Faial and Pico; flights to the other islands will be more expensive. SATA Air Açores offer tourists with an already purchased international air ticket a discount on inter-island fares, but the flights cannot be changed once booked. Staying over ten days triggers a discount of 10%.

By ferry Great fun if you have the time; there are always seabirds to look out for, and if you are lucky there is a chance of seeing dolphins or maybe even a whale.
   Throughout the year there are several sailings daily between Horta (Faial) and Madalena (Pico), a 30-minute crossing. In summer, in recent years, there has been a twice-daily Horta–Madalena–Velas service on São Jorge, less often in winter (usually once on three days a week).
   In summer there has been a ferry service between the eastern and central island groups, even very infrequently to Flores. Distances did not allow regular sailings on set days and, of course, all is subject to the weather so flexibility is needed if planning a holiday using ferries. For the latest information on sailing and prices, please check the Transmacor website (*www.transmacor.pt*).
   In 2006 the company opened ticket sales offices on the quays of all the islands except Flores and Corvo; the main office is in Ponta Delgada and from there it is possible to purchase tickets for all the ferries (*Gare Marítima Porto Comercial de Ponta Delgada;* ✆ *296 288644*). As well as having offices on the quay, Transmacor also have offices in the main town on each island (see individual islands for details). In Ponta Delgada this office is located on Rua da Misericórdia, 65–6 (✆ *296 628016;* f *296 288649;* e *saomiguel@transmacor.pt; open 09.00–12.00 and 14.00–18.00*). To avoid disappointment, it is advisable to carry your passport with you when reserving tickets for any ferry crossing as some ferry companies have started requesting ID cards in order to be eligible for government subsidies; you may get a discount by showing your passport.

By car As in Portugal, driving is on the right. At crossroads vehicles approaching from the right have priority. There is a maximum speed limit of 80km/h, 50km/h in built-up areas. Seat belts are meant to be worn at all times, including the rear passengers.
   You may come across the occasional idiot who thinks he is rally driving, and overtaking is often perilous. The new main roads are good but the small country roads can be pot-holed and narrow. One thing to be very careful about when driving in fog or low cloud and poor visibility is the Azorean black-and-white cow wandering on the road, either singly or in a scattered herd; in such conditions they are superbly camouflaged! Many of the minor roads are not signposted. Diversions for roadworks are signposted, but if the sign disappears after a few days it is seldom replaced because by then it is assumed everyone knows the way!
   A full UK driving licence is required and those aged under 25 years should check minimum requirements at the time of making a booking. Citizens from non-European countries similarly require a driving licence, along with a passport or other form of official identification. Normally there is no upper age limit but again this should be checked at the time of booking. In peak summer

season there is an acute shortage of hire cars, and reservations should be made well in advance.

There are many car-hire companies in the Azores, at least 15 on São Miguel, and some are very small. No one company has an office or cars on all the islands, therefore on Graciosa, São Jorge and Flores it is necessary to make separate hire arrangements which have to be paid for by clients on the spot. Larger companies are detailed under the individual islands and these have websites. Alternatively, your travel agent can of course make arrangements for you on all the islands.

Prices range per day for three to seven days according to season from around € 47 per day for the cheapest group A up to about € 78 for group D, and may be paid for in advance. Prices can differ between islands. Rates do not include insurance, CDW, TP, PAI and Super CDW. It should be noted that car-hire companies do not allow their vehicles to be taken on board the ferries.

Several islands have scooter hire, but this is not for the faint hearted or inexperienced. However, it is a cheap way to get around and rental starts from around € 20 per day. A driving licence is again required and helmets are supplied and must be worn.

ACCOMMODATION

This varies hugely, from standard comfort in conventional hotels, apartment hotels, resort hotels, interesting hotels, to the simple family hotel, and finally delightful old manor houses with character. There are no five-star hotels, but standards are high and the classification is from four- down to two-star. Family hotels (pensão, formally known as residencial and abbreviated to Res) are classified as 1a – better quality; 2a – middle quality; 3a – inferior quality. Some have been modernised and are comfortable, furnishings may be a little spartan while others can be gloomy and very conservative in the décor. Then come the rural categories:

TA – Turismo de Aldeia Accommodation in a group of at least five houses; the houses must be typical, and all the houses must be operated by the same owner.
TH – Turismo de Habitação Family type of accommodation in old manor houses with architectural, historical or artistic interest, representing a certain historical period. The owner has to live there.
TR – Turismo Rural Accommodation in houses with regional typical architecture and the owner must live there.
CC – Casa de Campo Private houses in rural areas in which the owner might or might not live in the house; the houses must be well integrated into the landscape/architecture of the area.
AG – Agro-turismo Accommodation in private houses as part of a farm. Guests can take part in the different farming activities. The owner must be resident.

Rural accommodation is becoming more available and there are now too many to list here; under the individual islands I have detailed the occasional one that has come to my attention. Some guest amenities can be simple, others are with en-suite bathrooms; they can be in the centre of a village, surrounded by pastures, or by the sea. They generally offer the least expensive accommodation, but remember they are usually in very rural locations which may be fine for a day or three, but could become frustrating without your own transport. Bed and breakfast tourism is getting itself organised and the Associação Turismo em Espaço Rural has a website up and running which is still in the process of development that will centralise all the information and eventually manage online reservations (*www.casaacorianas.com/ingles/index.php*). The government tourist office maintains a regularly updated and comprehensive list with websites of rural accommodation and are pleased to send copies on request (e *acoresturismo@mail.telepac.pt*). To be listed the establishments have first to be officially approved by the tourism department and then by their local municipality office.

Double rooms in four-star hotels vary in price from around €82 to €110 low season and €102 to €165 high season; three-star low season €63 to €102, high season €94 to €122; two-star low season €40, €90 high season. Apartment hotels and resort hotels fall into the four-star price range. Manor houses cost around €80 low season and €100 high season and *pensão* average around €50 low season, €68 high season. Quite a number of hotels offer special rates for children, or for an extra bed in a room. Rural accommodation varies hugely, and seemingly out of peak season can often be negotiated directly with the owner if not pre-booked. Please note well that in July, August and September hotels are very often fully booked and advance reservations are essential. Also, single room rates are generally only a little below the double room rate.

All islands have official campsites, most with amenities, and some are very attractive. Details are given under the respective islands. Charges are nominal. The sites are very popular with the local people – it's just nice to get away from home for a couple for days or so, read a book, go fishing, find a good restaurant or eat outside at the barbecues provided. They are also very popular with teenagers in the school holidays.

There are two youth hostels, one on São Miguel, the other on Terceira.

EATING AND DRINKING

EATING Eating out in the Azores is a very variable experience and is often surprising. Sometimes you can strike lucky in the more expensive eateries and be given a sophisticated and well-presented dish, depending on who is cooking that night; you will soon conclude it is rather a lottery. In the medium-priced restaurants there can again be surprises. Some islands are definitely better than others for eating out, and often a single establishment can shine like a beacon.

Sadly it cannot be claimed that the islands are a gastronomic delight. The lower and mid-priced restaurants all seem to share the same menu so that after a week you are beginning to look for novelties. To do so, instead of simply looking down one menu, menus of all the restaurants have to be examined – at least in Angra, Ponta Delgada and Horta where there are many restaurants to choose from. With such a good growing climate there should be a wonderful range of vegetables on offer but it seems most townspeople prefer simply to buy from the supermarket rather than grow much for themselves, and the supermarkets are not very adventurous. This is then reflected in the restaurants, which is no excuse, however, for serving rice and chips in combination, together with tinned diced mixed vegetables. Salads are mostly lettuce, some tomato, sliced onion, maybe grated carrot and if you are lucky some cucumber, rarely all together; dressing is usually left to you, from a bottle of olive oil and vinegar. Hotels often offer more variety, but even the best can include some of the routine cooked unimaginatively.

Portions are generally huge, sometimes overpoweringly so, especially meat. Fish including seafood is usually excellent, but there is a danger of fish being smothered in sauces or garlic so killing natural flavours. If you cannot find it plain grilled, often the most reliable ploy is to find it done as a local version of *bouillabaisse*; the *alcatra* on Terceira is an excellent example, and they make it with meat as well. *Bacalhau* (dried cod), the traditional village dishes and Azorean sausages can be very good indeed, as can the spicy *chouriço* (smoked sausage) and the black blood sausage, *morcelas*, with pineapple, but not too often in the same week! Mercifully Azorean cheeses are excellent and quality mainland Portuguese wines have been unsung for far too long, leaving the diner feeling very content with the world. Some chocolate desserts can be gorgeous. Whenever I am able I tend to seek the least pretentious, smallest, tucked away place I can find and there often discover superb Azorean fish cooked faultlessly to reveal the flavours only really fresh fish can give. Often, too, such places give amazingly good value for money although, like the fish, they are disappearing.

Restaurants are often tucked away down narrow alleyways and labelling them on maps is liable to confuse, rather than aid, a hungry traveller; but locals are friendly – don't hesitate to ask for directions.

DRINKING The settlers in the Azores had their priorities well ordered because wine has been produced since the very early days. On Pico grape varieties brought by the first settlers from mainland Portugal failed to acclimatise. The Verdelho grape was imported around 1500, possibly from Sicily, or maybe from Madeira, or perhaps by a Jesuit from Italy.

Vines were first planted on a large scale in the 16th century by the Catholic orders of Franciscans and Carmelites and by Jesuits in the following century. On Pico the vines were brought to Silveira, but here the surrounding land was too good for grapes and needed for essential foods such as wheat. Instead they went to the geologically youngest area of the island where the ground was very poor and stony, around the west coast. It is so heavily lava-strewn that it was only with great labour and difficulty sufficient stones were cleared, using them to make what became the characteristic walls, or *currais*, of small enclosures that provide such wonderful shelter from salty winds and at the same time extra heat. Surplus stone was neatly stacked into rectangular piles called *richeiros*. This was done mainly along the western edge of the island and now, almost half a millennium later, it is a protected zone because of its history. Other interesting features of this extraordinary memorial to the energy and persistence of the islanders include the *decansadouros*, the resting places for those carrying full baskets of grapes; made of stone, they are in two levels, one for those carrying on their heads and those carrying baskets on their shoulders. At the height of production some 30,000 barrels or 15 million litres were produced annually. Among countries it was exported to were Britain and famously to the Russian tsars, apparently by a German trading family. Quite what this wine was is not known as there were very few written records kept about how it was produced. Because of the rocky terrain transport of the barrels was difficult, and to get them onto the waiting ships wooden boards were laid over rocks that had previously been cut and roughly levelled. You might see old stone slipways or *rola-pipas* used to get the barrels into the sea, where they were then towed out to the waiting ship. Of the best Pico wine it was said to be 'so good it should be drunk in the middle of a prayer'.

When disease struck in the mid 1800s the first vines were replaced with the hardy Isabella grape whose strong aroma gave rise to the *vinho de cheiro* – fragrant wine. This is widely made throughout the islands for village consumption, and many a walker has staggered onward under the influence of spontaneous hospitality.

Twenty years or so ago small-scale experiments were conducted with new continental varieties, and some old stone enclosures replaced by long, straight rows supported by wires that always looked impressively immaculate in their level fields of cinders. However, it is the traditional method with its long history that is the remarkable showpiece and has most recently been rejuvenated in a number of ways, firstly by recognising various areas of vine growing and production, the *Zonas Vitivinícolas* and the establishment of a Regional Commission based in Madalena to guarantee quality and production methods, and certification. Named quality wines produced in a demarcated area VLQPRD (*vinhos licorosos de qualidade*

Monique Cymbron, São Miguel

The Azorean kitchen has more or less maintained the flavours of the Portuguese kitchen from the time of the Discoveries. There does not seem to be any influence of the early Breton or Flemish population. History tells us that they kept their language only for a generation and the same seems to be true about their food. One of the reasons may be that the Portuguese have always kept in touch with their continental homeland whilst other settlers perhaps did not.

The Azorean staple is soup. In the old times the main meal of poor rural inhabitants was often simply a thick vegetable soup with *chouriço* and bread. People are now better off but soup is still served as a starter twice a day, the thicker the better. There is a variety of vegetable soups, one of the most famous being *caldo verde*, a potato soup with finely shredded cabbage leaves cooked in it. Chicken broth is also popular and sometimes fish soup. Until the 1950s, the rural social structure was very archaic and the limited economic possibilities of the population meant that fish was the basic component of the daily meals, meat being a luxury served only on festive days, where tradition decreed three dishes of chicken, pork and beef, some boiled, others roasted, were served.

Interestingly, on the island of São Miguel, all dishes are flavoured with hot pepper (*pimenta*) in different forms: powdered, salted or as a paste.

Cod is one of the main raw materials on the islands. According to Portuguese tradition, there are 365 different recipes for cod, one for each day of the year. Even at formal dinners, it is usual to prepare a codfish dish. There is *bacalhau á braz* (fried potatoes, small pieces of boiled cod mixed with scrambled eggs), *bacalhau de natas* (fried potatoes, small pieces of codfish, olive oil-based bechamel sauce and cream on top) or *bacalhau na chapa* (a thick piece of codfish baked in the oven with olive oil, onion, garlic and red pepper).

There is a large variety of local fish. Small fish, *chicharros*, was regarded in former times as food of the poor since it was very cheap and eaten fried almost daily for lunch, on its own or with a garlic and lemon sauce or a hot pepper sauce, or parsley, olive oil and onions (green sauce). Recently its price rose astronomically – no-one could explain why the fish almost completely disappeared, only to return. Many medium-sized fish appear on restaurant menus, fried, grilled, steamed, sometimes filleted. They include *abrotea*, white hake, and *cherne*, 'wreck fish'. These are considered the best of the white fish. They are huge, so they appear mostly filleted. In summer one can find fresh tuna which is sliced as steaks and served fried. Swordfish (*espadarte*) is also a dark-flesh fish that is usually served fried.

As for seafood *marisqueira*, octopus cooked in the regional wine, *vinho de cheiro*, is very popular, as is barbecued European squid. There are *cracas* (a type of barnacle), a seafood typical of the Azores but increasingly rare, now found only in restaurants specialising in seafood. They are eaten as an appetiser, the tiny morsels retrieved with a special hooked tool from the shell that clings to a piece of rock. *Lapas* (limpets) are another shellfish eaten in various ways, most commonly baked with garlic and lemon juice. Rice with *lapas* is also popular, or *lapas de molho a fonso*, spicy sauce. There is *cavaco*, an endemic kind of crab, and *lagosta* (spiny lobster), and shrimps that are mostly imported.

produzidos em região determinada) covers *vinhos licorosas* or fortified sweetened wines recommended as an *aperativo*, and VQPRD is the white table wine Pedras Brancas from Graciosa, now welcolmely much reduced in price from a few years ago. The VLQPRD include the Brum wine from Biscoitos on Terceira and Pico's Lajido. Also from Pico is a more versatile red wine from Verdelho and Arinto grapes called Czar. Finally there are the certified Azores Regional Wines (Vinho Regional

For meat, pork, beef and chicken are all on the menu. Typical dishes here are *cozido a portuguesa*, that is pork, beef and chicken mixed mostly with cabbage, root vegetables and potatoes, all cooked together. Many restaurants serve this dish once a week as the dish of the day. In Furnas, *cozido* is a speciality but here it is cooked slowly in volcanic heat in the ground and called *cozido à caldeiras*. Terceira has *alcatra*, a special meat dish cooked in wine and spices.

A meal in an Azorean restaurant is often preceded with cheese, bread and pepper sauce offered whilst waiting for the meal. A local cheese is usually given; on Faial and Pico the cheese will be *São João do Pico*, on São Jorge it is *São Jorge*, a strong sharp-flavoured cheese, considered to be the best on the Azores. On Terceira the *Castelinhos* cheese and on São Miguel the *Agua Retorta* cheese or a fresh white cheese with the ever-present *massa de pimenta* are served.

The most typical appetiser on Faial, Pico and São Jorge is blood sausage with yams, a tropical vegetable cultivated on all the islands, while on São Miguel blood sausage comes with fresh pineapple.

Religious festivals have their own special dishes. During the Holy Spirit festival, a meat broth with bread is cooked on the islands of the Central Group. During the carnival, *malassados*, a rich dough like that for doughnuts is deep-fried and sugared. *Massa sovado*, sweet bread somewhere between bread and cake, is baked year round.

Formerly village people ate only home-baked bread, because corn was widely cultivated to feed both humans and other animals. Corn bread is a greyish, moist kind of bread that tends to mould rather quickly. Typical local restaurants often serve both corn and wheat bread. White Azorean bread tends to be too dry; the so-called home-baked bread, a big round loaf, is better.

There is a great variety of locally grown fruit in the Azores and many fruits were introduced following the disease that attacked orange trees in the last century. Pineapples were cultivated but it was soon found that the climate was not warm enough for outdoor growing, so greenhouses were built to obtain a reasonable crop. The Azores are now the only place in the world where pineapples are grown commercially in greenhouses. Economically they cannot compete with pineapples imported from Africa and South America and are heavily subsidised. They are generally sweet and juicy but can be acid in winter. Again, the Azorean climate is a little too cool for bananas which are generally smaller and sometimes brownish, but compensate by being sweet.

Other tropical fruits such as avocado, guava, mango, papaya, anona, maracuja (passion fruit) and diospyros (persimmon) are also grown. Citrus fruits including oranges, mandarins, clementines and lemons are still grown in quantity. Whilst bananas and pineapples are ripening all the year round, the others are mostly winter fruit starting in October and available until May or June. The typical summer fruit such as apples, pears, plums and peaches do not grow too well on the islands. A lack of a definite cold period means poor flowering; thus cherries do not crop at all although insects are abundant in summer, since insecticides are not generally used. Only in the higher altitudes such as the Furnas Valley can one get a reasonable crop.

Açores): the whites Viosinho e Gouveio, Frei Gigante, Terras de Lava and Maresia from Pico, Moledo from Terceira and the red from Pico, simply labelled Cabernet Sauvignon and Merlot.

On Pico a co-operative was formed, the Cooperativa Vitivinicola da Ilha do Pico and now has some 250 small growers. Their winery can be visited. Wine production is far from conventional, not just the lava habitat but complications affecting acidity, sugar content, maturation and other aspects are created by the extremes of cold air falling from Pico Mountain and the sun on the rocks and the salt in the air.

Terceira's first true vineyard was planted more than 400 years ago. A certain Pero Anes do Canto was in charge of the Portuguese navy and owned land at Biscoitos and it was he who introduced a Verdelho grape from Sicily. Production took off and records for 1693 show that taverns in Angra sold over 1,000 barrels of 500 litres each of Verdelho wine. It seems the same quantity was also sold to the island's eight convents! We could say, however, this may be a translation error, but wine was exported and taken to the Portuguese colonies. Subsequent introduction of the baco variety helped make the vineyards more resistant to disease.

Legislation ensures urban development is limited in the Biscoitos region to protect the vine-growing area. In 1993 the Biscoitos Society of Verdelho Wines was founded with the objective of promoting the Verdelho wines of Biscoitos as well as all of the quality wines of the Azores. Members are founders, honorary members, brothers and novices and wear a blue cape with a gold trim, blue representing the colour of the Azores flag and gold the colour of the Verdelho. The society's coat of arms in addition to the Azores arms includes a *tambolhadeira*, a drinking cup resembling the traditional clay *taladeira* used in Terceira to taste the new wine, a ritual that takes place on St Martin's Day. The Brum family wine museum is open to visitors.

Graciosa quietly produces wine from two wineries. Under the Terras da Conde name with its distinctive label showing a windmill comes a red and a white table wine, a welcome *aperitivo* and an excellent *aguardente*. The company was founded over 70 years ago and has its own vineyards, growing mainly arinto on *vinho brava* stock. The winery welcomes visitors. The second producer is the Adega Cooperativa da Ilhá Graciosa begun in 1960 with an initial production of 200,000 litres of dry white wine. By the 1980s this had languished and production ceased for a time but now with government support the situation is reversed, and its white table wine Pedras Brancas has certified status.

Several liqueur wines are also made, especially São Miguel's well-known *Maracujá* liqueur (passion fruit). This, mixed half and half with *aguardente* – fire and passion – is a great ending to a typical feast of traditional Azorean dishes! Others are made from local fruit such as Japanese plum (*Eriobotrya japonica*, the loquat), figs and blackberries. This last, called Amora, is less sweet than the others, and imbibed not in moderation has the kick of an island donkey.

☆ NIGHTLIFE

This is very modest, but the number of discotheques is increasing although their names are not emblazoned across the night sky and they are still few in number. A new phenomenon on São Miguel and Terceira, and spreading, is the entertainment bar with strip show. There is a handful of pubs, again scattered widely. This is not to say that nightlife does not abound; it does, and is lively, but is much more private than commercial and has a quite different meaning from that in the big city. There can be evening dress balls and other social events associated with the many organisations that thrive in the islands, of which the casual visitor remains unaware. As you travel around the islands you will see many barbecue sites at *miradouros* and in sylvan roadside glades where in summer these are busy after office hours when family and friends meet for an al fresco supper and evening together. At weekends and holidays they will again all be occupied, as will the woodland picnic sites laid out in so many lovely places by the forestry services. Summer is for outdoor living, which is also when the festivals and folklore gatherings mostly take place. On a balmy summer evening you can promenade around the harbours with their pretty lights reflecting on the water, or sit in a garden square and nibble a snack from a street stall or enjoy a drink at a pavement café – all happy pleasures where one is always going to meet friends and acquaintances. During your stay in Ponta Delgada check whether there is anything on at the recently restored Teatro Micaelensis, which stages everything from ballet to Fado. In Horta, on Faial, the *teatro* near the main square has also been recently restored and offers a mix of Hollywood and art cinema together with occasional orchestral and jazz music; see pages 71 and 166 for more information.

PUBLIC HOLIDAYS AND FESTIVALS

The main public holidays are 1 January; 25 April (marking the Revolution of 1974); Good Friday; 1 May (Labour Day); Corpus Christi; 15 August; 5 October (Proclamation of the Republic); 25 December. There are also municipal holidays, each municipality taking them on different dates so that there are some 18 of these during the summer, but they should not significantly affect the visitor. There are festivals throughout the year, and the principal ones are detailed under entries for individual islands.

SHOPPING

In addition to the handicrafts (see below), cheeses from the islands are always a popular purchase. Homemade jams are as good or better than grandmother's, while tea from the two tea estates on São Miguel is a very original gift and easiest of all to carry home. Somewhat heavier are one or two fresh pineapples in a presentation box, and island wine, *aperitivos*, liqueurs and *aguardentes*. For food gifts try the supermarkets, and at the airports on São Miguel and Faial there is at least one shop selling Azorean products, and new outlets are increasing all the time. Please note that many shops close from 13.00 on Saturday until Monday morning.

HANDICRAFTS – ARTESANTO There are many items common to all or most of the islands, with their own variations, while some handicrafts are specific to one island or village. All use natural raw materials; you cannot fail to see charming folk figures made from maize husks, wickerwork baskets, ceramics, various items from cut basalt, embroidery, delicate flowers made from fish scales or fig pith, simple rugs made from maize or rags, and superb woven bedspreads made on São Jorge. There are also models of whales and items to do with whaling, and some scrimshaw (products made from whalebone; see box overleaf). Shops offering these items have recently increased, but please be aware it is illegal to take these products out of Portugal and their purchase encourages this trade. Several shops now sell items made from environmentally friendly alternative materials.

ACTIVITIES

WALKING Walking in mid Atlantic is a most wonderful experience. Whether you are high in the mountains, following a coastal walk, or merely strolling along a country lane there is a purity in the air, an exhilaration in the light, and ever-changing cloud patterns. In places trails lie dark and dank between 2m-tall embankments, with hedges of cryptomeria, pittosporum and endemic shrubs while the banks themselves are moss-covered or draped with soft green curtains of selaginella, a primitive fern ally. At other times when high up in the mountains the scene is more akin to moorland, with low-growing grasses, rushes and mossy

Scrimshaw is an art born of boredom and loneliness on the whaling ships of the 19th century and links the Azores to many countries. Ships' crews would while away their time engraving on whales' teeth, and then rubbing lamp black into the lines to bring up the design. In the Azores this tradition continued, using the teeth taken from whales killed off the islands and brought ashore for processing. It has all but disappeared because time passes and also the supply of teeth is diminishing. Ten years ago divers could still find them on the seabed near old whaling stations on Pico and on Madeira, but now such finds are rare.

Modern artists sand down the tooth ridges, then use car polish to coat the tooth. A layer of Indian ink is applied to blacken the surface to be engraved. Machine-powered needles are used to engrave through the ink, the polish, and into the tooth. The engraved lines appear white and Indian ink is then applied a second time and this time it enters the unwaxed lines that form the design. The first coat of black is then removed. Prices vary for modern pieces in traditional style from € 50 to € 1,250.

flushes in the wetter areas, and elsewhere a knee-high scrub of heather, and often a view of the distant sea. Perhaps best of all is to file along a narrow path contouring a steep sea cliff, when the views are spectacular, very special and pure Azores. However, gentler walks along farm roads through patchworks of pastures with the sight of seemingly healthy, contented cows out to grass all year, and past farm buildings with ever-changing rural scenes, are equally as satisfying in their different way.

Buried beneath the vigorous alien vegetation of the islands lie many old cobbled trails, used long ago by the islanders to travel between the villages by donkey, oxcart and horse. The history and stories they could tell are as lost to the visitor as is the dustiest archive in the deepest cellar. Maybe one day local historians will make all this tangible and readily accessible, but meanwhile all we have are brief glimpses of this earlier age. If old trails happen to lead to pastures or to vineyards then their weathered surfaces can still be seen, perhaps for just a few metres, maybe for a hundred or more. They are there for the observant traveller to find, and then to let the imagination fill in the stories. Certainly if these hidden paths could be rediscovered they would make wonderful walks for our time and century. And if time and tide have in part destroyed them, then maybe new routes could be found to link them.

At present we are losing walks rather than gaining them. Every year more unsurfaced farm tracks are given asphalt surfaces with the help of EU funding; great for the farmer, but bad news for the walking tourist. Seismic tremors and flash floods cause human tragedies, and also send favourite walks permanently into memory, their imprint on the landscape forever destroyed by nature. There is a tremendous need for the existing walks to be better waymarked, be decently maintained and regularly monitored for damage by heavy rain and storms so they can be quickly repaired. Few long-distance walks exist that lead from an easily recognised starting place and ending in a village for refreshments and transport home. There is a real need for more coastal paths, and routes in the rugged hinterlands. The paths are there in part, the islands all have old road systems; they need identifying, cleaning and linking up. If and when this is done the islands will become a rambler's dream. The excellent news is that on São Miguel the Municipality of Povoação is taking all this seriously and has just restored and waymarked some 76km of trails. Even more important, they are committed to rigorously maintaining them and providing good information.

Elsewhere there is a number of designated paths but they are mostly of an hour or two's length and transport to the start and finish is often not easy; there are signposts and brochures describing these, but the directions can be difficult to follow and there is a risk of experiencing both pleasure and frustration in equal measure. Fortunately, by an accident of history we still have good walks on São Miguel, São Jorge and Flores. On Pico there is Pico Mountain itself to climb. On almost all the islands it is perfectly easy to park a car and explore inviting farm roads and tracks and thus make your own short walks. On little Graciosa there are limited walks, but the roads are still so quiet that really you can walk everywhere. One of the most useful items to have with you in the Azores is a mobile phone to call a taxi at the end of a walk.

WHALE AND DOLPHIN WATCHING Whale and dolphin watching has become a major focus of 'eco-tourism' and the increase in its popularity is awesome. Beginning as a commercial enterprise in 1955 on the southern California coast, by the year 2000 a widely cited study estimated over nine million people participated in some 87 countries generating at least US$1 billion, doubling in value since 1996. We are six years further on, and by dividing the number of whales on view into the cash generated now, each whale must be worth a small fortune. Good news in support of the conservation argument. I would love to be able to translate calls of the whales and know the word they have for us!

It is essential that these 'subjects' of our recreational curiosity are viewed with the respect they deserve. In the Azores, whale and dolphin watching has become a much-advertised and popular activity and there are now many operators offering whale-watching trips; some have more than one boat. This brings into question what effect this has on the cetaceans; they are sensitive animals surviving in a very tough environment doing the things we do, finding food, rearing young and socialising. They have highly sensitive hearing and are distressed and their communication interfered with, when speedboats tear around them, gunning their engines. Bothering them by too close a contact and in other ways can alter their migration patterns, separate groups and interfere with their reproduction. What the stress thresholds are is not known and more research is needed, so, given our ignorance, the best policy is: don't do it unless you know it is harmless. Whether we should swim with cetaceans is controversial and is banned in several countries.

A 2004 estimate revealed that some 30,000 people went whale watching in the Azores that year, supporting 35 boats and 85 jobs, worth a value to the islands of €1.53 million. The Azores government has passed two sets of regulations, in 1999 and 2004, controlling the number of boats allowed, passenger safety, and visitor behaviour when near the animals. The regulations also aim to encourage the companies involved to work more closely together, reduce competition and limit the number of boats around any one pod.

If you are going to visit them, there is an accepted etiquette to follow (see box overleaf). Rather than book a trip at random, study the notes about what you should know before you go out to sea, and how your boat crew should handle the situation. When you have absorbed these, check out the operators, ask the right questions, and when you find one that suits you, go ahead. Check whether they have an experienced biologist on board at all times; ask how many people they take as a maximum, if there is shade from the sun, a lavatory, and if drinking water is supplied. You can also ask if you are contributing to scientific research by choosing their boat.

For those who do not like the idea of venturing into mid Atlantic in a small rigid inflatable boat and enduring three hours banging into the waves as you speed along, there are now larger, more comfortable vessels that have cabins and decks

2

New legislation has recently been passed in the Azores to regulate the increasing demand but supervising behaviour out at sea and out of sight is not easy. You, the client whale watcher, can do this by reporting back any malpractice you encounter. The new economic significance of whale watching and the widening concern and support from those who participate is likely to do more than anything else to help protect these animals on the world stage and change political opinions.

- Cetaceans should not be chased.
- Boats should approach by maintaining direction parallel and slightly to the rear of the cetaceans, keeping an open field of 180° to the front of them.
- When approaching avoid changes in direction, keep at slow speeds of under 10 knots and when 400m from the area reduce to 4 knots.
- A maximum of only two boats are permitted inside a radius of 400m around an individual whale or group of whales.
- It is prohibited to approach cetaceans closer than 50m; when they are resting they may not be approached at all.
- Only one boat at a time is permitted to approach to the minimum distance of 50m from the whales, and the engine should be kept on low revs.
- Boats should not come between animals in groups thereby separating them, especially the young.
- Whales with small calves should not be approached closer than 100m.
- Movements of all boats must always be on the same side, parallel to and a little to the rear of the animals.
- Maximum time to be spent in the area observing is 30 minutes near the animal.
- After observation, boats must depart from the area to the rear of the animals, and maintain a slow speed within 400m of them.
- No swimming is allowed with cetaceans.
- Skippers must explain to clients the dangers of swimming with dolphins and that they do this at their own risk (there is no insurance available).
- When swimming with dolphins one extra crew member, apart from the skipper, must be allocated for surveillance of swimmers at all times and be equipped for swimming.
- Only two swimmers with dolphins should be allowed in the water at the same time and to be equipped with snorkels; they must remain quietly on the surface and not touch the dolphins.
- Swimming time with dolphins is limited to 15 minutes maximum.
- The boat's motor must be in neutral at all times when swimmers are in the water.

where you can move around. You are no less likely to see whales and dolphins this way and your view from the raised decks of these vessels is much better. Seeing whales and dolphins out at sea is a memorable and special experience; to really get the most out of your boat trip, do your homework first, read up about them, be informed; only then should you intrude upon them and with a clearer conscience.

Typically there are two departures each day, around 09.00 and 15.00, each lasting about three hours. Thirty minutes before departure there is usually a pre-trip briefing. Cost varies around € 40–50 per person.

Should you like more information, then the Whale and Dolphin Conservation Society, the world's most active charity dedicated to the conservation and welfare of all whales, dolphins and porpoises, has an excellent website (*www.wdcs.org*).

SWIMMING The steep rocky sea coasts mean that swimming opportunities are mostly focused on small beaches, little bays and a combination of natural and manmade rock pools. The more popular locations often have changing facilities and sometimes lifeguards, while amenities are improving rapidly all the time. The coveted European Blue Flags signifying the beaches or swimming areas that meet stringent standards have been awarded to many sites in the Azores. Few of the swimming places are really suitable for non-swimmers, and nowhere have I become more aware of so many very young children participating in swimming lessons in municipal pools. There are various adverse conditions and dangerous currents unknown to the visitor and swimming should be enjoyed only in clearly designated areas. The best locations are on São Miguel and Santa Maria.

DIVING For a long time few people thought of the Azores as a diving destination, but it is becoming increasingly recognised, although still in its infancy and really virgin territory. There is very little opportunity for try-diving, where a novice dives for the first time to see if they like it, and almost all centres cater only for certificated divers.

Because the weather is unpredictable dives usually take place in the mornings when the sea is most likely to be at its calmest. The seabed, being of volcanic origin, offers large areas of lava and various volcanic debris, tunnels, arches, vertical cliffs, small caves and rock needles. There are cold-water coral reefs and often colourful subtropical fish species and a huge diversity of other marine organisms. With a visibility range of up to 20m, the great joy of diving off the Azores is that you never know what you are going to see. Prices range from around €30 a dive. There are several diving centres and, because it is such a new thing, for details it is best to just type 'diving Azores' into Google. For the non-diver, a visit to the quite splendid Oceanarium in Lisbon (*www.oceanario.com*) is strongly recommended where, of their 450 species on show, some notable captives were caught in Azorean waters.

SPORT FISHING The Azores marine environment attracts large fish including 'granders', a fishing term for blue marlin weighing 1,000lb or more, and many world records have been caught in these waters. The season usually runs from early July to mid October when the water temperature is above 20°C and the weather is generally warm and calm. Apart from the Atlantic blue marlin various tuna species, several different sharks and numerous white marlin there are also small game fish. The sea is being overfished but after some years of disappointing results it seems 2005 proved one of the best years in the last decade for sport fishing. From the UK an eight-day package of seven nights' four-star bed and breakfast accommodation and four days' fishing costs around £2,500 per person.

CAR RALLIES Several rallies are held annually in the islands and those wishing to attend should make sure they have their hotel accommodation booked well in advance. Anyone coming to the Azores for a quiet holiday should plan their itinerary accordingly! Dates vary each year and should be checked with your tour operator or the Azores Directorate of Tourism.

São Miguel	Around 23–24 March: Rally of Ribeira Grande.
	End of June or early July: the SATA Azores Rally; counts towards regional, national and European rally championships.
	Around 13–14 October: Povoação Rally.
Santa Maria	First or second weekend of August, usually one week before the big religious festivities of 15 August: Rally Ilha Gonçalo Velho.

Terceira	Around 20–21 April: Rally Sical.
	Around 14–15 September: Rally Ilha Lilás.
Faial	Varying dates in May: Rally Ilha Azul.

SAILING These notes are made for the land visitor: sailors have their own cruising guides! In 1895 Joshua Slocum put into Horta while making the first single-handed circumnavigation of the world. Since then small boat arrivals have increased and with the construction of marinas and onshore facilities the number of yachts now visiting Horta is around 1,400 annually. Many are doing the milk-run, bringing boats over from Bermuda or the West Indies to the Mediterranean or similar for the summer, allowing their owners who do not like real sailing to fly across later. The Azores are also a major focus for several famous international races, and there are also local yachting events. The calendar is something like this:

Last Saturday in April	Competitors windsurf from Velas to Cais do Pico and then cycle via the coast road to Madalena and then kayak to Horta.
First week in July	Faial yacht club organises a race for cruising yachts from Horta to Velas on São Jorge and back, including an overnight party in Velas!
End of July	Atlantis Cup: São Miguel to Terceira.
Beginning first Sunday in August	Semana do Mar or Sea Week, with events connected with the sea as well as other cultural events.
Every four years	Clube Naval de Horta organises the race from Falmouth to Horta and back.
Every four years	Royal Cornwall yacht club organises the race from Falmouth to Ponta Delgada and back.
Every two years	Race from Brittany to Horta and back is organised by Société Nautique.
Further events	Include the Yachting World ARC Europe rally from the Canaries to the West Indies; Canaries–Bermuda–Horta–Ponta Delgada to either Plymouth or the Algarve; Rotterdam–Horta and back by Dutch Sports Planning International; rally by Ocean Cruising Club of England.

ℓ MEDIA AND COMMUNICATIONS

POSTAL SERVICES Postal services are efficient and reliable. A postcard sent by ordinary mail on a Monday at the airport in Ponta Delgada was delivered two days later in rural England, but realistically expect cards and letters to take around three to five days from Ponta Delgada or Lajes on Terceira, possibly longer from the other islands. There are post office counters at these airports: Terceira, São Miguel and Faial. There are two levels of service, and outside post offices you will see two post boxes, one for ordinary mail and one for blue mail.

The rates are:

Ordinary domestic	Up to 20g, €0.30; 20–50g, €0.46; 50–100g, 0.49
Ordinary mail Europe	Up to 20g, €0.57; rest of world up to 20g, €0.74
Blue mail priority domestic	Up to 20g, €45; Europe & rest of world up to 20g, €1.75

TELEPHONE SERVICES Excellent. The international code for the Azores (Portugal) is 351. The islands also have codes: 296 for São Miguel and Santa Maria; 295 for

Terceira, São Jorge and Graciosa; 292 for Faial, Pico, Flores and Corvo. You need to dial the whole nine-figure number no matter where you are.

Off-peak (economic) time is from 21.00 to 09.00. The cheapest way to make a call is to buy a telephone chargecard and use a public callbox. Many public phone boxes also accept debit or credit cards and, once inserted, there is a button with a flag to press until your chosen instruction language appears.

Mobile reception is generally very good, though the mountains do create blank spots.

Tourist helpline ❧ 800 296 296, calls free.

INTERNET Interest in IT is considerable and there are clubs on all the islands offering internet access and various courses; not so helpful for the visitor. The larger hotels offer internet services, either via sockets in the rooms or in their business centre, or in the lobby with rates from €3 for 15 minutes. Horta seems best served – see page 167. Wi-Fi systems are now becoming more common in airports and main towns and many require payment (the 'PT' network run by the Post Office) but some are free and often very fast. Many areas of the Azores now have ADSL broadband.

CULTURAL ETIQUETTE

Through the ages the Azoreans have had plenty of contact with the outside world, from pirates to tourists, and from their own travels for work abroad, family members in mainland Portugal, business, higher education and so on. For all this, the communities remain tight-knit, especially in rural areas. It is also a country with strong Catholic traditions. Simple courtesy and respect remain refreshingly important and the visitor will find these greatly contribute to first impressions. Boorish behaviour is not appreciated and will not go unremarked. Neither will topless sunbathing.

PHOTOGRAPHY If you are taking photographs of people, then do ask first; your smile will in most cases be returned and permission granted (see box on page 42 for further details).

Practical Information CULTURAL ETIQUETTE

2

Part Two

EASTERN GROUP

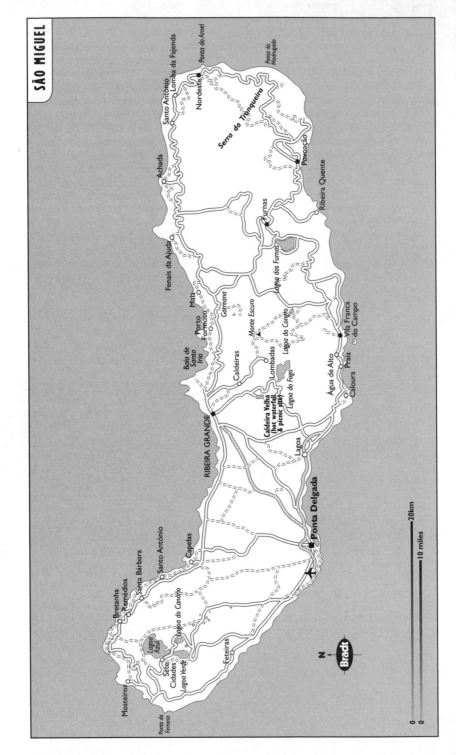

SÃO MIGUEL

Ponta do Arnel

Lomba da Fajenda
Santo António
Nordeste
Ponta da Madrugada

Achada

Serra da Tronqueira

Povoação

Furnas
Ribeira Quente

Fenais da Ajuda

Maia
Porto Formoso
Lagoa dos Furnas

Baía de Santa Iria
Gorreana

Monte Escuro

Caldeiras
Lombadas
Lagoa do Congro

Vila Franca do Campo
RIBEIRA GRANDE
Caldeira Velha
(hot waterfall
& picnic site)
Lagoa do Fogo

Água de Alto
Praia

Caloura

Lagoa

Santo António
Capelas

Santa Bárbara

Remédios
Bretanha

Lagoa do Canário

Ponta Delgada

Feteiras

Mosteiros
Sete Cidades
Lagoa Azul
Lagoa Verde

Ponta da Ferraria

Bradt

N

0 ━━━ 10 miles
0 ━━━ 20km

3

São Miguel

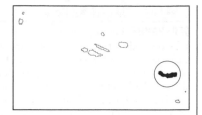

São Miguel is the largest island and has the greatest diversity of interests. It also has the largest town in the Azores, Ponta Delgada, and the busiest harbour. Although all the islands are green, São Miguel is known as the *Ilha Verde*, the Green Island, after the central area that has very good soil and is highly productive. There is a varied coastline, from small bays with black sand to precipitous sea cliffs and a mountain wilderness area of endemic plants on Pico da Vara, the highest point at 1,105m. Ponta Delgada, the capital of the Azores, is very charming and the pedestrianised streets, cafés, shops and long esplanade around the harbour all go to make it an enjoyable place to explore.

More cosmopolitan than the other islands, São Miguel has in recent years become increasingly sophisticated and is now the focus for the archipelago. Ponta Delgada's airport, towards the island's southwest, now receives most of the international air traffic. Yet, in spite of new marinas, new hotels, a second golf course, numerous restaurants, out-of-town supermarkets and so on, considerable rural charm is still to be found.

HIGHLIGHTS

Most famous are the two lakes of Sete Cidades, one blue the other green, in the caldera that dominates the western topography, and which have mythological beginnings. Ribeira Grande has a charming town centre that you pass through to reach the only tea estates in Europe, Gorreana and Chã Porto Formoso, midway along the north coast. In the southeast the small spa of Furnas, that has changed little physically over the years, is a must. Here, bubbling fumaroles of both mud and water and the smell of sulphur remind you that you are on a volcano in spite of the verdant surroundings; in fact you are in the centre of another large crater. Twenty-two mineral waters, all with different tastes, spout out of the ground; some have elaborate man made ornamental surrounds, while others just flow from between the native heather bushes. You can take a week's course of treatment at the medical centre. The 30-acre garden of the Terra Nostra Garden Hotel, mostly dating from 150 years ago but with beginnings in the late 18th century, with its naturally warm thermal swimming pool and meandering walks beneath almost 2,500 trees, is contact with the genteel life of earlier centuries. In the far northeast is Nordeste, a region not often visited by tourists, which has a spectacularly beautiful coast when viewed from the several splendid viewpoints and picnic sites. Vila Franca do Campo in the middle of the south coast was São Miguel's first capital, and is still a thriving and pretty town; the town square and the nearby harbour should be seen before taking a coffee and trying the local *queijadas* or Vila Franca cake. Pineapples are still grown under glass, and a nursery can be visited near Ponta Delgada. For the capital Ponta Delgada, you should allow at least one full day to explore the streets and buildings, and visit the museum.

GEOGRAPHY The largest island of the archipelago, São Miguel was once two islands as evidenced by the two large volcanic massifs, one at each end, and the low central area that emerged later from the sea following further eruptions. This low region is one of the best crop-growing areas of the island, and was the location of the first airfield. The highest point, in the eastern massif, is Pico da Vara at 1,105m. There are four large calderas, the famous Sete Cidades in the west, Fogo in the centre which last erupted in 1563, the very beautiful Furnas caldera – so large that many visitors to Furnas village do not realise they are in the middle of a dormant crater, and finally the much-eroded Povoação caldera in the east. The oldest rocks lie in the northeast, in the area of Pico da Vara, and date back as far as four million years. The Povoação volcano dates from around 800,000 years ago, while Furnas rose above the sea 100,000 years ago. Sete Cidades (Seven Cities) began some 290,000 years ago, and its caldera collapsed 22,000 years ago when legend alleges that seven cities were buried.

HISTORY São Miguel's first settlers came from the Estremadura, Alentejo and Algarve provinces of Portugal, and there were also Madeirans, Jews, Moors and French. The first capital was Vila Franca do Campo, but in 1522 a severe earthquake and mudslide that killed most of the 5,000 inhabitants was so destructive that the island's principal port, Ponta Delgada, took precedence and became the capital in 1546. Already there were some wealthy merchants, trading with mainland Portugal, Madeira, the Canaries, Flanders and elsewhere; some 25 English merchant ships are recorded as having visited in one year. Early crops included wheat, woad, sugarcane and there were also dairy products. The port area was fortified during the 16th and 17th centuries against the frequent atttacks by pirates and corsairs. Terceira was the key island in maritime trade and journeys, but with the restoration of Portuguese independence in 1640, São Miguel became the commercial centre although there were many economic difficulties. During the 18th and early 19th century the island prospered much of the time through the development of the new export crop, oranges, and many substantial homes and churches were built. In 1831–32 resistance to the Absolutist regime was organised from the island and it was from Ponta Delgada that the Liberal expedition with some 3,500 Azoreans sailed to northern Portugal.

Around 1860, oranges began to lose their share of the British market, partly to cheaper sources of supply from mainland Portugal and Spain, and partly because the orange trees succumbed to disease. This eventually caused an economic crisis and resulted in emigration to the Americas. New crops such as tea, pineapples, chicory, sugarbeet and tobacco then began to be introduced, together with livestock and, later, the development of fishing. Work began in 1861 to improve the port in Ponta Delgada which later stimulated industrial development, but it was after World War II in 1947 that it was greatly expanded. The basalt city gateway was removed to its present position in the nearby square (see *Town trail*, page 75), and the new Avenida do Infante D Henrique and the colonnaded buildings along the seafront transformed the town's appearance: truly a piece of excellent town planning much enjoyed today by townspeople and visitors alike.

GETTING THERE AND AWAY

BY PLANE Ponta Delgada is linked by daily two-hour SATA Internacional flights to Lisbon with onward connections to many European cities. There are also regular flights to Funchal on Madeira. In summer there are flights to Oporto and on Sundays there is a direct SATA Internacional return flight to Frankfurt; between

Even today there is evidence of the great orange-growing industry that dominated several of the islands in the 19th century; look in the numerous small gardens with their tall enclosing hedges of banksias and pittosporum. Grand town houses also reflect the wealth this crop generated, and the development of the countryside by land purchase for rural estates is significant history.

Far less known are the implications all these oranges had for transportation between the Azores and England, the major export customer. Citrus was a luxury fruit, available in season from November to May only, and its peak of desirability for the Victorians was Christmas when oranges and lemons were the fruit to have displayed on the table. And most of these came from the Azores.

'Buy my fresh St Michael's' was a common streetseller's cry, although it is doubtful that, like today, many customers would have known where 'St Michael's' was. Oranges were grown in the Azores already by the 16th century, brought in from Lisbon, in turn introduced by Portugal's Indian viceroys. From 1600 to 1800 the citrus trade steadily increased, with most oranges coming from Valencia and lemons from Sicily, but it was the ending of the Napoleonic Wars that accelerated exports from the Azores so that by the mid 1800s several hundred ships and several thousand seamen were employed in the trade. The topsail schooner was the favoured ship, one that could travel fast, for oranges are a quickly perishable cargo. The ships were of small tonnage since a larger vessel would have been no advantage; the boxes of oranges could not be stacked high otherwise those at the bottom would have spoilt, and the boats were loaded in the open roadsteads so speed was essential. Also, should a large consignment have arrived in one ship, the quantity would have swamped the market and reduced the price. In 1854, 60 million oranges and 15 million lemons were imported to London alone, using at least 70 vessels.

At first English merchants came out to the Azores at the start of the season to supervise purchase and loading, but by the mid 19th century many, along with their families, lived permanently on São Miguel in their large houses. Each fruit was picked as it turned from green to yellow and was wrapped in a dry sheathing leaf of the Indian corn cob. Loading was done with small boats from the shore taking the boxes out to the waiting ships. Speed in loading was vital, for should bad weather suddenly blow in, the vessel would have to stand out to sea only part-loaded, and several days might pass before loading could be completed. Typically a crew of not more than six under a master ran the ship, and it was tough sailing during winter in the north Atlantic. The average sailing time was ten–14 days, but it could sometimes be done in seven days. An added anxiety for the voyage home was to inspect the boxes daily for rotten fruit, since a clean cargo meant a bonus for the master. Today such an event would have been spun to equal the fame of the tea clippers, but there was a race each year to deliver the first oranges of the season. It is recorded that the first ship home sold all its cargo within six hours at three guineas a box (£3.15p). When others arrived, 47 ships within 40 hours, the price fell to 4/6d (22½p).

These schooners flourished until about 1860; steam was already transporting lemons from Sicily by the early 1850s, but there was no harbour suitable in Ponta Delgada for steam ships, a real problem in bad weather if they had to stand off burning coal, with no bunkering facilities onshore. About ten years later harbour construction began and the schooners' days were numbered, with an ever-decreasing number being chartered up until about 1870. Then in the 1880s disease struck the orange trees and harvests plummeted, by which time supplies from other countries, including California and Florida, became available, from orchards established with parent trees taken from the Azores.

April and October there is a direct flight every Tuesday between Ponta Delgada and London Gatwick. Increasingly new direct flights are being introduced to European cities. Between the islands, in winter SATA has daily flights to Santa Maria and several flights to Terceira with connections to the other islands, and on certain days direct flights to Horta and Pico. In summer there are more flights.

BY FERRY In the past there have been, between May and September, two or three sailings a week linking São Miguel (Ponta Delgada) and Terceira (Praia Vitória), sometimes at night, sometimes during the day. The journey took six hours. Between Santa Maria (Vila Porto) and São Miguel takes four hours and the service has been at least once weekly. For details of the current ferry service please check the website (*www.transmacor.pt*). Tickets are available from the office in town (*Rua da Misericórdia, 65–6;* ✆ *296 628 016;* e *saomiguel@transmacor.pt; open 09.00–12.00 and 14.00–18.00*) and from the office on the quay (*Gare Marítima Porto Comercial de Ponta Delgada;* ✆ *296 288 644*).

BY YACHT The new marina was opened in 1993, modelled on the one in Horta, and has already been expanded. There is a full range of services, and also good repair facilities. The Clube Naval Ponta Delgada also has a new building by the marina which has, in addition to offices and snack bar, an indoor swimming pool and gymnasium (✆ *296 283 005;* e *cnpd@mail.telepac.pt; www.cnpdl.pt*).

GETTING AROUND

BY CAR/TAXI Island tours by taxi generally fall into two separate programmes. One covers Sete Cidades in the west, often a half-day tour, while the second is a full day going to Ribeira Grande and the tea estates on the north coast, followed by Furnas and Vila Franca on the south coast, combined with some viewpoints in the mountains on the way depending upon the route taken. Nordeste is in the far northeast, in very beautiful countryside but perceived as so distant from Ponta Delgada that the region is often called the Azores' tenth island, and is best enjoyed as a day tour from Furnas. Visitors with a rented car can also advantageously divide their touring of São Miguel into three sectors: the western part including Sete Cidades and the northern coast to Capelas; the central area of Ribeira Grande, Lagoa do Fogo and Vila Franca; and the eastern part embracing Nordeste, Povoação and Furnas.

Car hire

Flor do Norte Estr Regional 14, Fazenda, Nordeste; ✆ 296 486 120 and Rua Dr Guilherme Poças Falcão 43, Ponta Delgada; ✆ 296 287 209; www.flordonorte-rentacar.com
Hertz Airport Ponta Delgada; ✆ 296 205 435, reservations 800 238 238; e reservas@hertz.com; www.hertz.com.pt

Ilha Verde Praça 5 de Outobro 19, Ponta Delgada; ✆ 296 304 800, central reservations 296 304 891; e reserve@ilhaverde.com; www.ilhaverde.com
Tourilhas-Rent-a-Car R Ernesto do Canto 37-D, 9500-312 Ponta Delgada; ✆ 296 304 949; e reservas@tourilhas.com; www.tourilhas.com

BY BUS São Miguel has a good bus service, with services running along both the north and south coasts. Many start not far from the tourist information office on the seafront, close to the fort. With an early start it is possible to enjoy a full day in Nordeste, Furnas, Povoação, Ribeira Grande, Sete Cidades and Capelas. To use the buses most effectively, get a timetable from the tourist office. The schedules may not always be very convenient for tourists, but they work well in combination with taxis, perhaps taking a bus for the outward journey and a taxi for the return. They

Departing Ponta Delgada at 06.45 in November; the streets are empty and there is only one other passenger and I waiting. After the strong and often howling winds of the previous two days, the pre-dawn gentle warm breeze softly caresses the face and is quite welcome. Travelling through town we soon pick up more passengers and, with the streets empty of traffic, and to a glorious fiery sunrise, we hurtle along and are passing the Gorreana tea estate after 40 minutes. Then come the many charming villages along the coast. We are now into rugged country, formed by volcanoes and subsequent erosion that has created a series of deep valleys and ravines. On the land between these ravines many of the villages have been established, but sadly we do not turn off and descend to their centres. It would just take too much time, and the bus is too long to wind easily through the narrow roads, although we do go down to Achada and have great problems negotiating a parked tractor. The bus becomes quite full as we get nearer to Nordeste, where it terminates. Arriving at 09.00, it gives a comfortable seven hours for exploration before catching the 16.00 return bus. This is time enough to visit the two museums, walk along to the Miradoura overlooking the Ponta do Arenal with its handsome lighthouse, and wander up to the forest park, perhaps with a picnic lunch. Recommended is to take a taxi to the Ribeira dos Caldeiroes, which the municipality has so charmingly laid out, and in the opposite direction to Ponta do Sossego near Pedreira, a lovely viewpoint equipped with picnic tables and barbecue pits, to see how well this authority cares for its countryside – the best kept in the entire Azores. The journey back takes an extra 30 minutes because of the traffic around Ponta Delgada, but the bus seats are comfortable so you are rested, and ready for the evening.

are rewarding because you see details of everyday life, and they slowly meander through villages that perhaps you would not otherwise see. Two thoroughly enjoyable day trips are outlined below:

By bus to Furnas Depart Ponta Delgada 07.15, arrive Furnas 09.00 via the north coast. The journey ends at the big school; walk to the end of this road and turn left to the Terra Nostra garden. This allows plenty of time to enjoy the famous garden, walk through the village to see the spa and on to the fumaroles, and time for lunch – maybe try the *cozido*, the Furnas speciality (see page 87 for details). Return 16.30 on the bus coming from Povoação (bus stop by the café before the entrance to the garden), via the south coast, arriving 18.00. Alternatively, get the bus starting from Furnas by the school at 17.10. A great day all for a fare of €6.66.

By bus to Nordeste This makes for a very happy full-day excursion, with the opportunity to see the north coast and a little of its villages, and explore the small town of Nordeste; all for a fare of €4 each way. (See the box above for an account of this trip.)

BY BICYCLE AND MOTORCYCLE

ABS – Azorean Bike Service m 96 346 14 86/91 633 33 23. Bicycles are Scott, BH and B-Pro. Rental or organised trips. One day € 18, down to 6 or more days at € 12 per day. Includes helmet, water bottle, lock, optional bike computer, air pump and repair kit and free delivery to your hotel.
Nuno Vasco Carvalho Rua Antònio Joaquim Nunes da Silva 55-A, 9500-022 Ponta Delgada (behind the theatre); ⌕ 296 628 304; e bikesrental@ yahoo.com. Mountain bikes (junior) €6 per day to € 30 per week; Especial 18 S € 10 per day to € 50 per week. Yamaha BWS 2 seats € 20/119 per day/week; Honda XBR 2 seats € 23/139 per day/week. Does not include insurance.

TRAVEL AGENTS See page 36.

 ## WHERE TO STAY

The principal hotels in Ponta Delgada I have grouped into: those in the west, in the centre and the east of the town. All are within ten–15 minutes' walk of the town centre, but those in the west are convenient for the public buses and those in the east for the marina and swimming pools. Prices show low and high season and many hotels have a children's policy offering various discounts. For classification details see page 45.

PONTA DELGADA
Hotels
In the west

🏠 **Hotel Vila Nova** *** (102 rooms, 5 suites) Rua João Francisco Cabral; ☎ 296 301 600; e vilanova@hotelcanadiano.com; www.hoteisplatano.com. Family owned and run, a nicely fitted, comfortable, modern hotel suited for both holiday and business use. Buffet restaurant, gymnasium, outdoor heated pool, parking. *Dbl € 90–110, sgl € 66–83.*

🏠 **Hotel Ponta Delgada***** (50 rooms) Rua João Francisco Cabral; ☎ 296 209 480; e hotelpdl@hotelpdl.com; www.hotelpdl.com. Some rooms with disabled facilities. Swimming pool, bar, restaurant next door, hairdresser, parking, conference rooms. *Dbl € 63–85, sgl € 52–68.*

🏠 **Royal Garden****** (193 rooms) Rua de Lisboa; ☎ 296 307 300; e royalgardenhotel@investacor.com. An extra couple of minutes' walk to town over the previous two, but a well-designed building with lots of light and feeling of space, built round an attractive inner enclosed garden planted with bamboos and cloud trees. Indoor and outdoor pools, tennis court, sauna, Turkish bath and gymnasium, offstreet parking. *Dbl € 110–150, sgl € 80–112.*

In the centre

🏠 **Hotel Talisman***** (44 rooms, 6 suites and 5 apts) Rua Marquês da Praia e Monforte; ☎ 296 308 500; www.hoteltalisman.com. The hotel is charming, stylishly converted in Art Deco from an old town house by a French architect. Some of the bedrooms can be a little dark, and there is no lift and quite a few quirky stairs. It is right in town on a pedestrianised street and many rooms overlook a pretty public garden. Quite different and the restaurant is excellent. *Dbl € 80–94, sgl € 66–79.*

🏠 **São Miguel Park Hotel***** (163 rooms) Rua Manuel Augusto Amaral; ☎ 296 306 000; e smgparkhotel.reservas@bensaude.pt; www.bensaude.pt. Situated towards the rear of the town with a good view over Ponta Delgada. Rooms all have balconies. Pool, fitness room, restaurant, bar. *Dbl € 102–122, sgl € 80–96 and all-seasons deal of stay 7 nights, pay for 6.*

🏠 **Hotel Colégio** **** (55 rooms) Rua Carvalho Araújo 39; ☎ 296 306 600; e hoteldocolegio@mail.telepac.pt; www.hoteldocolegio.com. Converted from a former convent, this is conveniently located in a quiet and narrow street. Good bar, restaurant; courtyard pool, Turkish bath, gymnasium, parking. *Dbl € 95–125, sgl € 72–98.*

🏠 **Hotel Canadiano***** (50 rooms) Rua do Contador 24A; ☎ 296 287 421; e canadiano@hoteisplatano.com; www.hoteisplatano.com. Rooms are all very spacious, most facing an inner open courtyard. Family-run hotel now in its second generation. Very friendly, bar, b/fast room, room service menu, buffet bistro, coffee shop, lounge, free parking. Near the museum, but foot access for a short stretch is along a busy narrow road. *Dbl € 80–100, sgl € 68–75.*

🏠 **Hotel Avenida****** (80 rooms) Rua Dr José Bruno Tavares Carreiro; ☎ 296 209 660; e h.atlantico@mail.telepac.pt; www.bensaude.pt. Good restaurant, bar. Efficient and comfortable, near Hotel Atlântico and the seafront. *Dbl € 110–122, sgl € 81–97.*

In the east

🏠 **Hotel Açores Atlântico****** (130 rooms and suites) Av Infante D Henrique; ☎ 296 302 200; e reservas@bensaude.pt; www.bensaude.pt. Almost all rooms have balconies, some seafacing. Restaurant, bar, piano bar, indoor swimming pool, fitness room, sauna, hairdresser, conference and banqueting rooms, computer centre, free parking. On the main seafront road at eastern end of town but still just a short walk from the centre.

🏠 **Hotel Marina Atlântico****** (184 rooms) Av Infante D Henrique; ☎ 296 307 900; e reservas@bensaude.pt; www.bensaude.pt. Next to the Hotel Açores Atlântico and part of the same group, this is a smart new hotel with external detailing influenced by the adjacent marina with, dare I say it, decking. A pedestrian bridge crosses the main road to give easy access to the marina and public swimming pools, and the 10-min harbour promenade walk into

the centre of town. Indoor and outdoor pools, health club, sauna, jacuzzi, Turkish bath, reading room, parking. *Dbl* € *127–165, sgl* € *102–134*.

🏠 **Hotel Holiday Inn****** (30 standard and 22 executive rooms, 2 suites) Av D João III 29; ☎ 296 630 000; e holidayinn.az@nsl.pt; www.holiday-inn.com/azores. On the edge of the main part of town, and a few minutes' walk down to the harbour promenade and marina. Rooms are designated smoking and non-smoking. Restaurant, sauna, jacuzzi, gymnasium, swimming pool. *Dbl* € *140–164, sgl* € *101–124*.

Pensão

Many *pensão*, some very small, are scattered throughout Ponta Delgada. Prices begin to overlap those of some three-star hotels. These three are long established and very central:

🏠 **Pensão São Miguel** (20 rooms) (2a) Rua Dr Bruno Tavares Carreiro 28; ☎ 296 286 086

🏠 **Pensão América** (20 rooms) (2a) Rua Manuel Inácio Correia 54/58; ☎ 296 284 351; f 296 287 353

🏠 **Pensão Sete Cidades** (34 rooms) (2a) Rua do Contador 20; ☎ 296 287 344; e residencial_sete_cidades@hotmail.com; www.residencialsetecidades.com

Youth hostel

🏠 Rua São Francisco Xavier; ☎ 296 629 431; e pja.acores@sapo.pt. In town, with easy access to

shops and transport. 90 beds in shared rooms and 2 family rooms with bathroom.

SÃO ROQUE

On the far eastern edge of Ponta Delgada, so still within relatively easy reach of the town.

🏠 **Aparthotel Barracuda***** (21 hotel apts) Praia das Millicias, São Roque, 9500 Ponta Delgada; ☎ 296 381 421. Hotel apts offer bedroom, sitting room, bathroom and kitchenette, telephone, cable TV,

minibar. Overlooking the beach, but with no swimming pool. Room service. Good restaurant. *Dbl* € *75–115, sgl* € *64–103*.

CAPELAS

🏠 **Solar do Conde***** (31 cottages) Rua do Rosário 36, 9545-142 Capelas; ☎ 296 298 887; e np95kd@mail.telepac.pt; www.multi.pt/azores/solar_do_conde. On the north coast, about 20 mins' drive from Ponta Delgada. Some cottages are

detached, some with open fires, all in a garden setting. Excellent restaurant. Small pool. 12km from airport, 6km from golf course. *Cottage sgl* € *54–92, 2 persons sharing* € *65–107, 3 persons sharing* € *87–139*.

ÁGUA DE PAU

🏠 **Hotel Caloura** **** (80 rooms and suites) Rua do Jubileu, 9560-206 Água de Pau; ☎ 296 960 900; e info@calourahotel.com; www.calourahotel.com. An ocean-front resort offering dbl rooms inc junior suites for 4 people, most with private terrace; panoramic restaurant, bar, swimming pool, fitness room, sauna, scuba-diving base, boating and tennis. The location is stunning, and you can walk the narrow roads

round to the pretty unspoiled harbour with its fishing boats and simple swimming facilities. Formerly an area of tiny vineyards, these have largely been removed in favour of pasture and very expensive housing. Sheltered and a sun trap, it is ideal for a winter holiday, but you will need a car if you want to explore the island. 17km (11 miles) from Ponta Delgada. *Dbl* € *67–113, sgl* € *52–89*.

The noted orange farmer Thomas Hickling built in 1770 a simple summer house on the high mound overlooking what is now the thermal swimming pool. It was surrounded by trees which would have sheltered fashionable summer parties and music; of those trees, we believe the old pollarded English oak in the corner by the pool is the only one that remains, and is therefore probably the oldest tree in the garden. Hickling died in 1834, and it was not until 1848 that the Visconde da Praia purchased the property and on the mound built the present house. The Viscondessa was a keen gardener, and over the years they enlarged the estate and laid out the garden in a grand style with water, dark groves of trees and parterres of flowers. After the Visconde's death in 1872 his son enhanced the house and laid out the garden more or less as it is today with its serpentine canal and grottoes, and walks. New tree species were introduced from around the world so many of these now-mature trees are at most 140 years old.

The newly built Terra Nostra Hotel opened in 1935, and soon after, Vasco Bensaúde, who was a very keen gardener, purchased the now neglected garden; the family's company still owns it today. With a head gardener from Scotland and a veritable army of workmen, he totally refurbished the house and restored the garden within two years. World War II came and ended the fashionable life of Furnas based on the hotel, casino, spa and gardens, and the place continued to slumber for years afterwards until tourism once more asserted itself.

In 1990 restoration began once again, this time with English gardeners, and a team of tree surgeons climbed vertically the equivalent of Mount Everest from sea level working on the 2,500 trees while local engineers refurbished the canals. Many new trees were planted, a garden of Azorean native species begun and, significantly, a collection of Malesian rhododendrons was planted. This is the only garden in Europe that can grow, out of doors without protection, these tender rhododendrons native to tropical mountains; they flower intermittently all year and come in spectacular colours and some are perfumed. The head gardener, Fernando Costa, continues with new developments: a fern garden, a formal flower garden, and most recently a garden of cycads, plants that peaked 200 million years ago and that would have been browsed by dinosaurs.

ÁGUA DE ALTO

🏠 **Hotel Bahia Palace****** (102 roooms) Água de Alto, 9680 Vila Franca do Campo; ☎ 296 539 130; e bahiapalace@azoresnet.com; www.hotelbahiapalace.com. On a little flat promontory by the sea 4km from the nearest town. Spacious common rooms and large suites and junior suites with sun terraces and sea facing, cocktail lounge, restaurant and grill, pool and good black-sand beach for sea swimming. *Dbl €89–120, sgl €72–104.*

VILA FRANCA DO CAMPO

🏠 **Hotel Marina***** (46 rooms, 3 suites) Rua Eng Manuel António Martins Mota, Vinha da Areia, 9680-029 Vila Franca do Campo; ☎ 296 539 200; e hotelmarina@mail.telepac.pt; www.maisturismo.pt/marina. Your hotel beside the seaside, with an extra view of the Aquapark right next door with water slides and pools. Rooms all have balconies, panoramic restaurant, bar, pool, conference facilities. 20-min drive to Ponta Delgada, and the same to Furnas golf course. *Dbl €82–120, sgl €62–93.*

FURNAS

🏠 **Terra Nostra Garden Hotel***** (79 rooms) Rua Pe José Jacinto Botelho 5, 9675-061 Furnas; ☎ 296 549 090; e recepcao.htnl@bensaude.pt; www.bensaude.pt. The hotel dates back to the 1930s and has a very strong period atmosphere. There is a new wing with large balconied rooms looking into the garden. Rooms in the original part of the hotel have recently been refurbished to a high standard in Art Deco style, some overlook the garden, some the front road with view to the old casino and its little formal garden. There is a restaurant, bar, comfortable residents' lounge, indoor heated pool and outdoor thermally heated pool. Residents have free access to the famous garden at all times. *Dbl €90–147, sgl €74–121.*

Camping

🛆 **Parque de Campismo das Furnas** Queimadas, Furnas; ☎ 296 549 010. By the Furnas lake, extremely popular with local people and very busy at weekends. *Open 15 Jun–15 Sep.*

POVOAÇÃO

🏠 **Hotel do Mar***** (36 rooms) Rua Gonçalo Velho, 9650-411 Povoação; ☎ 296 550 010; e hoteldomar@hoteldomar.com; www.hoteldomar.com. Located close to the sea near the harbour. Rooms have balcony and sea view, bar,

NORDESTE

🏠 **Estalagem dos Clérigos****** (20 rooms, 1 suite, 4 apts) Rua dos Clérigos, 9630 Nordeste; ☎ 296 480 100; e reservas@bensaude.pt; www.bensaude.com. A new hotel with views to the sea and inland to the Serra da Tronqueira. Restaurant and outdoor pool. *Dbl €72–122, sgl €60–100.*

🏠 **Casas do Frade** (CC) (9 cottages) Rua do Traitro 11, 13, 15, Lombas da Fazenda; ☎ 296 382 365; e casas.do.frade@mail.pt; www.geocities.com/casasdofrade. This is a small and very pretty complex of old cottages simply furnished and made

Camping

🛆 Ribeira do Guilherme, Nordeste; ☎ 296 480 060. Just before you reach Nordeste coming from the north road and tucked away at the bottom of a

🏠 **Quinta Vista do Vale**** (24 rooms) Rua da Palha 56, 9675-042 Furnas; ☎ 296 549 030. In a quiet location tucked away on the edge of Furnas near the forest department's nursery, it has a fine view over village rooftops and the valley and gives the visitor a real feeling of living in the village. Rooms all have balconies and view, central heating, private bathrooms. Only b/fast served, but restaurants are a short walk away. *Dbl €59–75, sgl €47–61; open 1 Apr–30 Sep.*

🛆 **Campsite Furnas** Lovely position overlooking the fumaroles, but rather confused site with hideously built facilities, tennis court, children's play area, small snack bar and large surfaced car park that mercifully weeds are already beginning to green over.

outdoor pool and jacuzzi. Not very inviting in winter, it needs a wood fire in the bar, but ideally placed for all the new walks promoted by the municipality. *Dbl €63–85, sgl €52–68.*

comfortable; each has dbl bedroom, living room, kitchen and bathroom. On the edge of the village and just 3km from Nordeste, it is a quite lovely rural scene. In March sitting on the little stone terrace in brilliant sun looking over meadows as lush and green as they can possibly be, bordered by trees, a few tiny houses and a blue sea beyond, the only sound that of cow bells and wild canaries, it would be hard to find a simpler place for a hideaway. *Per night each cottage Oct–Apr €65–78 and May–Sep €75–88.*

river valley, this pretty campsite is beneath trees by a stream with many watermills. Showers and WCs. Semi-natural swimming pool near the sea.

MANOR HOUSES In recent years, large country houses have begun to take in paying guests. There are now too many to detail here, but the Azores tourist office (see page 36) provides lists. The following are four establishments that I know or that have been recommended. All rooms have en-suite bathrooms.

🏠 **Estalagem Senhora da Rosa** (TH) (27 rooms, 1 suite) **** Rua Senhora da Rosa 3, Fajã de Baixo, 9500-450 Ponta Delgada; ☎ 296 630 100; e senhora.rosa@mail.telepac.pt;

www.estalagemsenhoradarosa.com. Open now for 9 years this is a very well-run rural property with bedrooms traditionally furnished, each one different, with a very comfortable guest lounge, bar, etc, an excellent restaurant with faultless service, and a large garden with tennis. Located on a quiet road on the outskirts of Ponta Delgada, a free minibus service is provided into town. The style and service give the feel of a *pousada*. *Dbl € 76–100, sgl € 61–86. A long, lingering dinner for 2 with drinks will cost about € 70.*

⌂ **Quinta de Santana** (AG) (10 rooms) Canada da Meca, 9600 Rabo de Peixe; ⟍ 296 491 241; e Quinta-santana@virtualazores.com; www.virtualazores.com/quinta-santana. On the north coast west of Ribeira Grande, a large property with purpose-built units nicely laid out and ideal for family use. Children's equipped play area, swimming pool, and a garden estate with enticing paths and lots of hidden areas to explore. *Dbl € 70–77, sgl € 52–65 and units up to € 138.*

⌂ **Quinta da Abelheira** (AG) (8 rooms, family room, 1 apt) Pico da Abelheira 17, Fajã de Baixo, 9500-701 Ponta Delgada; ⟍ 296 630 180/1; e info@ quintadaabelheira.com; www.quintadaabelheira.com. On the eastern side of Ponta Delgada and just a 10min drive to the centre, yet very quiet. A lovely old house, all rooms traditionally furnished, some within the house, others purpose built in an adjacent annexe. Games room and pool. Relaxing garden, decorated with tiled panels from 1932 and illustrated quotes from the Azorean poets. Dinner provided with 24hrs advance warning. No facilities for children. *Dbl in main building € 80–88; family room (4 persons) € 140–165.*

⌂ **Herdade N Sra das Graças** (AG) (4 rooms) Estaleiro, 9625-000 Lomba da Maia; ⟍ 296 446 165; e nsgraces@virtualacores.com; www.virtualacores.com/nsgracas. Enthusiastic feedback from Nico Olofsen in Amsterdam says it all: 'The 1920s' house is situated in farmland far off the beaten track and Lomba da Maia, the nearest village, can be reached by a farm road in about 30 mins' walk. Visitors are given a warm welcome and hospitality standards are high, with splendid evening meals with authentic Azorean flavours. The surroundings and peace are overwhelming, but a car would be useful as there is only one bus a day to Furnas and one to Lomba da Maia. English and German spoken.' *Dbl € 79–100, sgl € 70–86.*

✖ WHERE TO EAT

São Miguel has many restaurants, and several of the hotels also have restaurants open to non-residents. There are also good places to be found tucked away in several of the villages around the island, for details see under the village. In Ponta Delgada there are far too many to list, or even for your author to assess on your behalf, but two mid-priced eateries that have been established for many years are listed here.

✖ **Restaurante Nacional** Rua Açoreana Oriental; ⟍ 296 282 807. Recently won by popular vote a competition organised by the town hall for cooking the best steak. Very tender, ask for *bife à capitão do Porta*; it comes fried, so say if you prefer it grilled and unadorned. Sadly no fat; it seems butchers clean all of it away. Always consistent, with good service, very popular with locals as well as visitors, the restaurant has retained its sensible prices.

✖ **Restaurante Jordão** O Rei dos Bifes – The King of Steaks; Rua Hintze Ribeiro 17–19 (near Hotel Colégio); ⟍ 296 629 656. This snack bar is a newcomer. It is a small place with a nice atmosphere where I enjoyed the finest tuna steak ever.

More expensive are:

✖ **Hotel Talisman** Rua Marquês da Praia e Monforte; ⟍ 296 629 502. In summer you should reserve a table. Food here is consistently good, but better appreciated if the staff would smile more.

✖ **London Restaurante** 21 Rua Ernesto Canto, up behind the old Dom Pedro hotel; ⟍ 296 282 500

✖ **Hotel São Pedro** Largo Almirante Dunn; ⟍ 296 282 223. Now the catering school, formerly a hotel and originally the substantial 18th-century house belonging to Thomas Hickling, the American consul and orange grower who began the Terra Nostra property in Furnas. Worth a visit for its antique furniture, interesting old photos and prints, and attractive rooms. *Open 12.00–14.30 lunch and 19.00–22.00 dinner, every day.*

✖ **Casa Acoreana** Rua Hintze Rebeira; ⟍ 296 653 922. Included on good feedback from a reader.

Although Ponta Delagada is by far the most important and busiest town in the Azores, nightlife mercifully remains mostly quiet and traditional so you can fully appreciate how generally civilised everything is and enjoy an evening promenade by the harbour after a good dinner.

📺 **The Teatro Micaelensis** www.teatromicaelense.pt. Offers a wide range of cultural events throughout the year from ballet, musicals, fado, jazz and chamber recitals to fully staged operas, the programmes often linked with the Coliseums in Lisbon and Oporto.

☆ **Karamba** 46 Rua Hintze Ribeiro; ☎ 296 628 308. Bar/disco.

☆ **Escala** Av Roberto Ivens; ☎ 296 281 547. Restaurant and bar, live music after midnight.

☆ **Show Girls Gentleman's Club** Abelheira de Baixa, Faja de Baixa; ☎ 296 642 884; www.showgirlsclub.com. This is something new. It seems the girls from Brazil have arrived! *Open 23.00–05.00, couples always welcome.*

One of the most important festivals is that of **Senhor Santo Cristo dos Milagres** (literally Lord Holy Christ of Miracles) to whom intense devotion was given during the 17th century when the island was racked with frequent earthquakes and tremors, and whose celebration has strengthened through the centuries. The monastery and nearby 'Square of 5th of October' are illuminated and the street decorated with flowers and at the end of the week, on the fifth Sunday after Easter, a large procession passes round the town with the crown of golden thorns at the front. Behind come men in religious clothes, some barefoot, some carrying large, very heavy candles to declare their thanks for a blessing received during a period of affliction. These are followed by youth organisations with their brightly coloured banners, children, some dressed as angels, priests, then the figure of Senhor Santo Cristo dos Milagres carried under a dossel of velvet and gold decorated with 18th-century woven flowers.

A much less conspicuous celebration, but one that perhaps makes a greater impression upon the visitor by its gravity and simplicity, is that of the **Lenten pilgrims**. During the seven weeks of Lent, groups of men led by a 'master' walk right round the island and pray at the churches and chapels dedicated to Our Lady. As they walk they say the Ave Maria; you can ask them to say one for you, but in return you must say as many yourself as there are men walking in the group.

Of great significance in the religious calendar is the **Holy Ghost Festival** that climaxes on the seventh Sunday after Easter. It is a festival with German origins when an Imperial Brotherhood was set up to help people in times of calamity; it spread widely in Christian Europe including Portugal. On São Miguel its importance grew after the tragic consequences of the earthquake that virtually destroyed Vila Franca do Campo in 1522. The **Procession of Bom Jesus da Pedra** is one of the oldest religious festivals and attracts many emigrants from around the world.

Cantar ás Estrelas, Our Lady of the Stars, is celebrated by singing at night in the streets in thanks for the star that guided the Three Kings to Bethlehem.

In May is the festival of **São Miguel Arcanjo** which has been celebrated for more than 400 years. Its secular content involves a procession of different professional groups – fishermen, potters, shoemakers, barbers and farmers, etc. The **Festival of São João** on 24 June is also Vila Franca's municipal holiday; celebrations continue for a week with marching bands, dances, bonfires and barbecues.

Cantar ás Estrelas (Ribeira Grande)	beginning of February
Festa de São José (Ponta Delgada)	procession third week of March
Páscoa	April

Festa Sr dos Enfermos (Furnas); the streets are covered with azaleas and other flowers for the procession — end of April

Festa de São Pedro Gonçalves – Festa do Irró (Vila Franca); the fishermen process down to the harbour — end of April

Festa do Sr Santo Cristo dos Milagres (Ponta Delgada) — last week of May

Festa da Flor (Ribeira Grande); flower festival — May

Festas do Espírito Santo — May to September; intermittent

Festas de São João da Vila (Vila Franca); with popular singing groups and food stalls, dancing, bonfires and barbecues — middle of June

Império da Trindade (Ponta Delgada); ending of the Holy Ghost Festival — third week of June

Festa do Corpo de Deus (Povoação) — last week of June

Cavalhadas de São Pedro (Ribeira Grande); horsemen pay tribute to St Peter in traditional song asking protection for the island's governor — last week of June

Semana do Chicharro (Ribeira Quente); fishing festival — middle of July

Festa de N Sra de Lurdes (Capelas) — end of July

Festa de Santana (Furnas) — end of July

Festa de São Nicolau (Sete Cidades) — middle of August

Festa de N Sra dos Anjos (Agua de Pau/Fajã de Baixo) — middle of August

Festa de N Sra Conceição (Mosteiros) — third week of August

Semana da Cultura (Povoação); handicrafts and other activities — last week of August

Festa do Bom Jesus da Pedra (Vila Franca); one of the oldest religious festivals attracting many emigrants from around the world — last week of August

Festival de Bandas (Povoação); road show — first week of October

Dia das Montras (Ponta Delgada); shop windows are dressed for Christmas and prizes awarded for the best — second week of December

USEFUL NUMBERS

Emergency ✆ 112
Police Ponta Delgada; ✆ 296 282 022
Tourist information office Av Infante D Henrique, Ponta Delgada; ✆ 296 285 743; e info.turismo@drt.raa.pt
Post office Praça Vasco da Gama; ✆ 296 201 050
Hospital ✆ 296 20300

SATA Air Açores Av Infante D Henrique, Ponta Delgada; ✆ 296 209 720
TAP Air Portugal Av Infante D Henrique, Ponta Delgada; ✆ 296 205 233
Airport information ✆ 296 205 414; lost and found ✆ 296 205 413

WHAT TO SEE AND DO

MUSEUMS Museums seem to be opening all the time and they are all most charmingly staged and often in picturesque settings. The most interesting are in Ponta Delgada, Capelas, Ribeira Grande and Povoação.

Museu Carlos Machado (*Rua João Moreira, Ponta Delgada; open May–Sep Tue–Fri 10.00–12.00, 14.00–17.00, Sat/Sun 11.00–17.30; rest of the year Tue–Sat 10.00–12.00, 14.00–17.00*) Founded in 1876, this important museum is in the former convent of Santo André, named for the first patron saint of Ponta Delgada. Intended to house Clarissa nuns in the late 16th century, it has undergone several structural changes and its present appearance dates from the first half of the 19th century. The museum is named after its founder, Carlos Machado, whose natural history collections are now of only historical interest. The present collection has been greatly expanded and includes fascinating exhibits of regional ethnography detailing the traditions and customs of island life, while upstairs there is an interesting gallery of period and contemporary paintings and sculpture. Among the paintings are the locally famous *Os Emigrantes* by Domingos Rebelos (1892–1975) and *Os Regressantes* (The Returnees) by Thomás Viera, painted in 1988, both of which are vivid social comments.

Oficina-Museu M J Melo (*Rua do Loural 56, 9545-137 Capelas;* ⟍ *296 298 202; open Mon–Sat 14.00–18.00*) This is a most remarkable and extensive display of recreated bygone retail and artisan shops in the style of a street, all done by a retired schoolteacher of Capelas. Not only has Senhor Melo made the museum, he has also financed it, without any grant-aid. It is in part of his house, and from the outside does not look at all like a museum. You will find Rua Loural up from the main square of Rossio, in Capelas village. Well worth visiting.

Museu de Emigração (*On the right-hand side of the main road into Ribeira Grande from Ponta Delgada, next to the market, in a large building with museum flags flying; open weekdays 09.30–12.30 and 13.30–17.00*) At present the exhibitions change every few months, and concern different topics to do with the emigrants. The show I saw showed the tools and domestic items of the Azores at the end of the 18th and early 19th centuries contrasted with the items introduced by the returning emigrants, mainly tableware and glassware, and linen made in New Bedford but with typical Azorean crochet designs. The large car park opposite behind the wall used to be the cattle market.

Museu de Trigo (Wheat Museum) (*Signposted off the main road as you past the last houses leaving Povoação on the road to Nordeste. Located by the Ribeira dos Bispos, between the ridges of Lomba do Loução and Lomba do Alcaide. Open Tue–Sat 10.30–12.30 and 14.00–17.00, Sun 14.00–17.00; admission free*) Splendid watermill skilfully restored in a gloriously unspoiled setting of timeless pastures and hedgerows. Tea and local biscuits served. It is a triumph of restoration and capture of a past culture, and highly recommended.

The following all display their local cultural traditions and skills, and are most charmingly done.

Casa de Cultura da Ribeira Grande Rua São Vicente de Ferreira. *Open Tue–Sat 08.30–12.30 and 13.30–16.30.*

Museu Municipal de Vila Franca do Campo Rua da Visconde do Botelho. *Open Tue–Sun 09.30–17.30.*
Museu do Nordeste Rua D Maria do Rosario. *Open Mon–Fri 10.00–12.30 and 14.00–17.30.*

WALKING Staying either in Furnas or Povoação gives good access to several days of excellent and largely easy walking on marked, well-maintained trails and these two villages look as though they could become the best centres for walking in the Azores. From Ponta Delgada there are walks in the Sete Cidades area and access to the start of the ascent to Lagoa do Fogo. (See *Walks*, page 88.)

3

BIRDS AND FLOWERS The most famous rarity of São Miguel is the much-promoted Azores bullfinch, found only in the native shrubbery of the **Serra da Tronqueira Nature Reserve**. There are thought to be between 100 and 200 pairs, and they may be seen from along the unsurfaced road between Povoação and Nordeste – see *Walk* 4, page 96. As a gardener, I find some sympathy for the early farmers who shot it almost out of existence to protect their crops from its infamous depredations. Here one may also find the Azores woodpigeon. This mountainous area with its deep ravines and watercourses is densely covered with laurisilva or Macaronesian evergreen forest and the endemic species include laurel, holly, juniper, Portugal laurel and bilberry together with ferns.

Lagoa do Fogo Nature Reserve provides the most accessible site for endemic plants and even if not tempted by the steep and slippery path descending to the lake through this vegetation, exploration around the viewpoint can be rewarding enough. Juniper, laurel, frangula and erica shelter native hypericum and euphorbia and a patient search will reveal several more endemics. You cannot fail to hear the Atlantic yellow-legged gulls.

Sete Cidades and its varied sheltered habitats of fields and gardens can be productive for birds, while the lake offers respite for migrant species and in autumn occasional American vagrants.

The varied habitats around the village of **Mosteiros** are often rewarding, with migrating passerines in the cultivated areas and, on the lava beach, turnstones, whimbrels and little egret, less often sandpipers.

WHALE WATCHING For main entry see page 53. On the quayside in Ponta Delgada is a large notice listing the boat operators currently approved and licensed to offer whale watching. Off the south coast of São Miguel was once a profitable area when the islanders used to hunt whales and now, some three generations or so since the last whales were killed, they are again swimming past the killing shores. Some companies offer straight whale watching, others combine it with a sea cruise along to Vila Franca and back, others to Ribeira Quente with a stop for lunch in a noted restaurant. Often your hotel can advise you what is on offer during your stay, or in summer simply walk along the seafront to find operators' kiosks.

SWIMMING I repeat, the Azores is not a beach destination. On the north coast swimming can be dangerous as there are many currents and hazards; you will see local people swimming, but they know where the dangers are. Use only obviously developed swimming areas. All beaches are black sand.

Ponta Delgada At the eastern end of the harbour promenade, harbour swimming and in summer a complex of pools with full services.

Lagoa Originally this was a long, popular 150m stretch of irregular coastline, but the old complex was virtually destroyed during the winter storms of 1997. A new complex has been built with greater protection against storm damage with two pools, both heated to 24°C in winter. The largest is a four-lane, 25m pool; the second is for children. There is also an ocean swimming area surrounded on three sides by lava – swimming dependent on tides and strength of the sea. Sunbathing area, diving boards and slides complete the picture, together with a snack bar. EC Blue Flag designation.

Vila Franca do Campo Two beaches, Praia de Agua d'Álto and Praia das Francesa, known also as Vinha d'Areia. Here also is the Aquapark, with pools and slides. The Ilhéu da Vila Franca, an islet just offshore, has a naturally protected swimming area and is also good for scuba diving and snorkelling; note that this is a protected nature area and there is concern that increasing visitor numbers are damaging the habitat.

São Roque Beaches of Milicias or Areal Grande, and Areal Pequeno. Supporting facilities, and very popular, a short drive from Ponta Delgada.

Caloura Fishing harbour, natural pool, no beach.

Água de Alto Long stretch of sand between two promontories, by the Hotel Bahia Palace.

Ribeira Quente Fishing village at far end of which beneath steep cliffs is the Praia do Fogo. All facilities, and in summer there are several open-air restaurants. An extremely popular area.

GOLF There are two courses on São Miguel, one at Fenais da Luz just a few kilometres north of Ponta Delgada, the other at Furnas in the east of the island. (*Green fees 18 holes €55, 9 holes €36; set of clubs 18 holes €23.70; tuition 60 mins €31.20.*)

Golfe da Batalha Rua do Bom Jesus, Aflitos 9545-234, Fenais da Luz; ⤷ 296 498 559; f 296 498 284; e verdegolf@virtualazores.com; www.virtualazores.com/verdegolf. Designed by Cameron Powell Associates and built in 1996 with long fairways, large flowing greens and sinuously contoured bunkers, the course is a combination of links and woodland course with views over the sea on the first 9 and superb landscapes on the second 9 holes. 27 holes, par 72. Main competitions: SATA Air Açores Azores Open, VCC; International pro-am. The clubhouse has a restaurant with a stunning view, open to non-players (⤷ 296 498 540).
Golfe das Furnas Contact details the same as for

Golfe da Batalha. Designed by MacKenzie Ross (who also built the Estoril course near Lisbon and restored the Scottish Turnberry courses) and built in 1939 with 9 holes, it was extended in 1990 by Cameron Powell Associates to the full 18-hole course, par 72, and 6,232m long. It is an intimate course set in a glorious landscape with always verdant grass, forest and tree ferns. At 500m clouds and mist can often swirl around the course and present a different kind of challenge to the golfer. About 15 mins' drive from Furnas or one hour from Ponta Delgada; for a truly relaxing holiday stay at the Terra Nostra Garden Hotel and either taxi or drive to the course.

ITINERARIES
Ponta Delgada This is the largest town in the Azores, with a university established in 1975. The fastest and easiest way to get to know Ponta Delgada is to take the Lagarta Trolley (a toy train) or follow on foot my *Town trail*, see below.

The Lagarta stop is at the western end of the Avenida Infante Dom Henrique, opposite São Brás Fort. Between May and October five different circuits are offered at different times; heritage, historical, beach, gardens and outskirts (*open 09.00–23.00*). In winter, the choice is down to three routes (*open 09.00–19.00*). A commentary is given in English. Price is €3.

Town trail The following town trail should take about two hours, excluding the Carlos Machado Museum (see page 73).

We begin the walk at the tourist information office on the main promenade by the harbour, the Avenida do Infante Dom Henrique. The tourism department sells its own guide booklets to all the islands, illustrated with splendid photographs. Various other brochures and maps are also available free, as are the bus timetables for São Miguel.

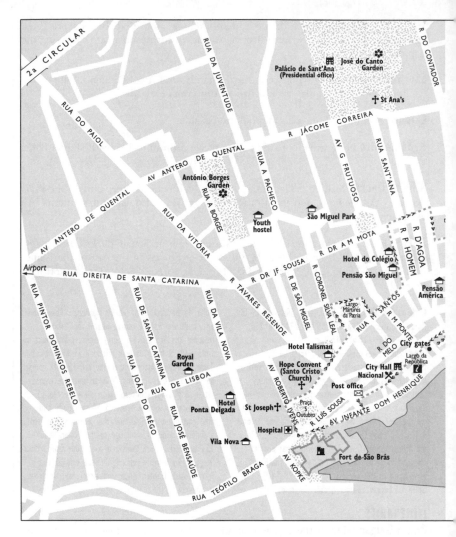

Upon leaving, turn left and left again around the corner where in the square, **Praça Gonçalo Velho Cabral**, you will find the three arches of the original (1783) gates to the city which once stood by the old harbour wall. The modern statue commemorates the man after whom the square is named, supposedly the discoverer of São Miguel and Santa Maria.

Ponta Delgada had become important as a trading port, and in the 18th and early 19th centuries it was especially significant for the export of oranges. On several of the houses you will see square attic-like structures on the roof; here a servant would be stationed to watch for and give early warning of the approach of an orange schooner. This gave the grower or merchant valuable extra hours to harvest the fruit as it had to be picked fresh to travel well. Ships had to moor offshore and lighters (transportation barges) conveyed passengers and cargo from shore to ship. The harbour then was very small, and the square where you are now standing was the harbour. The bank on the east side and the buildings adjacent all have many internal arches which once fronted the sea. Land reclamation has pushed the sea

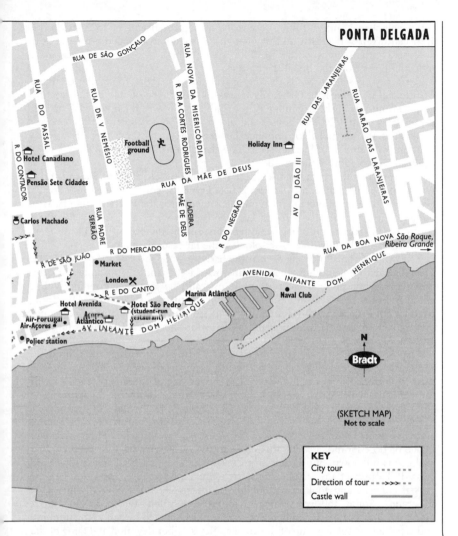

RUA DE SÃO GONÇALO

RUA DO PASSAL

RUA DR V NEMÉSIO

RUA NOVA DA MISERICÓRDIA

R DR A CORTES RODRIGUES

RUA DAS LARANJEIRAS

RUA BARÃO DAS LARANJEIRAS

🏃 Football ground

Holiday Inn

RUA DA MÃE DE DEUS

AV D JOÃO III

🏨 Hotel Canadiano

R DO CONTADOR

🏨 Pensão Sete Cidades

LADEIRA MÃE DE DEUS

R DO NEGRÃO

🏛 Carlos Machado

RUA PADRE SERRÃO

R DO MERCADO

RUA DA BOA NOVA *São Roque, Ribeira Grande* →

R DE SÃO JOÃO

• Market

AVENIDA INFANTE DOM HENRIQUE

London ✕

R E DO CANTO

• Marina Atlântico

• Naval Club

Hotel Avenida

• Hotel São Pedro (student-run restaurant)

Air-Portugal

Açores Atlântico

AV INFANTE DOM HENRIQUE

Air-Açores •

• Police station

N

Bradt

(SKETCH MAP)
Not to scale

KEY
City tour   ▪ ▪ ▪ ▪ ▪
Direction of tour ▪ ▪ ▪ ≫ ▪ ▪
Castle wall   ────────

back and allowed the new bank and other buildings, as well as the main promenade road, to be built in 1947.

Cross the square, and stand with your back to the Parish Church of São Sebastian. You are now facing a run of buildings that once fronted the sea. The city gates originally joined these. On your left, facing the São Sebastian Church, is a tiny entrance to the **Café Mascote** (previously known as the Café Chesterfield); go into the old part, No 66, and see the arched roof while enjoying a coffee. This was once part of the original colonnade at the harbour's edge. Murals in the café show what it all looked like.

Exit the café and turn right and then right again down a small side street. On the left at the end is the police station, formerly the customs house. Take the little turning on the right about halfway along to go to the rear of the Café Mascote. Again you will see some arches in the outside wall, part of the colonnade at the edge of the harbour.

Return the same way as you came, to **São Sebastian Church**. This began as a very small chapel built to fulfil a vow made during the plague of 1523–31; in the 18th century it was greatly added to in the Baroque style and the interior was decorated with ornate woodcarving. The exotic timbers used, especially jacaranda, reflect imports from the Brazilian colonies.

Retrace your steps towards the city gates and turn right, to see the **Câmara Municipal** or town hall. Originally it was the residence of one of the wealthy families and only at the beginning of the 20th century was it converted. The bell tower dates from 1724 and houses the oldest bell (16th century) in the Azores. Look in at the ground-floor entrance between the steps; here there is often a temporary exhibition of local interest. The statue in front of the building is of St Michael, patron saint of the island.

Continue past the town hall taking the road on your left, **Rua de Santa Luzia**. At the end, on the left, is the old post office. Leave the square, the Praça Vasco da Gama, and continue along the main promenade towards the **Forte de São Brás** at the end of the present-day harbour. Looking back provides a pleasing view of the continuity of architecture along the waterfront and by the post office. Please avert your eyes from the intrusive tower block at the far eastern end.

You will see a small floating deck at the harbour edge and café tables; this is the **Cais de Sardinha**, and was where sardines used to be landed. Continue along the avenida, past the present-day customs house, and see a corner building with a circular tower, the local headquarters of the Ministry of Defence. The 16th-century Forte de São Brás was built to defend the village against corsairs and pirates, including some from England. Enlarged in the 19th century, it is now the army headquarters.

Opposite the fort is the square of **Praça 5 Outubro** (formerly the Campo de São Francisco), the traditional site for festivals and overlooked by the fine, green-washed, former Franciscan monastery. On the far side of the square, parallel with the seafront, is the **Convent and Chapel of Nossa Senhora da Esperança** (Our Lady of Hope), completed in 1541 and occupied by the nuns of the order of St Francis. The chapel is decorated with magnificent 18th-century tiles and gilding and is associated with the worship of the Christ of the Miracles. There is also an image of Ecce Homo, a statue that came to the Azores in the 16th century. The sculptor is unknown, but it came from Paris into Caloura to a convent that then existed. To protect the statue against frequent pirate attacks, the nuns left the coastal convent and took it with them to the newly built Nossa Senhora da Esperança. Some 150 years later a young girl called Teresa da Anunciada (1658–1738), from a rich family in Ribeira Grande, devoted herself to the nunnery and especially to the worship of this image. News of her devotion and fame of the miracles granted carried to all the islands and even as far as mainland Portugal. Subsequent emigration spread the worship of the Christ of the Miracles, and now pilgrims come from Azorean communities overseas to join the annual festival. The image may be seen between 17.30 and 18.30 every evening when a nun opens the internal gates to allow visitors in to see it, as well as the vestments and treasures. There is also a splendid ceiling and Baroque ornamentation. Once a year the image is taken on procession through the city, passing along the narrow roads carpeted with fresh flowers in geometrical designs.

Outside, in front of the chapel, there is a statue to Madre Teresa da Anunciada. Behind, at the first seat, the poet and political activist Anthero de Quental shot himself in 1891, aged 29. The church to the left of the convent, **São José**, was part of the Lady of Conception convent and in the 16th century took 60 years to build. The façade is 18th century. Inside, it has a fine ceiling and much 18th-century decorative art. It is the major church of the old village and parish of São José.

From the square and by the convent, the pedestrianised road leading off is and has always been called the central road or **Rua Direita**, although today it is not central. Pass along the convent buildings and you come to green metal gates. Here you will find the side entrance to view the Ecce Homo.

Continue along the Rua Direita which becomes the Rua Marques de Praia e Monfort, where even now traditional shops are still to be found. On the right you will come to the **Royal Palace**, once belonging to the Marques, opposite the Hotel Talisman. It is now used by the Department of Social Services. Walk past the palace and then look back and you will see on the roof an observation tower looking in all four directions. This was for defence. The car park was once part of the garden. It was the Marquis de Praia who in 1843 purchased the land in Furnas and began the great expansion of the Terra Nostra garden. Keep straight, passing the little garden square dedicated to the writer and orator Padre Sena de Freitas, and take the next road on the left, up the **Rua Comandante Jaime de Sousa**. Note one of the largest lookout towers on a private residence. You come to Martyr's Square at the far side of which is a secondary school, originally the grand home of the wealthy 'Fonte Bela', so nicknamed because of his many water installations on the island. He was one of the first and most important of the orange growers and the largest landowner. The cream-coloured building on the left, to the west, is the old government or **Parliament House** of the autonomous region. Note the church with its ornate Manueline façade.

Take the **Travessa de Conceição** and then turn left into the Rua Machado dos Santos. A very small chapel at the top of a short flight of basalt steps is the **Chapel of Santa Luzia**, dated 1584. Luzia was the daughter of a rich family and was losing her sight; she promised that if she could keep her sight she would build a chapel in gratitude.

Turn left into the **Rua Carvalho Araújo**; at the far end you will see the splendidly ornate **Franciscan convent** in the 18th-century style of Pombalino; the interior is currently under major reconstruction. Enjoy the many wrought-iron balconies as you walk up this street. Next to the convent is the memorial garden to the poet Anthero de Quental with its elegant Art Deco sculpture, *Emotion and Reason*.

From the convent go eastwards along the Rua Dr Aristides da Mota and the Rua Dr G P Falcão and keep going until the narrow road opens out and you see a large building to the right surrounded by a tall whitewashed wall enclosing a garden. This is the **Carlos Machado Museum** (see page 73); turn right and follow the wall round to the entrance. If you have time, do make a visit for it is well worth seeing; if not, then make a point of returning.

Out of the museum turn left and right down the hill and, at the first crossroads, turn left. You will see on the right the tall **Teatro Micaelense**. This was originally the site of a military fortress, destroyed by fire in the early 1900s. The theatre was opened in May 1917 and is modelled on the Coliseum in Lisbon. It has been recently restored and seats 1,500. If you want to visit the **market** selling fresh fruit, vegetables, flowers, meat, fish, cheese and handicrafts, continue along the Rua Mercado for about 100m and you'll find it on the right-hand side of the road. There are also very clean public lavatories, and a snack bar. Afterwards, retrace your steps back to the theatre.

Walk down the hill and turn left into the **Rua Misericórdia** and you will come to the **city library** on your left with the red gates at the top of the steps. Take the right fork along to the **Hotel São Pedro**, now a catering school. This was the residence of Thomas Hickling, built 1799–1812 in Georgian style. Hickling was the wealthy Bostonian who built a summer house at Furnas and began what later became the Terra Nostra Park. Opposite on elevated ground is a church, the main **church of the parish of São Pedro**. Climb the steps for a good view out to sea.

Ponta Delgada has over the years absorbed the surrounding villages and today has three parishes, two of which we have now met, and the central parish of São Sebastião.

From here walk down to the seafront and continue right along the promenade to return to the tourist office.

Gardens During the middle years of the 19th century at least three great gardens were developed in Ponta Delgada, and their owners vied with each other to have the latest introductions and the rarest plants. They are within walking distance of the town centre.

Jardim António Borges (*Open daily 09.00–19.00, 20.00 in summer*) This remains by far the most ornate, or rather fanciful, of the gardens. Now a public garden managed by the municipality, it is an anachronism given the present-day demands made by users of public open space in a crowded town. There remains the great fern ravine with its romantic bridge, and the small lakes and various watercourses can readily be detected, although they are now dry. Boating and garden parties must have been huge fun. Most of the original trees have long gone; a great buttress-rooted India rubber tree, *Ficus elastica*, and a huge *Albizia* sp. are well worth seeing. The garden is being refurbished and it will be a challenge to retain as many of the historical features as is practicable and commensurate with the demands and expectations of modern times.

The Presidential Palace or Sant'Ana Palace (*Open Mon–Fri 09.00–12.00 and 14.00–16.30; admission free*) Now the office of the president of the autonomous region of the Azores, this was once a family home of the Correia family who commissioned an English architect to build it in 1846. With three wings, it is in a neo-Classical style with sculpture and statuary on the front elevation. Inside, in the main entrance and stairway, there are paintings by the Lisbon artist Ernesto Ferreira Condeixa commemorating the royal visit of King Don Carlos and Queen Dona Amélia in 1901. In the first-floor dining room an *azulejo* panel depicts the 1831 Liberal victory over the Absolutists at Ladeira da Velha, on the north coast east of Ribeira Grande. The 7.5ha garden is attributed to the work of two gardeners, the first from Scotland for the general design, and the second, later, from Belgium who notably introduced many camellia cultivars. For the visitor, much of the original 19th-century layout remains, there is a number of good trees, a substantial attempt at a garden of native Azorean plants, and an impressive long *allée* of box trees. For the sharp eyed, there are interesting shrubs to discover. To view the house an appointment must be obtained from the president's office.

Jardim José do Canto (*Open daily May–Oct 09.00–18.00; Nov–Apr 10.00–17.00; modest entry charge*) José do Canto was probably the most knowledgeable gardener of his time and from the mid 1800s began to build a plant collection of several thousand species, importing them from nurserymen in London, Paris, Belgium and Rio de Janeiro. Not only did he compile lists of the species he wanted to acquire, he even kept a long list of the plants he did not want to grow! His garden was originally intended to include a large modern house, but this was not pursued. Much of the design was supervised by English gardeners. The garden remains in private ownership, is next door to the Sant'Ana Palace, and is now the grounds of the Pensão Casa do Jardim. Without doubt the finest specimen trees of the three gardens are to be found here, in maturity a noble memorial to the man who worked so hard to introduce them.

Pineapples were introduced as a replacement crop for oranges around 1850 and became so successful that after ten years they were being exported to northern Europe including England where they featured in royal banquets. The Azores are not warm enough for their outdoor cultivation, and there were some 3,000 glasshouses producing yearly about 2,000 tonnes of fruit. With the high capital costs of new greenhouses, it is doubtful if this crop will continue when existing houses need to be replaced. The main area is in Fajã de Baixo on the edge of Ponta Delgada, also in Lagoa and Vila Franca do Campo. It takes two years to produce a ripe fruit with an average weight of 1.5–2kg. Earlier, heather, ferns and moss were taken from the mountains and made into a thick growing bed but nowadays, to protect the mountain vegetation, leafy branches of pittosporum and other shrubs are used. As these decay they give off heat, and in a closed or carefully ventilated glasshouse this is sufficient for the plants to thrive. Old stems are used for propagation, which take six months to produce young plants. These are planted out to grow on for another 12 months, when in old oil drums ivy and other vegetation is burned to create a dense smoke. This triggers the plants to flower all at the same time, and in six months they are ready for harvesting. Without 'smoking' flowering would occur intermittently and it would take much longer before the crop could be cleared and the cycle begun again.

Arruda Açores pineapple plantation (*Rua Dr Augusto Arruda, Fajã de Baixo, 9500 Ponta Delgada;* \ *296 384 438; open Jun–Sep 09.00–20.00; Oct–May 09.00–18.00*) Admission is free to see the greenhouses and includes tasting of pineapple liqueur and delicious pineapple boiled sweets. There are pineapple fruits for sale, loose and in presentation boxes, plus various handicrafts.

The western part of the island

Lagoa do Canário On the way to Sete Cidades from Ponta Delgada you will notice a forestry services sign to this lake on your right after you have passed a lovely old stone aqueduct. An unsurfaced narrow road lined with azaleas leads down to a car park, where there are picnic tables and barbecues. There are several things to see here. As you drove in you will have passed a small lake on your left down amongst the trees; not only is this a lovely spot, around the lake is a very healthy community of royal fern, *Osmunda regalis*. From the car park another wide road leads you further on between the cryptomeria forest; it is a 15-minute walk to one of the finest *miradouros* (viewpoints) in all the Azores, a truly stunning view of the Sete Cidades lakes and village. As you return to the car park, on your left is a small track leading down; this takes you to a deep, very narrow ravine filled with a gurgling stream, tree ferns, several endemic plants and many ornamental azaleas. It is cool and moist, and wonderful for ferns and mosses.

Sete Cidades Mythology provides a romantic history. In the kingdom of the Seven Cities, once long ago there was a king. He had a very pretty daughter who loved the countryside and happily roamed the fields, the little valleys and the surrounding hills. One day she came across a handsome shepherd boy tending his animals, and they shyly spoke. As the days went by she saw him again, and then again, and slowly romance blossomed and they fell deeply in love. Unfortunately, her father came to hear of this romance and was furious, because he intended his daughter to marry a neighbouring prince who was heir to a large kingdom. He forbade his daughter ever to see her shepherd boy again, but she pleaded so well

3

that he agreed they could meet for one last time. At the final parting, they both cried so much two lakes were formed, one blue from the princess's eyes, the other green from those of the shepherd boy, and although they were parted forever, their tears have remained united. Inevitably you will stop at the main viewpoint, the **Vista do Rei**, named from King Carlos's visit in 1901, where you can see both lakes of tears. The circumference of the caldera is roughly 12km.

The northwest coast along to Capelas Out beyond the airport the whole of this coastline is very pretty, and there are some especially lovely stretches of road running beneath tall, elegant plane trees with grass banks solid with blue agapanthus and topped with blue hydrangeas. At **Ponta da Ferraria** you can view the *fajã* from the road at the top of the cliff. In the rocky parts by the sea there are thermally heated natural pools. The old bath house is where a doctor would visit twice a week, descending by donkey along a little trail where now the road winds down. The level track leading from the sea was used by horse-drawn water carts to carry water to the bath house, used by patrons who could not afford to travel to Furnas. **Bretanha** is a pretty area originally settled by the French from Brittany; in the village is a restored windmill. Pass through **Remédios** and come to **Santa Bárbara**, where there is a very good restaurant, the **Cavalo Branco**, with regional food; take the first street right up a steep hill after the sign. They do a set regional meal which provides a taste of many good dishes, and is presented as a long sequence of small servings. In summer reservations are essential (✆ *296 298 365*). The **Miradouro Santo António** overlooks small fields, the village and the sea beyond. Finally you come to the large village of **Capelas**, which once was an important whaling centre with a factory for processing the animals. Don't forget the Museu M J Melo, see page 73. Just beyond the village is the **Solar do Conde**, which is an old manor house with a formal garden. Here there is another excellent restaurant with a really good ambience well worth travelling to (✆ *296 298 997*).

The eastern part of the island: Ribeira Grande, Nordeste, Povoação and Furnas
Ribeira Grande The fast-flowing stream that now runs along the side of the very nice-looking town square and past one of the prettiest town halls anywhere originally attracted early settlers to build their watermills here. In 1507 it received its town charter. In France during the second half of the 17th century Colbert, Louis XIV's Minister of Finance, gave considerable support to numerous industries to boost economic development, but the subsequent religious intolerance made many skilled workers emigrate. With the arrival of French workers, linen and wool weaving brought great prosperity to Ribeira Grande in the following 18th and early 19th centuries. Today it is expanding with light industrial development, but still manages to keep tucked away much of its old charm. Visit the main church of **Nossa Senhora da Estrela**, where there is a curious work of art made by a nun in the 19th century using gum arabic mixed with bread and egg white. It is called *Arcano* and it tells the story of the Old and New Testaments. Now rather faded, you have to ask the caretaker to let you see it as it is hidden away upstairs. Also see the sacristy and its paintings of the Flemish School. The misericórdia church, the **Church of Espírito Santo**, in the main square, has one of the best Baroque façades in the Azores; curiously it has two doors. The **Ethnographic Museum** (*Rua São Vicente de Ferreira; open Tue–Sat 08.30–12.30 and 13.30–16.30*) is located in one of the little backstreets nearby, and is excellent. As you leave the village you pass by in the road an enclosed fountain partly buried by lava from the eruption in 1563 that destroyed the village.

   Cerâmica Micaelense (*42 Rua do Rosário;* ✆ *296 472 600*) on the road out to Furnas, is a ceramic workshop making excellent tiles. Numerous original and ambitious designs are displayed in their showrooms and around the workshops, and they will make any design to your order: pictures of your garden, your house, figurative, abstract; no end of fun.

Caldeiras and Lombadas Valley A 5km drive inland from Ribeira Grande, this tiny spa village of large old houses surrounds a central square where there is a hot spring and a thermal pond. Now a little tired, it must have been delightfully romantic in its social heyday. The road continues to Lombadas and takes you into really wild country along a narrow cobbled road, slippery when wet. At the head of the valley is a small hut where a mineral water spring comes out. This was formerly the main source of bottled mineral water on the island, coming from a length of domestic garden hose whose further end disappeared somewhere under the heather on the adjacent hillside. I watched just three men washing, filling and capping the bottles; the whole enterprise was charming and the water delicious. From here you must either return towards Ribeira Grande and continue east along the north coast, or take the mountain road over the Cumeira Massif to the south coast.

Geothermal plants From the area around Ribeira Grande you will have seen steam rising in two or three places from the green hillsides heading up to the mountains. As you drive up to Lagoa do Fogo on the cross-island road to Lagoa, one of them is very close: the complex of silver-painted structures is part of the geothermal energy supply to the island.

Caldeira Velha This is a strange place hidden among trees down a side turning a few kilometres along the main road crossing the island from Ribeira Grande to Lagoa. There is a small warm-water waterfall which runs into a small artificial pool; there are plenty of iron deposits and sulphurous smells, and it is a popular place to bathe. There are picnic tables beneath the trees.

Lagoa do Fogo Also along the same road to Lagoa, is this well-named fire lake. It is a caldera with a lake at the bottom. The caldera walls are steep, but there is a narrow, very slippery path to the bottom; it is a protected area and several endemic plant species can be seen here. On a day when there are clouds and a strong wind blowing it is good fun to stand at the viewpoint on the edge of the crater and watch the clouds pour into the crater and then get sucked up out again.

Miradouro de Santa Iria This is one of the loveliest viewpoints along the north coast. In summer on a balmy night you can stand here for ages listening to the cry of Cory's shearwaters as they swoop around the cliff below you and, at the same time, become intoxicated by the perfume of the Himalayan ginger lilies. If you have just arrived via Lisbon and are transferring to your hotel in Furnas, always ask your driver to stop here; the pressures of the big city fall away and after just five minutes of these scents and sounds you already feel at peace and rejuvenated.

Porto Formoso You are advised not to do this at weekends in summer because so many people come here and parking is a nightmare. Rather than continue along the main road, take the smaller road leading off down to the coast. At the T-junction turn right to drive slowly through a typical village to find an excellent fish restaurant, the **Cantinho do Cais** (*29 Rua Padre Botelho do Couto;* ⟍ *296 442 631*) run by Jorge Silva. Returning up the hill to the other end of the village you will come to the Praia dos Moinhos where you will find fishing boats pulled up on a small sandy beach. An old watermill has been converted into a simple restaurant,

O Moinhos (✆ *296 442 110; open daily*), and recently extended by a glazed seating area, and often in winter with a log fire; in summer there are tables outside. Note that the bay is sunlit only in the morning, the hill behind casting it into shadow later in the day.

Gorreana tea estate (*Plantações de Chá Gorreana, Gorreana, 9635 Maia, São Miguel;* ✆ *296 442 349; www.azores.net/gorreana; the factory is open to visitors Mon–Fri 08.00–17.00; there is a small shop and fresh tea is served*) The first records of tea growing in the archipelago date from towards the end of the 18th century, although it is thought to have been known before then because of the Portuguese ships passing through on their return from Asia. It was the demise of the production of oranges and their export that stimulated the development of new crops, including tea. The Gorreana estate was founded in 1883 and is now one of the last of several estates that once thrived on São Miguel; 50ha remain, producing some 30 tonnes of tea. The first plants were introduced in 1874, grown from seeds brought directly from China. By 1883 these were producing their first crop and the drink proved so popular further varieties were brought from India. To manure the shrubs lupins which can fix nitrogen in the soil were grown around them. Tea plants have thrived so well in the Azores that an especially aromatic variety has developed. The leaves, or rather the young shoot tips, are harvested between April and September by a simple machine operated by three or four men that straddles the rows of bushes; previously they were hand-plucked by women and girls. The leaves are then processed in the usual way in what are now old but beautifully engineered machines, and finally sorted and packed by hand. The distinctive packets are exported to the other islands, continental Portugal, Germany and Azorean communities in North America. In Germany an association has been formed – the Friends of Azorean Tea.

Chá Porto Formoso (*open Mon–Sat 10.00–17.00*) A second small estate nearby, towards São Brás, which also has a visitor centre, shows an interesting video of tea production and has a charming tea room and lovely view.

The Gorreana walking trail Soon to open is a waymarked trail from the Gorreana factory through the old areas of tea production up to Lagoa de São Brás and back. It takes about three hours and involves some uphill walking. There will also be a shorter circuit, through the tea plantation.

Maia This is a small fishing village where the large pink building houses a theatre, meeting hall and other community facilities.

Fenais da Ajuda If you have time, drive down to the village and past the main church until you come to a much simpler, smaller, church which was the first one to be built in the village in the early 19th century. Behind is a cemetery at the far end of which is a splendid view along the coast to Maia and Ponta do Cintrão in the middle distance, and way beyond to the Ponta da Bretanha which is the far northwest tip of the island.

Miradouro do Salto Farinha Clearly signposted from the road, this is another good place for a view. After heavy rain the 40m waterfall flows briskly and becomes a twin fall. You can walk down the path to the valley bottom and to the sea.

Ribeira dos Caldeirões, just before Achada You cannot miss this charming valley as you drive along the main road, with its lovely tree ferns, watermill, and in February the heavenly scent of all the pittosporum trees in flower. In 1986 severe floods destroyed most of Nordeste's watermills. More than 100 once existed, now only seven remain. Three have been acquired by the municipality to help restore the natural park area of Ribeira dos Caldeirões and to preserve the area's heritage and connect with a past traditional way of life. One mill has been restored as a working museum, two remain to be done.

Santo António To see the local weaving, take the road going up, opposite the church.

Lombada Fajenda If it is lunchtime, then the **Casa de Pasto Cardoso** is a handy restaurant (↘ *296 486 138*).

Ribeira do Guilherme Just before you get to Nordeste, look out for the signpost on your left. There is a camping site below, and a picnic site. Also from above, you will see the semi-natural swimming pool by the side of the river where it joins the sea. To see watermills, follow the sign marked *Zone Balnear*. There is also a most charming garden laid out parallel with a stream feeding a watermill.

Nordeste Nordeste is so far from the rest of the island and further isolated by the then poor roads that, until the end of the 19th century, boat was the preferred means of travel. This has always been a charming, sleepy little place that few tourists ever reached, but now this princess has been kissed by progress and is slowly awakening, with a new restaurant and other small developments, and in 2002 a new small hotel. The town centre is dominated by the 18th-century church, and on one occasion I happened across a wedding, just after the service. Near the altar the bride and groom and all their guests were gathered drinking champagne and the choir above was singing merry songs, a very happy scene.

Located below the left side of the church is a small **museum** (*open Mon–Fri 09.30–12.30 and 13.30–16.30*) with old ceramics from Lagoa and Vila Franca, early clothes, weaving and other items pertaining to the area. There is a **tourist information office** nearby (*open 10.00–12.00 and 14.00–16.00, weekdays only*).

Where to eat Restaurante Tronqueira (↘ *296 488 292*) is a modern restaurant with large windows looking into the surrounding garden. A much superior venue for lunch is the **Estalagem dos Clérigos** (↘ *296 480 100*). The **Parque Florestal** offers an attractive picnic area beneath cryptomeria trees, adjacent to neat rows of tree seedlings and formal hedges.

Serra da Tronqueira Here you have a choice, either to continue along the main road which is very pretty indeed with lovely *miradouros* and views of the coast, or to turn off from Nordeste and experience the Serra da Tronqueira.

This road runs through the mountains from Nordeste to Povoação, about 20km. It is unsurfaced and can be badly affected by heavy rain at any time of the year. However, should it have been recently graded and in good condition it is a wonderful drive on a clear day. If the clouds are low you will not see anything so do not waste your time. You can deviate and take the side turning 8km to Pico Bartolomeu, at the summit of which is a radio mast. In spite of the height it is a relatively limited view, but it is wild country with a mix of plantation cryptomeria and native forest. To the south you look over Água Retorta. Continue towards Povoação, and you reach a *miradouro* where you have a close direct view of Pico da Vara, the highest point of São Miguel at 1,105m. Covering the hills and valleys is the largest remnant of native vegetation, now a protected area; it is from this *miradouro* that I watched the rare Azorean bullfinch (*priôlo*) flitting in and out of the dense foliage.

Viewpoints of the southeast coast There are several *miradouros* and picnic sites along this road, and they are constantly being improved and added to. The Nordeste municipality has always taken a great pride in these, and deservedly so.

Ponta do Arnel provides a dramatic view down upon the lighthouse. **Ponta da Madrugada** is one of my favourites; on a sunny day the contrast between the bright colours of the flowers, the rich green grass and the deep blue sea is wonderfully vivid. Twenty years ago when Azores tourism was really in its infancy and few tourists explored this road, we used to have a picnic lunch at this viewpoint. The head waiter would come with a colleague in a van from the Terra Nostra Hotel and set it all up on one of the tables. It would be a Lucullan affair, with several courses and linen napkins; and formally dressed waiters wearing white gloves would pour the wines. Alas, no more. The coast between Faial da Terra and Ponta do Arnel is a special protected area; it is an important nesting site for shearwater and common tern, and there are some endemic plants and invertebrates.

Povoação This was the first settlement on São Miguel, and now has a pretty little town square and old streets leading down to the harbour. The church of Nossa Senhora do Rosário, built in the 15th century but restored in the 19th century and again recently, is thought to have been the first building of worship on the island. Don't forget the Wheat Museum (see page 73).

Ribeira Quente The valley down which you approach the village is very green and on the way you will pass beneath two tunnels where there is a waterfall. There is a new, long seafront and if you drive to the end there is a good black-sand beach with all amenities. Maybe one of the locals will tell you where the thermal area is; here, at low tide, the sea is very warm. You will notice considerable redevelopment for tourism and of the old harbour. Offering excellent seafood are several restaurants; in summer with outside tables they are very popular. The village physically divides into two, by the harbour and then by the church and beach. As you go along the seafront from the harbour to the beach area you will pass the Nucleo Museologica da Pesca Artesanal, part of one of Ribeira Quente's two schools. Exhibits include a typical fishing boat, nets and equipment used for local small-scale fishing.

Furnas Along with the view of Sete Cidades, this village in its huge caldera is among the best-known images of the Azores, and especially of São Miguel. Two places appear in all the brochures: the hot springs with their bubbling water and burping mud, and the Terra Nostra garden. Popular as a spa in the 19th century, Furnas attracted patients from as far as England. The bath house from the earlier part of the 20th century has been restored and it is possible to take a week's course of treatment under the attending doctor's supervision. The largest, noisiest and perhaps most fearful of the many hot springs or fumaroles is named *Pêro Botelho*, a 16th-century nickname for the devil. Around the calderas area some 22 different mineral waters emerge from the ground, the best-tasting from fountains, the lesser ones out of simple plumber's pipes. At the edge of the village is a forest services' immaculately maintained tree nursery and trout farm; visitors welcome. A local large flat soft roll called *Bolos Levedos* is made in Furnas and it is delicious, especially in the Café Atlantico when filled with cheese and ham and toasted.

At the end of December 1839 Joseph and Henry Bullar spent a winter in the Azores and later published in London a detailed account of their travels. Here is their description of a thermal bath at Furnas, or the 'Baden Baden of St Michael' as they named it.

After looking at the calderas, we took our bath, and it was certainly never my good fortune before to bathe in an invigorating warm bath. It produced a feeling of strength instead of lassitude, and the skin seemed not alone to have been cleansed and rendered most agreeably smooth, but to have been actually renewed.

While bathing, our man cooked eggs for us in one of the small boiling springs, and we afterwards went to the iron-spring for a draught [of mineral water]. This flows from a stone spout into a hollow stone basin, and trickles down a bank into a stream below: it has a strong but not disagreeable iron flavour, effervesces slightly, and is extremely grateful and refreshing. The bath and the spring seemed the two things best suited to the outside and inside of man, on first rising from his bed: natural luxuries when in health, natural remedies when sick; – luxuries without after-pain, remedies without misery in taking them; – both which evils seem to be inseparable from the luxuries and the remedies of our own invention. Most invalids feel that before-breakfast existence is burdensome; but this bath and draught of liquid iron were as breakfast in producing serenity and happiness, and were more of a breakfast in giving warmth and briskness, and a feeling of health, as of the flowing of younger blood through the veins…

There are several large summer homes built by grandees in the 19th century, some with once lovely gardens. Terra Nostra garden, belonging to the Terra Nostra Garden Hotel, has a long history; it is open to non-residents for whom there is an entrance charge.

Furnas Lake This is São Miguel's second-largest lake at almost 2km². On the far side from the road, and signposted, are the calderas, where for generations people have come to cook the famous *Cozido nas Caldeiras*. Holes are made about 1m deep in the hot earth into which a container is lowered filled with different meats, sausage and some vegetables, mostly kale, cabbage and potatoes. It is all left to cook gently for around seven hours. Cooked slowly, and so evenly, all the flavours and delicious juices are retained, although those with timid appetites can find it a little daunting. Across the lake you can see a pseudo-Gothic chapel dedicated to Our Lady of Victories built by José do Canto, one of the Azores' great gardeners. It is a family vault and he and his wife are buried there. Nearby is a private garden largely devoted to camellias; sleeping for years, it has a melancholy charm. You may visit the garden with the owner's permission, but beware: the paths can be very slippery. In early spring the magnolias and camellias give the impression they are in their native wild forest.

Vila Franca do Campo Located on a fertile plain or 'campo' it was once a duty-free zone whose residents were exempt from paying taxes. It was also the island's first capital. There is good swimming and a large programme of tourist development is planned including an aquarium theme park, a marina near Vinha d'Areia, health centre and Clube Naval expansion. There is a harbour with small fishing boats and there are fish restaurants, and good local cakes called *Queijadas da Vila*. Among many buildings of historical architectural merit is the Matriz, the Church of São Miguel Arcanjo or St Michael the Archangel. Completed in 1537, it has an impressive façade built completely of basalt, with a carving of Christ on the cross. On the edge of the town by a pretty little public garden is the old church and convent of São Francisco, dating from 1525; it is now a hotel.

Just off the beach is the **Ilhéu da Vila**, the remains of an old volcano where the sea has breached the crater wall creating a protected swimming area. Extremely popular with local people, it is accessed by a regular boat service between June and September. The island is also a nature reserve, and there is a conflict of interest between conservation and recreation.

If you have time, it is well worth driving up to the **Chapel of Nossa Senhora da Paz**, which can be seen from Vila Franca high on the hillside behind the town. From here there is a splendid panorama of Vila Franca and its surrounding pineapple glasshouses, and of the green landscape spreading down to and along the coast.

Lagoa Lagoa has long been the centre of São Miguel's pottery industry, which began in the 19th century. Crockery, pots, bowls, vases and other items in traditional designs and colours are made here and visitors are welcome to tour the factory, showrooms and museum of Cerâmica Vieira, founded in 1862. The old town's harbour was once busy with exports of woad and wheat.

Caloura This is a pretty area with a tiny fishing harbour and a natural swimming pool at the end of the breakwater, surrounded by old vineyards each with its own stone wall. In the past few years substantial new homes have been built and it is now obviously a very desirable place to live; for the property curious, it is interesting to see how a severe, stony landscape can be transformed. There is also a charming little convent by the sea, dating from the 16th century, now privately owned.

WALKS

Right from the early years of walking holidays in the Azores there existed the walks around Sete Cidades, the walk up to Lagoa do Fogo and the circuit of Furnas Lake. Two favourites from that time were the cliffside walk from Gaiteira along to Ribeira Quente, what is now called the Lobeira/Praia da Amora trail, and from Furnas up over the rim of the caldera and down to Ribeira Quente, the Pico da Areia trail. Sadly these two were destroyed in the tragic flash flood and landslides that swept down upon part of the village of Ribeira Quente in 1997. Now repaired, they are part of the network of restored and new walks by the Povoação Municipality; under this initiative so far 11 trails have been formally designated for the Furnas and Povoação areas. These are well marked, are to be regularly maintained, supported by explanatory brochures with information on the state of the trails constantly updated and readily available from the tourist information offices in Furnas (by the hot springs in the village) and in Povoação (Rua do Infante Sagres, close to the old church and ocean front).

These are the designated trails developed so far for Povoação and Furnas:

Lobeira/Praia da Amora, distance: 7km, time: 2½ hours, difficulty: medium.
Ribeira do Faial da Terra, distance: 6.5km, time: 2 hours, difficulty: medium. Starts near the Água Retorta Forest Park, ends in Faial da Terra.
Sanguinho Trail, distance: 4.7km, time: 1½ hours, difficulty: medium. Starts and ends in Faial da Terra.
Agrião trail, distance: 4.9km, time: 1½ hours, difficulty: medium. Starts in the square of Lombo do Cavaleiro, ends Ribeira Quente.
Lagoa das Furnas, distance: 10.7km, time: 3½ hours, difficulty: easy. Starts and ends in Furnas.

Pico da Areia, distance: 8.5km, time: 2½ hours, difficulty: medium. Starts Furnas, ends in Ribeira Quente.
Redondo trail, distance: 3.2km, time: 1 hour, difficulty: easy. Starts from along the regional road between Furnas and Povoação, ends Ribeira Quente. Can be combined with the Agrião trail.
Pico da Vara, distance: 8.5km, time: 2½ hours, difficulty: difficult. Routes and feasibility depends on weather; please get the latest advice from the tourist office in Povoação.
Pico de Água Retorta, distance: 6.7km, time: 2 hours, difficulty: medium. Start or end in Faial da Terra. Can be combined with the Sanguinho and Ribeira do Faial da Terra trails.
Lombo Gordo, distance: 3.9km, time: 1 hour, difficulty: easy. Starts Água Retorta, ends Lombo Gordo.
Vigia da Baleia, distance: 8km, time: 2½ hours, difficulty: medium. Starts Faial da Terra, ends Povoação.

Some of the trails are short, which means they can be easily accessed by car and walked on an out and back basis, never boring because the views are always so enchanting or varied. Exploring São Miguel using these trails offers the opportunity to gain many insights into the rich history of the countryside that still influences life in the islands. Before the advent of roads these trails were the economic and social lifelines for the villages, for the fishermen of Ribeira Quente carrying basket loads of fish to Ponta Garça and Vila Franca, for the workers walking to their fields, to the vineyards, their fruit and orange orchards, and for religious pilgrimages. You pass through pastoral landscapes and woodland, following streams, seeing indigenous vegetation, all often enhanced by a backdrop of mountains or a view of the sea, even a sight of Santa Maria across the ocean.

High in the mountains, I have experienced more rain and cloud white-outs than on any other island, so always take waterproofs and be aware of the possibility of sudden loss of visibility. If you are staying low, then a good supply of drinking water is even more important, together with a sun hat.

Described in this guide are: the walk up to and round Furnas Lake which can be done more or less spontaneously – late afternoon is a good time to set out so as to enjoy the evening shadows and get up a good appetite for dinner; the whole day walk along the forest road between Povoação and Nordeste – not a recognised walking route; a walk at Sete Cidades; and the ascent to Lagoa do Fogo since these last two are not well maintained.

WALK I THE MYTHICAL LAKES OF SETE CIDADES (*Time: about 4½ hours; distance: about 13km*) There are numerous choices when it comes to exploring this area for there are several roads going down into the caldera and to the village of Sete Cidades, and there are various roads leading from the caldera rim down to villages along the coast. You will doubtless find various published descriptions of these. I think the walk described here is best, since, in one route, you have the most magnificent caldera views which constantly change as you progress along the rim, and the end of the day offers the contrast of approaching the sea with fine views of Mosteiros and the chance to see what living on a *fajã* is like. Even on a national holiday, at most you will meet a farmer or two attending their cows and maybe another walker.

Footpath conditions are easy, more or less level, with some steep pitches at both the start and finish.

If the weather is very windy it can be very unpleasant, and if there is low cloud, do wait for another day since you will miss all the wonderful views. Half the fun is identifying all the landmarks.

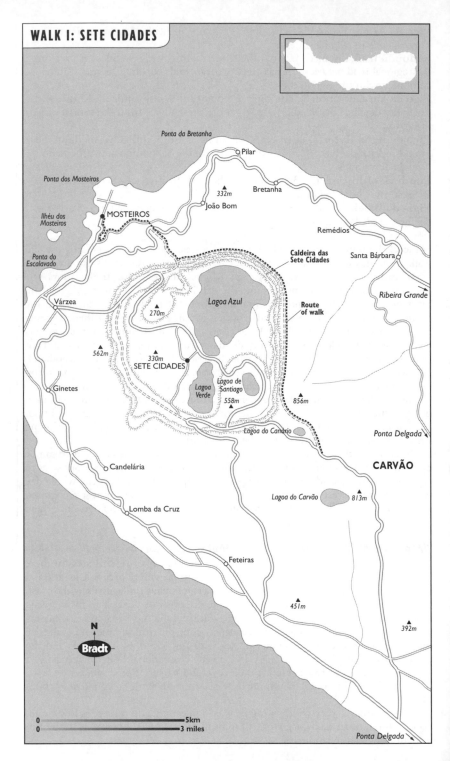

WALK 1: SETE CIDADES

Ponta da Bretanha

Pilar

Ponta dos Mosteiros

332m

Bretanha

João Bom

Ilhéu dos Mosteiros

MOSTEIROS

Remédios

Ponta do Escalavado

Caldeira das Sete Cidades

Santa Bárbara

Várzea

Lagoa Azul

Ribeira Grande

270m

Route of walk

562m

330m

SETE CIDADES

Lagoa Verde

Lagoa de Santiago

558m

856m

Ginetes

Lagoa do Canário

Ponta Delgada

Candelária

CARVÃO

Lagoa do Carvão

813m

Lomba da Cruz

Feteiras

N

Bradt

451m

392m

0 ———————5km
0 ———————3 miles

Ponta Delgada

Take a taxi to the area known as Carvão. Approaching from Ponta Delgada go past the Miradouro de Carvão, past the sign on your left to Lagoas dos Empadadas and then take the second asphalt-surfaced turning on your right. This soon curves round in front of an old and rather beautiful stone aqueduct and then into cryptomeria forest. Stop at the first unsurfaced farm track on your left – it is on a bend in the road.

You begin the walk here, slowly ascending through the forest and upon emerging come to a cement road making a very steep ascent up to the caldera, finishing by a building. You may be lucky and have an enthusiastic taxi driver prepared to risk damaging his car; mine had never been there before and insisted on driving all the way to the top where there is a level turning area. He ran to the caldera edge and was dumbstruck by the stupendous view; it is so much more dramatic than from the usual viewing place at Vista do Rei. On a clear day with no wind this has to be the finest view in all the Azores.

From here you simply follow the farm road going anticlockwise around the caldera rim; it soon forks and you bear round to the left. Continue ignoring all roads and tracks leading off from the main road around the caldera. In about two hours you reach a *miradouro* with some picnic tables and a road descending off on your right.

Continue on round the caldera and in about another 30 minutes you see the Ilhéu dos Mosteiros just off the coast, and near here you are above a tunnel that runs from the blue lake out of the caldera above Mosteiros. The track descends a little to come to a junction by a large smooth face of grey tuff with names carved into it. Two roads go down on your right, one either side of the bluff; take the second of these. The road you were following continues on round the caldera.

You now descend, at times between high walls of tuff and, lower down, reeds, to reach an asphalt road after 20 minutes. Cross this and continue down on the track and within two minutes come to a T-junction. Turn left, and the road forks either side of a fountain bearing the sign 'Rua Direita Pico de Mafra'. Take the left fork and follow this steeply down to the houses and continue on quickly to come to a *miradouro* giving a splendid view over Mosteiros, its white houses contrasting with the black lava and blue sea. To go down to Mosteiros take the small concrete road going steeply down on the right, about 50m below the Espírito Sancto chapel. From Mosteiros you may get a bus back to Ponta Delgada, or phone for a taxi.

WALK 2 ASCENT TO LAGOA DO FOGO OR FIRE LAKE, IN THE CENTRE OF SÃO MIGUEL
(*Time: about 5 hours; distance: about 14km*) This moderately difficult walk starts from Ribeira da Praia on the south coast; the route is uphill most of the way, the steepest part at the beginning up a farm track. The return is by the same way to either Ribeira da Praia, where you could leave your car, or to Água de Alto where there is a small bar from which to telephone for a taxi. The lake is at the bottom of a large crater. The walk begins almost down at sea level and climbs up through dramatic scenery to the lake, an ascent of some 600m. By the lakeside on a sunny day it makes a different place to picnic and, in summer, locals like to swim. If, however, upon reaching the lake you get pouring rain and dense mist, it is very atmospheric, but can be very cold.

Take a bus or taxi to **Ribeira da Praia**. If you have a car, then there are places nearby where you can park. The walk begins just before the bridge crossing the Ribeira da Praia and at the road sign saying 'Praia'. There is a farm track ascending steeply which should be signposted to Lagoa do Fogo. Take this, and shortly another track goes off on your left; ignore this and continue, passing a stone building on your right and then through a cutting in the rock, emerging into a field of vines. Shortly there are lovely views out to sea providing an excuse to stop and recover your breath. The track then divides and you take the left fork.

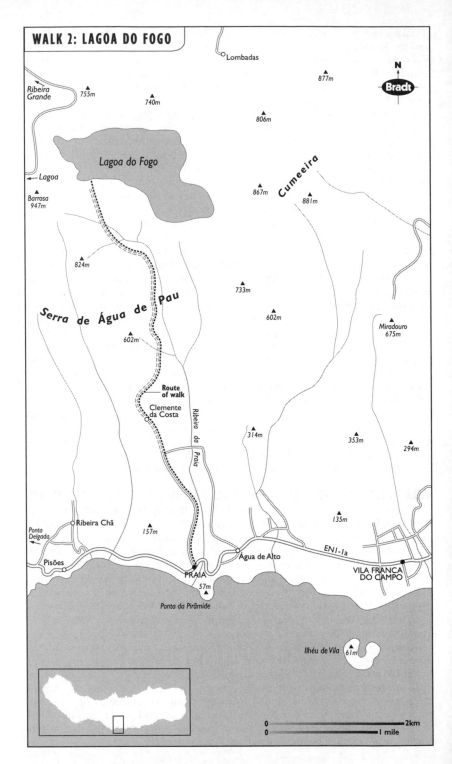

WALK 2: LAGOA DO FOGO

Lombadas

877m

N

Bradt

Ribeira
Grande

755m

740m

806m

Lagoa do Fogo

Cumeeira

Lagoa

867m

881m

Barrosa
947m

824m

Serra de Água de Pau

733m

602m

Miradouro
675m

602m

Route
of walk

Clemente
da Costa

Ribeira da Praia

314m

353m

294m

Ribeira Chã

157m

135m

Ponta
Delgada

Pisões

Água de Alto

ENI-1a

VILA FRANCA
DO CAMPO

PRAIA

57m

Ponta da Pirâmide

Ilhéu de Vila

61m

0   2km
0   1 mile

Continue always by the main track and ignore smaller side tracks until you reach a cattle trough. Turn right and, ignoring all the tracks coming in from the left, continue until you come to some ruined houses. Go past these and a little further on you will find the route is marked with cement arrow posts. You will come to the *levada*, or watercourse; follow the trail alongside this carefully – it is broken in places. At the end of the *levada* simply follow the track until you reach the lake, passing hills of black scoriae and dark vegetation.

Return the way you came; do not be tempted to take the wide 'road' as the owners object to walkers crossing their land. If, however, you do not have a car, you can walk down to Água de Alto where there is a bar from which you can phone for a taxi, or walk along the main road into Vila Franca; when you get to the end of the *levada* and have passed the ruined houses and begun to lose height, watch out for a wide road coming in from the left. Take this and you soon come to a stream crossing over the road. Cross by the stepping stones. The old electricity generating works were installed here in 1903. Follow the stone path on the other side and after a short ascent the track forks. Take the right fork and after another short climb the track levels out and follows the ridge down. The Ribeira da Praia is on your right, where you look down upon the waterfalls, the water tank and the length of the ribeira out to sea. If you look behind you to the hill above, there is a building with a small tower – it is another generating station. By a stone water trough the path joins another and you go on down the hill to come out on the main road into Água de Alto.

WALK(S) 3 AROUND LAGOA DAS FURNAS

The walks to Furnas Lake can easily be varied according to the time you have and how far you want to walk.

Option (a) (*Time: about 2 hours; distance: about 5km*) The easiest option is to take a taxi from Furnas to the chapel of Nossa Senhora das Vitórias at the far side of the lake, and then walk back along the lake edge at the side of the main road to Furnas, downhill all the way, reversing the descriptions below under option (b).

Options (b), (c) and (d) The following walks begin at the pretty petrol station with its *azulejos*, near the Teatro das Furnas, just a short distance from the Terra Nostra Garden Hotel. At the garage the main road bears round to the left and a cement road leads off very steeply up the hill. Take the cement road. Regrettably there has been an asphalt outbreak and what was a simple farm track is now surfaced, but there is virtually no traffic and the scenery remains as lovely as ever. Keep to the main route until it bears strongly round to the left with a good track on your right going steeply up into the shade of a belt of trees towards the top of the ridge. From here the road very quickly goes down the other side to the lake. You will smell sulphur and may notice steam coming from fissures in the banks. Now you have a choice of how long a walk you want to make; approximate times are given from the petrol station.

Option (b) (*Time: about 3½ hours; distance: about 11km*) To walk around the lake, turn right and pass the cooking area of the famous **Furnas Cozido**, and straight ahead come to a gateway. Simply continue along this track, first along a small stream, following more or less the edge of the lake. You will have noticed an old house by the water on the far side, and a chapel. These once belonged to the family of José do Canto, who created here yet another fine garden. There are many fine old camellias, some magnolias and a fern gully, but alien species have invaded and it is interesting to imagine how beautiful it must have been more than a century ago. Access only with the owner's permission. The road continues to join the main south coast road from Ponta Delgada, which has so far been left in its original

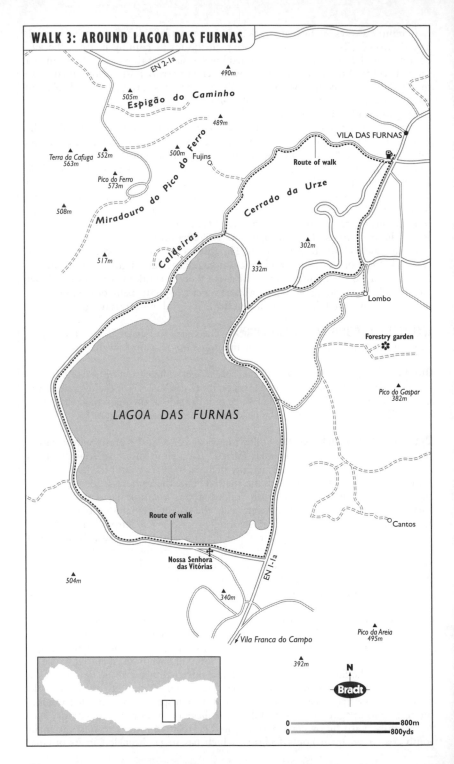

WALK 3: AROUND LAGOA DAS FURNAS

EN 2-1a

▲ 490m

▲ 505m
Espigão do Caminho

▲ 489m

VILA DAS FURNAS

Terra da Cafuga ▲ 552m
563m

▲ 500m
Fujins

Route of walk

Pico do Ferro
573m

Miradouro do Pico do Ferro

Cerrado da Urze

▲ 508m

▲ 302m

▲ 517m

Caldeiras

▲ 332m

Lombo

Forestry garden

Pico do Gaspar
382m

LAGOA DAS FURNAS

Cantos

Route of walk

Nossa Senhora
das Vitórias

EN 1-1a

▲ 504m

▲ 340m

Pico da Areia
495m

Vila Franca do Campo

▲ 392m

N

Bradt

0 ——————— 800m
0 ——————— 800yds

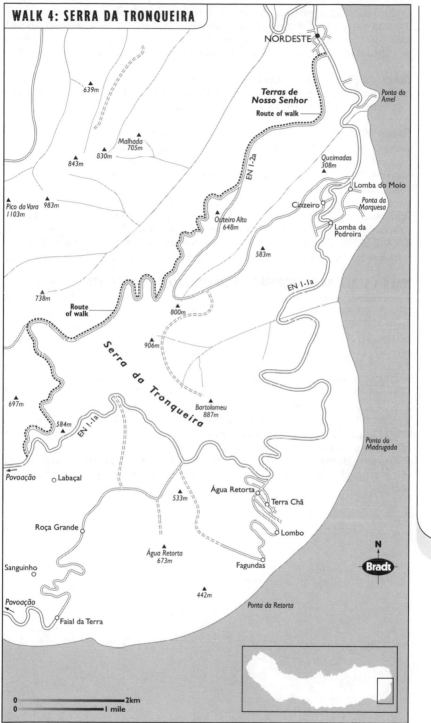

WALK 4: SERRA DA TRONQUEIRA

NORDESTE

639m

Terras de
Nosso Senhor

Route of walk

Ponta do
Amel

Malhada
705m

830m

843m

Qucimadas
308m

Lomba do Moio

Pico da Vara   983m
1103m

Outeiro Alto
648m

Cinzeiro

Ponta da
Marquesa

Lomba da
Pedroira

583m

EN 1-1a

738m

Route
of walk

800m

906m

S e r r a   d a   T r o n q u e i r a

Bartolomeu
887m

697m

Ponta da
Madrugada

584m   EN 1-1a

Povoação   Labaçal

533m

Água Retorta

Terra Chã

Roça Grande

Lombo

Sanguinho

Água Retorta
673m

Fagundas

Povoação

Faial da Terra

442m

Ponta da Retorta

N

Bradt

0 ————————2km
0 ———————— 1 mile

cobbled state. Turn left to complete your circuit of the lake, but some distance after the road has left the lake on its descent into Furnas you come to a low wall painted white on your right running alongside the road. Where it begins there is a wide asphalted track going steeply down. If you take this it is a short cut into the village.

Option (c) (*Time: about 2 hours starting from the Furnas garage; distance: about 5km*) For the fastest return to Furnas, leave the lake in a clockwise direction to join the main road into Furnas. Take the short cut described above.

Option (d) (*Time: about 4 hours starting from the Furnas garage*) As for option (b) but after you have left the chapel and are walking along the main road, you will see a road off to your right, cut through the scoriae hillside, and signposted to the Serviços Florestais. Follow the road round to the forestry garden, which is charming and has interesting plants. To return to Furnas, retrace your steps along the road, but this time take the road off on your right that goes steeply uphill. When you emerge from the cryptomeria trees at the top of the hill, the road turns steeply down to your left. Before following this, just walk ahead for a short distance to get a beautiful view of Furnas. The steep road down to Furnas takes about 15 minutes, but be very careful because it is very easy to slip on the loose stones.

WALK 4 SERRA DA TRONQUEIRA, FROM POVOAÇÃO TO NORDESTE (*Time: about 4½ hours; distance: about 12km*) This is in the far northeast, and is easy walking along an unsurfaced road steadily climbing, then steadily descending. The road surface often becomes badly damaged by heavy rains so even in the peak summer months of June to September there should not be too many cars using this road, and certainly in winter you will have it to yourself. It is the perfect winter walk because, even if the clouds descend after you have started out, you cannot miss your way.

The road passes through plantation and natural forest, and provides views of hills and deep valleys covered with native vegetation. The scents and sounds and also silence are wonderful, often enhanced when the clouds swirl around you. It is a protected area, and home of the rare bullfinch (*priôlo*). Although you can begin from Nordeste, it is better to start from Povoação because the walk starts 7km out of the town, and ends in Nordeste where it is easy to get transport. Get a taxi from Povoação to drop you where the unsurfaced road (the EN 1-2a) to Nordeste leaves the main road. There is an obvious international 'No entry' sign. Then just keep walking!

4

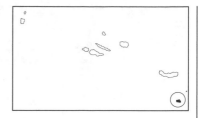

Santa Maria

Santa Maria sees itself as the sun island, claiming that, being a little further south than all the other islands, it receives more sun and sea temperatures are higher. Certainly it has been very sunny on every visit I have made, and photos of the long sandy beach at Praia Formosa complete the image. In the east are idyllic, picturesque, tranquil, verdant landscapes of forests and pastures. These may be sprinkled with glimmering white traditional houses that are either scattered, in little clusters or in small villages. In places there are no buildings at all, or perhaps just a time-weathered basalt shelter tucked away in a corner of a field.

HIGHLIGHTS

To hire a car and meander along almost empty winding roads through such glorious countryside, stopping for views and parking the car at the end of a farm road and just walking to the sound of birdsong, makes for a wonderful three or four days' holiday. High sea cliffs provide precipitous views and you can drop down to the coast at Maia and São Laurenço for glorious sea swimming in manmade pools with their own natural wave machine. In contrast, the western sector of the island is flat, calcareous, and an altogether different landscape. Between exploring these environments you have the white sandy beach at Praia Formosa, and the sea pools at Anjos in which to relax. Other interests include the little chapel at Anjos associated with Columbus's first landfall on his return from the Americas and the quite remarkable stone terraced vineyards at Maia, an extraordinary work of such great skill and energy you are left wondering at the effort humankind is prepared to make to produce wine! And the amazing red soils and almost desert landscape of Paul da Cerra.

GENERAL BACKGROUND

GEOGRAPHY The island first rose above the sea some five million years ago and then sank again, so allowing sedimentary deposits to form. Subsequent uplift a million years later means that Santa Maria is the only Azores island with sedimentary deposits and fossils. The potters on São Miguel import some of their clay from here, and from deposits at Santana and Figueral came the lime to whitewash all the archipelago's houses. Where the airport is located and sheep graze the surrounding land, the area is flat and relatively arid. This changes rapidly on the approach to the central peak of Pico Alto, the highest point at 590m. Here once more is the typical Azorean green landscape with cryptomeria trees and pittosporum mixed in places with native shrubs. Then comes the eastern half that is visually such a pastoral idyll. There are dramatic coastlines, proud headlands and sheltered bays, and another novelty for the Azores, white sand.

HISTORY Santa Maria is generally considered the first island of the archipelago to be discovered by the Portuguese, sometime between 1427 and 1432, and is so

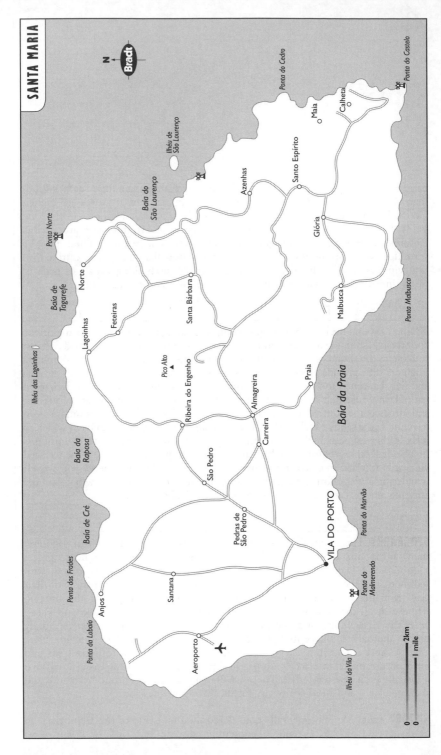

SANTA MARIA

Bradt N

Ponta do Cedro

Ilhéu de São Lourenço

Baía do São Lourenço

Ponta Norte

Baía de Tagarete

Ilhéu das Lagoinhas

Baía da Raposa

Baía de Crê

Ponta dos Frades

Ponta da Labaio

Norte

Lagoinhas

Feteiras

Santa Bárbara

Pico Alto

Ribeira do Engenho

São Pedro

Anjos

Santana

Pedras de São Pedro

Aeroporto

Ilhéu da Vila

VILA DO PORTO

Ponta do Malmerendo

Ponta do Marvão

Carreira

Almagreira

Praia

Baía da Praia

Glória

Malbusca

Ponta Malbusca

Santo Espírito

Maia

Calheta

Ponta do Castelo

Azenhas

0   2km
0   1 mile

named because it was sighted on the Feast of the Assumption of Our Lady. It was also subsequently the first island to be settled. The initial settlement was made in 1439 by people mainly from the Algarve and Alentejo, on the northwest coast at a place named Praia do Lobos, just west of what is now Anjos, by the Ribeira do Capitão. This river is now called Ribiera de Santana. However, between 1460 and 1474 Vila do Porto became the principal administration centre of the island. Exports were woad and urzela for dyeing. In the 16th century, land in the west was developed for wheat. Needless to say, during the 16th and 17th centuries French, Turkish and Moorish pirates attacked and destroyed the settlements many times. By the 19th century demand for Santa Maria's exports had dwindled and emigration increased. It was the American wartime air base built in 1944 that brought real change, and later it became an international airport for transatlantic flights; in 1977 it received its first visit from Concorde. Currently it is an air-traffic-control centre for the north Atlantic. The population has dropped considerably due to emigration: in the 1960s it was around 14,000 inhabitants; now it is down to some 6,000.

GETTING THERE AND AWAY

BY PLANE SATA Air Açores makes the 30-minute flight from Ponta Delgada every day, sometimes twice daily, and there are flights to Terceira. There is also a direct flight to Lisbon.

BY FERRY In summer expect a more or less twice-weekly sailing between São Miguel and Santa Maria, taking four hours. For details of the current ferry service please check the website (*www.transmacor.pt*). Tickets can be purchased from the office on the quay in Vila do Porto (*Gare Marítima Porto de Vila do Porto;* \ 296 883 150).

BY YACHT There are anchorages at Vila do Porto, where a large breakwater gives protection except from the southeast. Clube Naval has a clubhouse and bar by the harbour (\ 296 883 230; e cnsm@mail.telepac.pt).

GETTING AROUND

There is a very limited island bus service weekdays linking some of the villages, mainly for bringing people into Vila do Porto in the mornings and returning them late afternoon, which is of little help to the visitor. My experience is the drivers do not expect tourists as passengers so if you are alone at a bus stop they tend to drive past and not stop. Use a taxi, but this is an island best explored with a self-drive car.

TAXIS
Santo Espirito \ 296 884 027

Vila do Porto \ 296 882 767/199

CAR HIRE
Ilha Verde Airport; \ 296 886 528; www.ilhaverde.com

Rent-a-Car Ilha do Sol; Salvaterra, 9580 Vila do Porto; \ 296 882 021; e reservas@ilhadosol.com; www.ilhadosol.com

TRAVEL AGENTS
Micaelense Rua M, Vila de Porto; \ 296 882 040/284 636. Their office is next to the Hotel Praia

do Lobos (same building) and provides guided tours and car hire.

🏠 WHERE TO STAY

There are now three conventional hotels, one in town and two about 35–40 mins' walk outside Vila do Porto. If you have a car, then this is not a problem, otherwise I would recommend staying in town. There is also some rural accommodation, two with email addresses.

🏠 **Hotel Praia de Lobos***** (34 rooms) Rua M, 9580 Vila do Porto; ✆ 296 882 286. Good-sized rooms, very light and airy in a building sympathetic to local architecture; bar, convenient location. *Dbl* €52–65, *sgl* €37–47.

🏠 **Hotel Santa Maria***** (46 rooms, 2 suites) Rua Do Horta, 9580-421 Aeroporto de Santa Maria; ✆ 296 820 660; e commercial@ hotelsanta-maria.com; www.hotelsantamaria.com. Restaurant and bar. Built on the site of the old wartime officers' mess this hotel has the advantage of all being on ground-floor level, each room with access to a large garden and a short walk to the pool and tennis courts. The bedroom floors are tiled and this strikes cold and uninviting in winter, but could be an advantage in summer because this part of Santa Maria can be hot. *Dbl* €57–80, *sgl* €41–51.

🏠 **Hotel 5****** (64 rooms plus senior and executive suites) Cruz Teixera, 9580 Vila do Porto; ✆ 296 820 200; e santamaria@hotel-5.com; www.hotel-5.com. Restaurant, bar, coffee shop, pool, gym, Turkish bath, jacuzzi, massage and children's room with inflatables, PlayStation, ping-pong, etc. Also bicycle hire. The building is an awful intrusion into the landscape and the restaurant is a bit bleak, but it is a comfortable hotel. *Dbl* €60–95, *sgl* €47–73.

🏠 **Apartamentos Turísticos Mar e Sol** (10 apts) Praia Formosa, 9580 Vila do Porto; ✆ 296 884 499. Apts with balconies, laundry and cleaning services in an uninspiring rectangular block overlooking the beach.

🏠 **Casa São Pedro** (4 rooms) (TH) 9580 Vila do Porto; ✆ 296 884 044; e garajau@ virtualazores.com. This is a rebuilt family-owned manor house on the São Pedro road 3.5km from Vila do Porto. On the upper floor leading from an inner covered courtyard are en-suite rooms, 2 twins, 2 doubles. There is a guest lounge with TV. Outside there is a large lawn beneath trees for relaxation, and a swimming pool. Their excellent restaurant, Rosa Alta, is 100m distant. Casa São Pedro has its own horses for hire to experienced riders, and a fully equipped 9m boat for big-game fishing with an experienced captain.

🏠 **Casa do Norte** (1 room) (CC) Apt 566-9580 Vila do Porto; ✆ 296 886 338; e info@lauristur.com; www.lauristur.com/casa-do-norte.htm. A beautifully restored typical small house with an Algarve chimney.

CAMPING

⛺ **Praia Formosa** Near the sea; all facilities; restaurant nearby in village.

✖ WHERE TO EAT

VILA DO PORTO

✖ **Central Pub** Rua Dr Luís Bettencourt; ✆ 296 882 513. Does pizza and things Italian, as well as the usual fare.

✖ **Restaurante Atlântida** Rua Teóf Braga; ✆ 296 882 330. Good menu for both fish and meat. *Closed Thu.*

✖ **Clube Naval** Down by the harbour. Has a bar; open winter evenings.

CRUZ TEIXEIRA

✖ **Pub Candeia** ✆ 296 884 804. In the village of São Pedro, near the church of the same name; a nice simple restaurant.

SÃO PEDRO

✖ **Restaurante Rosa Alta** ✆ 296 884 990. 3.5km from Vila do Porto. Excellent, with a lighter, very different menu from anywhere else on Santa Maria plus a good selection of wines. Has a small comfortable bar for *aperitivos* and coffee.

PRAIA FORMOSA

✗ **Restaurante Praia** ℡ 296 884 965. Located in the village just before the seafront. Open 12.00–15.00 and 19.00–22.00, otherwise just snack-bar services.

✗ **Beach Parque** Snacks and bar. With a disco in summer.

SÃO LOURENÇO

✗ **Snack Bar O Ilhéu** ℡ 296 884 383. Open every day Apr–Oct until 04.00; in winter, weekends only.

NIGHTLIFE

Very little. There is the **Paquette Disco** on the front at Praia Formosa (*open 1 May–end of Oct 10.00–midnight*), and a very small one in the Fort de São Brás in Vila do Porto.

FESTIVALS

Festas de Santo António (Santo Espírito)	second week of June
Festas de São João (Vila do Porto)	last week of June
Festa do Sagrado Coração de Jesus (Santa Bárbara)	first week of August
Festa N Sra da Assunção (Vila do Porto)	middle of August
Festival Maré de Agosto (Praia Formosa)	third week of August
Festa das Vindimas – grape harvest (São Lourenço)	first week of September
Festa N Sra da Anunciação (Vila do Porto)	third week of September

USEFUL NUMBERS

Emergency ℡ 112
Police Vila do Porto; ℡ 296 883 000
Hospital ℡ 296 820 100
SATA Air Açores Rua Dr Luis Bettencourt, 9580-529 Vila do Porto; ℡ 296 886 501/2

Airport ℡ 296 886 504
Airport information ℡ 296 820 020/886 335
Tourist information ℡ 296 886 355 (information office at the airport)

WHAT TO SEE AND DO

MUSEUMS The island's **Ethnographic Museum** is well worth seeing, and can be combined with a visit to the craft co-operative for some of their delicious handmade biscuits since both are in the village of Santo Espírito.

WALKING Good walks are waiting to be discovered on Santa Maria. One or two have been identified and promoted, with the route waymarked. However, these trails are not rigorously maintained, the signs are lost, and they quickly become overgrown. Since they often pass through a network of small roads, it is easy to quickly become confused in unfamiliar territory which just leads to frustration, or worse.

The most talked-about walk is from **Pico Alto to São Pedro**. There are printed brochures and it should be waymarked. When I checked it out in November 2005 the beginning, near the mountain's summit, was signposted but the trail was completely buried by the dreaded Kahili ginger. Later, at an important junction, we found the critical paintmark on what had become the undersurface of a large rock, itself at the bottom of a pile of rocks, the remains of what was once the end of a stone wall. Hopefully, the route might just be repaired, so check it out first with the tourist office and the taxi drivers. Someone may know! Azoreans visiting from São Miguel told me they enjoyed the walk, but got lost and had to ring friends on their mobile for guidance.

A relatively unknown walk from **Vila do Porto to the beach of Praia Formosa** is not waymarked, but is fairly straightforward, follows well-used tracks and offers terrific views from cliffs high above the sea. Parts are so lovely visitors have been known to dally all day along its route. See page 105.

BIRDS AND FLOWERS Being the least visited by ornithologists the island has few records, but it is home to a subspecies of goldcrest that is endemic to Santa Maria. One of the most interesting sites is the small islet of **Ilhéu de Vila** just off Vila do Porto, which can be viewed from the shore or better still a small boat. There are petrels and shearwaters, roseate and common terns and it is thought from earlier records to be the only breeding site in Europe for the sooty tern. Other islets good for birds and observable from land include **Lagoinhas** near Tagerete Bay, part of the North Coast Protected Landscape Area.

Ponta do Costelo on the southeastern corner and its designated area of 300ha combines a coastal strip of steep cliffs some 200m high with an immediate offshore marine area. Particularly known for shearwaters and Madeiran storm petrel, it is also a passage point for bottlenose dolphin and loggerhead turtle. The cliffs and stony beaches support a number of endemic plants including herbaceous spurge, spurrey, lotus, tolpis and azorina. The *miradouro* makes an excellent place from which to look for whales.

SWIMMING

Praia do Formosa With its white-sand beach it is very popular in summer. There is an area marked off for surfboards. Changing facilities with showers; snack bars and ice creams.

Anjos There are two pools, sunbathing areas, changing rooms and showers, and a snack bar (*open 10.00–22.00 in summer – from Apr/May–Oct/Nov according to the season's weather*).

Maia Facilities include sea swimming pool with changing rooms and showers, and two bars; Bar Prazeres da Maia has a restaurant and is open during the summer while the Flor da Maria at the farthest end of the bay is open all year.

São Lourenço In addition to a sea swimming pool with changing rooms and showers, and a snack bar, there are also small white beaches between the rocks.

ITINERARIES As you travel around the island note the different house chimneys, especially the squarish ones topped with tall slender round chimney pots. Some of the parishes have their houses painted in the same colour: Santo Espírito, green; Santa Bárbara, blue; Almagreira, red; São Pedro, yellow; and Vila do Porto, tile coloured.

Vila do Porto Known originally simply as Porto, it became Vila do Porto in the 16th century when it was given its charter, the first town in the Azores to have this status. What is left of the old town runs uphill from the fort overlooking the harbour, now a modern port. The façades of the old grand houses give an idea of what it must have been like, together with the tiny cottages in the streets behind. All these are protected but sadly many owners of the large houses left for Lisbon in the 1950s and records have been lost, so by default their houses have become ruins. The government is now being urged to regain the initiative, and graffiti on the walls says *restaur* (restore). As you walk down from town (along the Rua Teófilo Braga) look out on your left for the façade of the 15th-century building that supposedly belonged to the Governor João Soares de Sousa. It may be recognised by its Gothic windows. Nearby houses have interestingly carved lintels and other details. The Fort of São Brás was built in the 17th century and of course provides a good view out to sea; with the cannon in position it is a fertile place to imagine early events. If you are staying at the Hotel Praia do Lobos then a stroll down to the fort after dinner is a pleasant ending to the day. In summer the cooling evening contrasts with the still-warm stones and makes a different but parallel smell to rain on sun-scorched earth. If you have time, take the old cobbled road down to the port and continue right round to the end of the mole (breakwater); there is a splendid view of the fort.

The modern part of the town, which starts roughly around the beginning of the Rua Teófilo Braga, is a linear development which looks as if it will go on growing longer. All the usual small shops are here including several small-scale supermarkets, and a market, just by the Hotel Praia do Lobos. The square in front of the town hall might give it some future focus. If the Camara Municipal is open, do step inside for a peep as it is a grand building. It was the first Franciscan monastery to be founded in the islands by the monks who came with the settlers; it successively grew wealthy, was looted, then rebuilt, then finally converted into a town hall. This is a history repeated throughout the islands, the converted uses also being hospitals and charities.

At the opposite end of the town there is a forestry park with a children's play area, picnic tables and washrooms beneath pine trees. There is also a small sterile aviary and some alert-looking deer. A belvedere offers a view of Vila do Porto and the immediate countryside.

The airport No, not quite, but the area surrounding it! This is limestone country and was once the most productive wheat area. Now the modern civilian airport takes a large percentage of the land while beyond the boundary remains of the wartime airfield linger in the form of old Nissen huts and concrete slabs. There is also the big radio station, and much new housing greatly in need of tree planting to soften it. The old officers' mess was the only hotel on Santa Maria until recently; it burned down a few years ago. Now the farmland is down to cattle, that are thought by the locals to be better eating than those on the higher pastures, and Romney Marsh sheep, farmed for wool, and originally imported from England. If you leave the airport road and take the minor road to Santana you pass through this utterly different countryside; in the height of summer when all is brown and the sun blazes down it can seem quite hostile, but in October/November to May it is green. From Santana the road continues and joins the main road down to Anjos, but before it does you pass through an area of acacia forest which shows a splendid example of wind pruning.

São Pedro This small village near Vila do Porto is noted for its *mata-mouras*, literally 'moor killers'. These are pits in the ground once used to hide grain and other desirables from pillaging pirates.

Anjos Once a tiny fishing village, Anjos then became a centre for tuna; now the factory is closed. The little bay has recently been very nicely developed for swimming. The island of São Miguel, 52 nautical miles away, can be seen on the horizon. On the roadside above is a picnic site with barbecue facilities.

The village is historically very significant as the first landfall of Christopher Columbus on his return from the Americas. A modern statue commemorates the quincentenary (1493–1993). The chapel of Nossa Senhora dos Anjos is possibly the first place of worship built in the Azores, being 15th century and rebuilt in the

17th century and again restored at the end of the 20th century. The small chapel has a triptych (recently restored) representing the Holy Family, St Cosmo and St Damien which, according to tradition, is from Gançalo Velho's caravel. On the outside wall is built a porch dedicated to the Holy Ghost; bread is distributed from here on the feast day.

Santa Bárbara This is among the prettiest parishes of the island; in July/August the roadsides are flaming with orange-red montbretias and yellow gingers and there are photo opportunities every 200m. There is wonderful silence apart from the occasional crowing of a cockerel.

São Lourenço Bay On the northeast coast, the bay is well worth visiting for the spectacular descent by road down the cliff face. On the way down, stop at the Miradouro do Espigão for a splendid bird's-eye view of the bay and its cliffside vineyards. There are swimming facilities.

Santo Espírito A pretty village surrounded by pastures and green hills. The **Church of Nossa Senhora da Purificação** is well worth visiting and must rate among the best kept of all parish churches. Go inside and be welcomed by the scent of wax-polished floors and pews with a gilt chapel reflecting sunshine from the windows. Originally constructed in the 16th century and beautifully restored in 1966, it is 17th-century Baroque with stone ornamentation on the front façade. It is also noted to be the church linked to the first Holy Ghost festivals in the Azores. The **museum** (*open Tue–Fri 10.00–12.00 and 14.00–17.00, and 1 May–30 Sep at weekends 14.00–17.30*) is located behind the church. Exhibits include early Santa Maria pottery, period household items and costumes. For handicrafts, the local *Cooperativa da Artesanto de Santa Maria* sells delicious bread and *biscoitos* from its own bakery, and from several looms traditional woven items. Find it about 400m into the village from the church, past the games area and almost opposite the school. There is a snack bar in the village.

Maia Many of the houses are now holiday homes, but there are still fishing boats on the quay of the tiny harbour. It is the stone terracing for grapevines that is truly amazing. Walls enclose areas just a few metres square and these reach up the cliffside almost until it becomes vertical. At intervals there are very narrow stairways between the vine enclosures running in straight lines up the cliff face to provide access. A book of photographs of the stones of Maia is for sale at the Santo Espírito Museum. The wine, purely for local consumption, is *vinho de cheiro*, plus a very pleasant sweet *aperitivo*. There are swimming facilities plus a restaurant and a bar.

Pico Alto The side road up to the highest point of the island, at 590m, leaves the main road between Almagreira and Santo Espírito where it forks to Santa Bárbara. Here the landscape is utterly different from anywhere else on Santa Maria, as you ascend through dense cryptomeria plantations to arrive at a tiny summit with fine views and where some native plants can be found.

Praia Formosa In a wide bay at the foot of steep cliffs is a very clean, pale sandy beach with rock pools at the eastern end, and it is the best-known swimming beach. Commercial development is really quite limited compared with a similar situation elsewhere in the world, and the road, with parking, runs along behind the beach. Vineyards tumble down the hillside to meet it. There is a small apartment hotel and campsites. In the close-by village there is a restaurant. At the western end are the remains of the 16th–17th-century Fort São João Baptista, which the sea has almost demolished. In summer the cliffs here, normally dark with pittosporum and myrica trees, are marked with 4m-tall yellow flower spikes of agave.

WALKS

Santa Maria offers lovely short walks, best accessed by car. As you drive, you will see farm roads heading off between pastures; some lead to small settlements, others to fine views. See also my note on page 101.

VILA DO PORTO TO THE BEACH OF PRAIA FORMOSA *(Time: 2'/2–5 hours; distance: 11km)* This can be done in 2'/2 hours, but much nicer if you allow four to five hours and maybe stop and watch for whales on the way. Walk always with the sea to your right.

Starting in the Fort de São Brás, face the little church and round to the left you will see some buildings between the church and a second small church. These were until December 2005 an abattoir; the double parallel metal railings was where the cows and pigs entered. There are two gates in these railings; go through these and follow the trodden path down. Turn right at the bottom of the slope, then first left by a house. This wide path takes you across the Ribeira Grande and diagonally up the opposite side. On the shore you will see some old machinery and ramps, the Calhão de Ropa; this was where the caterpillar machines were brought ashore for the construction of the wartime airport. Inland, higher up the ribeira, are the remains of old watermills. Continue on the track that goes round in front of the wind turbines. As you pass the turbines, you see a volcanic hill ahead, the Facho de Vila, that is being slowly demolished for rocks and gravel for building materials.

As the main track bears left, take the smaller track off to your right to walk on the seaward side of the mountain. If you miss the path it does not matter because the main track simply goes round the hill on the landward side. Follow this grassy road between two stone walls and soon you will see Praia Formosa with its sandy beach and above, just before the bay, the Miradouro of Marcela. It is made in black stone and is a little difficult to see against the hillside. This is your next objective. The track joins a main dirt road with some concrete farm buildings; you continue right. Look out on your left in the field for an old stone construction; this is an old *barro*, or kiln, used for firing roof tiles and other ceramics. The road takes you to a swooping valley with brilliant white houses, the village of Fonte do Mourato. When you come to a small track off to the right, take this to come to the main asphalt road just above the *miradouro*. Go down asphalt road a short way to another asphalt road going off to the right which takes you straight down to the sea and past the ruins of an old fort fast losing a final battle against the sea, and so along to the seaside amenities.

Part Three

CENTRAL GROUP

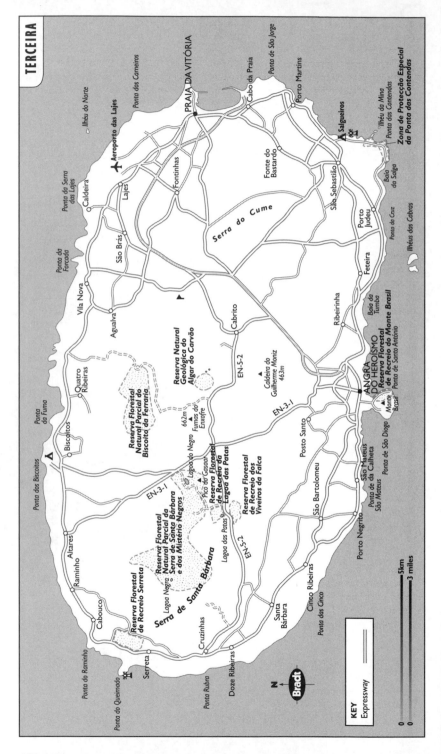

Ilhéu do Norte

Ponta da Serra das Lajes

PRAIA DA VITÓRIA

Ponta dos Carneiros

✈ Aeroporto das Lajes

Ponta de São Jorge

Caldeira

Lajes

Cabo da Praia

Porto Martins

Ponta da Forcada

São Brás

Fontinhas

Fonte do Bastardo

Ilhéu da Mina

Ilhéu dos Contendas

Salgueiros

Ponta dos Contendas

Zona de Protecção Especial da Ponta das Contendas

Vila Nova

Serra do Cume

São Sebastião

Baía da Salga

Ponta da Fuma

Agualva

Quatro Ribeiras

Reserva Florestal Natural Parcial do Biscoito da Ferraria

Reserva Natural Geológica do Algar do Carvão

Cabrito

EN-5-2

Caldeira do Guilherme Moniz 463m

Porto Judeu

Feteira

Ponta da Cruz

Ilhéus das Cabras

Biscoitos

662m

Fumas do Enxofre

EN-3-1

Ribeirinha

Baía da Tumba

Ponta dos Biscoitos

Lagoa do Negro

Pico do Gaspar

Reserva Florestal de Recreio da Lagoã das Patas

Reserva Florestal de Recreio dos Viveiros da Falca

Posto Santo

ANGRA DO HEROÍSMO

Reserva Florestal de Recreio do Monte Brasil

Monte Brasil

Ponta de Santo António

Altares

Raminho

EN-3-1

Reserva Florestal Natural Parcial da Serra de Santa Bárbara e dos Mistério Negros

Lagoa das Patas

São Bartolomeu

São Mateus

Ponta de São Diego

Cabouco

Serra de Santa Bárbara

EN-5-2

Porto Negrito

Ponta da Calheta

São Mateus

Ponta de São Mateus

Lagoa Negra

Ponta do Raminho

Reserva Florestal de Recreio Serreta

Cinco Ribeiras

Serreta

Cruzinhas

Santa Bárbara

Ponta das Cinco

Ponta do Queimado

Ponta Rubra

Doze Ribeiras

N
Bradt

KEY
Expressway

0 ___ 5km
0 ___ 3 miles

5

Terceira

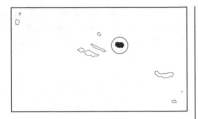

Terceira is best known for two things: the international airport and American airbase at Lajes and the historic UNESCO World Heritage Site of Angra do Heroísmo. This is unfair because, like all the other islands, there is much else waiting to be discovered for those not in a hurry. There are lovely villages, really wild country in the centre, volcanic caverns, comfortable places to stay and a golf course. It is an ideal island on which to hire a car and explore at your own speed.

HIGHLIGHTS

It is easy to spend a whole day seeing the historic buildings of Angra do Heroísmo together with the fort opposite and the whole of Monte Brasil. The drive around the west coast looking in at villages and charming museums is another joy and, if you choose to linger, a day is easily spent. The wild centre is a must, too, and a car gives access to some interesting areas and a chance to see something of the indigenous vegetation. Praia da Vitória is another town to explore, smaller and very different but no less charming, and if there is time seek out the view from the top of the Serra do Cume across the whole of the eastern part of the island. Between May and September some 220 Azorean bullfights will take place on the island so there is a fair chance you will experience one – remember, the bull is not killed or even wounded; it is the young men who run the risk of damage.

GENERAL BACKGROUND

GEOGRAPHY Terceira's origins go back one million years, but the oldest surface rocks are no older than 300,000 years. Like São Miguel, Terceira is made from four volcanoes. The youngest is Santa Bárbara, 1,021m, in the west; almost every day the summit is hidden in cloud. Its upper 300m is covered with typical scrub vegetation of juniper, erica, ling and bramble. On the northwest side of Santa Bárbara is the Serreta Forest, a mix of planted cryptomeria and eucalyptus and large patches of remnant native vegetation with many Azorean native species. It is a good area for birds.

Terceira's oldest volcano is in the east, around Serra da Cume. It is an area now covered with pastures, and most of the rim of the Cinco Picos caldera has long gone; there remain only the ridges of Cume da Praia (550m) and Ribeirinha (410m).

More or less at the island's centre is the region known as Terra Brava, the Wild Land, and aptly named because of the bewilderingly broken country and dense vegetation in places. The highest point is Pico do Juncal (706m). This tumultuous landscape was created by the violent action of the Guilherme Moniz and Agualva volcanoes. First, the eruption that created the Guilherme caldera destroyed most of the Cinco Picos caldera. Later, but relatively recently, the Agualva volcano erupted and crushed the northern rim of the Guilherme caldera. Lava flowed down through the caldera and spread three ways to the coast: in the south to what are now São Mateus and Feteira, and in the northeast to Caparica at the end of the Lajes airstrip.

HISTORY Originally known as the Island of Jesus Christ, the island was later named Terceira or Third Island since it was the third island to be 'discovered'; it is also the third in size. The first settlers in about 1460 were led by a Fleming, Jácome de Bruges, with the first settlements around Porto Judeu and Praia da Vitória. Like the other islands, farming became of paramount importance with cereals and woad the prime crops. For centuries it was the most important island because of its sheltered harbour, protected by Monte Brasil. In 1534 Angra was the first settlement in all the Azores to be formally designated a town and the same year Pope Paul III made it the seat of the bishopric. Terceira was a stronghold of resistance to the Spanish authorities when they annexed Portugal in 1580, holding out for the Portuguese claimant, Dom Antonio, who was being helped by the French. It was the last Portuguese territory to submit to Spanish rule, when the Spaniards defeated the French fleet at Terceira in 1582, overrunning the island the following year and inflicting a terrible retribution. As a consequence of the later 16th- and 17th-century Spanish exploitation of the New World, the island's harbour became even more important. Ships bringing back gold and silver at this time assembled off Terceira to form a convoy for escort to Cadiz, to reduce the danger of attack by pirates from the north African coast. Later in the 17th century this practice ceased and the island's economy plummeted, followed by emigration to Brazil. After Portuguese liberation in 1640 the islands became a staging post for British trading ships, until the opening of the Suez Canal in 1863. Oranges also came to the rescue and their export led to renewed prosperity, but as in the other islands their demise led once more to further emigration.

Along with São Miguel, Terceira played an important role in the struggle of the Liberals and Absolutists; at one time Terceira was the only Liberal stronghold in all of Portugal. In 1829 the Absolutists attempted to land at what was then called Vila da Praia and their defeat was marked by the new name of Praia da Vitória. In 1832 it was from Terceira and São Miguel that the Liberal forces from the Azores left for northern Portugal in their fight against the Absolutists. In 1766 the government of the Azores had been unified and based in Angra, remaining the capital of all the Azores until 1833 when the islands were divided into three districts. For a short time that year it was also the capital of Portugal when King Pedro IV was in residence – commemorated by the change of name to Angra do Heroísmo.

Lajes airport was constructed in 1943, as a transit point for airborne troops flying to Europe, and today contributes to NATO's strategic role. It has three runways, the largest 3,600m long, and is used by both civil and military aircraft.

On New Year's Day 1980 a severe earthquake inflicted substantial damage, affecting also Graciosa and São Jorge. Many of the important buildings in Angra do Heroísma were badly damaged and have taken years to painstakingly restore. In 1983 Angra was declared a UNESCO Historic World Heritage Site.

GETTING THERE AND AWAY

BY PLANE From Lisbon TAP Air Portugal flies direct seven times a week.

Terceira is the hub airport for the archipelago, and SATA Air Açores fly from here to almost all the islands on most days, and several times to São Miguel and Faial, even in winter.

BY FERRY There have been – during May to September – six-hour direct sailings about twice a week between Terceira and São Miguel, and connection to Santa Maria. There are also more or less weekly sailings direct to Graciosa (three hours 15 minutes), and onward sailings to Santa Maria. For details of the current ferry service please check the website (*www.transmacor.pt*). There are three ticket offices on Terceira. Two are situated in Angra do Heroísmo (*Rua do Galo 58;* ⟍ *295 217 380;* f *295 217 380;* e *terceira@transmacor.pt and also: Porto das Pipas;* ⟍ *295 215 022*) and one on the quay in Praia da Vitória (*Porto Comercial da Praia da Vitória;* ⟍ *295 543 590*).

BY YACHT Two new marinas have recently opened, one in Praia da Vitória with 175 berths and the other in Angra with 260 berths. This second is rightly controversial and you cannot but have considerable sympathy with the view that it is an unnecessary and quite ghastly modern intrusion into an important historical setting. For further information contact Clube Naval de Praia da Vitória (⟍ *295 512 993*).

GETTING AROUND

If you are without a car, and especially if you are making a short stay, then the best place to stay is Angra, because in addition to that city, you can visit Praia da Vitória which makes a pleasant excursion wrapped around a good lunch. There is a regular on-the-hour bus service between 07.00 and 19.00 from the main square in Angra to Praia da Vitória which takes less than an hour and is a pretty drive around the southeast corner of the island. The bus stops opposite the fire station. Walk back in the direction from which the bus came and you soon come to a big junction; turn left and you are in town along the Rua de Jesus. The return bus is from the same stop, leaving again on the hour, between 06.00 and 19.00. There are also less regular buses to Biscoitos and Porto Judeu. It is, however, an island much better enjoyed if you have your own transport, and options are detailed under *What to see and do* (see page 114).

CAR HIRE
Ilha 3 Rua das Minhas Terras, Angra do Heroísmo; ⟍ 295 213 114; e ilha3@mail.telepac.pt; www.ilha3.cidadevirtual.pt

Ilha Verde Praça Velha, Angra do Heroísmo; ⟍ 295 215 823; www.ilhaverde.com

BICYCLES AND MOTORCYCLES
Cruserve Rent-a-Car Rua da Igreja de São Bartolomeu 45, 9700-570 São Mateus da Calheta; ⟍ 295 206 360; e cruserve@cruserve.com; www.cruserve.com

TRAVEL AGENTS See under *Local travel agents* in *Chapter 2*, page 36.

WHERE TO STAY

The main hotels are in Angra, and in Praia da Vitória which is just five minutes' drive from the airport. In Angra there is a city hotel conveniently on the main square, a small one by the harbour, two neighbouring resort hotels about 30 mins' walk along a busy main road west of town and a brand-new Pousada in an old fort to the east with an easier and shorter walk into town. Then there are numerous *pensão* and some manor houses within driving distance.

HOTELS
Angra do Heroismo
⌂ **Angra Jardim Hotel*** (120 rooms) Praça da Restauração, 9700-201 Angra do Heroísmo; ⟍ 295 206 600; e angrahotel@mail.telepac.pt; www.angrahotel.com. Restaurant, bar, lounge, health

club, sauna, Turkish bath, jacuzzi, indoor pool, conference room and private parking. On the town's main square it is perfectly sited for the exploration of Angra. Rooms to the rear are quiet, overlooking one of the best public gardens in the Azores. *Dbl* € 85–110, sgl € 56–94.

🏠 **Hotel Beira Mar***** (23 rooms) Largo Miguel Corte Real, 9700-191 Angra do Heroísmo; ✆ 295 215 188; e reservas @ hotelbeiramar.com; www.hotelbeiramar.com. Excellent restaurant. Located by the harbour, which could be noisy in summer. *Dbl* € 70–80, sgl € 43–63.

🏠 **Pousada São Sebastião** (30 rooms) Formerly the Castelo de São Sebastião, overlooking the bay of Angra; e guest@pousadas.pt; www.pousadas.pt. Pool, restaurant. *Dbl* € 83–185, sgl € 70–146.

🏠 **Hotel Terceira Mar** **** (139 rooms) Portões de São Pedro, São Pedro, 9700-097 Angra do Heroísma; ✆ 295 402 280; e terceiramarhotel@bensaude.pt; www.bensaude.pt. By the sea in a bay, 30 mins' walk on pavements along a busy main road to the centre of Angra. Rooms with sea-view balconies, restaurant, bar, gymnasium, and splendid outdoor pool next to the sea, tennis courts, jacuzzi, Turkish

bath, sauna, massage, hairdressers. *Dbl* € 99–128, sgl € 79–101.

🏠 **Hotel do Caracol****** (100 rooms) Estrada Regional, Silveira, 9700-901 Angra do Heroísmo; ✆ 295 402 600; e hotel@hoteldocaracol.com; www.hoteldocaracol.com. At the western end of Angra, about 30 mins' walk from the centre along a main road. It has a fine view across the small bay to Monte Brasil and out to sea. Design of hotel ties in with the setting and it has a different feel from the average conventional hotel. Rooms include 17 suites and 2 for disabled guests, restaurant and bars, health centres and spa, massage, therapy treatments, anti-stress programmes, sauna, jacuzzi, 2 gymnasia, squash, adults and children's outdoor pools, indoor heated pool, conference room. Diving centre and fishing trips arranged. Direct access from health centre to the sea. Sea bathing perfect with access by ladder, and by the old boat ramp when it was a harbour. No beach, but area nicely enclosed in a small bay called Silveira. Floating platform in summer. Caracol is a spiral shell or land snail, and the small garden has a steep mount with a spiral path to the top for an elevated view over the sea. *Dbl* € 94–116, sgl € 77–101.

Praia da Vitória

🏠 **Hotel Verandas do Atlântico***** (30 rooms) Rua da Alfândega 19, 9760-411 Praia da Vitória; ✆ 295 540 050; e reservas@hotelvarandas.com; www.hotelvarandas.com. In front of the beach, 50m from the main square and the marina, 5 mins' drive from the airport. Some rooms balconied, some with connecting rooms for children. *Dbl* € 53–79, sgl € 42–64.

🏠 **Hotel Apartamentos Praia Marina******(268 apts) Av Beira Mar/Largo José S Ribeiro Santa Cruz, 9760-412 Praia da Vitória; ✆ 295 540 055; e reservas@hotelpraiamarina.com; www.hotelpraiamarina.com. Overlooking the beach. Allergy-free rooms and apartments with equipped kitchenettes. *Dbl* € 65–85, sgl € 52–74.

MANOR HOUSES

🏠 **Quinta do Martelo** (10 rooms) (TR) Canada do Martelo 24, 9700-576 São Mateus da Calheta; ✆ 295 642 842; e quintamartelo@mail.telepac.pt; www.acores.com/quintadomartelo. This is a private and remarkable crafts centre, once an orange farm. The numerous outbuildings have been set up as a series of workshops inc blacksmith/farrier, tinsmith, carpenter, joiner, cooper, cobbler, basket-maker, weaver, broom-maker, even a barber's shop. It is a good historical exposition of the everyday life of a rural homestead. There is a restaurant with a splendid ambience, providing traditional and festive meals cooked on wood-burning stoves with home-baked bread. The owners' idea is to give their guests a feel for the atmosphere of a rural house on Terceira while providing comfortable accommodation. Less traditional are the swimming pool, tennis court,

gym and sauna, but they also have traditional Azorean games. Not a luxury stay, but a very interesting one and utterly different. Each room has a bathroom, all are differently furnished, and are provided in 2 houses. *Dbl* € 100, sgl € 93 per day inc car hire with unlimited kilometres.

🏠 **Quinta da Nasce-Água** (10 rooms) (TH) Lugar da Nasce Agua – Vinha Brava, 9700-236 Angra do Heroísmo; ✆ 295 628 501. Some of the rooms are in the house, some in adjacent cottages. A gracious house set amidst rolling hills and pastures, with a charming formal garden, there is a 20m 3-level swimming pool, tennis court, Turkish bath and golf training. A short taxi ride takes you to the centre of Angra, or every 30 mins there is a public bus or it's about 20–30 mins' walk. Dinner by arrangement. *Dbl* € 70–112, sgl € 52–87.

🏠 **Quinta dos Figos** (10 rooms) (TR) Rua das Pedras 34, 9760-118 Cabo da Praia; ☎ 295 542 708; ℮ reservas@quintadosfigos.com; www.quintadosfigos.com. Dating from the 19th century it has been a store, a barracks and an elementary school, but is now well converted to en-suite rooms, with furniture made from local woods and soft furnishings by Azorean artisans. Bicycles available for hire. *Dbl € 80–90, sgl € 60–70 and 3–4-person apt € 112–140.*

🏠 **Quinta de Nossa Senhora das Mercês****
(6 rooms, 1 suite, 1 self-catering house) Caminho de Baixo, São Mateus, 9700-559 Angra do Heroísmo; ☎ 295 642 588; ℮ geral@quintadasmerces.com; www. quintadasmerces.com. Between Angra and São Mateus it is a short drive to either town. The farm goes back to the 16th century, and the manor house together with its chapel was built in the 17th century. Set between the sea and woodland it has various common rooms, b/fast and dining room, library, games room and an inner courtyard. Outdoor pool and tennis court in a remarkable stone-walled enclosure with an all-weather artificial grass surface. There are 4 rooms with private garden, 2 with a sea view and 1 suite, Turkish bath, jacuzzi, gymnasium and woodland walks. Also a self-catering house with 2 bedrooms, kitchen and living room. Dinner upon request 24 hrs in advance. Probably the top manor house in all the islands, favoured by a reigning monarch (albeit the whole house), it is a place for a special occasion. *Starting from dbl € 85–120, sgl € 68–99.*

YOUTH HOSTEL

🏠 **Pousada de Juventide de Angra do Heroísma** (70 beds) Negrito, São Mateus, 9700 554 Angra do Heroísma; ☎ 295 642 095; ℮ pja.angra@oninet.pt. Also has 1 family room with bathroom. About 25km west of Angra, near the sea.

CAMPING

🏕 **Baia de Salga** Near Porto Judeu; ☎ 295 905 451. Good facilities inc electricity. Sea swimming. Closed in winter. Popular, necessary to book in high summer.
🏕 **Cinco Ribeiros** On the southwest coast; ☎ 295 907 200. New all-year campsite on grass beneath tamarisk trees. Full amenities, inc laundry.
🏕 **Biscoitos** A new site with amenities.

✖ WHERE TO EAT

There are many restaurants and much competition so choice is generally wider on Terceira than the other islands. Too many to list, these below are just a few pointers. Some village restaurants are also mentioned under the car tours.

ANGRA DO HEROÍSMO
✖ **Beira Mar** By harbour; ☎ 295 642 392
✖ **Adega Lusitânica** Rua de São Pedro 63–65; on the road between Angra and the two resort hotels; ☎ 295 212 301

SÃO MATEUS A short drive from Angra, or an even shorter one from the two resort hotels.

✖ **Adega São Mateus** Opposite church; ☎ 295 642 345
✖ **Quinta do Martelo** Cantinho, São Mateus; ☎ 295 642 842. Good Azorean food in typical farmhouse setting, reservations advisable.

ALTARES In the northwest.

Pastelaria Caneta ☎ 295 989 162. It is tight on the right-hand side of the road with a not very obvious sign, on the corner of the Canada José Romeira. The small bar entrance leads to a charming garden area and upstairs is the restaurant. Recommended.

SÃO SEBASTIÃO In the southeast, about a 15-minute taxi ride from either Angra or Praia.

Os Moinhos Rua Arrebalde, 9700-610 Vila de Sâo Sebastião; ✆ 295 904 508. Restaurant with terrific ambience in a converted watermill. Charcoal-grilled meat and fish, an excellent *alcatra*, and make sure you keep room for the *sobremas*, delicious desserts including a chocolate mousse to travel for; finally a wine list, the best I have seen in the Azores. Prices are sensible, yet service comes with panache, and if the downstairs restaurant is busy the owner will open an intimate upstairs room for that special dinner. In winter, wood-burning fires. If you are staying in Angra or Praia, then well worth the 15-min taxi ride, but better reserve a table. Widely considered as probably the finest restaurant in the Azores. *Closed Tue, Nov–Mar.*

NIGHTLIFE

🄴 **Classic Bar** Rua São João, Angra
🄴 **Etis Bar** Praia da Vitória. Live music, sometimes theatre.

🄴 **Foxis Bar** São Mateus. In a typical house with space outside, before the harbour, near the tennis club.

FESTIVALS

The Holy Ghost Festival held on the eighth Sunday after Easter takes place not only in Praia da Vitória but all over the island in villages wherever the crown of the Holy Ghost is held, either in church or in a private house. The Vine and Wine Festival in Biscoitos on the first weekend of September marks the grape harvest and also offers traditional foods. There are also many more smaller celebrations held all over the island for saints' days and secular events.

Carnaval (all over the island)   last week of February
Touradas á corda (throughout the island)   May to end of October
10 Bodos (Praia) First event of the Holy Ghost Festival   May
Festa de Sanjoaninas (Angra) Includes many cultural
activities   June/July
Festival de Folclore, Gastronomia a Etnografia
(Angra)   August
Angrajazz (Jazz Festival)   first week in October

USEFUL NUMBERS

Emergency ✆ 112
SATA Air Açores Rua da Esperança, Angra; ✆ 295 212 016
TAP Air Portugal Rua da Sé, Angra; ✆ 295 216 489
Police Praça Dr Sousa Junior, Angra; ✆ 295 212 022

Hospital ✆ 295 212 121
Tourist information office Rua Direita, Angra; ✆ 295 213 393; e turter@mail.telepac.pt
Tourist hotline ✆ 800 296 296
Airport information ✆ 295 540 047; lost and found ✆ 295 540 032

WHAT TO SEE AND DO

MUSEUMS

Museu de Angra do Heroismo (*Ladeira de São Francisco; open Tue–Fri 10.00–12.00 and 14.00–17.00, additionally May–Sept, Sat and Sun 14.00–17.30; Sun free*) Housed in the old Convent of São Francisco, once the headquarters of the Franciscan order of the Azores, the building itself is well worth the visit. Furniture and military exhibits are included in the permanent displays and there are frequently changing exhibitions.

Os Montanheiros (*Sociedade de Exploração Espeleológica, Rua da Rocha 6/8; www.montanheiros.com; open summer 10.00–16.00, winter 09.00–12.30 and*

13.30–17.00. Closed weekends and public holidays) The geological museum and headquarters of this very enthusiastic and active society; to view are topographical models of the islands, photographs and rock specimens.

Museu do Vinho dos Biscoitos (*www.Casaagricolabrum.com; open Tue–Sun 10.00–12.00 and 13.30–16.00, until 17.30 Apr to Sep and closed during the third week of Sep during the grape harvest; admission free*) Good small private museum showing most interesting details of the family business and wine production going back over 100 years. There are small demonstration vineyards, and other fruit orchards.

Quinta do Martelo (*Centro Etnográfica e Gastronómico;* ✆ *295 642 842;* e *quintamartelo@ mail.telepac.pt; www.acores.com/quintadomartelo*) This is a private museum and restaurant with an excellent exposition of the traditional way of living. Open only to residents, and diners upon request. Telephone booking essential.

WALKING On Terceira feedback suggests there are rather too many bulls for comfortable cross-country walking and in any case there are no really satisfactory trails. The **Mountaineering Society** offers a guided walk from 09.30 to around 17.00 every Sunday between March and October. You will need to be reasonably fit and with transport to get to the start of the walk (e *montanheiros@montanheiros.com; www.montanheiros.com; photographs on www.olhares.com/osmontanheiros*). There are also **private guides**: Filipe Ribeiro Laurenço (✆ *963 289 993;* €*20 per person for half day plus transport*) and Miguel Mendonça (✆ *967 317 024*).

BIRDS AND FLOWERS The best-known site among dedicated birders is a rather grotty disused quarry at **Cabo da Praia** that supplied the stone for the harbour at close-by Praia da Vitória in the 1980s. If you are visiting for the birds and not the scenery then it is worth a look, although feedback has reported disappointment. Godswits, whimbrels, plovers, turnstones, sandpipers, grey herons, the odd duck and more might be seen. However, one informant tells me that it is important to visit the quarry at the correct time since tidal times are important to your chances of success. The special thing about this quarry is that it was dug to a depth where the sea seeps through fissures in the rock and enters from underground. Water does not come over the cliffs from the sea just 100m away, but the twice-daily sluicing in rhythm with the tide has created a remarkable wetland habitat. Protected from the wind and excellent for waders, species usually seen only in Africa and North America seem to be able to find this quarry so if you visit two to five weeks either side of mid September and go during the two- to three-hour period either side of low tide you could be rewarded with very interesting sightings. As yet, it has no protected status, and the salt plants, weeds and grasses will add quite a few species to a holiday plant list.

To salve your aesthetic sense drop down to the Special Protected Area of **Ponta das Contendas** and the **Baia das Mós**, the southeast corner of Terceira. Originally there was a 500m-long peninsula created by lava flow and through erosion and chemical change it is now discontinuous, the furthest point being Ilhéu da Mina. Many species of both resident and migratory birds may be seen, but it is botanically uninspiring.

As compensation, botanists will be pleased that **Lagoa do Negro** and the surrounding **Mistérios Negros** is mentioned here for their benefit alone. West of centre, this remarkable volcanic area has formed a swamp and other special ecosystems rich in mosses and lichens; of special interest are the bog lovers *Littorella uniflora* and *Isoetes azorica*. However, if birders continue on towards **Pico Alto**, 808m high with a collapsed caldera, woodcock and snipe might make a change from their usual observational menu.

SWIMMING Around the coast there is a mix of semi-natural rock pools and artificial pools, many with WC and changing rooms open in summer. The long sand beach at **Praia da Vitória** is popular.

Silveira By the Hotel do Caracol, has a public bathing area in the deep inlet protected by Monte Brasil

Negrito Harbour swimming facilities, changing rooms and a small café/bar

Ponta da Cinco Ribeiros Harbour swimming, changing rooms and a small café/bar. Campsite nearby.

Biscoitos Natural rock pools amidst interesting volcanic rock formations; changing facilities

Baia das Quatro Ribeiras Natural swimming pool, changing facilities and nearby campsite

Porto Martins Near the harbour. A natural swimming pool, like a conventional pool but with a wave machine! There are changing rooms and a restaurant.

Baia de Salga Near Porto Judeu. Sea swimming with changing facilities. Campsite nearby.

GOLF

Club de Golf da Ilha Terceira Fajãs Agualva, 9760 Praia da Vitória; ☎ 295 902 444/299; e info@terceiragolf.com; www.terceiragolf.com; green fees for non-members: daily pass €25; set of clubs €15; clubhouse with restaurant open to non-members, small pro shop. Designed by Cameron and Powell and opened in 1954 at 350m above sea level, it is set in another Azorean landscape of tall trees, lakes, colourful azaleas and hydrangeas and with its wide fairways is reckoned to be the easiest of the three Azores courses. 18 holes, par 72. Handicap requirements: men 28, women 36.

ITINERARIES The programmes suggested below take a total of three days, but can certainly be done in less time. Alternatively, you can easily select your own itinerary from the notes. Angra do Heroísma is a must and will take you a morning. You could then spend the afternoon and early evening on Monte Brasil. Travelling slowly around the west coast to Biscoitos will never fail to delight, passing through small villages and past many houses, their whitewashed exteriors sparkling in the sun, even when the hills of the interior are covered with cloud. Including the museums and a reasonable lunch this will take an easy day. If the skies are clear or the clouds are not too low then a day could be spent exploring the wild hinterland, with many old volcanic cones and extensive areas of broken and tumbled land covered in grasses, mosses or tree heathers. This gives the opportunity to judge which day to do what, according to the weather. Since almost every visitor goes to Angra, the two car tours begin from the city.

Angra do Heroismo Given the setting, it is difficult not to slip back through time to the period when Angra was the centre of the Atlantic universe. Trading and treasure ships gathered and passed through here from both the East Indies and the New World, and the town grew ever more prosperous. It was central, too, to the Azores archipelago until usurped by Ponta Delgada. Ban the cars, change the shop windows, clamber into period costume, and all you need is a pirate ship to come sailing into the bay! Well, perhaps not quite, but it is fun to

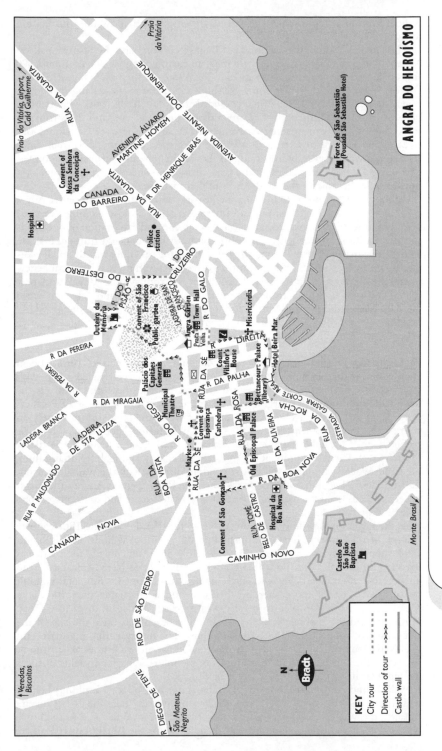

ANGRA DO HEROÍSMO

KEY
- - - - - - City tour
- - >>> - - Direction of tour
————— Castle wall

Praia da Vitória

RUA DA GUARITA

Praia da Vitória, airport,
Cald Guilherme

AVENIDA ÁLVARO
MARTINS HOMEM

AVENIDA INFANTE DOM HENRIQUE

Convent of
Nossa Senhora
da Conceição

RUA DA GUARITA

CANADA
DO BARREIRO

RUA DR HENRIQUE BRÁS

Hospital

Police
station

R DO
DESTERRO

R DO
PISÃO

LADEIRA DE SAN
FRANCISCO CRUZEIRO

R DO GALO

Outeiro da
Memória

Convent of São
Francisco

Public gardens

Angra Gáfeten

Town Hall

R DA PEREIRA

R DA PEREIRA

Palácio dos
Capitães
Generais

Praça
Velha

DIREITA

Misericórdia

R DA MIRAGAIA

Count
Vilaflor's
House

R DA SÉ

R DA PALHA

Hotel Beira Mar

LADEIRA BRANCA

LADEIRA
DE STA LUZIA

Municipal
Theatre

Convent of
Esperança

Cathedral

R DA ROSA

Bettancourt Palace
(library)

ESTRADA GASPAR CORTE REAL

RUA DA ROCHA

RUA P MALDONADO

Market

R DA SÉ

Old Episcopal Palace

R DA OLIVEIRA

RUA DA
BOA VISTA

CANADA NOVA

Convent of São Gonçalo

R DA BOA NOVA

RUA TOMÉ
BELO DE CASTRO

Hospital da
Boa Nova

NOVA

CAMINHO NOVO

Castelo de
São João
Baptista

RIO DE SÃO PEDRO

R DIEGO DE TEIVE

São Mateus,
Negrito

Veredas,
Biscoitos

Monte Brasil

Forte de São Sebastião
(Pousada São Sebastião Hotel)

N

Bradt

117

wander around at night when the streets are empty, and allow the imagination to fly.

The Duke of Cumberland's flotilla of English corsairs sank the Spanish galleon *Nuestra-Señora de Guia* off Terceira in 1589, an example of just one of almost 900 ships recorded lost from various causes in the Azores in the past 500 years. In the Bay of Angra alone there are some 80 shipwrecks, the deepest lying in 60m of water, the oldest from 1543. Angra provided the safest haven but, when storms blew in from the southeast, it became a dangerous dead end and disastrous for those ships too slow or unable to leave in time. It seems there are few doubloons to be found because any treasure was recovered soon after the shipwreck since such losses would severely impact upon the Portuguese and Spanish economies. These wrecks, however, represent the most marvellous site of marine archaeology, time capsules because of the suddenness of their demise.

Although no-one wants to live in a theme park, what a stimulating centre Angra could have become for the study and interpretation of a most exciting and vivid period of history: the exploitation, colonial expansion and exploration of new lands and the maritime consequences of politics and war on mainland Europe. Instead, an ugly new marina intrudes upon the bay harbouring in winter mostly small boats that are normally seen cluttering suburban driveways. And more, an execrable new restaurant climbs the harbour wall. Look across from Monte Brasil, and new orange-red roof tiles scream out against the weathered old, and this is a World Heritage Site. Although it is hard to ignore such cavalier intrusions, the grand old buildings mercifully retain their gravitas and a morning's wander with a coffee break or two is highly pleasurable.

Angra city tour During summer several of the buildings are open to visitors. Begin at the centre of the city in the **Praça Velha**, the most attractively paved square with a Renaissance influence. At the western end and built in the 19th century is the town hall, with one of the largest and finest great halls in the whole of Portugal (*Open to visitors*). Leave the square by the Rua Direita and almost immediately on your right is the balconied house of the **Count of Vilaflor**, later Duke of Terceira, commander of the Liberal armies and leader of the Liberal army at the Battle of Praia in 1829. The visual unity of the front elevation is satisfying, but I do not think the count would have approved of the condom dispenser on the wall along from his front door! The house is open to visitors. The Rua Direita is Angra's first main street and leads from the harbour directly to the main square and to the governor's house a little beyond.

At the lower end of the Rua Direita on the left is the dominating 18th-century **Misericórdia Church**. The first hospital in the Azores was built on this site in 1492, supported by the Brotherhood of the Holy Spirit; one of the founders was Joã Vaz Corte-Real, Governor of Angra who is thought to have been the first to discover Newfoundland. The present building dates from the 18th century, built by an association of the earlier brotherhood and a charitable institution, the Misericórdia. Badly damaged in the 1980 earthquake, it is again open to visitors. Further round the harbour wall the small sandy beach was once the site of the shipyards that supported the early trading ships. The new yachting marina begun in 2000 is seen by many as an ugly intrusion and violation of a historical patrimony, and when the constant metallic rattling from the masts of berthed yachts disturbs the night air historical reverie can be difficult.

Walk round until you come to the blue-and-white-painted building behind which is a flight of stairs taking you to the upper road. Take the Rua Carreira Cavalos, the Way of the Horses, so named because a festival devoted to the horse was held here; at the far end on the right-hand corner is the **Bettencourt Palace**.

Built at the turn of the 18th century it has a fine portico above which is the Bettencourt family coat of arms. It is now a public library and open to visitors. On the other corner is the old Episcopal Palace, with little remaining of the original dating from 1544.

Go along the Rua da Rosa and at the end you are outside the walls of the massive **Convent of São Gonçalo**, founded in 1545 for the nuns of the Order of St Clare. It is Angra's oldest and the largest in the Azores. The small side door should be unlocked, and it is well worth entering. There are figured choir stalls, 18th-century Portuguese tiles, 17th-century silver crucifix, paintings and ornamental ceiling.

Turn left at the crossroads along the Rua da Boanova to quickly find the **Hospital da Boa Nova**, a military hospital built by the Spanish for the soldiers stationed in the castle.

Retrace your steps and continue straight along the Rua Gonçalo Cabral passing the modern sports centre on your left. At the main road turn right along the Rua da Sé to come to the cathedral church of Angra, **Santissimo Salvador da Sé**, founded in 1570. Of interest are the 16th-century painted panels, the Indo-Portuguese-style lectern made in the Azores of Brazilian jacaranda wood and whale ivory, and the altar's early 18th-century silver antependium made on Terceira. The church was finished in 1618 while Angra was under Spanish dominance, and its craftsmanship is influenced by Flemish, local and Spanish Baroque styles. There is also a museum of religious objects.

Continue down the road, taking the first turning off left to find the splendid **Palácio dos Capitães Generais**. The original building was a Jesuit college, and the island's governor had it modified during the second half of the 18th century and made into a palace. Two kings have stayed here, King Pedro IV in 1832 and King Carlos I in 1901. The interior is richly decorated and is open to visitors.

Nearby you will see the entrance to a public garden, the **Duque da Terceira Gardens**. Initiated in 1862 as an experimental garden for agricultural development, it 20 years later also provided space for public use, which became a garden that was enlarged in 1888. This garden was developed by a Belgian, Francisco J D Gabriel, who began his early horticultural career in a Liège nursery before coming to the Azores aged 18 to work on São Miguel. He managed the garden for 15 years, until his death in 1897. A wonderful urban period garden of the late 19th century, it was noted in its heyday for its many exotic ornamental species. In February/March the magnolias are at their best and, of course, never get damaged by spring frosts. If you walk through the garden you can climb the steps that take you steeply up to **Outeiro da Memória**, the Memorial Hill.

This was the site of the first fort built in the Azores around 1474; the obelisk was erected in 1846 in memory of King Pedro IV. The reward for making the climb is the fine view over Angra and across to Monte Brasil.

Go out of the garden and take the small road off on the right, the Rua do Pisão. Once there was a stream flowing in this area, and early in the town's development this was put into an open conduit and served for some 500 years the industries that sprang up alongside: watermills, tanneries and other enterprises. The narrow winding streets here are fun to explore and at the bottom you come to the **City Museum**, housed in the Convent of São Francisco; the entrance is off the Ladeiro de São Francisco, the road running up from the main square beside the public garden. The building alone is well worth seeing, and the museum offers permanent displays about the Azores and temporary exhibits. After, you can simply walk down the hill to the square where this walk began, or go up the hill, the Rua da Guarita, to see the impressive exterior of the 17th-century Convent of Nossa Senhora da Conceição, built in the 16th century with 17th- and 18th-century alterations.

Monte Brasil During the Spanish occupation Sir Francis Drake unsuccessfully attacked Angra and eight years later, in 1597, the Earl of Essex with around 100 ships failed to seize a fleet of Spanish treasure galleons anchored in the bay. To defend the harbour against such attacks and at the same time secure control of Angra, King Filipe II constructed the Fort of São Filipe at the foot of Monte Brasil, later given its more familiar name of São João Baptista. The exterior wall is 4km long and some 400 artillery pieces defended it. Three other smaller forts along the coast including that of São Sebastião provided crossfire so completing the defence. Inside the fortress is the **Igreja de São João Baptista**, commemorating the restoration of Portuguese sovereignty in 1640 and the Governor's Palace.

If you are in a hurry, then drive up or take a taxi up to **Pico das Cruzinhas**, the highest point at 205m to enjoy the view of Angra. You can clearly see the old historical core; look for the last-century pyramid erected on the first fort to be built, then below the governor's palace, the Santissimo Salvador da Sé Church, then down to the harbour at the bottom of the Rua Dirieta to the Misericórdia Church. To the right on higher ground is the conspicuous Convent of São Francisco; to the left is the Convent of São Gonçalo, close to the large modern indoor sports complex. Note also the 17th-century Castelo de São Sebastião that once protected the eastern approaches, now a *pousada*. To the left, westwards, is an area known as Caminho de Baixo where the rich people of Angra once had their summer houses. Behind you on the grass mounds are British gun emplacements from World War II. The tall stone cross dated 1492 and the surrounding wall again incorporating the cross is a typical monument that the Portuguese built wherever they landed and claimed new lands.

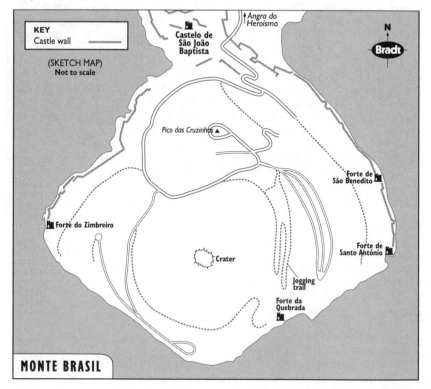

MONTE BRASIL

With a car there are several walks available. Equally, you can spend a very enjoyable full day exploring this old volcanic hill on foot, walking easily from the centre of Angra, or from Pico das Cruzinhas. You can also incorporate a guided visit of the Fort of São João Batista, starting daily on the hour during summer.

Following the surfaced road, these are some of the walks you can do. The first signposted side road will take you to the little chapel of St Antonio at the end of the asphalt road. From here to the end of the unsurfaced track it takes about 45 minutes to walk there and back; you will have good views of Angra and views eastwards of the south coast.

Return to the main road and continue until you reach the rim of the caldera. The caldera itself is used by the military and you are not allowed to go down. Look for the signpost to the **Vigia da Baleia**; it takes about an hour to walk there and back. It is a good walk often in the shade of trees, and the reward is a commanding view seaward; if you have binoculars and the time, try your hand at whale watching. You can also walk in the other direction up to **Pico do Zimbreiro**.

When you return to the main road continue round the caldera until you come to another large track on your right. There is a children's play area, picnic tables and a WC. From here it is another very pleasant walk up to **Pico da Facho**.

Return to the main road and it is a short walk to **Pico das Cruzinhas**.

The west coast tour: Angra do Heroísmo to Biscoitos
São Mateus Just two miles west of Angra is this pretty village and harbour, one of the most important fishing harbours in the Azores. Between 16.00 and 17.00 the boats land their catches to sell on the quayside. The colourful little boats create a cheerful scene and there is a small fort overlooking the harbour. Take time, too, to explore the nearby backstreets. There are two good fish restaurants.

Negrito This is a small village with an old fort by the harbour, with swimming facilities and a small café/bar. An old small trying area has been preserved where in basalt are the fireplaces and pots for reducing the whale blubber. On the nearby headland is Terceira's youth hostel. As you continue, you should be able to see São Jorge on the horizon.

Cinco Ribeiras Early into the village on the left site is the **Casa Typica** owned by Dr Marcelo Moules. This is a private house that is sometimes open to visitors in summer and shows typical life as it was once lived on Terceira.

Soon on your right is Azulart, the **ceramics studio** of Aurelia Rocha (✎ 962 582 930). Her pots are all wheel thrown and in stoneware are traditional Terceiran designs, and in earthenware traditional shapes and designs of the Azores. All are hand painted, and commissions are accepted. Reflecting the enterprise needed for life on an island in mid Atlantic, she has built her own kilns. Ceramics in the early days on Terceira used clay imported from England, shipped over in the empty sailing boats coming for the orange crop, and clay is still imported from the continent as the island clay from Santa Maria does not take glazing and can be used only for *alcatra* pots and similar that do not need a glaze.

Further on, on the left, is the **Canada da Pilar** (*open 08.00–22.00, weekends 15.00–22.00*), a narrow road between houses going down to the coast. The small factory making Vaquinho cheese is along here, where you can sample and buy the three cheeses made and enjoy a coffee and the delicious traditional small cake of Terceira, made by a lady in the village. Quejo Vaquinho is the traditional cheese and sold in small blocks like butter and is made with salt only on the outside. O Ilha cheese, cheese of the island, has the salt incorporated into the milk, and Quejo Vaquinha Picante has red peppers added. The dairy does not make any butter, so all the milk, not separates, goes into the cheese. Cheese was first made on Terceira in 1912, and Vaquina translates as a small cow.

At the end of the road you get to **Ponta da Cinco Ribeiros**, a harbour with swimming facilities, also the remains of a small fort that the sea has almost washed away. Close by is a camping site under trees with electricity and amenities.

Rather than return to the main road, you can continue parallel with the sea following always the asphalt road. It is a very pretty drive through a landscape of stone-walled fields and pastures, and eventually you will come to Pezinho da Senhora, a recently developed parking area with picnic tables and barbecue facilities, and an old-style oven for people to use who no longer have them in their modern houses. There is also a bullring, and the red-painted boards with white circles are the only means of defence from the bull! The arena is also used for music and folklore events.

From the picnic area take the road going inland and the left fork to quickly come to a little chapel with white tiles, with an adjacent large house on the Largo Na Sa da Ajuda. There were no springs in this area, so water was at a premium. To the left of the large house is a small cistern; you will see steps going up to a small door. Look inside and you can see where a bucket can be lowered into the water, stored from rainfall falling onto the roof. The name Pezinho da Senhora comes from a rock in the river that has the imprint of a girl's foot; follow the steps down on the right of the chapel and you will see a small grotto, where the Senhora is supposed to have appeared. The large house next to the church, originally a small priest's house but later enlarged, was for pilgrims to stay visiting these miraculous places, an equivalent to a *Romeiro* house on São Miguel.

Continue on the asphalt road to come into Santa Bárbara. If you missed all this, you can pick it up turning from the main road signposted to Largo Na Sa da Ajuda, opposite the Mercado Bárbarense.

Santa Bárbara As you continue around the coast you come to the farming community of Santa Bárbara, with their white-painted houses so startlingly bright in the sunshine. The Spanish colonial influence in the architecture of the parish church suggests the 16th century. Inside there is a 17th-century organ from the Convent of Nossa Senhora da Conceição in Angra and the furniture in the vestry is made from jacaranda and other tropical hardwoods. You can find beautiful New World woods used in often unexpected places, brought to the Azores as ballast. Near the church is a 19th-century *império*.

Doze Ribeiras Some 200m before the church on the right-hand side of the road look out for the oldest house; there is no sign. In front of the stone building is a large tank for rainwater with a half-dome catchment roof; on the roof a washing tub and pots used for bread making. There is an oxcart, a windmill that would have ground *burra de milho* or donkey corn, used for feeding farm animals; note the sheets of zinc on the corn store to keep the rats away. In summer there are folk-dance performances. Nearly all the adjacent small houses were built with the help of the Portuguese military for the elderly unable to afford to rebuild after the disastrous earthquake in 1980. Houses are painted annually for the Holy Ghost or summer festivities.

Serra de Santa Bárbara Beyond Doze Ribeiras take the right-hand EN 5-2 turning inland, eastward, to the impressive volcanic area behind Santa Bárbara. Look on the left-hand side of the road for a signpost to Serra de Santa Bárbara; take this side road (5km) to go to the top of the mountain where, if the weather is clear, you may see the most beautiful views of Terceira Island. Return to the main road and turn right to rejoin the main road running along the coast.

Serreta This is a small village with its important Church of Our Mother of Miracles where promises are made by people from all over the island. Beyond the village you will come to a sign to a *farol* or lighthouse which makes a nice walk, or you can continue to Raminho and take the trail back to the lighthouse. It was off this stretch of coast that the undersea Serreta volcano was recently active, and the volcanic bombs could be seen coming to the surface.

Raminho The signposted Miradouro do Raminho is a substantial viewpoint looking along the coast and is a good place for seabirds, with WC, parking and picnic tables beneath the trees. There is also a *vigia* (a simple look-out shelter) for spying whales. In the distance on a clear day you can see São Jorge and Graciosa.

Altares The local **museum** is just past the blue-and-white church (*open Wed–Sun 14.00–17.00*). This is a small village with an excellent restaurant, the Pastelaria Caneta (listed under *Where to eat*, page 113). You will see a hill on the coast called Pico de Altares (on maps called Matias Simão) with a monument at its summit. This was once a *vigia*. If you have time, climb to the top (153m) for the view along the coast.

Biscoitos This area was always intriguing because of its volcanic origins and black lava; *biscoito* means 'biscuit'. This came from the last eruption in 1761 when lava flowed down from the area around Pico do Gaspar. It was also known for its *Verdelho* wines, and is again becoming recognised in the Azores for its wine production and wine museum. Francisco Maria Brum (1860–1928) first began making wine over 100 years ago and was the first to graft grapes after the disastrous *Phylloxera* outbreak that decimated the vines. The years between 1910 and 1960 saw the maximum production. The family make white wines including a special small production of only 500 litres. However, by the time it is put into bottles only 400 litres are left, so it goes into half-bottles to provide 800 for sale! The museum is on your left as you turn into Biscoitos village.

At the end of the village there is a small roundabout; turn left towards the sea to view the vineyards, the tiny walled enclosures called *curraletas*. There are also natural rock pools for swimming. Turn east to continue parallel with the sea. Near the harbour are changing facilities for more natural swimming pools. Left of the harbour is an unsurfaced track leading westwards along the coast; this is a pleasant walk above the rocks. Turn left to rejoin the main road and when you again come to the wine museum turn right to take the main road inland to Angra. In July and August this road is made spectacular with all the flowering hydrangeas.

The wild hinterland tour, with Praia da Vitória
Setting out from Angra, take the EN 3-1 road heading for Biscoitos. At the crossroads near Pico do Gaspar turn left to take the EN 5-2 leading to Doze Ribeiras; this road is called the Estrela dos Ribeiros. Continue until the road off to your left signposted to São Bartolomeu; take this to reach a forestry park with picnic tables beside a lovely clear and sparkling stream beneath lofty cryptomeria trees. There is also a forest nursery here.

Returning to the Doze Ribeiras road, turn left and continue as before for a short distance to the turning off on your right to Lagoa do Negro; it goes across to the EN 3-1. This is a beautiful road, particularly in July and August when much of its length is lined with hydrangeas. First passing pastures, you soon enter wild country with native vegetation, especially the area called **Mistério Negro**, an extensive area of black cinders thrown out by the last major eruption on Terceira in 1761. You will find the Lagoa do Negro on your right, and opposite is a stone house by the road. This is the entrance to the cave, the **Gruta de Natal** (*open 31 Mar–31 May*

15.00–17.30; 1 Jun–30 Jun 14.30–17.45; 1 Jul–31 Aug 14.00–18.00; 1 Sep–30 Sep 14.30–1745; 1 Oct–4 Nov 15.00–17.30), a 697m-long, branched lava tube with stalactite- and stalagmite-like structures.

Continue on the same road until you come to a major junction. Turn right to go to Angra (left goes to Altares, opposite to Biscoitos). Just before you get to the crossroads you came to earlier, take a left turning to an area for car parking where there is a *tentadeiro*, an area where bulls are selected for the bullfight. On summer mornings you are likely to find plenty of activity here.

Now continue on the main road to the crossroads. At the crossroads, turn left towards Cabrito. If you would like a sharp reminder that you are on a volcanic island, then take the wide unsurfaced road you soon come to on your left signposted to Furnas do Enxofre; this road ends in a turning area. The route can be slippery so take care. A small path leads in about 15 minutes' walk to several small caves. Do not enter these or be tempted to explore them – the gases emitted are very dangerous. You will find the ground quite hot, and steam emissions have often turned the grass brown. The area is a geological protected zone.

Return to the main road and continue, ignore the first road off to your left to Agualva, and take a later turning on your left, signposted to Algar do Carvão. The **caves** (*open 1 Jun–30 Sep 15.00–17.00*) are a huge lava tube about 100m long, the remains of an eruption some 2,000 years ago; there are stalactites and stalagmites, formed by silica. Opposite is the Caldeira de Guilherme Moniz, a primary volcano with a crater perimeter of 15km that is among the largest in the archipelago.

When you leave the caves and get back to the main road, turn right to find the turning to Agualva, now off on your right. This is a really good drive passing a tumultuous volcanic landscape covered with native vegetation. Growing along the Ribeira Agualva are the most impressive tree ferns.

Although Agualva is a large village, you cannot miss an interesting privately owned handicraft workshop on the main road. Here you can see the artisans at work. Follow the main road along to Vila Nova and Lajes, and to Praia da Vitória.

Praia da Vitória In contrast with other towns in the archipelego, Praia always feels open and bright. It has an attractive main square and a long pedestrianised shopping street. The extensive lowlands of this eastern half of the island produced large quantities of wheat, and the wealth created is reflected in many fine houses in the town. At first called simply Praia, it gained town status in 1640. In 1581, after bombarding Angra, a Spanish fleet of ten ships was reconnoitring the Terceira coast and anchored in Salga Bay, in the southeastern corner. They were seen and the alarm given but by the time the Portuguese arrived 1,000 Castillians had landed and were already bent on destruction. After a morning's fierce but indecisive fighting an Augustinian friar had the idea to drive cattle at the enemy. Over 1,000 animals were stampeded at the Spaniards, who fell back in disarray and were killed or drowned on the shore. Thus ended the Battle of Salga. Again battle came to Praia in 1829 when the town, supporting the Liberal cause, successfully resisted an attempted landing by an Absolutist fleet of 21 ships. In commemoration, the town was called Praia da Vitória in 1837. The nearby Lajes airport now covers much of what were the great wheatfields of earlier days.

In the main square, the Praça Francisco Ornelas da Câmara, is the Liberty Statue, erected on the first centenary of the 1829 battle won by the Liberals in homage to the heroes. Overlooking the square is the attractive town hall, and further along on the Rua de São Paulo is the parish church, the Santa Cruz Church. This was founded by one of the first settlers and has a 15th-century Gothic doorway and a 16th-century Manueline side doorway. Inside there are fine carvings, rich gilt ornamentation and various works of art. Further along on the

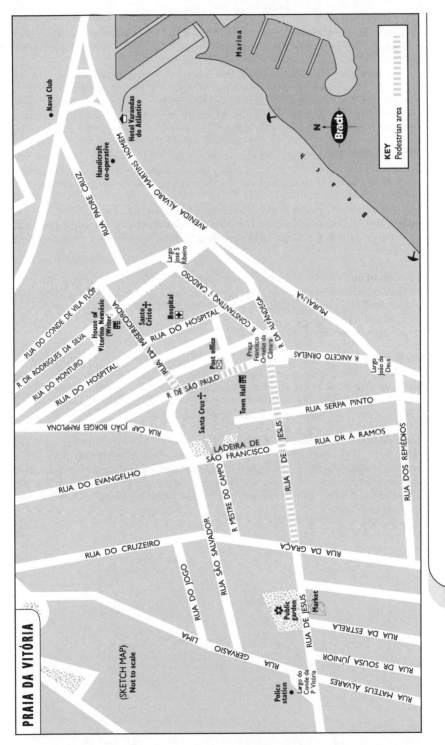

PRAIA DA VITÓRIA

(SKETCH MAP)
Not to scale

Police station

Largo do Conde da P Vitória

RUA GERVASIO LIMA

RUA DO JOGO

RUA DO CRUZEIRO

RUA SÃO SALVADOR

R MESTRE DO CAMPO

Public garden

RUA DE JESUS

Market

RUA DE JESUS

RUA MATEUS ALVARES

RUA DR DE SOUSA JÚNIOR

RUA DA ESTRELA

RUA DA GRAÇA

RUA DOS REMÉDIOS

RUA DR Á RAMOS

RUA SERPA PINTO

Santa Cruz ✝

Town Hall

LADEIRA DE SÃO FRANCISCO

RUA DO EVANGELHO

RUA CAP JOÃO BORGES PAMPLONA

R DE SÃO PAULO

Post office

Praça Francisco Ornelas da Câmara

R DA ALFÂNDEGA

R ANICETO ORNELAS

Largo João de Deus

R CONSTANTINO J CARDOSO

RUA DO HOSPITAL

Hospital

Santo Cristo ✝

RUA DA MISERICÓRDIA

RUA DO HOSPITAL

RUA DO MONTURO

R DR RODRIGUES DA SILVA

RUA DO CONDE DE VILA FLÔR

House of Vitorino Nemésio (Writer)

RUA PADRE CRUZ

Handicraft co-operative

Naval Club

Hotel Varandas do Atlântico

AVENIDA ÁLVARO MARTINS HOMEM

Largo José S Ribeiro

MURALHA

Marina

N

Bradt

Beach

KEY
|||||| Pedestrian area

Terceira WHAT TO SEE AND DO

5

same road on the left is the house where the writer Vitorino Nemésio (1901–78) was born. He held several senior academic posts in Lisbon and was a novelist, poet and scholar and also a popular television personality; his novel of 19th-century life on Faial and Pico, *Stormy Seas*, is in English translation.

The **local Handicraft Co-operative** has its showrooms and shop on the Av Álvaro Martins Homem (*open weekdays 13.00–18.00*). In the opposite direction, towards the far end of main pedestrianised Rua de Jesus, is the town market, built in the final quarter of the 19th century. Alternatively, in the opposite direction, take the Rua da Alfândega which leads down to the beach and along to the new marina.

Porto Martins The area was once covered in vineyards, of which there are still some small traces, but now there are many new houses, summer houses for people in Praia da Vitória. Near the harbour is a natural swimming pool and a restaurant.

Salgueiros Take the minor road to Ponta das Contendas, passing a field of *Strelitzia reginae*, the bird of paradise flower, grown for cut decoration. From the headland there are views of the three rocks, the Três Marias, which are a protected bird sanctuary.

São Sebastião The 15th-century parish church has interesting internal features including frescoes on the walls and unusual ceilings, and in the facing square is a monument to the Battle of Salga. Note also the nearby *império* with its depictions of food and hydrangeas.

See also under *Where to eat*, page 114.

Porto Judeu This is a small fishing village, a happy place to visit because of its simplicity. It also has a good restaurant, **O Ninho**, with a 180° sea and coastal view. **Restaurante Snack-Bar Rocha**, Caminho da Esperança, is next to the infants' school on the main road (✆ *295 905 185; open until 23.00, closed Wed*). It is especially noted for octopus cooked in red wine (*Polvo guisado*).

Serra do Cume If you have time, it is worth making the side trip to drive along this elongated hill top; the highest point is 545m. The view is of small, rich green fields enclosed by stone walls and hydrangeas, and the harbour of Praia with breakwaters appearing like a crab with two claws. Behind is a view of the largest flat area in the whole of the Azores, lying between the Serra do Cume and the Serra da Ribeirinha northeast of Angra.

6

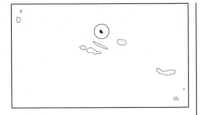

Graciosa

The general opinion is that Graciosa, meaning 'gracious', is the most relaxed of all the islands. Most certainly it is where I would choose to stay in all the world if ever strife and tribulation became too great and I needed to recuperate. I can record little change in the 23 years since my first visit. A rectangular island lying southeast/northwest and the least humid of the archipelago, Graciosa's highest point is Pico Timão at only 398m. As a result, villages are distributed more or less equally across the countryside, and not located only around the coast. The pace is slow, men can still be seen travelling in pony traps or riding donkeys along the roads, there are good eateries, the walking is easy and everyone recognises the visitor second time round. The scenery is picturesque, an idyll of pastures and enclosures, little clusters of whitewashed houses around village churches, occasional windmills with their distinctive red, onion-shaped domes – there were once 36 – and all surrounded by a glittering blue sea. Only after descending within the caldera to a huge cavern 80m high and an underground lake in the very bowels of the island do you confront Graciosa's violent geological past. Like rare wine, it is an island to be enjoyed slowly.

HIGHLIGHTS

Of greatest attraction is the Furna do Enxofre, the cavern at the bottom of the caldera, first seriously explored in 1879 by Prince Albert of Monaco. The winery of Terra da Conde should not be missed, nor the Ethnographic Museum, both in Santa Cruz. Otherwise, just relax and enjoy being on Graciosa.

GENERAL BACKGROUND

GEOGRAPHY Roughly oval in outline, the highest point of Pico Timão is to the south of centre while in the southeast is the caldera, at the bottom of which is the deep cave for which Graciosa is probably known best. The western sector is relatively flat, where most of the vines were grown and to a much lesser extent still are today. The oldest rocks around the Serra das Fontes date from 620,000 years ago, while the eye-catching caldera is thought to have begun as a separate island; its walls and rim may be no more than 20,000 years old.

HISTORY There had always been a strong relationship between Graciosa and Terceira and so doubtless it was sailors from Terceira who first discovered the island and encroached upon it. The leading settler and man responsible for clearing tracts of vegetation was one Vasco Gil Sodré who came originally from Montemor-o-Velho in Portugal along with his family and household retinue and established himself at Carapacho. He was not, however, given the governorship; this went to Christopher Columbus's brother-in-law. It is thought many of the first settlers came from the Beiras and Minho regions of Portugal and from Flanders.

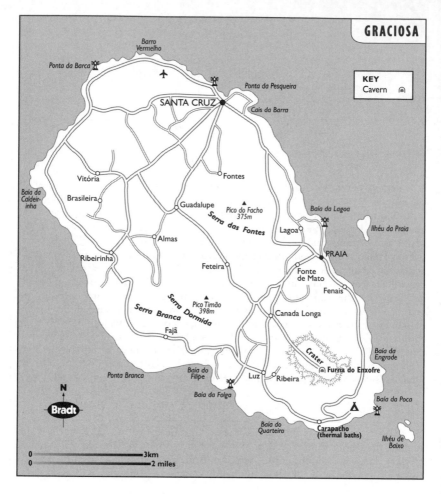

Graciosa soon proved very suitable for the cultivation of cereals and vines, and well within a century of first settlement was already exporting wheat, barley, wine and brandy. These exports were first shipped to Terceira, the economic and administrative centre that also had the harbour frequented by large ships. Needless to say the wealth this generated attracted pirates, and some 13 forts were built to protect the island and its women. Grain had to be stored in hidden underground chambers. These crops remained dominant for very many years, but now, apart from grapes, like the rest of the islands beef and dairy products are the main farming outputs. Fishing has become difficult in recent years because of the decline in fish stocks.

At one time the population numbered around 14,000 inhabitants, but emigration reduced this substantially and again there was a considerable exodus in the 1950s. At first only one member of a family was allowed to leave, but this was relaxed by 1959. The population is now about 5,000 and has stabilised; today mothers go out to work and families are small.

Graciosa proudly claims visits from three historical figures. Firstly Chateaubriand stopped over when fleeing to America from the French Revolution, afterwards to become known for his political writings as secretary to Cardinal

Fesch and in 1822 ambassador to London. In 1814 the poet Almeida Garrett wrote some of his earliest poetry during his stay with an uncle on the island, and lastly the hydrographer Prince Albert of Monaco visited in 1879 and descended the Furna do Enxofre Cave at the bottom of the caldera.

GETTING THERE AND AWAY

BY PLANE SATA Air Açores flies between Graciosa and Terceira at least once a day, sometimes twice, throughout the year. Onward connections to other islands vary according to the days of the week.

BY FERRY Previously there were more or less weekly sailings direct to Graciosa (3½ hours) and onward sailings to Santa Maria. For details of the current ferry service please check the website (*www.transmacor.pt*).

Tickets can be purchased from the office on the quay in Vila da Praia (🕾 295 732 455).

BY YACHT Praia is the best-protected port. It has some bunkering but no repair facilities. There are proposals to construct a marina.

GETTING AROUND

There are buses to every village but for the tourist, the times are often not very convenient. A printed timetable is available from the tourist information office, or the bus company in Rua Boa Vista. Your hotel should also have details. The best way to use the buses is to make the outward journey by bus from Santa Cruz, and return by taxi. Taxis are available in Santa Cruz (about 12), Luz (2) and Praia (2), and any bar will telephone for one. The distances are not great and therefore taxis are not expensive.

CAR HIRE
Rent-a-Car-Medina & Filhos Rua Almeida Garrett, 9880-362 Santa Cruz da Graciosa; 🕾 295 712 094; e medina_filos@hotmail.com

Rent-a-Car Graciosa Ger 138 St Anto – Vitória, 9880 Guadalupe; 🕾 295 712 274, and at airport 🕾 295 712 970

SCOOTER AND MOUNTAIN-BIKE HIRE
Rent-A-Car-Medina & Filhos Rua Almeida Garrett, 9880-362 Santa Cruz da Graciosa; 🕾 295 712 094;

e medina_filos@hotmail.com

TRAVEL AGENTS
Turangra Rua Conselheiro Jacinto Cândido 12, Santa Cruz da Graciosa; 🕾 295 732 401;

e miguelfonseca@turangra.com; www.turangra.com
Via Graciosa Rua Marques de Pombal; 🕾 295 732 981

WHERE TO STAY

All hotels are within a pleasant ten-minute walking distance of the main square in Santa Cruz.

HOTELS
⌂ **Pensão (Res) Ilha Graciosa** (15 rooms) (1a) Av Mousinho de Albuquerque 49, 9880-320 Santa Cruz da Graciosa; 🕾 295 712 675/6; e gracitur@grwonline.com; www.graciturgrwonline.com.

Well-restored manor house. Rooms come with TV and direct-dial telephone, comfortable lounge and bar with a lovely old basalt wine press. Small garden courtyard. *Dbl € 65, sgl € 53.*

🛏 **Pensão (Res) Santa Cruz** (18 rooms) (2a) Largo Barão de Guadalupe, 9880-344 Santa Cruz da Graciosa; ☎ 295 712 345; f 295 712 828. Rooms with satellite TV and direct-dial telephone, 100m from the sea, and close to town.

🛏 **Pensão (Res) Mira Mar** (8 rooms) (3a) Rua Comandante Carlos Pereira Vidinha, 9880 Santa Cruz da Graciosa; ☎ 295 712 632; e residencialmiramar@hotmail.com. Half of the rooms are sea facing, just 8m across a little-used road bordering the sea by the harbour. All rooms with TV and direct telephone line, guests' lounge with bar.

RURAL Currently there is one listed rural accommodation, in Vitória, a few kilometres inland from Santa Cruz:

🛏 **Quinta dos Frutos** (4 rooms) (CC) Carreira Aberta 10 Vitória – Guadalupe, 9880 Santa Cruz da Graciosa; ☎ 295 712 557

CAMPING

▲ **Carapacho** ☎ 295 712 125. A lovely small site on three levels with sea views and sheltered by trees. Showers, toilets, electricity, stone barbecue. Go first to the Dolphin Snack Bar to register. Carapacho Spa is immediately adjacent, as is the sea swimming pool.

▲ **Praia** Above the town with a sea view, but an uninviting site with even less-inviting amenities, seemingly funded by EU money.

✕ WHERE TO EAT

Although all three residencials are in Santa Cruz, almost all the good restaurants are out of town. However, a taxi to and from each is not expensive and takes only minutes. Fish is excellent, but fresh, crisply cooked vegetables seem even more of a rarity on this island. Islanders living in Santa Cruz like to get out at weekends in summer, so the restaurants can be busy.

SANTA CRUZ

✕ **O Coluna** Largo Barão de Guadalupe; ☎ 295 712 333. Some Brazilian dishes. The lady is a very good cook but it can take 1½ hours from ordering to serving. The trick is to order in advance and fix the time. However, it is one of the very few restaurants to offer Pedras Brancos wine, so the waiting can pass very pleasantly. The atmosphere is very different too, rather like dining in a family's front parlour.

✕ **Snack Bar Santa Cruz** Rua da Boa Vista. Specialities *frango no churrasco* (a kind of barbecued chicken) and *alcatra peixe e carne* (a very slow-cooked stew). A tiny place, very friendly, very good prices and they serve a large mixed salad! Fun and recommended.

✕ **Costa do Sol Restaurante** Largo da Calheta; ☎ 295 712 694

✕ **Clube Naval da Graciosa**, Cais da Barra. This is a basic facility with a straightforward menu. It is very pleasant on a summer evening to walk along the coast to the ruined building that you can see in the distance and return to the club for a beer. *Open every day in summer at about 16.30 until closing time, depending on customers. In winter, open earlier every evening.*

BAÍA DA FOLGA

✕ **Restaurante Estrela do Mar** Folga; ☎ 295 712 560. Very simple small restaurant near the harbour. Great atmosphere, very casual, good fish and lobster. *Open throughout the year 07.00–midnight; closed Mon. On summer weekends it is advisable to book.*

PRAIA

✕ **Panificação Graciosense** In the street behind the beach; ☎ 295 712 589. Tables outside, but in the back of the front bar is a super restaurant with nice atmosphere. Menu with lots of fresh fish and seafood, and sells Pedras Branco, the VPRD island wine to accompany. In the bar are all the island's special pastries, plus a lot of other calorific temptations.

CARAPACHO

✕ Dolphin Just above the campsite; ☎ 295 712 014. Modern, simple and good, both restaurant and an open terrace with wide sea view. Fish always very fresh. Very busy on summer weekends.

FONTE DE MONTE

✕ Green Light Signposted from the main road. In a potentially nice situation surrounded by woodland, but the building is new and very ugly, so it is a

⊟ Caterina Where you can get a beer; lovely situation in the village with a terrace between trees immediately overlooking the sea. Plaque commemorating the first landing and settlement of Vasco Gil Sodré in 1450.

missed opportunity. It is included here as you will inevitably hear about it because it is new.

NIGHTLIFE

There is very little nightlife, and what there is is mainly found in Santa Cruz. On summer evenings many islanders gather in the spacious centre of town to stroll and talk until after midnight. There are several bars, some of which have small discos – identified by their music. Near the airport is a discotheque-pub, the **Vila Sacramento**, open at weekends. It has seating beneath trees in a garden, and the dance area inside. One constant pleasure comes from just sitting on a wall above the harbour and listening to the sea, especially if there is moonlight.

FESTIVALS

As with all the other islands there are small festivals throughout the summer but two are of especial interest for the visitor. When the **Espírito Santo** or **Holy Ghost** celebration takes place one can enjoy participating in the island's hospitality, taking the special bread and local wine. This occurs widely over the island, but especially in Santa Cruz, Luz, Guadalupe and São Mateus. The Festival of **Santo Cristo** is celebrated with boat races, *touradas* or bullfights, plus cultural and musical happenings. Santa Cruz really decorates itself for the celebration, and becomes wonderfully busy with visitors from the other islands as well as North American emigrants.

Espírito Santo
Festival of Santo Cristo

seventh Sunday after Easter
early August

SHOPPING

Graciosa wines, of course. Graciosa cheese. *Queijadas da Graciosa*, small cakes delicious with an espresso coffee and rather like a treacle tart mix in a crisp, thin pastry cup. With ingredients of flour, sugar, eggs, milk, butter and *canela e sal*, they make a fantastic energy source when descending calderas. The little factory making them, together with another speciality only to order for weddings, is in Praia and visitors are welcome. The Filnor Supermercado in Santa Cruz has Graciosa products and the Supermacada Melo in Luz has a good range of Graciosa T-shirts and other island memorabilia.

USEFUL NUMBERS

Emergency ☎ 112
Police Santa Cruz; ☎ 295 712 527
Airport information ☎ 295 712 457/8
SATA Air Açores ☎ 295 712 456
Resident doctor ☎ 295 712 525/294

Tourist information Rua da Boavista, Santa Cruz; ☎ 295 712 509
Post office Av Mouzinha Albuquerque, Santa Cruz; Rua Rodrigues Sampaia, Praia.

MUSEUMS By the old harbour in **Santa Cruz** is another splendid **Museum of the Azores**, established back in 1983 and housed in a late 19th-century traditional building of a wealthy family that they used for storing corn and for making wine. Here you will find, in several rooms devoted to times past, furnished family rooms, various antiques and paintings, the tools of several important trades and all the gear to make wine in the old way. Close by in the road opposite fronting the sea is an annexe where there is a whaling boat and exhibits to do with whaling; because this is so simply done and in a shed by the harbour you get the feeling that if a rocket were to be fired a crew would come rushing down to launch the boat.

At Rochela, in **Vila da Praia**, just up from the beach, is the **Núcleo Marítimo** displaying items to do with fishing and whaling. At **Fontes**, a short drive from Santa Cruz, is a restored working windmill, standing resplendent in the landscape with its white base and bright red cupola. On the road to the **caldera** in a low basalt building with paintwork of traditional Graciosa green is the **Tenda do Ferreiro**, a museum devoted to the work of the blacksmith.

The main museum in Santa Cruz is open weekdays 09.00–112.30 and 14.00–17.30; in June, July and August it's also open weekends 14.00–17.00; ✆ 295 712 429. The other museum branches are open in summer only, or by request for a small group. In winter, when there are few visitors to the island, the museum concentrates its services on the island's schools.

WALKING Two walks are described below, and there is still so little traffic it remains a pleasure to walk along any of the island's roads, especially in the late afternoon/early evening when the shadows bring out the beauty of the island landscapes. I particularly like strolling along the coast from Santa Cruz harbour round to Cais da Barra, perhaps finishing with a beer in the Clube Naval.

BIRDS AND FLOWERS With little high ground and almost everywhere farmed it seems there is not a great deal known, through lack of observation. It is while on Graciosa some years ago I concluded ornithologists had a pretty easy time as I watched a most handsome yacht sail by close inshore with half a dozen pairs of binoculars trained on the low cliffs below me; I later discovered they were a research team engaged upon a long-term study of the roseate tern.

The basalt islet of **Ilhéu da Praia** is a Special Protected Area of 11ha and is said to have one of the richest and most diverse concentrations of seabirds in the Azores with many migratory species. It is a little more than 1km out from Praia. Breeding colonies have declined through human disturbance so while it is nice to know they are there, it is best they are left in peace. However, from the opposite shore or the harbour quay it is easy to observe the action with a good telescope. Another possible area in the far southeast is the Special Protected Area of the **Ilhéu de Baixo** and adjacent rocky shoreline.

Disappointed wildflower enthusiasts will just have to resort to applied botany – the grape vine and its products.

SWIMMING Santa Cruz has a new public open-air swimming pool with all facilities at the near end of the harbour quay.

There are natural and manmade rock pools at **Barro Vermelho**, with showers and changing facilities, at most 2km from Santa Cruz, and the area is backed with tamarisk trees which makes it nicer. **Praia** is Graciosa's only beach and is very popular, although the sand can sometimes disappear after a winter storm. There are changing rooms and showers, and a counter selling ice creams etc; across the road is a café/bar with a restaurant deeper inside – see *Where to eat*, page 130. Carapacho has good access to protected sea swimming.

THERMAL BATHS Carapacho Spa thermal baths (✆ *295 712 272; open 1 May–30 Sep*) was renovated in 1993 and has some 20 individual bathrooms. No appointments are needed for a single bath, which is a very relaxing 15 minutes, the maximum recommended time. Main treatments are for rheumatism and skin disorders; a course of treatment can be arranged with the consulting doctor, and a first appointment should be made with the receptionist.

SEA CRUISING Built in the early part of the last century the *Estefânia Gorreia* played an important part in Graciosa's economy during the whaling period when it went out supporting the small boats, towing the whales back to shore. The last whales were caught in 1974. At Cais da Barra, by the Clube Naval you can see the slipway, and next to it the trying area. The large buildings nearby are all to do with whaling. The boat also played an important role in emergencies, taking people to the hospital in Terceira before the time of the air services. Now beautifully restored, it is planned to operate summer cruises around the island. Check at Clube Naval for possible excursions.

ITINERARY

Full-day tour A day tour by taxi will take in, among other places, the caldera and Furna do Enxofre, the view of Santa Cruz from Sra da Ajuda, Praia, the lighthouse at Pta da Restinga Carapacho, the Serra Branca, Porta Afonso (the track is too rough for cars and you will have to walk) and the lighthouse at Farol da Ponta da Barça with its whale-like rock formation. If you like to swim, I suggest you arrange with your driver a morning itinerary starting at 09.00 and stopping at Carapacho around 12.30. As soon as you arrive book your lunch for say 14.00 at the Dolphin Restaurant, then have a swim and a shower or try the spa. You can arrange to be collected at 16.00 and continue the tour with a stop at Praia for coffee and the museum, to return to Santa Cruz around 17.00–17.30. If you don't want to swim, then take your midday break at Folga and enjoy exploring the harbour and its surrounds and isolation, before continuing again at 15.30 to Praia. About € 100 for a whole day, € 60 for half a day.

Santa Cruz The town focuses on the main square of cobbles laid beneath large metrosideros trees, elms and araucarias, and two large water tanks, originally used for watering cattle accessed by a sloping cobbled road. There are several small bars and cafés nearby, and some shops. The shops are rather scattered and are not always obvious, which is inconvenient if you need something in a hurry, but a most charming and welcome contrast to the ubiquitous commercial form. The taxi rank is in the square, with a line of telephones each housed in a little model windmill. Roads leading off are often lined with grand town houses and domestic buildings with interesting wrought-iron balconies and other architectural detail.

The tiny harbour with its simple quay and a semi-natural swimming pool has an early charm; above is a narrow cobbled street and pairs of seats in the wall. It is on a small and intimate scale. The pool can be rough with a big swell, and there are no facilities. In early summer a frequent sight is several species of seaweed looking like tufts of wool laid out to dry. These are sent to continental Europe for use in medicine and cosmetics, according to quality and species. Gathering these from the sea can be dangerous as lost fishing nets become entangled with the seaweed and swimmers have been caught and drowned. Further round is a modern quay, built in the 1960s. Graciosa's own Terra da Conda winery is adjacent to the Residential Ilha Graciosa, open for tasting and sales.

On the hill above, the Monte da Ajuda, are three chapels: São João, São Salvador and Nossa Senhora da Ajuda, all floodlit at night. The last can be likened to a castle; it is 16th century and has 18th-century *azulejos*. All three are usually closed, but sometimes, if anyone is around to ask, a key may be found. There is a surfaced road to the top where a splendid view can be had of the whole town. A little below the chapels is a small bullring, used during festivities in August; a stepped path leads down and continues on into town.

If you take the coastal road from the square leading to Praia, Rua Infante D Henrique, and walk for about ten minutes you will come to a large building on your right that was until recently a noisy power station. On the same Rua Infante D Henrique is the Associacão de Artesãos da Ilha Graciosa; you will see a silver nameplate on the building. The entrance is towards the end of the side passage. Here you will find the women working, and a display of their completed work and items for sale. It is open weekdays during normal business hours.

Take the turning to the left down to the old harbour, the Cais da Barra. It is a pretty bay with several small boats moored during the summer. Here you will find the Clube Naval building and maybe refreshments. You will soon realise this is on the site of an old fort, Fort Santa Caterina, and there are old rusty cannons still threatening the ghosts of long-dead pirates. Peer over the wall and in the black lava you will discern an old ramp where the whales were once hauled ashore. On the headland beyond (reached by the farm track along the coast) are the remains of a large house and defensive walls, which the sea is slowly undermining. This was once a Jewish settlement, the Fort Deis Judeus, and there is a tiny cemetery in black basalt engraved 'Cemetario Judaica' nearby. Threatening to shatter this historical tranquillity is a proposal to build an overlarge hotel. The walk back along the asphalt road following the coast is a pleasant evening walk.

Praia Praia is a fishing port with a high sea wall, and an arched gateway leading from the beach through the wall into a long street with a café/bar (see under *Where to eat*, page 130). The usual cobbled square is in the road behind, before the Church of São Mateus, rebuilt in the 19th century; inside there are Flemish images of St Matthew and St Peter and a pietà, all 16th century. A second eatery is to be found a short way up the ascending road to the right as you exit from the beach. The beach itself is almost white sand and very popular. In the near distance is the modern Negra Quay, the island's main port.

Inside the caldera and Furna do Enxofre Either take a taxi to the caldera and drive down to the entrance of the Furna do Enxofre ('Sulphur Cavern'), or go by bus from Santa Cruz to Canada Longa on the Luz–Praia road.

As you enter the caldera from the tunnel, made in 1953, a dramatic landscape confronts you. Small meadows are grazed by cows and all around cryptomeria forest climbs the steeply enclosing slopes towards the sky. The road soon forks, to the left down to a picnic site, the right down to the entrance of the Furna do Enxofre (*the kiosk is open 10.00–16.00 weekdays, 11.00–16.00 weekends; nominal entrance fee*). For walkers there is a short cut through the woods, which leaves through a gap in the wall on the left-hand side at the only hairpin bend in the road and which descends quite steeply to the entrance kiosk. Please note the gas emissions are closely monitored and sometimes it may be too dangerous to visit; more likely in winter. Unfortunately there is no way of knowing this until you get to the entrance.

The best time to visit is between 11.00 and 14.00 when sunlight enters. Descend a concrete spiral staircase of 184 steps to the cave floor. This was officially opened on 30 July 1939, a great improvement over the rope ladder used on the first descent by the Prince of Monaco 60 years earlier. It seems that it was built to enable farmers to get water for their animals. The narrow opening allows a few ferns and mosses to grow. A little into the cave is a small gently bubbling mud pool, sounding rather sinister in the darkness. The ropes preventing further descent into the cavern result from the deaths of two visiting sailors some years ago who were overcome by an unexpected emission of sulphurous fumes deeper inside the cave. There is a lake, and at one time a rowing boat enabled further exploration when the lake was 130m across and 15m deep. In recent years the lake has gone down 11m, and there is speculation there may be an underground connection with the thermal area of Carapacho. The floor of the lake is below sea level.

After leaving the cavern, a day can be spent very happily exploring and enjoying the peace of the caldera. Alternatively, see *Walk 1* below.

Ilhéu da Baleia If you walk out of Santa Cruz along the north coast you first pass what was once the main vine-growing area and a stretch of coastline that is a popular bathing area among the rocks near the few houses of **Barro Vermelho**. Beyond this you come to **Ponta da Barca**, with its lighthouse, about 5km from town. Close to the shore is a rocky islet that looks, with a little imagination, like a whale; there may be some seabirds as well. It is a walk along the road, but there is little traffic; in summer the best time to do this is in the cool of the evening.

View of the other islands The best and most readily accessible view is from the main road as it skirts the Serra Branca following the south coast between Luz and Ribeirinha. Pico, São Jorge, Faial and Terceira can all be seen on a clear day.

WALKS

There are two walks, one taking you through ancient agricultural land, old gardens and woodland, the other going round the outside of the caldera with wonderful views of the island. This can also be done by taxi. There is really so little traffic that you can walk with pleasure along all the roads, providing the day is not too hot.

WALK I AROUND THE OUTSIDE OF THE CALDERA, AND DOWN TO THE COAST (*Time: about 2½ hours; distance: roughly 7km*) Although the route is along a wide, intermittently tarmac-surfaced road, there is hardly any traffic. As you encircle the caldera the view is constantly changing and it becomes a very rewarding walk.

If you are coming from the caldera, leave the tunnel and walk down the road for a short distance to find the road going off on your left. If you have a taxi, your driver will put you down at this road junction. If coming by bus, get off at Canada Longa, on the Luz–Praia road, and walk up the asphalt road leading to the caldera until you reach the turn-off.

About 100m along this road, as it climbs upwards to meet the road that encircles the outside of the caldera, you will pass a small *furna* (cavern), the Furna do Abel. When you reach the encircling road, turn right. You are accompanied down to the coast by constantly changing tranquil views over pastures divided by a jigsaw of stone walls and farm tracks and scattered white houses. After about 3.5km take the wide road, now surfaced, down to Fenais. At Fenais you have a choice: turn left to walk along the road to Praia, which takes about an hour, or turn right for the longer walk to Carapacho (although this might prove tedious). There are restaurants and good swimming at both Praia and Carapacho.

WALK 2 ALMAS TO PEDRAS BRANCAS (*Time: about 3 hours; distance: roughly 6km*) This walk takes you into old rural Graciosa on a trail of ancient farm roads and past now deserted homes and gardens.

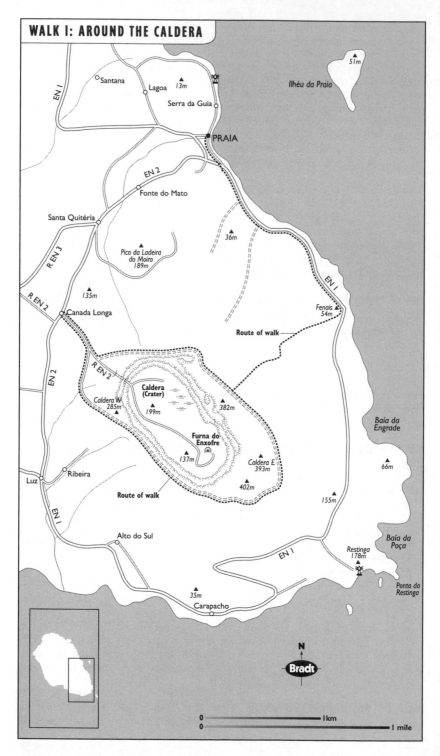

WALK I: AROUND THE CALDERA

Santana
Lagoa
13m
Serra da Guia
PRAIA

51m
Ilhéu da Praia

EN 1

EN 2
Fonte do Mato

Santa Quitéria

R EN 3

R EN 2

36m

Pico da Ladeira
do Moiro
189m

135m

Canada Longa

EN 1

Fenais
54m

Route of walk

R EN 2

Caldera
(Crater)

Caldera W
285m

199m

382m

Baía da
Engrade

Furna do
Enxofre

EN 2

137m

Caldera E
393m

66m

Luz

Ribeira

402m

Alto do Sul

155m

Baía da
Poça

EN 1

EN 1

Route of walk

Restinga
178m

Ponta da
Restinga

35m
Carapacho

N

Bradt

0 ———————— 1km
0 ———————————— 1 mile

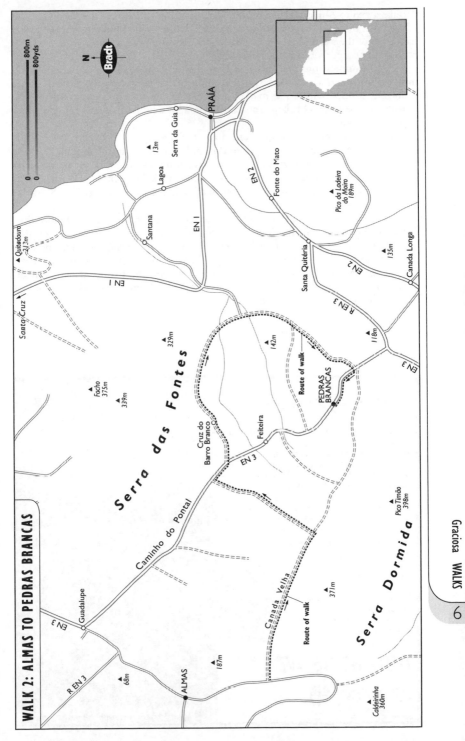

WALK 2: ALMAS TO PEDRAS BRANCAS

Bradt

N

0 800m
0 800yds

PRAÍA

Serra da Guia
13m

Lagoa

Santana

Quitadouro
213m

Santa Cruz

EN 1

EN 1

Fonte do Mato

EN 2

Pico da Ladeira
do Moiro
189m

Santa Quitéria

EN 2

Canada Longa
135m

R EN 3

118m

EN 3

329m

Serra das Fontes

142m

Route of walk

PEDRAS
BRANCAS

Focho
375m

339m

Cruz do
Barro Branco

Feiteira

EN 3

Caminho do Pontal

Pico Timão
398m

Guadalupe

EN 3

Canada Velha

Serra Dormida

371m

Route of walk

R EN 3

68m

187m

ALMAS

Calderinha
360m

Take a taxi to Almas and ask for the Canada Velha which is at the far end of the village; it is by a *casa da água*, or water house, a whitewashed building on the right-hand side of the road. Opposite is a path between stone walls with a concrete lamp post on the corner – this is the Canada Velha.

Fifteen minutes into the walk you join a wide farm road; continue left. At 20 minutes go down a small grassy track going off to your left, the Canada Jorge Nunes, identified with a red-marked post. At 35 minutes you come out on the asphalt road between Guadalupe and the caldera, by a house painted grey and white with green doors.

Immediately opposite is another small track going up between stone walls climbing the Serra das Fontes. Ignore this and turn right up the asphalt road. As you go over the rise in the road in about five minutes you will see an araucaria growing in the middle of the road. Take the track branching off to the left, downhill, passing cottages and high stone walls and then small fields. The Serra das Fontes is on your left.

At 45 minutes a track comes in from the left by a deserted house. Ignore this, but soon the track forks and here you turn right, into quite dense woodland that has invaded old stone-walled enclosures. The track becomes quite wide and after about an hour following this track through the wood you come to a large pig farm hidden amongst the trees. Soon after it emerges onto the main Guadalupe road. Turn left, and shortly you will walk down into Pedras Brancas to find a welcoming bar where you can ring for a taxi.

7

São Jorge

Town of Velas so beautiful
Leaning on the sea side
More beautiful I have yet to see
Not kissed by the moonlight

Oh, island of infinitive grace
Far away from you, thinking with obsessive thoughts
My longing has no end
In my beating heart

The days: eternity
In the heart separation ...
being more 'cold' in the friendship,

is more 'warm' the absence to be alone ...
when the sweetest is the missing
the heart is more crucified.

Anselmo da Silveira, Angra, November 1949.
On *azulejo*, in the town garden, Velas.

A friend of mine in Velas greets his visitors with 'Welcome to São Jorge, my island with 10,000 people and over 20,000 cattle'. Known widely beyond its shores for its delicious, strong, Cheddar-like cheese, São Jorge's many other attributes are far less recognised. Every visitor will react in his or her own way to each island they see, but to me São Jorge is an island of mystery. Perhaps because, before ever setting foot, I saw it first across the channel from Pico, a long cliff wall rising from the sea and invariably disappearing into cloud or mist. I also caught glimpses from Graciosa, Terceira and Faial. Finally, one summer, I went across in a small boat from São Roque to Velas and watched with fascination as the slow voyage gave diminishing detail of Pico's coast behind me and an increasing but narrowing view ahead of São Jorge and of the little port and main town of Velas. Approaching the harbour I could not but be aware of the huge presence of Pico Mountain behind me now that I was distant from it, its sharp cone at the forefront of the island, the high plateau behind like a girl's long hair in the wind or like the carved figure on the prow of an ancient sailing ship. Trying to look in opposite directions at the same time, Velas harbour became prettier with every chug of the engine. Tying up at the quay, the imposing gateway and walls dating from the time of pirates promised quiet pleasure. While my bag was whipped away in a truck to the hotel some little distance away, I walked the few metres into town; narrow streets, small shops, the main church, some manor houses, a little square or two, the sound of voices coming from smoky bars. Clouds hung heavily upon the uplands beyond,

SÃO JORGE

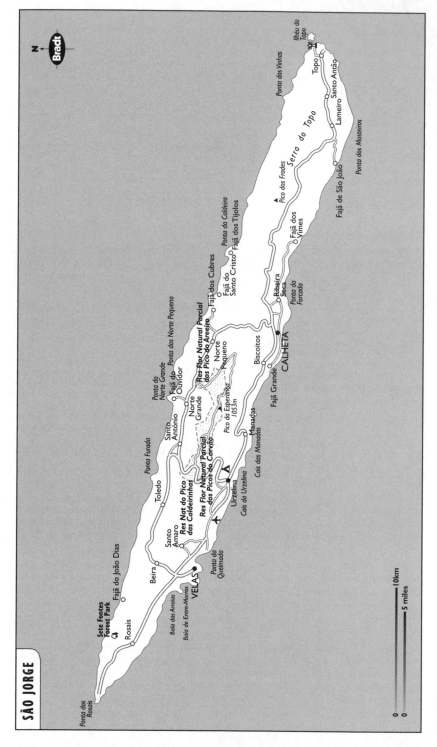

N

Bradt

Ponta dos Rosais

Sete Fontes Forest Park

Rosais

Fajã do João Dias

Baía dos Arrais

Baía de Entre-Morros

Beira

Santo Amaro

Toledo

Ponta Furada

Ponta da Queimada

VELAS

Res Nat do Pico das Caldeirinhas

Santo António

Urzelina

Cais da Urzelina

Norte Grande

Ponta do Norte Grande

Fajã do Ouvidor

Ponta dos Norte Pequeno

Res Flor Natural Parcial dos Picos do Carvão

Pico da Esperança 1053m

Manadas

Cais das Manadas

Norte Pequeno

Res Flor Natural Parcial dos Pico do Areeiro

Fajã dos Cubres

Fajã do Santo Cristo

Ponta da Caldeira

Fajã dos Tijolos

Biscoitos

Fajã Grande

CALHETA

Ribeira Seca

Ponta da Forcada

Fajã dos Vimes

Pico dos Frades

Pico do Espigão

Serra do Topo

Ponta da Caldeira

Fajã de São João

Ponta dos Mosteiros

Lameiro

Santo Antão

Topo

Ponta dos Vinhas

Ilhéu do Topo

10km

5 miles

0

0

concealing them in spite of my coming closer. Perhaps tomorrow the clouds would repent and reveal all.

Even on dull days there is an intense pleasure to be derived from walking along little-used farm roads in utter, total silence with stone walls, hedgerows, cows, and occasional trees giving depth to the stage. In sunshine and with a deep-blue sea beyond, the cliff paths are magnificent for scenery, combining landscape grandeur and intimate vignettes together with unexpected human interests while steep descents to *fajãs* on tiny tracks give a tender appreciation of the hardships of the islanders.

Although it is an island with good walks, graded unsurfaced roads have in recent years ramified throughout the island and in reasonable weather allow the motorist to explore many of the previously hidden beauties of the island. The best of these are shown on the latest maps prepared by the tourist offices, and there are other newer ones not shown. Many very happy days can be had exploring these back roads as well as the little-trafficked main roads from which side roads lead into small, often charming villages.

On a full moon the island comes into its own; the channel across to Pico reflects and shimmers, while the great black unequal-sided triangle of Pico massively provides the theatre setting. In Velas, drop down to Neto's Bar by the harbour, and on the tiny terrace, if you are lucky, thrill to the haunting mew of Cory's shearwaters as they fly just above your head in the dark.

HIGHLIGHTS

By car, São Jorge is an island on which to spend slow days relaxing, stopping to explore the accessible little settlements along the coast, and to enjoy the scenery. The *fajã*, while not unique to São Jorge, is a very special feature of this island and their microclimates and settlements are most rewarding to explore. There are numerous viewpoints, the two ports of Velas and Calheta, lovely sites for picnics, and opportunities to make easy short walks. In Brown's guidebook of 1926 he laconically says: 'The Lisbon steamers touch alternately every fortnight. There are no carriage roads.' Now there are plenty to take you to lovely places.

GENERAL BACKGROUND

GEOGRAPHY São Jorge is cigar-shaped, 56km long and at most 8km wide. A long ridge running along its length characterises the island, arising abruptly from the sea and ascending to Pico da Esperança (1,053m) at about the centre. The average height of this central ridge is 700m. Unlike all the other islands, there are no dominating calderas. The Serra do Topo making up the eastern third of the island is considered to be the oldest part, formed up to 550,000 years ago. Much more recently, about 30,000 years ago, came Rosais in the far west, with the central part 6,000 years later.

The coasts are very steep, in places over 400m, particularly on the north side, and small rocky platforms, *fajãs*, occur at the base of these cliffs. *Fajãs* are formed either by lava flowing into the sea, or from fallen debris from the cliffs above, and are valued for their microclimate and the cultivation of vegetables and fruit, as well as for overwintering cattle. São Jorge has 46 in all – 30 on the north coast and 16 on the south – but many were abandoned following the 1980 earthquake and now only the larger and safer ones are inhabited. The north coast is more eroded than the south and the sea has cut back the cliffs to a greater height, while to the south the slope is gradual. One theory is that a huge slice of the island sheared off from the north coast, creating the almost vertical cliffs. However, much of the land

7

surface is above 300m and villages are at much higher altitudes than anywhere else in the Azores, so that they can be nearer the fields. It is 16km across the channel from Pico, 30km from Graciosa and 34km from Terceira.

HISTORY Velas was founded around the middle of the 15th century and developed sufficiently within 50 years to be given its town charter with an economy based on exporting wool and archil, a lichen used for dyeing, and growing wheat and grapes. Three centuries later oranges became an important export crop, with schooners coming to Urzelina from England to load the boxes of fruit. As with some of the other islands, the lack of a good harbour meant isolation until the airport was built. The principal products are now cattle and, most importantly, cheese. Nine factories now make the famous São Jorge cheese. Like all the other islands, São Jorge suffered from the predations of pirates; it also suffered earthquakes and three major volcanic eruptions, in 1580, 1757 and 1808.

GETTING THERE AND AWAY

BY PLANE SATA Air Açores has regular flights between São Jorge and Terceira and São Miguel.

BY FERRY In summer there are often twice-daily crossings between Faial (Horta) via Pico (Madalena and Cais do Pico) and São Jorge (Velas); single fare around €13, return €17; time: 105 minutes. On certain days expect services between Terceira and Velas, taking 4½ hours. For details of the current ferry service please check the website (*www.transmacor.pt*).

Tickets can be purchased from two offices on the island situated on the quays of Velas (*Gare Marítima do Porto de Velas;* ⑴ *295 432 225*) and of Calheta (*Porto da Calheta;* ⑴ *295 416 490*).

BY YACHT There are harbour moorings in Velas, but no facilities. Contact Clube Naval de Velas (⑴ *295 432 169*).

GETTING AROUND

There is a limited **bus** service which very much serves to bring passengers to and from work, some leaving Velas in the afternoon and returning the following morning. However, it is possible to do some touring, giving you time in Calheta and Rosario. Buses leave from the main square and you should confirm the times with your hotel.

VELAS–CALHETA On Wednesdays and Fridays a bus leaves Velas at 08.30 and via the north coast arrives Calheta at 09.30. The return bus leaves Calheta at 15.30, arriving Velas 16.30.

VELAS–ROSARIO On Monday through to Friday a bus leaves Velas at 09.45 and arrives at Rosais Church 10.15 and returns at 14.45, arriving in Velas 15.15. You can ask the driver to put you down at the road leading to Rosais Forest Park, to save you walking back from the church. For the return, it is better to get the bus at the church.

Otherwise you can use **taxis** or **car hire**. If you want to make a tour of the island by taxi, or use taxis to access the walks, then it is better to book it through the local travel agency who will ensure you have a driver to explain things, and who will know the walks. Taxi prices start around €60 for a half-day tour, €100 for a full day going down to Topo. If you are travelling alone or as a couple in summer it is possible to join with others and share a minibus: contact Aquarius (see *Travel agents*, below).

CAR HIRE

Rent-a-car Almeida Azevedo Av Livramento, Velas; ✆ 295 430 159
Rent-a-car Ribeiro e Sá Rua Infante D Henrique, Velas;

✆ 295 432 470; e rentacarribeiroesa@hotmail.com
Urzivelas Largo Dr Duarte Sá, Urzelina; ✆ 295 414 101; e urzivelas.commercio.aluguerauto@clix.pt

MOTORSCOOTER HIRE

Diogo Soares at Hospedaria Austrália Rua Teofila Braga 25, Velas; ✆ 965 708 954;

www.acores.com/australia

TRAVEL AGENTS

Aquarius Rua Infante D Henrique, Velas; ✆ 295 432 006; e aquariustravel@mail.telepac.pt;

www.viagensaquarius.com. Will arrange tours, walks and boat trips.

🏠 WHERE TO STAY

VELAS

🏠 **Hotel São Jorge***** (58 rooms) Rua Dr Machado Pires, Velas; ✆ 295 430 100; e hotelsaojorge@clix.pt; www.acores.com/hotels.jorge. In a good situation overlooking the sea and across the channel to Pico and a few mins' walk from the centre of town. Rooms have balconies, TV, AC, swimming pool, bar, b/fast room but no restaurant; includes airport transfers. *Dbl* € 69–98, *sgl* € 59–85.

🏠 **Pensão Neto** (23 rooms) (3a) Rua Cons Dr José Pereira, Velas; ✆ 295 412 338. Close to the harbour, TV, bar and small seawater swimming pool.

🏠 **Pensão Livramento Casa de Hospedes** (12 rooms) Av do Livramento, Velas; ✆ 295 430 020. Near the fire station.

🏠 **Casa do António** (8 rooms) Rua Infante D Henrique, 9800-554 Velas; ✆ 295 430 330; e antonio@viagensaquarius.com; www.viagensaquarius.com. This is a wonderfully eccentric and personal well-designed, well-built new extension to an old building so there are quirky stairs and corners and the whole thing comes together in a mock Art Deco style. A really fun place and right by the harbour with, in summer, Cory's shearwaters whipping by overhead to their nesting sites in the nearby cliff face. The owner/designer has invested considerable thought into making guests comfortable, and the rooms are all en suite. There is a b/fast room (with excellent varied b/fast) and a small elevated garden. *Dbl* € 55–80, *sgl* € 39–64.

🏠 **Quinta do Canaval** (21 rooms) (CC) On Baía de Entre os Morros, near Velas; ✆ 295 412 981; e info@quintadocanaval.com; www.quintadocanaval.com. High vantage point over sports ground and camping site and across the channel to Pico. Offers guided walks, horseriding and sailing. Rooms, in the house or in terraced cottages, some with attached kitchen and dining room, dbls and triples. When all let, it could feel very congested. Small pool. Restaurant for residents. In Nov 2005, looking very much in need of some tender loving care. *Dbl* € 60–130, *sgl* € 40–68 inc b/fast.

🏠 **Quinta do Canário** (3 rooms) (CC) Caminho do Carregadouro 16, Santo Amaro, 9800-345 Velas; ✆ 295 412 800/1; e geral@quintadocanario.com; www.quintadocanario.com. About 10 mins' drive from Velas, close to the airport, a really short walk from the sea. Original house built for a wealthy farmer in 1884, modernised and extended in 2004 by the present owners whose home this is. The high-quality contemporary treatment has been done in style and merges well with the old, creating a gracious whole. Land to the rear includes a terraced garden area with nice pool and view across to Pico, banana garden, orchard and a summer house plus beehives providing honey for b/fast. In the house there is 1 dbl room with private bathroom, and 2 dbl rooms with a shared bathroom, a comfortable lounge. There is also a self-contained suite in a small building in the garden. Light meals are available in the evenings, and more elaborate with advanced warning.

CALHETA

🏠 **Pensão Solmar**, Rua Domingos d'Oliveira 4, 9850-036 Calheta; ✆ 295 416 120

CAMPING

⚐ Fajã Grande Calheta; ☎ 295 416 324; f 295 416 437. Close to the sea, there is a good natural rock pool with European Blue Flag status. The campsite is supervised 24hrs, with all facilities inc a children's playpark, and tents can be hired. There are also bungalows for 4 persons. It is very attractive with a pergola and belvedere, a great place to sit and watch the sunset. To find the campsite take a steep cement road down to the sea; there is no signpost. Shops are very limited, there is no bakery, but there is a kiosk and a snack bar.

⚐ Urzelina camping ground ☎ 295 414 401. All amenities and resident warden. Swimming pool and natural rock pools. Close by are several windmills.

⚐ Velas now has a new camping site, located near the football ground in the Baía de Entre os Morros and about 15 mins' walk from town. With simple facilities, but it appeared to me in winter to be rather bleak, without trees and could be hot and dusty in summer.

✖ WHERE TO EAT

This is difficult because it seems that more than on any other island, the restaurants keep changing with some closing and new ones opening. Choice has improved enormously in the past few years and at the end of 2005 there were 14 restaurants on the island, plus numerous small snack bars. There is also the lovely story from some years ago of several hundred visitors arriving by ferry for the day to attend a festival who found all the restaurants closed because their owners were also attending the festival! However, in Velas, always reliable over many years and open every day, is the **Restaurante Velense** down by the harbour, adjacent to the tourist office. Velas is a nice tiny place to explore, and you will find enough choice of places to eat.

If you want to eat outside of Velas, then here are some ideas, otherwise ask at your hotel or keep a look out as you travel around:

SANTA AMARO

✖ **Fornos de Lava** Travessa de S Tiago, Santa Amaro, not far from Velas; ☎ 295 432 415. A delightfully rural place, with luxuriant views over pastures; the owners are really trying hard and, a true novelty for the Azores, they are growing their own vegetables and herbs for the restaurant.

FAJÃ DE SANTO AMARO

✖ **Restaurante da Escola Profissional das Velas** 100m from the airport, on the main road; ☎ 295 430 240. In a stone building: serves a normal menu and also traditional food, but for this in winter advance warning is required. Operated by the local school of tourism, so student staff are nervous but usually efficient.

URZELINA

✖ **Manazanho's** On the south coast road just 200m from Urzelina's little port, heading southeast; ☎ 295 414 484. It offers a good selection of dishes, as well as a good buffet on some days. Very popular at weekends with the local people.

✖ **Fajã do Ouvidor** Near Norte Grande
✖ **Café Amilcar** Close to the harbour; ☎ 295 417 156. This simple café is open every day all year and offers good fish — the owner is also a fisherman.

CALHETA

✖ **Os Amigos** Ponta de São Lourenço, in Calheta near the museum; ☎ 295 416 421. Café restaurant. Good food and service, sea view.

RIBEIRA SECA

✖ **Café – Ponto de Encantra** Canada dos Vales, on the main road just before Ribeira Seca; ☎ 295 416 240. Does a buffet meal *Almoco e Jantar*. Inviting restaurant with views across to Pico. *Open 07.30–midnight every day except Tue.*

NIGHTLIFE

Discotec Zodiac (*not far from the Hotel Velas;* ☎ *295 412 677*) is the main option. Otherwise, uniquely, there are several small pavement cafés where you can listen to the shearwaters.

FESTIVALS

Velas is making quite a local name for itself with the *Semana Cultural* or week-long cultural festival held in early July to coincide with the annual Horta–Velas–Horta yacht race, when numerous events are staged including cultural conferences and exhibitions as well as more usual pop, rock and folk music and bullfights. There is another in April. Also in July, in Calheta, is the biennial festival with processions, cultural and sports events. The dates of many festivals vary each year, so please check with the tourist information office. There is also some criticism of the way these festivals have developed, with too much imported rock music to the detriment of traditional Azorean culture.

Festa de São Jorge (Velas)	week around 23 April
Espírito Santo	June
Semana Cultural (Velas)	first week of July
Festa de São Tiago (Ribeira Seca and Calheta)	fourth week of July
Festa do Sant'Ana (Velas)	last week of July
Festival de Julho (Calheta)	third week of July
Festa de N Sra Rosário (Velas and Norte Pequeno)	middle of August
Festa da Caldeira do Sr Santo Cristo (Calheta)	first week of September
Festa de N Sra das Dores (Velas)	second/third week of September
Festa de N Sra das Neves (Velas)	third week of September
Festa de N Sra Rosário (Topo)	second week of September
Festa de Santa Catarina (Calheta)	last week of November

USEFUL NUMBERS

Emergency ☎ 112
Police Velas; ☎ 295 412 339
Hospital Velas; ☎ 295 412 122
Tourist information office Rua Conselheiro Dr José Pereira, Velas; ☎ 295 412 440. *Open Mon–Fri*

19.00–12.30 and 14.00–17.30.
SATA Air Açores Rua de Santo André, Velas; ☎ 295 412 125
Airport information ☎ 295 412 395

WHAT TO SEE AND DO

MUSEUMS
Sacred Art Museum Housed in an annex of the Matriz de São Jorge Church, Velas. Exhibits include sacred images, silver, censers and monstrances.

Museum of São Jorge Occupying a house built in 1811 in Calheta. There is a permanent exhibition about the history and ethnography of the island and a supporting library.

WALKING São Jorge has some memorable walks and they are long established so fairly well-worn, although waymarking and maintenance leave much to be desired. See *Walks*, page 151, for details of six walks.

BIRDS AND FLOWERS The most interesting areas are the famous *fajãs*. Best known is **Fajã dos Cubres** on the north coast east of Norte Pequeno, formed largely by the 1757 earthquake and subsequent erosion and with a biologically rich very indented lagoon. Groundwater enters the lagoon but causeways built across it have created two habitats, essentially marine to the west and fresh water in the east. It is among the most important wetland habitats in the Azores. Growing amongst the pain-inflicting sharp rush, *Juncus acutus*, is goldenrod, *Solidago sempervirens*, or cubres after which the *fajã* is named. Wild celery, wild carrot, orache and the submerged herb beaked tasselweed are among the varied plants. Eurasian coot and greenshank, snipe, terns and a long list of rarities can make this a rewarding site for birds, especially coming as it does at the end of a beautiful cliff walk – see *Walk 6*, page 157.

A little further eastwards along the coast is the **Fajã de Santo Cristo**. Its lagoon is well known for being the only place in the Azores where cockles are found, but these delicious molluscs are now protected. It is also one of the best places for surfing. This nature reserve has one of the largest populations of endemic scabious, *Scabiosa nitens*.

Ilhéu do Topo off the far eastern end of São Jorge is a Special Protected Area because of its birdlife. The islet has in excess of 2,000 Cory's shearwaters among its many breeding seabirds.

At the other island extremity, the high coastal cliffs at **Ponta dos Rosais** support an interesting vegetation that can only without difficulty and danger be glimpsed from a distance. It is an important site for migratory birds and is a passage point for whales, dolphin and turtles.

SWIMMING Remember, natural rock pools are subject to wave action.

Velas Artificial pool, and also natural rock pools near the Hotel Velas

Urzelina Natural pools and harbour swimming with changing facilities. About 100m further on at **Portinhos** is another access to the sea with facilities and a grassy relaxation area.

Fajã Grande Natural rock pool with all facilities

Fajã do Ouvidor Natural swimming pool with facilities near harbour; restaurant

ITINERARIES São Jorge is an attenuated island so to travel everywhere takes a disproportionate amount of time. Many visitors are based in Velas and content themselves with seeing Rosais in the far west, and then a central circuit taking in both north and south coasts but not going further east than Calheta.

Velas Velas, the main town of São Jorge, remains very small, and the old part around the pretty harbour has been generally well cared for and is most charming. The narrow backstreets, some fine houses with their wrought-iron balconies, the little shops, and the inviting, intriguing and imposing 18th-century gateway, or Portão do Mar, all go to make a pleasing whole. You will even find a boat or two parked on the road along with the cars. Some of the little streets have been very prettily pedestrianised, and paved in the traditional manner of small black setts with designs in white depicting activities of the island. One street is now a pretty shopping area, with hanging baskets filled with flowers, a good cake shop at one end and the attractive town square at the other, and a fine replica now replaces the time-battered classic old bandstand. At a little distance the unmistakable and very modern community building declares Velas is really part of the 21st century; inside is the public library, meeting rooms and a splendid 220-seat theatre. There is an imposing parish church, the Church of São Jorge no less, which has been built and modified from the 17th century and of particular note is the carved wooden retable. The 17th-century Church of Nossa Senhora da Conceição was a former Franciscan monastery and is now cared for by nuns and well worth seeing. Tucked away in one of the small streets is a museum of sacred art, showing Indo-Portuguese items and silver altar vessels. Built upon a *fajã*, the harbour and old town is beautifully set against surrounding high cliffs.

Rosais Rosais itself is a very linear village running along the road, but this is also the name given to the whole of the end of the island west of Velas. After you pass through the village you will come to the signposted Miradouro Pica da Velho, and at 493m this gives a commanding view over this part of the island. The viewpoint is generously planted with camellias, hydrangeas, azaleas and agapanthus so it is also very pretty when they flower.

Farol dos Rosais This lighthouse is at the far western end of the island, and is also the end of the road. It is now abandoned, after the earthquake of 1980 made the cliffs unstable. Be very careful if you walk near the lighthouse as there are deep holes in the ground.

Sete Fontes Forest Park Here, at the Seven Fountains, the forestry department has laid out an attractive park with ornamental planting sheltered and shaded by trees. There are picnic tables, a barbecue area, and some animals. The surrounding countryside is a mixture of meadows and forestry. Many of the roads are unsurfaced, and a relaxing day can be spent exploring the area on foot.

The central part of the island between Velas and Calheta Leaving Velas, take the road to the north coast signposted to Norte Grande, and go first to **Beira**, to visit one of the nine cheese factories here. It is open seven days a week – cows do not stop producing for weekends – and in the morning you can see the whole manufacturing process. Founded in 1927, this is the oldest co-operative cheese factory in the Azores and in the whole of Portugal. You will find it on the far side of Beira, clearly signed Cooperativa Leitaria da Beira. Here 6,000 litres of milk are converted into 60 cheeses each weighing 10kg, taking three months to mature. In another building, 150,000kg of cheese can be stored. There is a blind-tasting room for quality control and that not up to the standard to carry the São Jorge label is sold simply as island cheese. All the nine factories join together to co-ordinate their exports; container ships take full containers to Lisbon and lesser quantities to São Miguel, Santa Maria and Flores, while smaller trading vessels supply Terceira and Graciosa and the ferry Pico and Faial.

Continuing on the north road you pass through **Toledo**, now just a tiny village, which was probably first settled by Spanish immigrants soon after King Philip of Spain invaded Portugal. The settlement of **Santo António** was destroyed in the earthquake of 1980, and rebuilt.

Norte Grande is the largest village in the north. Do visit the church, Nossa Senhora das Neves, Our Lady of the Snows, dated 1762; it has a quiet and beautiful interior with splendid *azulejos* and modern stained-glass windows. Note the weathervane in the shape of a fish; this is peculiar to São Jorge and is the symbol adopted by early Christians. Take the road steeply descending by the side of the church and signposted to **Fajã do Ouvidor**. Stop first at the *miradouro* for a fine view of the village below; on a clear day you can see Graciosa and to your right,

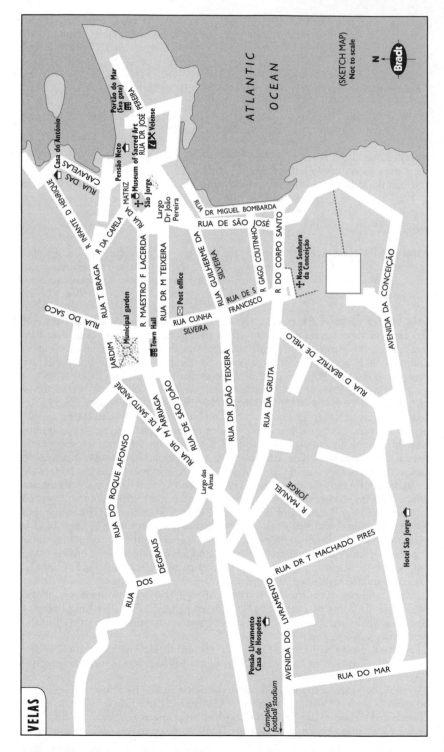

VELAS

Casa do António

RUA DAS CARAVELAS

Casa do António

RUA T BRAGA

R INFANTE D HENRIQUE

RUA DO SACO

R DA CAPELA

Pensão Neto

Portão do Mar
(Sea gate)

Museum of Sacred Art

RUA DR JOSÉ PEREIRA

✠ RUA DA MATRIZ
São Jorge

Largo
Dr João
Pereira

✗ Velense

ATLANTIC

OCEAN

RUA DR MIGUEL BOMBARDA

RUA DE SÃO JOSÉ

JARDIM
Municipal garden

R MAESTRO F LACERDA

RUA DR M TEIXEIRA

Town Hall

RUA GUILHERME DA SILVEIRA

RUA DE S FRANCISCO

R GAGO COUTINHO

R DO CORPO SANTO

✠ Nossa Senhora
da Conceição

Post office

RUA CUNHA
SILVEIRA

RUA DR M ARRIAGA

R DE SANTO ANDRÉ

RUA DE SÃO JOÃO

RUA DR JOÃO TEIXEIRA

RUA DA GRUTA

RUA D BEATRIZ DE MELO

AVENIDA DA CONCEIÇÃO

RUA DO ROQUE AFONSO

RUA DOS DEGRAUS

Largo das
Almas

R MANUEL JORGE

RUA DR T MACHADO PIRES

Hotel São Jorge

Pensão Livramento
Casa de Hospedes

AVENIDA DO LIVRAMENTO

RUA DO MAR

Camping,
football stadium

N

Bradt

(SKETCH MAP)
Not to scale

DECORATIVE PAVING

Decorative paving has long been a feature of Moorish Spain and Portugal, although today it is the latter where it is most popular. It first appeared in the Azores in 1825 when the governor had it laid in front of his residence in Horta. The idea soon spread but most of the present paving dates from the 1940s. The black stones are of course basalt from abundant local sources but the white are limestone and have to be imported. A full container load costs around €4,000. On mainland Portugal the situation is reversed, and white dominates. A knapping-hammer is used to shape the individual stones which are then laid on a thick layer of sand and dry cement, with the gaps filled with dry sand. It is always fascinating to watch the paviors at work for they apply their considerable skill in a seemingly most nonchalant manner to give great charm to the archipelago's streets.

further along the coast, Fajã da Ribeira de Areia. Go down to the *fajã* where there is a small harbour and a natural swimming pool. From the harbour yams were once exported to Graciosa in exchange for clay roof tiles. There are waterfalls along the coast; if you are enjoying a gloriously sunny day and a period without rain, bad luck! You will not see much. Come instead when it is raining in torrents and you will see good waterfalls. The lava here came from what is now called Pico da Esperança, 1,053m, which you can see high above you, but the eruption is lost in pre-history. There are two short walks you can do here over the lava, taking the path next to the house with the new conspicuous stone driveway.

In the middle of the next village, **Ribeira da Areia**, there is a stone sign pointing the way down to Fajã da Ribeira da Areia; it takes about 45 minutes to descend, somewhat longer to climb back up. It makes you appreciate just how isolated some of these communities were and still are.

Move on to the large village of **Norte Pequeno** where the road turns south to Calheta. Look out for the asphalt road signposted down to Fajã dos Cubres; from the top there is probably one of the finest views of the coast. The *fajã* beyond is Fajã da Caldeira de Santo Cristo, another isolated settlement with its nearest road an hour's walk from the road ending below you. Its lagoon is well known for being the only place in the Azores where cockles are found; these delicious molluscs are now protected, but harvested in strictly limited numbers. It is also one of the best places for surfing.

Cross the island to Calheta, but before you get there take the main road left signposted to Topo and then go down to **Ribeira Seca**. On the skyline above you will see five wind turbines generating 20% of the island's energy requirement. The road is very pretty, lined with flowering azaleas, hydrangeas, escallonia and tibouchina shrubs. Near the church is a large private house covered with painted tiles, and a 17m-tall chimney inspired by the Royal Palace at Sintra. It was built in 1905 in French colonial style by Gaspar de Silva, a Hawaiian emigrant who returned very wealthy – the current epidemic of pretentious new building would seem to be nothing new! Another house belonging to him with the same kind of exterior tiles may be seen in the centre of Velas. Francesco Lacerdo, the Azores' greatest composer and friend of Claude Debussy, was born here in 1869 and later lived in Urzelina.

Go along the lower road into **Calheta**, in size second only to Velas. Calheta developed as a town, but Velas has the better harbour and so became the principal town, later reinforced by the construction of its nearby airport. There remains a healthy rivalry. Calheta is on Fajã Grande, one of the flat coastal plains around the island. There is a recently extended busy harbour, with its small fishing fleet, near which may be seen an old tuna factory. There are public toilets, post office, and a café/bar serving light meals. The museum is open Tuesday–Friday 10.00–12.00 and 14.00–17.00, Saturday and Sunday 14.00–17.30, marginally longer in summer. The tourist information office is next to the municipal offices, open weekdays.

Continuing on the lower road from Calheta you pass through **Fajã Grande** itself where upon leaving on the left is a blue-and-white-painted factory that cans tuna fish in an old style; the brand name is Santa Catarina and is held to be among the best; production is seasonal and come winter the shops quickly sell out.

Following the main road back to Velas, you will come to **Manadas** (meaning a group of cows) where you must stop to see the 18th-century parish church dedicated to Santa Bárbara. It is very small and in a most beautiful setting by the sea adjacent to the ruined remains of a fort that once defended the little harbour. This gem of Azorean Baroque is the finest in the archipelago, and the interior has remained almost unchanged for many generations. There are splendid tiles telling the story of Santa Bárbara, a rich gilt carved altar and a cedarwood ceiling. Legend has it that in 1485 a sailor, Joaquim António da Silveira, found an image of Santa Bárbara in a wooden box off the coast of São Jorge and thought a church in her honour should be built. Work started in 1510, but it was later enlarged to its present form about 1770 and of the original there remains a window and a font. The church may be locked, but someone in the nearby houses just past the bottom of the hill on the right will know who has the key!

At **Terreiros** is a small harbour with picnic tables and two restaurants. **Urzelina** suffered tremendously in the eruption of 1808 when the lava flowed down and buried everything except the church tower and this remains today as a monument to the buried village. Many of the villagers sheltered inside the church and were either buried or suffocated. It is on the right, close to the main road, surrounded by a pretty little garden. Overlooking the small harbour is a seating area with two commemorative stones. The first concerns a former harbour master. A British schooner, the *Tamar Queen*, anchored offshore and was boarded by the harbour master Amaro Soares but bad weather quickly blew up and the ship set sail for England. Sadly, Senhor Soares was murdered, and the crew later punished. The second gives the names of early settlers. Immediately above the harbour are the remains of an old Portuguese fort, now a summer café/bar. On the harbour's other side is a house with a large tile picture on its wall; this was once a temporary store for oranges before they were exported to England. There are some manor houses in the village that reflected the wealth of the orange farmers. Urzelina gets its name from the lichen that was such an important export in the early days after settlement. A small ethnographic museum by the harbour is open in summer.

Ribeira do Nabo is a small village beyond Urzelina where the Cooperativa Artesanto Sra da Encarnação offers a good range of nicely handmade goods including knitted pullovers, appliqué, macramé, ceramics, items in wood, jams and many other things. Before you reach the airport at Queimada there is a road going down to the sea and a very primitive landing place called **Cais da Queimada**. In summer there used to be a boat that ferried between here and Velas. The blackened stone tower that looks as if it might once have been a windmill is an old lime kiln. The best thing though is the sea-level view of Velas, worth seeing if you travel by air and do not come or go by the ferry.

The eastern part of the island To reach **Fajã dos Vimes**, going down from the main road to Topo, is a most beautiful drive though luxuriant forests of largely acacia, the high humidity offering shelter for ferns and mosses. Stop at the Miradouro dos Vimes; 300m below is Fajã Fragueira and in the distance your immediate destination of Fajã dos Vimes. As you further descend note two old watermills and the overhead wires still used today for transporting forage and fuelwood to the houses way below. In the village, find the **Café Nunes**; here they make arabica coffee from beans grown in the village. The plants produce two crops a year. Close by is the small weaving centre where the famous woollen bedspreads are woven. Made with natural colours and traditional designs and looms, and wool imported from Santa Maria and mainland Portugal, they are not only collectors' items but a great pleasure to use. Sadly, there are now only two people weaving and it takes 1½ weeks to make a double bedspread. These cost around €350 and their order books are full, so you must be prepared to wait but you will have an excuse to return to São Jorge, to collect the finished item! Towards the cliff you will see growing many pollarded willows that are used for basket making; *vimes* means withy or osier. From the end of the village there is an obvious footpath eastwards to make the short walk to **Fajã dos Bodes** and its watermill.

Return to the main road and continue eastwards; if you have time, drop down to Fajã de São João with its mixed orchards enjoying the microclimate, the watermills and dragon trees. Back on the main road, you will pass extensive areas of pasture to come to **Santo Antão** and finally **Topo** with its lighthouse. Just off the end is the **Ilhéu do Topo**, a strictly protected sanctuary for birds. The very first settlement on São Jorge was at Topo, but the Serra do Topo so separated the people from the rest of the island that it was easier to go by boat to Terceira for their supplies rather than travel by land.

On the way back to Velas, above Faja dos Vimes, you will see an unsurfaced road going off on your right by the side of the turbine parks. This ranks highly among the many beautiful roads of the Azores, as it winds along through a gentle landscape of small pastures surrounded by hedges, especially lovely in July and August when the hydrangeas are flowering. It is not a long drive, so do stop along the way and enjoy late afternoon shadows and the tranquillity. You will come to a junction. Turn left to Silveira; if you turned right you would go to Norte Pequeno. Soon you will see signs marking the way to the Silveira Forest Park, a beautifully green semi-gardened area to stroll around. Should you arrive earlier in the day, then it is a cool place to enjoy a picnic.

A short drive above Velas From Velas take the short drive up to Santo Amaro and then the dirt road continuing east. Saint Amaro (Sant Maurus or Maur) is famous for the miracle when he rescued a young monk who was drowning in a flooded river near Rome. He brought the boy back to the bank and saw that his own clothes were dry – unnoticed, he had walked on water. Passing through beautiful pasture landscapes, a right fork leads you to a simple *miradouro* or viewpoint giving a marvellous view along the coast to Urzelina, while below you is the airport. Rejoin the main track and it soon becomes asphalt; continue straight on and be intrigued by the tall endemic heather (*Erica azorica*) so abundant here. Ignore the road off to the right, this goes down to Urzelina, and continue to a T-junction. Turn left to Santo António on the north coast, right to Urzelina. Continue straight on, and you follow the route of walk 4, see map, page 154.

WALKS

Given reasonable weather the coastal walk, walk 5, and the walk across to the north coast, walk 6, described below are the finest and just being up on the route of walk 4 with its ever-changing views never ceases to inspire, while the others will certainly not disappoint. Walks 2 and 3, although now largely on asphalt, remain popular and are easily done from Velas.

WALK I SHORT WALK FROM VELAS TO THE SUMMIT OF MORRO GRANDE (*Time: about 1 hour*) This is an ideal walk if you would like to get a good view of Velas, or across the channel to Pico, or to find a sheltered spot to settle down with a book. Morro Grande, 161m, is the volcanic peak overlooking Velas.

The track to the summit where there is an old *vigia* can be seen clearly zigzagging up the hillside. To join the track, simply walk out of Velas past the new housing on the road that leads to the new sports stadium. At the top of the peak there is a small caldera, partly covered by tree growth and grassland.

WALK 2 TERREIRO DA MACELA BACK TO VELAS (*Time: about 1 hour*) An easy walk with views across São Jorge's Channel to Pico through the interesting village of Serroa. Mostly following unsurfaced forest roads which are now changing to asphalt, but notwithstanding this it remains a very popular walk and is therefore included here.

Take a taxi to **Terreiro da Macela**, which is beyond Beira, where there is a little whitewashed church, São Antão.

Begin the walk here, taking the left fork, an unsurfaced forest road leading uphill between cryptomeria and large tree heathers. On your left is **Pico Barroca** with a radio mast on its summit. Soon you will pass on your left a surfaced track leading up to the mast; you can ascend for a good view of this part of the island.

In 2km there is a small road off to the left (walk 3 joins here, approaching from the opposite direction). Take this left-hand road to cross the island, and soon you will have a view over the south coast, with the sun and cloud shadows playing on the sparkling water, with Pico beyond. In about 1km you come to four stone cottages and, where the road forks, you go round to the left. There are tranquil views either side over meadows and grazing cows, and Pico is across the channel. Keep straight on this narrow road to take you to the almost deserted village of Serroa, everyone having been evacuated following the severe earth tremors on São Jorge in 1964. Many people from the village emigrated, and only a few families live here now.

You will come to a fork in the road; keep to the right. Keep descending and for the last kilometre or so the road narrows and becomes an old track. This comes down to the asphalt road coming from Rosais. Turn left along this road for a short distance to the junction with the main road to Velas. Turn right and very shortly cross São Pedro Bridge. Immediately on your right you will find a cobbled path between stone walls, with a double metal gate. Take this to return to Velas, passing the new sports stadium.

WALK 3 DOWN TO FAJÃ DO JOÃO DIAS AND RETURN TO VELAS (*Time: about 3 hours*) This walk begins with a steep descent, slippery after rain, of 400m down the sea cliffs of the north coast. At the bottom is the little settlement of Fajã do João Dias where people cultivate small gardens taking advantage of the markedly warmer microclimate. After climbing back up the cliff, there is an easy walk back to Velas. Alternatively, arrange a time for your taxi to collect you at the clifftop. There is no road access to the *fajã*.

Take a taxi to the path leading down to Fajã do João Dias – the drivers will know where it is. The unsurfaced narrow road ends by meadows, which is where your driver will stop. Cross the field by the worn path to the clifftop where you will see the path continuing down to the *fajã*. The descent takes about 45 minutes. Allow longer for the climb back up!

From the start of the road, where the taxi left you, walk down the road to where it forks. Take the left fork. The road passes fields and where you come to gates, this is a public right of way; proceed, closing the gates behind you, and continue until

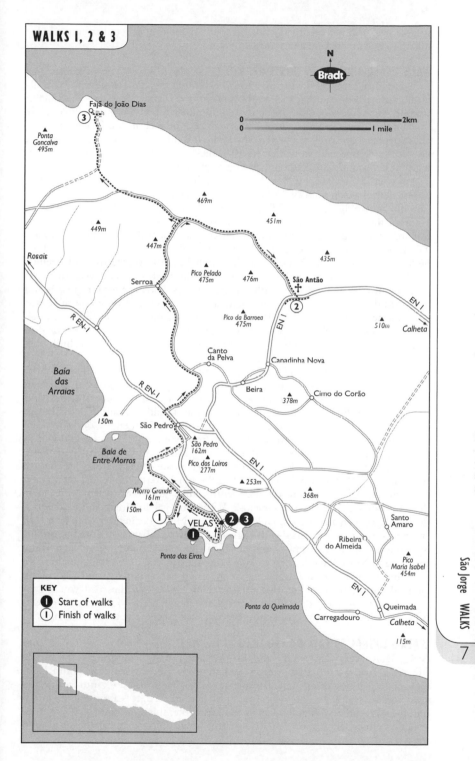

WALKS 1, 2 & 3

Bradt

Fajã do João Dias
③

Ponta
Goncalva
495m

0 _____ 2km
0 _____ 1 mile

▲ 469m

▲ 451m

▲ 449m

▲ 447m

▲ 435m

Rosais

Serroa

Pico Pelado
475m

▲ 476m

São Antão ✝
②

▲ 435m

▲ 510m   Calheta

R EN-1

Pico da Barroea
475m

EN 1

EN 1

Baia
das
Arraias

R EN-1

Canto
da Pelva

Canadinha Nova

Beira

▲ 378m   Cimo do Corão

▲ 150m

São Pedro

São Pedro
162m

Pico dos Loiros
277m

▲ 253m

▲ 368m

Baia de
Entre-Morros

Morro Grande
161m

EN 1

▲ 150m

① VELAS
② ③
①

Santo
Amaro

Ribeira
do Almeida

Pico
Maria Isabel
454m

Ponta das Eiras

EN 1

KEY
① Start of walks
① Finish of walks

Ponta da Queimada

Carregadouro

Queimada

Calheta ➞

115m

São Jorge **WALKS**

7

153

you come to a wide forest road going off to the right. Take this and continue as for walk 2 to cross the island and return to Velas.

WALK 4 CALDEIRINHAS TO NORTE GRANDE (*Time: about 5 hours*) The walking is easy, with a gradual ascent followed by a long descent all the time along a wide, well-made, unsurfaced road that follows the spine of the island. At up to some 1,000m altitude, this walk should be made in good weather otherwise mist will certainly obscure the views, and these are truly magnificent on a clear day. In winter, it is a photographer's dream. It can be very atmospheric if mist engulfs you. This happens, but take care, especially in winter, for then these high places are deserted; only in the summer months are cattle brought up to graze and people are about.

Ask your taxi to put you down at Caldeirinhas. This is just to the east of Pico das Caldeirinhas, on the EN 3 road that crosses the island from Urzelina to Santo António, where the unsurfaced farm road begins, signposted to Pico da Esperança.

Cross the cattle grid at the beginning of the black dirt road, and just keep walking! The road later changes to softer coloured, less threatening, red stones. The large volcano of black scoriae – you can see that some has been quarried for building use – is the one that so tragically erupted in 1808 and destroyed Urzelina. As you move on past this rather sobering place the road snakes between different small peaks and gives you constantly changing views. Look out for Graciosa Island on your left, and then Pico on your right, and for the villages down on the coast; you will soon see Urzelina with its small harbour and blue-green swimming pool, and Norte Grande on the opposite north coast. When you reach the base of Pico da Esperança there is a path to the summit should you feel tempted to climb it; at 1,053m it is the highest point of São Jorge.

Following the road round its base the most fabulous view awaits: the rest of the length of the spine of São Jorge and all its grassy calderas. It is an amazing landscape, and has to be seen to be believed. In the far distance are the wind turbines above Ribeira Seca and to their right you should just be able to make out the tiny white church of Loural, and to the left Norte Pequeno. Continue along the spine, and when a dirt road comes in from your right, this leads down to Manadas. You could of course take this road, and end your walk on the south coast, it takes about 1½ hours to descend, but do carry on and then, as you start to leave the island's spine and begin to descend to the north coast, the road winds down through an amazing dwarf forest of endemic juniper and tree heathers. On a clear day you can see Terceira and Graciosa. When you get to where the road forks, ignore the right-hand fork which leads down to Norte Pequeno. At the next fork the right-hand road is marked with a green signpost to Norte Pequeno. Ignore this and continue until you come to another road going down to your right signposted this time to Norte Grande. Drivers must take this to drop down to the main road, then turn left to the village. Walkers have the privileged option to avoid a 2km walk along the main road by ignoring this turn-off and follow the road you are on straight ahead over a cattle grid. In about 2km you will come to a road going down on your right. Take this to come into Norte Grande, where you can get a taxi.

WALK 5 LOURAL TO FAJÃ DE SÃO JOÃO (*Time: about 2 hours, and about 1 hour to drive back to Velas*) Not only a good walk, this path also reveals something of the simple life of the farmer using these steep slopes to produce crops or pasture animals. In summer this is best done in the late afternoon, so that as you walk into Fajã de São João you can watch the sun beginning to set behind Pico. It is almost all downhill and the path can be difficult when wet. Please note: this walk used to begin from Fajã dos Vimes, but a short length of cliff is now subject to rockfalls and should be avoided.

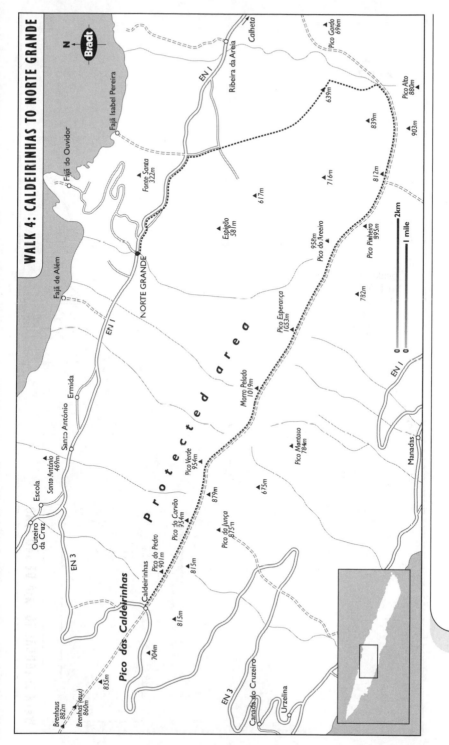

WALK 4: CALDEIRINHAS TO NORTE GRANDE

N

Bradt

Fajã Isabel Pereira

Fajã do Ouvidor

Fajã de Além

Outeiro da Cruz

Escola

Santo António
469m

Santo António

Ermida

EN 1

NORTE GRANDE

Fonte Santa
322m

Ribeira da Areia

Calheta

Pico Gordo
696m

639m

Pico Alto
880m

839m

903m

716m

812m

Espigão
581m

617m

Pico do Areeiro
958m

Pico Pinheiro
995m

732m

Pico Esperança
1053m

P r o t e c t e d   a r e a

Morro Pelado
1019m

Pico Verde
954m

879m

Pico Montoso
784m

675m

Pico do Carvão
954m

Manadas

EN 1

0   2km
0   1 mile

Pico do Pedro
901m

Pico da Junça
873m

815m

815m

Caldeirinhas

704m

Pico das Caldeirinhas

Brenhaus
882m

Brenhos (aux)
860m

835m

EN 3

Canada do Cruzeiro

Urzelina

EN 3

São Jorge WALKS

7

155

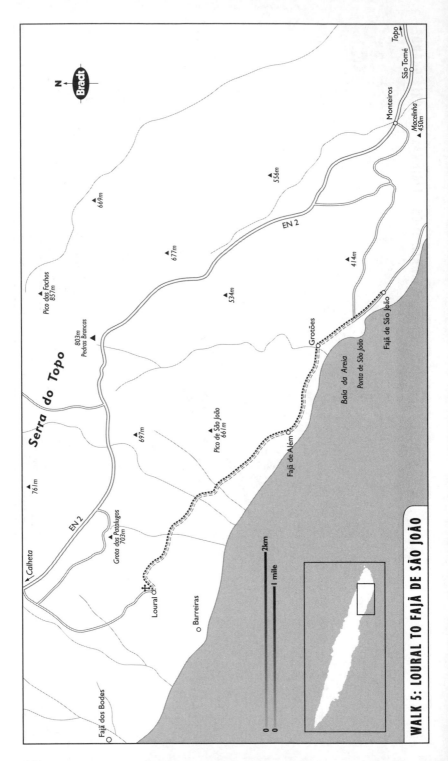

WALK 5: LOURAL TO FAJÃ DE SÃO JOÃO

N

Bradt

Serra do Topo

Calheta

EN 2

761m

Grota dos Patalugos
703m

Pico dos Fachos
857m

803m
Pedras Brancas

669m

677m

EN 2

556m

534m

697m

Pico de São João
661m

414m

Monteiros

São Tomé

Topo

Macelinho
450m

Loural

Barreiras

Fajã dos Bodes

Fajã de Além

Grotões

Baía do Areia

Ponta de São João

Fajã de São João

0   1 mile

0   2km

You can either ask your driver to meet you at a pre-arranged time at the end of the walk in Fajã de São João, or you can walk 5km up the asphalt road into São Tomé which is a small village on the main road with a bar from where you can telephone for a taxi.

If you are driving yourself, go to **Loural** and begin the walk from the church. Follow the farm road for about 700m and you come to farmhouses and a little stream.

The other option is to take a taxi to the place on the main road near the old cheese factory above Loural, where a grassy farm track 3m wide between two low stone walls sets off downhill for 100m or so, then veers round to the left. The drivers know it. It is about 1.5km after the sign to Lourais; Lourais is the plural of Loural because there are three Lourals! Follow the farm trail and soon on your left you can hear a stream flowing with its banks covered by tall shrubs, remnants of the laurisilva forest that would once have covered these hills. Rounding the bluff, there is the sea, and a lovely view of the church at Loural. Head on down the path to where you come to farmhouses and a little stream. Thanks to over-generous EU money, you will see the newly asphalted road leading up to Loural Church.

From this point continue on the farm road winding down the hill and when you come to a turning off to the left by a cattle trough take this and go down an old paved donkey trail.

In 15 minutes you pass a waterfall, and then caves enlarged with small boulders used as shelters for a horse, or a couple of cows and even a pig. Continue, and the village of Fajã de São João comes into view at the foot of a high cliff. You pass small stone houses where their owners live for two or three months twice a year: in the winter to grow their beans and potatoes and again in September–October to make their wine. Then just above the beach pass a stone watermill and you are in the village.

WALK 6 DOWN TO FAJÃ DA CALDEIRA DE SANTO CRISTO AND ALONG THE COAST TO FAJÃ DOS CUBRES (*Time: about 2 hours down to Caldeira de Santo Cristo and 1 hour to the end of the walk in Fajã dos Cubres. It takes about 1 hour to drive back to Velas*) It is magnificent country and you will want to stay and enjoy the ever-changing views, and the contrast between the high grasslands where you begin the walk and the fascinating villages at sea level, in their microclimate.

This walk begins above Fajã dos Vimes on the Topo road, EN 2, at a point about midway between Ribeira dos Vimes and Ribeira do Capadinho. Ask your driver to take you to the *canada* or old trail leading down to Fajã da Caldeira de Santo Cristo. It begins on the other side of the road from a concrete shelter, now well signposted at the start of the walk, about 5km on from **Silveira**. Arrange for a taxi to collect you at the end of the walk from **Fajã dos Cubres**.

The old stone track climbs for a short distance and very soon you have left the south coast behind and at around 700m altitude you look down over the Caldeira de Cima to the north coast. The land falls away before you and you are atop an amphitheatre enclosed by hills. About 20 minutes into the walk you come to a ridge between two ravines. The path, now narrow, starts winding down through a mixture of grazed grassland, juniper and tree heather. There are several gates along the path, with self-closing devices made from gnarled tree stems that look as though they have come straight from a children's book of illustrated fairy tales. About 45 minutes into the walk you come to a fork in the path and you bear round to the left. In another 20 minutes you are down to a tumbling brook, and a good place for a picnic with somewhere to cool a bottle of wine. Almost immediately another stream comes down from the right with a small bridge over it.

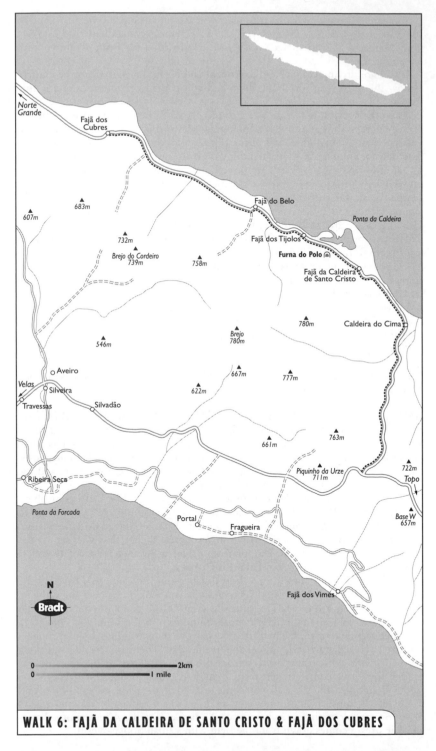

Norte
Grande

Fajã dos
Cubres

▲ 683m

▲ 607m

Fajã do Belo

Ponta da Caldeira

▲ 732m

Fajã dos Tijolos

Brejo do Cordeiro
739m

Furna do Polo 🏠

▲ 758m

Fajã da Caldeira
de Santo Cristo

▲ 780m

Caldeira do Cima

Brejo
780m

▲ 546m

▲ 667m

▲ 777m

Aveiro

Velas

Silveira

▲ 622m

Travessas

Silvadão

▲ 661m

▲ 763m

Piquinho da Urze
711m

▲ 722m
Topo

Ribeira Seca

Ponta da Forcada

Portal

Fragueira

Base W
657m

N
Bradt

Fajã dos Vimes

0 ━━━━━━━━━━2km
0 ━━━━━━━━━1 mile

WALK 6: FAJÃ DA CALDEIRA DE SANTO CRISTO & FAJÃ DOS CUBRES

Ten minutes later you reach two watermills by the side of a larger stream, and a splendid grassy bridge crossing it. Note the large plants of New Zealand flax, *Phormium tenax*, growing around the mill houses, once used for tying the flour sacks. Continuing, you will come to a view looking down into the Fajã da Caldeira de Santo Cristo and its lagoon; the path follows the cliff. Another 20 minutes and you are by the church.

This must be one of the most isolated villages in the Azores, and having got down to it you have now to leave as do the villagers. This is by a clearly worn track running along the coast. In half an hour you pass the remaining buildings of Fajã do Belo and in another 40 minutes you reach Fajã dos Cubres.

São Jorge WALKS

7

8

Faial

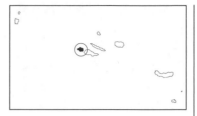

Known as the Blue Island because of its abundant hydrangeas, Faial is quite spectacular when they are blooming from mid July though August. My taxi driver said he had calculated there are 56km of hydrangea hedges. Some years ago a letter appeared in *The Times* London newspaper bemoaning the abundant hydrangeas in the Azores and appealing for something else to be planted!

Although the island is dominated by its central caldera and nearby highest point of 1,043m, the visitor is not really aware of this, travelling around the island past its pretty villages, lush pastures and vigorous hedgerows.

Picturesque Horta has long been a major port of the Azores and it is really this town that has dominated the island; today its recently enlarged marina is a major tourist attraction. More than 1,100 yachts put in each year for supplies and repairs as they make the Atlantic crossing and in summer this influx of mostly young visitors certainly enlivens the evenings, especially between May and July.

History is everywhere among the streets and old buildings, and always across the channel is the great cone of Pico. Sometimes it is totally clear of cloud, seeming arrogantly to challenge the elements to renew their erosive attacks. More often, it is adorned with a fast-changing wardrobe of clouds, engulfing its summit, encircling its midriff, or clothing it from apex to base, and obscuring it from our sight but not our consciousness; you never tire of glancing across the channel. In winter with its uppermost quarter briefly dusted with snow and fronted with a travel-brochure blue sea the mountain is breathtakingly beautiful.

HIGHLIGHTS

Horta, the only town, will take at least a half day to explore, easily a full day with the museums. Seeing the highlights of the rest of the island can be done on a half-day taxi tour. The view into the caldera, green and a nature reserve, and the reverse view down to Horta, across the channel to Pico island and up to its volcano summit with São Jorge beyond, make it well worth a drive up. Then there is Capelhinos, the site of the major 1957 eruption which added another 2km² to Faial; the half-buried lighthouse and village houses, slowly becoming exposed once more by wind erosion from their smothering of ash, bear witness to the human drama.

GENERAL BACKGROUND

GEOGRAPHY The island is dominated by a central massif that rises to 1,043m; there is a large caldera from which a line of secondary volcanic cones runs westwards to the latest eruption site at Capelhinos. Faial is the nearest island to the Mid-Atlantic ridge, some 100km to the west. The basalt bed upon which Faial is built is some 5.5 million years old, and the island is less than 1 million years old. Much of the landscape is pasture, although there is now some forest; at one time the tree cover

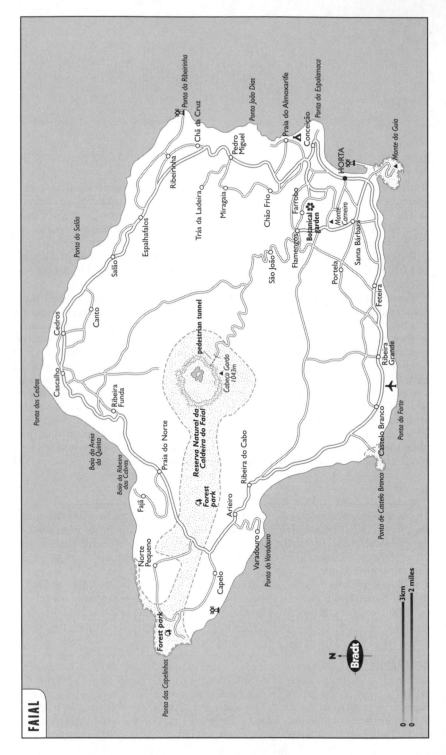

FAIAL

162

Ponta dos Cedros

Ponta do Salão

Baía da Areia da Quinta

Baía da Ribeira das Cabras

Cascalho

Cedros

Canto

Salão

Espalhafalos

Ribeirinha

Trás da Ladeira

Ponta da Ribeirinha

Chã da Cruz

Pedro Miguel

Ponta João Dias

Praia do Almoxarife

Ponta do Espalamaca

Conceição

HORTA

Monte da Guia

Miragaia

Chão Frio

Farrobo

Botanical garden

Monte Carneiro

São João

Flamengos

Santa Bárbara

Portela

Feteira

Pedestrian tunnel

Cabeço Gordo 1043m

Reserva Natural da Caldeira do Faial

Forest park

Ribeira Grande

Ribeira Funda

Praia do Norte

Ribeira do Cabo

Ponta de Castelo Branco

Castelo Branco

Ponta do Forte

Fajã

Arieiro

Varadouro

Ponta do Varadouro

Norte Pequeno

Capelo

Forest park

Ponta das Capelinhos

N

Bradt

3km

2 miles

0

0

was so depleted that wood for fuel was imported from Pico. There is only one town, Horta.

HISTORY Early maps present the island as *Insule de Ventura*, and the Portuguese discovered it in the first half of the 15th century. Led by Josse Van Huertere, Flemish settlers came to Faial in 1468, and just 20 years later their number had grown to 1,500. Establishing themselves first at Praia do Almoxarife, they soon moved inland to the Vale dos Flamengos, not far from Horta, and the parish still called Flamengos reflects this early settlement. The first two areas developed were at either end of what is now the main port and marina of Horta. The Azores has always played an important role in the history of the Atlantic. Laden Portuguese ships returning from the West Indies would seek protection from the many pirates awaiting them off the African coast. As both the new English settlements in North America and the West Indies and the Portuguese Empire grew, Horta became a busy sea port, then the only really safe anchorage in the Azores. Horta was not only trading but also victualling, supplying good fresh water and fresh vegetables, repairing ships and providing crews for East Indiamen, West Indiamen, codfishers, slavers, ships carrying wine, or sugar, or salt, or miscellaneous cargoes, and men-of-war. In addition, there has always been a great deal of inter-island trading, as well as between the islands and mainland Portugal.

Of course, it was not always peaceful; in 1583 the Spanish attacked and fought a battle for the Santa Cruz fortress. This still overlooks the harbour, but is now a hotel. During Spanish rule English privateers attacked several times including, in 1597, Sir Walter Raleigh, who razed Horta by fire. A far more peaceful English visitor was Captain James Cook who, in 1775, checked his navigational instruments onshore before sailing off to explore the South Seas.

Early whaling fleets came to Horta for supplies, rest, to offload whale oil and recruit crews, anchoring in Porto Pim. Later, entrepreneurs developed warehouses and other facilities to further attract ships to Horta. Among these was American John Dabney who arrived at the beginning of the 1800s, and whose family influenced commerce for 100 years. Oranges and Pico wine were two important exports they handled, as well as whale products, whale fishing, ship's chandlery, and much else. Extremely successful, they lived life on a lavish scale building several large houses. The number of whalers increased, especially from New Bedford, which is now twinned with Horta. Work began in 1876 on the docks and sea wall to better protect the port so that steam ships could also call as well as sailing ships, and so bunkering services were added with much of the coal shipped out from Liverpool, England.

The first reliable transatlantic telegraph cable connection was laid in 1866, and more quickly followed during the next 50 years linking many regions of the world. In 1893 the first cable was laid linking Horta with Ponta Delgada and on to Carcavelos on the Arrabida coast south of Lisbon. This was operated by an English company, the Europe and Azores Telegraph Co, which eventually became, in 1934, part of Cable & Wireless.

These early telegraph cables had a relatively short operational range, and Horta's mid-Atlantic position was ideal for a relay station for transatlantic cables. It was also a good interchange location, and Deutsch-Atlantische Telegraphengesellschaft, founded in 1900, laid its first cable to link the USA and Germany via the Azores. Further cables followed, between Horta and Waterville in Ireland, Horta and Porthcurno in Cornwall and on to Mindelo in the Cape Verde Islands to connect with other cables to Africa and South America.

In the early 1900s there were some 300 employees – British, Germans, Americans and Portuguese. The last cable connecting Horta was laid in 1928, the latest technology allowing simultaneous transmission of five messages in each direction, a total of 500 words per minute. Now Horta was one of the most important cable centres in the world. It was in 1969 that the last cable company left, superseded by new technology. Today something like 70–80% of telephone and data communications are made through submarine fibre optic cables, the remainder via satellites. Modern systems can cross the Atlantic without the need for intermediate landing stations. The cables cross the Mid-Atlantic ridge spaced well apart where there is a low occurrence of volcanic activity, and faults due to seismic tremors are rare.

The 1893 cable linking the Azores with mainland Europe also meant the meteorological observations made in the Azores, so far out in the Atlantic, could be transmitted rapidly; this had a tremendous influence on the development of weather forecasting. In 1901 construction of the Prince Albert Observatory began on the summit of Monte das Moça, above what is now the Fayal Resort Hotel, and it is still in use today.

The first transatlantic crossing by seaplane was made in 1919 by the American Albert C Read, who landed off Horta en route, to be followed by many others. In 1933 Charles Lindbergh flew to Horta seeking an acceptable year-round route for Pan-Am's seaplanes from America to Europe. Soon after Horta became the regular stopover for the Pan-Am clipper flights, to be followed by Lufthansa, Air France and Imperial Airways, now British Airways. However, there were disadvantages: the harbour was not large enough for landings and take-offs and the big flying boats had to use the open ocean, taxiing in and out of the harbour. Ocean swells could delay flights and in December 1939 four clippers were stranded for three weeks. This romantic era of travel ended with improved land-based aircraft and a runway constructed on Santa Maria.

Now the summer yachts crossing the Atlantic make the cosmopolitan life of Horta, and tourism generally is the new growth industry. Meanwhile, cattle and fishing continue in the background.

GETTING THERE AND AWAY

BY PLANE TAP Air Portugal has direct flights between Lisbon and Horta. SATA Air Açores operates direct flights between Terceira and Faial every day and between Ponta Delgada and Faial on certain days.

BY FERRY There is a regular 30-minute service between Horta and Madalena on Pico throughout the year, and on some days between Velas on São Jorge. In summer there is a daily crossing between Horta via Pico (Madalena and Cais do Pico) and São Jorge (Velas); time 105 minutes. For current summer schedules to the other islands please check the website (*www.transmacor.pt*) or contact one of the two offices on the island (*Rua Nova 29, Angústias, 9900-023 Horta;* ✆ *292 200 380;* f *292 200385;* e *transmacor@mail.telepac.pt or Gare Marítima do Porto da Horta, Angústias;* ✆ *292 200381*).

BY YACHT Horta has an excellent marina with full facilities (*secretariat open 09.00–12.30 and 14.00–18.00*). The yacht club is the most active in the Azores (*Clube Naval da Horta, Cais Velho, Rua Vasco da Gama;* ✆ *292 391 719*).

GETTING AROUND

There are buses, but you will need to check the current timetable with the tourist office.

The best way to see the island is to take a half-day taxi tour, which will cover more or less the same ground as described below under touring by self-drive car. Allow about 30 minutes for the drive from the airport to Horta; taxi fare around € 10.

One thing you can do which is fun, weekdays only, is to take the 11.45 bus going westwards from the stop close to the tourist information office. This will take you round the coast to Praia do Norte, from where it continues clockwise in line with the coast back to Horta. The whole circuit takes 1½ hours. When you board the bus, ask for a ticket to go right round the island; you get two tickets, total cost € 4.53. It is a very pretty ride anytime and on a really hot day under a clear blue sky in early November the island was especially beautiful. First following the coast and a sparkling blue sea you get to Capelhinos, and a good view of the 1958 eruption site and the half-buried lighthouse. Twenty years ago the area was petty well deserted, with damaged or destroyed houses lying abandoned or buried in ash. Now people are returning, and either restoring the old houses or building new and it is becoming very attractive. On to Praia do Norte and to Cedros, passing through some well-forested areas, it is then down to Ribeirinha before climbing up to Espalamaca, looking down to Praia do Almoxarife on your left, to Pico, and opposite, the splendid view of Horta.

CAR HIRE

Ilha Verde Rent-a-Car Rua das Angústias 70, 9900-018 Horta; ℡ 292 392 786; www.ilhaverdecom

Rent-a-Car Colombis Faial Resort Hotel, Rua Consul Dabney, 9901-856 Horta; ℡ 292 392 786

SCOOTER AND MOUNTAIN-BIKE HIRE

Fayal Radical Rua Nova 12, 9900 Horta; ℡ 292 292 715; e fayalradical@mail.pt; www.fayalradical.com. Main rental office located in marina, in front of Café Sport.
Peters – Café Sport Rua Jose Azvedo. Offer a trip up

to the caldera where they leave you and a mountain bike to cycle back down, on the tarmac road. The record is 33 mins; an attempt on this is not for the faint hearted but the ride is good and barely 500m of actual pedalling is required.

TRAVEL AGENTS

Agência Viagens Hortatur Rua Conselheiro Medeiros, 9900-144 Horta; ℡ 292 391 531;

e hortatur@mail.telepac.pt; www.ciberacores.pt/hortatur

WHERE TO STAY

⌂ **Faial Resort Hotel****** (143 rooms) Rua Consul Dabney, 9901-856 Horta; ℡ 292 207 400; e geral@faialhotel.com; www.fayalhotel.com. Bar, snack-bar, lounge, shop, games room, beauty salon, conference rooms, indoor pool, fitness room. Going since 1973, with part occupying buildings once belonging to one of the cable companies, plus addition of new wings, all set in grounds with tennis courts and swimming pool. The restaurant in the main building has a stunning view looking across the channel to Pico. Dbl € 105–140, sgl € 78–106.
⌂ **Hotel Horta****** (80 rooms inc 4 suites) Rua Marcelino Lima, 9900-122 Horta; ℡ 292 208 200; e info@hotelhorta.com; www.hotelhorta.com. Nicely appointed new hotel, all rooms with balconies and sea view; heated outdoor swimming pool in a garden setting; located near the Azorean General Assembly

building immediately above the town centre, entailing a short uphill walk. Very quiet. Dbl € 77–129, sgl € 62–105.
⌂ **Hotel do Canal** **** (103 rooms) Largo Dr Manuel de Arriaga, 9900-026 Horta; ℡ 292 202 120; e reserves@bensaude.pt; www.bensaude.pt. New hotel, by the busy harbour, across from the ferry quay, perfect for visiting Pico. Restaurant, bars, winter garden, games room, fitness centre, sauna, jacuzzi, Turkish bath, hairdresser, conference room, garage. Dbl € 94–133, sgl € 76–111.
⌂ **Pousada de Sta Cruz****** (26 rooms) Rua Vasco da Gama, 9900-017 Horta; ℡ 292 202 200; e recepcao.stacruz@pousada.pt; www.pousadas.pt. A 16th-century fort declared a national monument in 1947. Done to the high standards of Pousadas de Portugal, not all rooms have a sea view; the

restaurant offers regional dishes, there's also a bar with terrace and pool overlooking harbour and view across to Pico. *Dbl € 95–180, sgl € 69–142.*

🏠 **Pensão (Res) São Francisco** (32 rooms) (2a) Rua Conselheiro Medeiros, 9900-144 Horta; ☎ 292 200

980; e reserves@residencialsaofrancisco.com; www.residencialsaofrancisco.com. Simple but comfortable rooms, in the centre of town so may be noisy. French spoken. Long established with a good reputation. *Dbl € 56–79, sgl € 47–60.*

CAMPING

⚡ **Praia do Almoxarife** ☎ 292 292 131. This valley is very charming and the village has several good eating places, the small beach is nice, and there is a lovely

view across to Pico, all within a 15-min taxi drive from Horta or by local bus. The campsite is 24hrs supervised, with all facilities and tents can be hired.

✕ WHERE TO EAT

In Horta, there is quite a number of restaurants, and of course the main hotels are open to non-residents; the **Faial Resort Hotel** has a stunning view across to Pico from the restaurant, and **Hotel Horta**, rather out of sight but with a good restaurant, should not be out of mind.

✕ **Restaurant O Marineiro** Rua Almeida Garrett 4, Horta; ☎ 292 392 580. A simple restaurant with excellent service, good basic food (inc vegetarian if requested), and quietly hidden away in the backstreets of town off the main tourist route. Easiest way to find it is to walk almost to the end of the harbour esplanade until you come to the Rua Bom Jesus, at the side of the Domus Lusitae, a large new building and its statue holding the scales of justice; you can see the restaurant at the end of this short street.

✕ **Restaurante Kabem Todas** Rua Bombeiros

Voluntários; ☎ 292 292 120. In the pink wedding-cake building to the left of the fire brigade station, in the market squre (Praça da Republica), recently opened and obviously a triumph with the locals, so best to reserve a table. Sensibly priced. Heartily recommended. *Open 12.00–15.00 and 19.00–23.00, closed Sun.*

✕ **Café Porto Pim** On the road by the port and overlooking the bay. Another easily missed restaurant; tables outside. Excellent for a snack lunch offering good soup and a welcome range of different sandwiches.

Readers have also written in recommending these three:

✕ **Canto do Doca** Rua Nova, Angústias; ☎ 292 292 444. Located in the corner of the harbour, this offers a very different meal where you cook your own dinner of fish or meat on a very hot lump of basalt. Reportedly great fun and no complaints

about the chef!

✕ **Baia do Vista** ☎ 292 945 140. 'Serves the best barbecued chicken on the island at a very reasonable price, with great sunsets thrown in.'

CEDROS

✕ **O Escondiejo** ☎ 292 946 505. A cosy little restaurant with good food as long as you can find

it! Signposted from the main road in the centre of Cedros.

NIGHTLIFE

🍺 **Bar Canto da Doca** (Pub/Snack Bar) Rua Nova, Angústias, Horta — by the harbour, near the ferry quay; ☎ 292 292 444

🍺 **Crazy and Company** (Pub/Disco) Av 25 de Abril — next to O Capote Restaurant towards the eastern

end of the seafront esplanade; ☎ 292 293 295

🍺 **XF Bar** (with recorded music) 14 Rua Ladeira, Horta — a small street just above the harbour and below the Faial Resort Hotel; ☎ 292 392 697

CINEMA The Teatro near the main square in Horta with its ornate music-hall style rows of boxes and Art Deco ceiling has recently been restored and offers a mix of

Hollywood and art cinema, together with occasional orchestral and jazz music. See the website for their current film programme (*www.cineclube.org*).

FESTIVALS

By far the busiest celebration is Sea Week at the beginning of August. Primarily a yachting regatta with whaling boat races, the channel between Faial and Pico is a mass of fluttering sails. Different musical groups perform each evening, including bands from mainland Europe, local bands and folklore groups. There are exhibitions too, and the road along the seafront is closed allowing thousands of people to promenade. On the first Sunday at the beginning of Sea Week the Festival of Nossa Senhor de Guia, Protector of the Fishermen, takes place with a procession from Porto Pim. The dates of many festivals vary each year, so please check with the tourist information office.

Sports and Cultural week (Horta)	end of April
Festa de N Sra Angústias (Horta)	sixth Sunday after Easter
Festa de São João da Caldeira (Horta)	24 June
Sea week (Horta)	first to second Sunday in August
Festa de N Sra Lurdes (Feteira)	last week in August
Festas do Espírito Santo	August/September, intermittently
Festa de N Sra Saúde (Varadouro)	first week September
December festival (Horta)	December

USEFUL NUMBERS

Emergency ☎ 112
Police Largo Duque d'Avila e Bolama; ☎ 292 208 510
Tourist information office Rua Vasco da Gama; ☎ 292 292 237; also at the airport Jun–Aug.
Post office Largo Duque d'Avila e Bolama; ☎ 292 200 770

SATA Air Açores Largo do Infante; ☎ 292 293 912; also at the airport ☎ 292 943 112
TAP Air Portugal Rua Vasco da Gama; ☎ 292 292 665
Hospital Estrada Príncipe Alberto do Mónaco; ☎ 292 201 000
Airport Information ☎ 292 943 111; lost and found ☎ 292 943 112

COMMUNICATIONS

INTERNET Horta, conscious of its historical pivotal role in transcontinental communications, intends again to be at the centre of information technology thus countering any risk of information exclusion resulting from the island's isolated geographical position. The Horta Municipality over the last two years has invested heavily in modernising its technical and administrative services, creating multi-channel access for residents and visitors, extending internet broadband access, and implementing a system to distribute institution and tourist information. The city-wide Wi-Fi net is an essential part of the strategy enabling residents and visitors to access the net free of charge via the municipal portal (access the 'CMH' server as the 'PT' one is the local paysite). This portal is composed of two parts, a citizens' site and a municipal site aimed at tourists. Citizens can access local government services etc (some of these may require a password) and reports of committees and other proceedings thus enabling e-democracy. The municipal site has information on numerous topics about the island and maps. There is also an island-wide project to identify and signpost places of interest such as walking trails, monuments, parks, etc. For the developing site go to www.cmhorta.pt and follow links to 'municipio'.

Faial COMMUNICATIONS

8

More conventional and accessible for the visitor is this shop on the main street:

⒠ Hortanet Serviços de Informática Rua Walter Bensaúde 2 r/c, 9900 Horta; ↘ 292 292 304; www.hortanet.com. According to Miguel Figueiredo, IT student/marine biologist, 'This is Linux country. On a quiet night you can hear Windows reboot.'

WHAT TO SEE AND DO

Wandering the streets of Horta, enjoying the present and past harbours, and making a tour to see the caldera and the scene of the last eruption is what most visitors do. If you have a car, then there are little villages to explore, tempting places to stop from which to make your own short walks, and whale watching from the clifftops. For pleasure boat and fun fishing trips, check with the tourist information office to see who might be offering what.

MUSEUMS

🐚 **Museu da Horta** Largo Duque D'Avila e Bolama. *Open Tue–Fri 10.00–12.00 and 14.00–17.00; additionally in May–Sep, Sat and Sun 14.00–17.30.*
🐚 **Museu de Arte Sacra** Rua Conseleiro de Medeiros. *Open Tue–Fri 10.00–12.00 and 14.00–17.00; additionally in summer Sat and Sun 14.00–17.30.*

🐚 **Museu Scrimshaw** Café Sport. *Open Mon–Sat 09.30–20.00, Sun 09.00–13.00.*
🐚 **Museum of the Capelinhos Volcano** Capelo. *Open Tue–Fri 10.00–12.00 and 14.00–17.00; additionally in summer Sat and Sun 14.00–17.30.*

Just beyond Porto Pim, **Ecoteca** organises activities for the local children when their school is closed in summer, when excursions are made to the caldera, Pico and other places of natural history interest. You might have spotted these before on other islands. Some act as quite large teaching resource centres, attracting the occasional volunteer student from overseas.

BIRDS AND FLOWERS The **Caldeira do Faial Nature Reserve** is good for the smaller endemic or rarer plants and in the grassland by the footpaths and around the viewing area inside the tunnel *Lactuca watsoniana*, *Daboecia azorica*, *Thymus caespititius*, *Centaurium scilloides*, *Hypericum foliosum*, yellow pimpernel and more can be found. The two most common birds are chaffinch and blackcap. The new volcano at **Capelinhos** regularly has nesting common terns and the roseate tern has also been recorded. Waders and ducks put into the beach at **Porto Pim**, and at the back of the beach grow sea daffodils.

SWIMMING

Varadouro On the southwest coast, on the way to Capelhinos. Natural rock pools, changing facilities and occasional lifeguard. There was also a thermal bath here, but the spring stopped flowing after the 1988 earthquake; the hunt is now on to find where it is presently coming out.

If you are wondering about the municipal indoor swimming pool at the far eastern end of the seafront esplanade, users are first required to produce a medical certificate to show they are in good health.

Porto Pim The relatively long sandy beach in the bay with almost sand-coloured sand which was once the original harbour. Shallow water for some way out, so water is warmer. Very popular, and on the edge of Horta town. No facilities.

Praia do Almoxarife Very small sandy beach, near the camping site. Some 15 minutes by taxi from Horta; facilities and restaurant nearby. See also page 173.

WHALE WATCHING For main entry see pages 53–4. There is a large sign by the harbour listing all licensed operators for whale watching, and also a summary of the whale-watching code of behaviour. There were 12 companies listed (covering Horta, and Madalena and Lajes on Pico) in December 2005, but none quite rightly operates in winter because the weather is unpredictable and leads to client disappointment.

The tourist department is beginning to signpost locations of old *vigias* – look out for them especially around Cedros. This is a splendid initiative, for they are the perfect places for a picnic and binoculars; amazing how many waves turn into dolphins by the end of a bottle of wine.

ITINERARIES

Horta The only town is made up from two adjacent bays, one small and rounded, Baía do Porto Pim, the other larger and more open. The remains of a volcano crater divides them, the Monte da Guia, from which may be had splendid views of both. The smaller is intimate, and was an American whaling centre from the end of the 18th century and during the 19th century. As many as 400 ships have been recorded in the harbour. Even by the beginning of the last century two-thirds of all sperm whales harpooned were caught off the Azores. The remains of the old whale factory and the slipway where whales were landed and hauled up for processing after being caught by the Azorean open boats can be seen. In the town itself there are some fine buildings, and there is a walk eastwards along the esplanade out to a pleasant little park.

Audio tour Under development is an audio tour of Horta that will encompass the whole city and eventually be extended to areas beyond. Audio equipment will be available for rent from the front desk of the municipal building (next door to Horta's main church and museum, close to the post office). Rental will be around €3, and a deposit required together with identification – eg: passport. The equipment is unobtrusive, and users will be given a map of the city with the audio tour locations identified by colour-coded numbers for churches, architecture, gardens, etc. At each of the 56 locations there will be a photograph posted and a short description for those without the equipment. Initially it will be in the Portuguese and English languages. Check with the tourist office to see whether it is up and running.

Town trail This conveniently divides into two walks, and we begin with the central and northern parts of town.

Central and northern Horta Start at the **Pousada de Santa Cruz**, the castle built in 1567 to defend the harbour. Opposite the castelo is the tourist information office. Go right, passing the little garden on your right overlooking the marina and take the left fork along the Rua C Medeiros at the side of the pastel green wedding cake of a building, charming with its wrought-iron balconies. One of its shops, round the corner facing the sea, is my favourite coffee bar with its Art Deco interior.

Soon on your left you will see towering above you the church and former convent of St Francis, built at the end of the 17th century; the original convent was destroyed by Essex and Raleigh in 1597. To its right is the charming St Francis Church, built in 1696; scheduled for restoration, it is currently closed to visitors.

From the church continue eastward and you soon come on your left to the old Jesuit college, founded in 1719 for the training of missionaries to serve in the Portuguese colonies. It is now the **Museum of Horta**, plus government offices. Although a small museum, it is well worth visiting. On display are some early maps

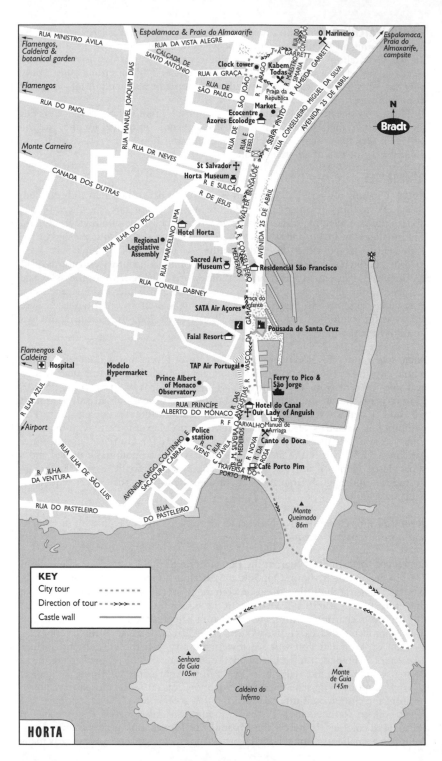

Espalamaca & Praia do Almoxarife
O Marineiro
Espalamaca, Praia do Almoxarife, campsite

RUA MINISTRO ÁVILA
Flamengos, Caldeira & botanical garden
RUA DA VISTA ALEGRE
CALCADA DE SANTO ANTÓNIO
RUA DO CONCEIÇÃO
T-A GARRETT

Flamengos
RUA A GRAÇA
Clock tower
Kabem Todas
RUA MAESTRO
R T ARAÇÃO
R MARIA GARRETT
RUA SIMARIA GARRETT

RUA DO PAIOL
RUA MANUEL JOAQUIM DIAS
RUA DE SÃO PAULO
Praça da República
RUA DE SÃO JOÃO
R SERPA PINTO
RUA CONSELHEIRO MIGUEL DA SILVA
AVENIDA 25 DE ABRIL

N

Bradt

Monte Carneiro
RUA DR NEVES
Market
Ecocentre
Azores Ecolodge
RUA E REBELO

CANADA DOS DUTRAS
St Salvador ✝
Horta Museum
R E SULCÃO
R DE JESUS

RUA ILHA DO PICO
Hotel Horta
R WALTER BENSAÚDE
AVENIDA 25 DE ABRIL

Regional Legislative Assembly
RUA MARCELINO LIMA
Sacred Art Museum
RUA CONSELHO MEDEIROS
Residencial São Francisco

RUA CONSUL DABNEY
Praça do Infante
SATA Air Açores
R GAMA

Faial Resort
Pousada de Santa Cruz
R VASCO DA GAMA

Flamengos & Caldeira
✚ **Hospital**
Modelo Hypermarket
TAP Air Portugal

R ILHA AZUL
Prince Albert of Monaco Observatory
Ferry to Pico & São Jorge

Airport
RUA PRINCÍPE ALBERTO DO MÓNACO
Hotel do Canal
Our Lady of Anguish
Largo Manuel de Arriaga
R F CARVALHO

RUA ILHA DE SÃO LUIS
Police station
RUA E SILVEIRA DE MEDEIROS
R C RUA D'ÁVILA
R NOVA
R DA ROSA
Canto do Doca

R ILHA DA VENTURA
AVENIDA GAGO COUTINHO E SACADURA CABRAL
IVENS
TRAVESSA DO PORTO PIM
Café Porto Pim

RUA DO PASTELEIRO
RUA DO PASTELEIRO

Monte Queimado
86m

KEY
City tour — — — — —
Direction of tour ⇒>>>= ▪
Castle wall —————

Senhora da Guia
105m

Caldeira do Inferno

Monte de Guia
145m

HORTA

of the Azores, recent secular paintings, an exhibition of remarkable models made with the soft inner tissue from fig stems by Euclides Rosa, who was from Faial, together with various other items. Examples from Horta's impressive collection of sacred art including statuary of several centuries are also exhibited. Some originate from Flanders but many were carved from cedarwood in the Azores. The Friends of Heart School in Angra made figures which were taken to the other islands and the figures come not only from churches and chapels no longer extant, but also private homes. Next door is the Church of São Salvador, the principal or mother, *Matriz*, church of Horta, begun in 1680 and finally completed in 1760.

Leaving the Horta Museum turn left and take the road along the right side of the post office, the Rua Serpa Pinto, to come to the marketplace on your left. Next to this is a little garden square, the **Praça da Republica**; on the diagonally opposite corner is another wedding cake of a building, this time pink, with splendid white balustrades. In earlier times houses painted pink were owned only by the aristocracy. Go up the road coming steeply into the square by this building. Take the first right, and you will see a clock tower at the top. This is the **Torre do Relógio**, built in the early 18th century; it is a symbol of Azorean perseverance in the face of seismic forces which destroyed the 16th-century mother church. The adjacent public garden dating from 1857, the **Jardim de Florêncio Terra**, has fine dragon trees, while the massive building behind is the **Hospital da Misericórdia**, now empty and awaiting a new role. Leave this area by the road behind the clock, which you will find goes steeply down the Ladeira da Paiva. At the bottom go left to cross a small stream, the Ribeira da Conceição, near which Faial's first settlement was begun in the 15th century. You will see the small church, the **Igreja de Nossa Senhora da Conceição**, inscribed with the dates 1527, 1597, 1749, 1926, 1933. This church has suffered a traumatic history. Originally built by the early settlers it was destroyed during the first sacking of the town in 1597. A church built much later was destroyed in 1926. Its replacement was built in the Art Deco style of the time and this in turn was damaged in 1941 by an explosion in a nearby army barracks. Following a major restoration in 2001/02 it is now pristine and most elegant. From here, either return along the roads through the town, or go south to the sea and return along the esplanade.

Southern Horta To explore the second, southern sector, again leave from the **Pousada de Santa Cruz**. This time turn left and walk down the road to pass the Café Sport. Some 20 years ago this was a small bar known to all sailors who called in at Horta, and a visitors' book was maintained which had many amusing entries. Now there is a shop and other enterprises including a museum of scrimshaw, and the guest book with all its early entries is posted on the internet; with good self-publicity the café is now known to a much wider circle around the world.

Proceed on and keep to the higher road and you will soon come on your left to the **Igreja de Nossa Senhora das Angústias**, the Church of Our Lady of Agony, just recently restored. Continue straight and you soon reach **Porto Pim**, the original harbour of Horta. Note the defensive walls and the remains of the Fort of **São Sebastião** constructed during the 17th century as protection against pirates and other attackers. You should try to visit at night when the gateway is floodlit and very pretty. Construction of the new harbour began in 1876.

Take the road running behind the sea wall left of the gateway to access the beach. You will see the small houses of one of the oldest remaining parts of Horta, all nestling at the foot of **Monte Queimado**; *queimado* means burned, referring to the cinders. Walk along the beach to the far end to visit the old whale factory. This was built only about 50 years ago and there is an earlier factory dating from 1836 built originally for drying cod. It is now a cultural centre, the Centro do Mar, with

In 1875 a house burned down and the governor was so angry that no-one came in time to extinguish it he offered a reward to the first eight men to come with a pump and a lesser sum to the first 12 men with buckets. This was how a rudimentary fire service began, and continued until 1912 when Horta's water supply was improved and the Associaçao Faialense de Bombeiros Voluntarios could be established. Church bells would sound the alarm and each district in Horta had its own signal; 4 bells for Angusuas, 6 for Matriz, 8 for Conceição, until they were replaced by a siren in 1966.

Extinguishing shipboard fires was and still is their responsibility. Their payment for dealing with a fire on a World War I Italian troopship enabled the volunteers to purchase in 1930 their first two motorised fire engines. Shipboard fires were frequent between 1958 and 1968 because of the number of ships transporting fishmeal, which had a tendency to self-combust. Today's very professional association of *bombeiros* is one of more than 450 departments nationwide supervised by the Portuguese National Fire Authority, the SNB.

The firemen are still volunteers who give their time and risk their lives thus continuing a long tradition. Horta has 54, all with understanding employers. Volunteering tends to run in families, sometimes three generations serving at the same time. They are called by the siren that continues to sound until enough firemen arrive to crew the engines. Volunteers can join the association from age 14 and remain until 60. Training is done on the island, often with imported specialists. The department is also involved in civil rescue service and disaster simulations from fires to earthquakes and volcanic eruptions are undertaken twice a year. Volunteers also visit each school on the island at least once a year to teach the children how to respond in emergencies. The service is now funded by a combination of private, municipal and central government sources, supplemented by demonstrations and firefighting courses around the island to raise money. The fire department is also responsible for the ambulance service, whose crews are the only permanently paid members of staff.

occasional cultural events and exhibits to do with the sea. This small area is full of history, for you can find near the museum the point where the submarine cables came out to connect to relay stations, and also the ruins of a summer villa and its garden, once belonging to the influential Dabney family.

From the whale factory take the road that climbs to the summit of **Monte da Guia**. There is a discreet visitor centre at the start of the climb. On the way you will pass a little chapel, dedicated to Senhora da Guia, also once used as a lookout for whales. The summit of Monte da Guia is 145m but it is closed to visitors. To return, follow the road all the way down and as you descend enjoy the splendid views of Porto Pim and Horta. Look also across Porto Pim Bay and to the hill behind, **Monte das Moças**, where you will see an observatory. The building dates from around 1901, and has been in use as a meteorological observatory since 1915. It was named Prince Albert of Monaco Observatory in 1923, a year after the prince's death. Just below this are the buildings and tennis courts of what is now the Faial Resort Hotel; previously these buildings were the residential compound belonging to the American Western Union Telegraph Co, built in the 1920s with reinforced concrete to withstand earth tremors. Hotel Faial opened in 1973, and has had new buildings added in recent years.

As you return to town and pass the harbour, pause to view the drawings and cartoons on the walls left by visiting yacht crews. This free outdoor art gallery exists because it is said to be bad luck to sail away without leaving your mark. Sadly, however, one or two have become memorials. Considerable care and time have clearly been taken by some artists, others are rushed scrawls, but all show a record of the many crews that have put in at Horta on their travels across the oceans.

Praia do Almoxarife Just the other side of the ridge immediately to the north of Horta is one of the prettiest valleys on the island. Long settled, the houses have charming gardens and in the past few years several restaurants have opened. There is a small sandy beach with changing facilities, and the camping site is nearby. It is a relaxing place from which to enjoy a fine view of Pico. You can walk back, first up the surfaced road to the top of the ridge. Here you will see a trodden path leading down to the old eastern sector of Horta, but only do this if there is not much traffic about. A bus runs to Praia do Almoxarife from the stop at the eastern end of the Horta marina at 07.15, 12.45 and 18.15, returning 07.30, 13.00 and 18.30 weekdays and on Saturday there is one bus only from Horta at 07.15, and one back at 07.40.

The Botanic Garden at Flamengos This is in the grounds of the Quinta de São Lourenço, with an extensive area of old gardens sheltered by magnificent hedges to protect them from the salt-laden winds. Established in 1989, the small botanic garden, the Jardim Botânico do Faial, is devoted to the endemic and indigenous plants of the archipelago, and is most attractively designed with gentle hills and a ravine filled with ferns. Here in season can be enjoyed some of the more showy species such as *Thymus caespititius*, the native thyme, *Azorina vidalii*, the native campanula, dramatic *Euphorbia stygiana* and the most desirable shrub of all, the endemic bilberry *Vaccinium cylindraceum*. In addition, if you (understandably) have

JARDIM BOTÂNICO DO FAIAL

The garden was established to fulfil the following objectives:

- by cultivation and propagation conserve those Azorean species threatened with extinction
- to build and maintain a collection of plants native to the Azores and Macaronesia
- to establish typical plant associations found at different altitudes
- to maintain a collection of native species for the interest of visitors

Because of its location the garden is able to grow species that are found at both sea level and at various altitudes in the mountains, and four altitudinal zones are represented. The coastal vegetation represented in the garden includes such Azorean endemic species as *Festuca petraea*, *Euphorbia azorica*, *Azorina vidalii* and the non endemics found outside the Azores *Juncus acutus* and *Solidago sempervirens*. *Erica scoparia* ssp. *azorica* and *Myrica faya* are also growing in this zone, although they merge with the next, intermediate zone. This second zone is not very clearly defined in nature and in addition to the two previous species also includes *Picconia azorica*. The third zone represents the vegetation found in the higher altitudes of the islands' mountains, above 600m. Here are found *Ilex perado* ssp. *azorica*, *Vaccinium cylidraceum*, *Juniperus brevifolia*, *Erica scoparia* ssp. *azorica* and *Laurus arizorica*, species typical of the laurisilva forest unique to Macaronesia. For those species that demand wind shelter, shade or more humidity comprising a fourth zone or category an artificial ravine was made where can be grown such rarities as *Lactuca watsoniana* and *Sanicula azorica*.

There is also a small visitor centre with photographs and some explanation about the different ecosystems.

been struggling to identify all the different evergreen shrubs native to the islands, here is an excellent opportunity to study them close at hand and compare them; they have labels!

Capelinhos This is the site of the 1958 eruption and it is fascinating to see how it is, years later, with a few hardy pioneering plants trying to establish themselves, and the effects of wind erosion. Come here on a blustery day and you see the fine particles blowing on the wind and indeed feel them stinging your face. Any work being done to the ruined lighthouse is towards its eventual conversion to a new home for the small museum in the nearby village of Capelo. It is worth walking or driving down to see the small fishing harbour below Capelinhos. Also near the village is the forest park which is a pleasant place to walk.

Feteira You will often see this place mentioned in brochures. Lying between the airport and Horta, it is a length of coast with contorted lava rocks and rock arches of some curiosity.

CAR TOUR Faial is small, and this itinerary provides a fascinating half-day tour. If you can, take a picnic to enjoy in the forest park at Capelinhos.

Horta–Espalamaca–Ribeira Funda–Praia do Norte–Capelinhos–Castelo Branco–Horta
Leave **Horta** and begin by driving up to the ridge that overlooks the town from the east and stop at the belvedere **Espalamaca**. Here you have a fine view over Horta, the harbour, and of fields nudging their way up to the houses, so quickly does town end and countryside begin. Along the ridge of Espalamaca are several windmills and, neatly nestling in its valley, **Flamengos** village. Turn around and look down upon a pretty valley and Praia do Almoxarife.

Take the EN 1-2a which will lead to the caldera and the little **Chapel of São João** is your next stop, after a cool drive beneath cryptomeria trees. São João is at the junction, where you have a view down over meadows to Horta across the channel to Pico. In early summer the hedgerows here are bedecked with tiny double red roses, coinciding with the Festa do São João in June.

Turn right in front of the chapel (EN 2-2a) and drive up to the **Caldera** along a narrowing road lined with tall hydrangeas. You will pass a road off to your right leading to Quebrada and Ribeira Funda on the north coast. There are wonderful views across to Pico and São Jorge. The road ends by a **tunnel**, at an altitude of 900m. The tunnel is very short, so walk through and view the caldera which is now a nature reserve. The large crater is 400m deep and 1,450m in diameter. The common native shrubs are juniper and erica. Above the tunnel on the caldera's rim is the Oratory of São João. On a clear day Pico, São Jorge and Graciosa can be seen; almost due west from the summit is a line of cinder cones marking the fracture along which eruptions have occurred in recent geological time.

Drive back down to the the the turn-off previously mentioned, now on your left, leading to **Ribeira Funda**. For flowers, this is one of the prettiest roads, and during July and August the hydrangeas are at their best. There are good views from two viewpoints along this road, and between trees and hydrangeas there are glimpses of villages and the sea beyond. Stop and enjoy, too, the glorious view over the Ribeira das Cabras and note the extensive lava beds before coming to **Praia do Norte**.

Praia do Norte is a good place to stop for coffee before going to Capelinhos, held to be one of the most interesting volcanic sites in Europe.

At **Capelinhos** stop by the old lighthouse. Here, in 1957–58, an eruption added another 2km^2 to Faial, and looking back you will see the line of cones leading up

THE CAPELINHOS ERUPTION

Earthquakes began on 16 September 1957 and on 27 September the sea began to boil near the Capelinhos rocks. On 29 September explosions began and cinders were thrown into the air. By 1 October cinders were thrown 600m high, the eruption cloud rose to 6,000m and an islet began to form round the crater. By 7 October there was a cone-shaped island 60m high and 640m across, but already the sea was destroying it. Two days later it was 100m tall and over 700m across in the shape of a horseshoe, opening to southward. The sea entered this break so that the vent of the volcano was underwater, causing very violent explosions and fragmenting the new lava into ash and cinders. By 30 October the sea had washed away the entire island.

In early November, eruptions began again and by the middle of the month a new island was linked to Faial by a narrow bar of black ash. Eruptions continued through the winter and by March 1958 more than 2km² of land had been added. During the following months lava flowed into the ocean, and, with the vent protected from the sea, incandescent lava was thrown up most spectacularly more than 500m, continuing intermittently until 24 October. In one period of 36 hours over 300 earth tremors were registered, shaking the whole island. In total some 300 houses were destroyed and almost every house on the west side of Faial was damaged; 2,000 people were rehoused. Crops were destroyed and a 5m layer of ash and rocks buried houses and many of the fields around the villages of Capelo and Norte Pequeno. Wind erosion is now slowly exposing these once more. The eruption changed the lives of many islanders when hundreds emigrated to the USA and Canada.

towards the big caldera. Continue on to the village of **Capelo** which has a little museum with interesting exhibits of the eruption (*open 10.00–12.00 and 15.00–17.00; closed on Mon*). Beneath the museum is a small handicrafts showroom, with items such as hand-painted silk scarves for sale.

Continue more or less parallel with the coast on the EN 1-1a to **Castelo Branco** where there is a fine view of the coastline before proceeding to **Feteira** to enjoy the coast and to see the caves in the lava.

Before returning to Horta drive up to **Monte Carneiro** (267m). The views are lovely from here over Flamengos and of Horta, Pico Island across the channel and, in the far distance, São Jorge.

Faial **WHAT TO SEE AND DO** | 8

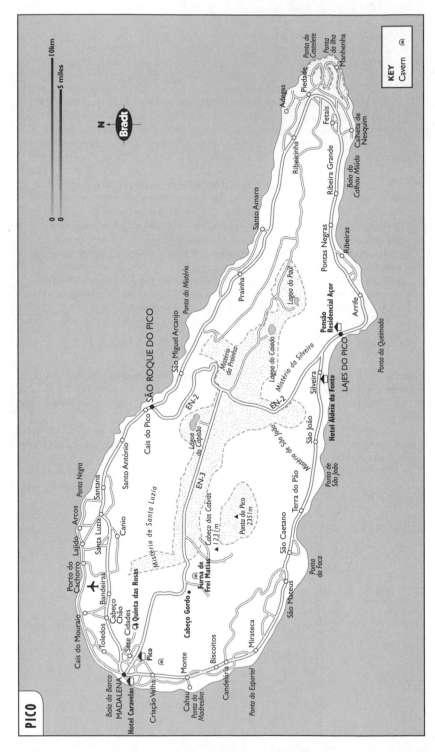

PICO

KEY
Cavern @

10km
5 miles

N

MADALENA

SÃO ROQUE DO PICO

LAJES DO PICO

Ponta do Pico
2351m

Cabeço Gordo

Furna de
Frei Matias

Cabeço das Cabras
1231m

Lagoa do Capitão

EN-3

EN-2

EN-2

Mistério de Santa Luzia

Mistério da Prainha

Mistério da Silveira

Mistério de São João

Baía da Barca

Hotel Caravelas

Cais do Mourajo

Toledos

Porto do
Cachorro

Lajido

Arcos

Santa Luzia

Santana

Ponta Negra

Canio

Santo António

Cais do Pico

Bandeiras

Cabeço
Chão

Sete Cidades

Quinta das Rosas

Pico

Monte

Biscoitos

Candelária

Mirateca

Cahau

Ponta da
Madresilva

Ponta do Espartel

São Mateus

São Caetano

Terra do Pão

Ponta
da Faca

São João

Ponta de
São João

Silveira

Hotel Aldeia da Fonte

Arrife

Ponta da Queimada

Pensão
Residencial Açor

Lagoa do Caiado

Lagoa do Paúl

Prainha

Santo Amaro

Ponta do Mistério

São Miguel Arcanjo

Ribeirinha

Adegas

Piedade

Ponta do
Castelete

Ponta
da Ilha

Manhenha

Fetais

Calheta de
Nesquim

Baía do
Calhau Miúdo

Ribeira Grande

Ribeiras

Pontas Negras

Criação Velha

176

9

Pico

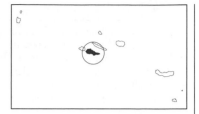

Pico is to most visitors the Pico mountain itself, a remarkable, steep-sided, dormant volcanic cone rising to 2,351m, and Portugal's highest mountain. Certainly this peak and the numerous black lava flows in different parts of the island make Pico the most distinctive of all in the archipelago. The finest views are to be had looking across the channel head-on from Faial, or the long side view from São Jorge; on the island itself, I love the view of the summit from Lajes. In the western end of the island you are always aware of Pico's overshadowing presence, whether dense clouds hang just above Madalena's rooftops obscuring everything above 40m, or the sky is at its bluest and all is revealed. The mountain always looks over your shoulder.

Of all the islands this is the most obviously volcanic, especially around Madalena and along the coast by the airport where the black stones have been gathered and made into tiny walled enclosures, square ones for vines, round ones for figs. Long ago, red and pink scrambling roses, the dark purple-blue trumpet flowers of the climbing ipomoea, and carpets of nasturtium escaped from cultivation, and now add wild colour for many weeks if not months of the year. Houses are of black stone, dressed around the windows, whitewash on the walls. Pico, with nearby Faial, was the centre for land-based open-boat whale hunting; some seven years after the last whale was killed boats again went to sea hunting whales, only this time just to watch, and again Pico has become one of the main centres.

For the naturalist, Pico has the most easily accessible areas of endemic vegetation where you can begin to imagine just how the islands might have appeared to the very first settlers. To explore the island's uplands by car, to find the lakes and other beautiful areas, just to stop and enjoy the grand scenery and the ever-changing cloud patterns around the mountain, is reason enough to come to Pico. But added to this are the cultural and historical interests and, for the experienced walker, the extraordinary experience of being on the summit of Pico where on a clear day the stupendous views embrace the sister islands of Faial, São Jorge, Graciosa and Terceira. Much closer, below, daughter cones and craters pockmark the plateau giving a tiny hint of what an extraordinary scene this must have been when it was most active. The mountain is only dormant; at the very summit on Pico Piqueno, the little peak that is a small cone in the summit crater, there are fumaroles, rocks are very warm to the touch and there is a sniff of sulphur. Escaping gases and flowing hot magma when the surface lava was cooling have created caves and tube-like tunnels; several are known and named, but others are buried beneath vegetation or a thin tumble of rocks so great care is needed and it is essential not to wander from paths. The second-largest island in the Azores surely has something for everyone.

HIGHLIGHTS

An island tour by car or taxi is a must, driving as high as the road reaches on Pico Mountain and down to sheltered areas by the sea, enjoying impressive landscapes and exploring villages and country life. For the botanist, the central mountain road running the length of the island offers endless interest, with side excursions off to small lakes and viewpoints. The museum in Lajes tells the fascinating story of whaling in the Azores and is another must, and the more adventurous can go whale watching and attempt the ascent of Pico. Pico was once famous for its fortified *Verdelho* wine and, in the last several years, new methods of cultivation and production are once again making saleable table wine. Originally the vines were grown in very small stone-wall enclosures to protect the plants from salt winds and to gain extra heat, and are an extraordinary memorial to the tenacity and hard work of the earlier settlers. Extensive areas stretching along the western coast from just outside Madelena are so impressive that in 2002 UNESCO designated them a World Heritage Site. A visit to the winery followed by a tasting completes the picture.

GENERAL BACKGROUND

GEOGRAPHY There is no better place to begin than with the aesthetically satisfying cone of Pico, the dominant feature of all the central group of islands. Pico was probably formed by repeated eruptions at different intervals, creating a massive conical volcano or *stratovolcano*. All the Azores islands except São Jorge have *stratovolcano*. They are usually built up of lava and beds of tephra (magma fragments created by exploding gases), but the magma erupting in such volcanoes varies in composition. Pico lava flows have been basaltic which have a low viscosity and therefore can flow for great distances, but probably they were erupted slowly and so did not travel for long before cooling and piling up around the vent. Other *stratovolcano* include Mount St Helens, Fujiyama, Etna and Vesuvius. Lavas at the summit of Pico are thought to be possibly less than 1,000 years old. The volcanic ridge to the east is older, but considered not more than 37,000 years old. Pico is the youngest of all the islands of the Azores.

At Pico's summit is a crater, Pico Grande, with a perimeter of around 700m and 30m deep. To one side is the secondary peak, the cone called Pico Pequeno, 70m tall. Steep-sided, especially in the south, the slopes flow quickly down to the sea except to the east where, after the initial fall to about 1,000m, there continues a long ridge slowly losing height until sea level some 33km distance from the peak.

The lower slopes show a pattern of forest and pasture; above 1,500m low shrubs and higher dwarf herbs abound; the final pull to the summit features bare lava and cinders. Most of the mountain, including the summit area, is a nature reserve. The southern slopes of all the island are more sheltered and less windy and so protective enclosures go high above the coastal villages. In contrast, the northern slopes are far more forested. Pittosporum and native myrica have invaded the lower slopes where there were once extensive vineyards among the stones, adding further large areas of tree cover. On the uplands most of the native vegetation has been cleared for cattle pasture, helped by subsidies from a then embryonic European Community – a dubious investment, since the resultant grass is very poor. However, there are pockets of native and endemic plants and hopefully current measures will be sufficient to save them; 1,500ha above the 1,200m contour are a designated protected zone. The coast has numerous headlands, some of which provide spectacular *miradouros*, and also curious lava formations, the best known being at Cachorro, near what is now the airport, and further along the coast. During historical times there have been three eruptions, in 1562, 1718 and 1720, to the east and south of the main peak that gave rise to the *mistérios* of Santa Luzia, Praínha, Silveira and São João.

HISTORY The first houses are thought to have been built in Ribeiros, but real settlement began in the area of what is today Lajes, in about 1460, and was for many years the principal port and town. Later it was to develop as the centre of the whaling industry in the Azores. São Roque dates back to 1542, possibly because it is opposite Calheta on São Jorge, just 18km away. It is thought to have been first populated by people from Graciosa. Again, later, it was a whaling base with a large processing factory.

Until the latter half of the 19th century wine production was a very important economic activity and its Pico Madeira wine was exported in substantial volume, to England and famously Russia. The vineyards, especially those along the west coast south from Madalena, were owned by some half-dozen families from Horta who came over for the summer to oversee the grape and wine production. Their large summer houses may still be seen today. Ever-increasing use of the important harbour on the adjacent island of Faial brought greater prosperity to that island and allowed the development of Horta, which in turn influenced the development of Madalena. Horta was the export centre for Pico's wine. Facing each other across the channel, the two towns have always been closely linked. Even today people go across from Pico on the ferry for hospital appointments, to shop at the supermarket or to buy their microwave oven or hi-fi system in Faial and carry it home via the afternoon sailing.

In 1852 disease (*Oidium tuckeri*, a mildew) nearly destroyed the vines and 20 years later when the aphid insect Phylloxera struck the remaining vines were destroyed. This brought terrific hardship to the islanders, for at the time of maximum wine production Pico's population was 32,000, and caused a massive emigration to Brazil and California. Those who could afford to paid their way on passing ships, the less fortunate embarked illegally on whaling ships serving a minimum contracted term of two years. With the vines gone, the families sold their large land holdings and so people were able to acquire small plots of their own. Later, returning islanders brought with them the American Isabela grape, which thrived, and so the smallholdings began producing a wine for local consumption known as Vinho de Cheiro, a low-alcohol partly fermented wine. Around this time, with skills gained from working on the American whalers, land-based whale hunting began from Pico, using small open boats. This soon spread to other islands, and whaling made a substantial contribution to the economy until world demand fell for the oil for lamps and machinery when cheaper synthetics became available. Many factories closed, while hunting continued on an ever-decreasing scale until the final whale was killed in 1984.

Today, like all the other islands, cattle and dairy produce drive the economy, despite the relatively poor quality of the land. In Madalena there is a tuna fishing fleet, and tourism is increasing.

GETTING THERE AND AWAY

BY PLANE SATA Air Açores have daily flights to Pico from Ponta Delgada and from Terceira. There are also direct flights from Lisbon to neighbouring Faial.

BY FERRY Frequent daily crossings operate throughout the year between Madalena and Horta on Faial, sailing time 30 minutes. In summer there are at least daily crossings between Faial (Horta) via Pico (Madalena and Cais do Pico) and São Jorge (Velas). In winter there are generally three sailings a week between Madalena and Velas. Tickets should be purchased on the quayside from the sales office just prior to departure. In summer there are also services to Terceira and other islands and for details of the current summer schedules please check the website (*www.transmacor.pt*). Tickets can be purchased from one of the two offices on the quays of Madalena (*Gare Marítima do Porto da Madalena;* ✎ *292 623 340*) and São Roque (*Gare Marítima do Porto de São Roque do Pico;* ✎ *292 642 482*).

BY YACHT Madalena, the main town, is a busy port because of the tuna fishing boats and regular ferry service to Horta on Faial. There are plenty of moorings, but no services for yachts. The Clube Naval de Madalena has its offices and a snack bar nearby (✎ *292 623 042*).

São Roque (also known as Cais do Pico) is the safest port on the island, with a large quay for container ships. Again, there is no real service for yachts and yachts should be very careful if using the commercial quay because of the overhang built into the dock wall. The Clube Naval São Roque de Pico is opposite the old quay and has a snack bar (✎ *292 642 105*). Plans for new marinas are under consideration.

GETTING AROUND

There is a bus service which follows two circuits, the north Madalena–São Roque–Piedade and the south Madalena–Lajes–Ribeirinha, but the times are infrequent. To make a round-the-island tour from Madalena both the south and north coast buses leave the harbour at 08.45 and arrive at Piedade at 10.45 and 10.50 respectively. Change at Piedade to continue round the coast. The south coast bus leaves Piedade at 12.25 and, via the north coast, the bus leaves at 13.00 so either way you get a chance to walk around and get refreshments. Both buses arrive back at Madelena at 15.00 From Lajes to Madalena the times are 06.45/08.00 and 13.40/15.00, and Madalena/Lajes 08.45/09.55 and 17.45/19.00.

The island divides quite easily into a half-day car tour – Madalena–Santa Luzia–São Roque–Lagoa do Ciado–Lajes/Madalena or variations – and a full-day tour taking in most of the above plus going down to the little-visited far eastern end of the island. The price for a taxi is around €100 for a day, €60 for a half-day tour. If you have a hire car, then there are three days of happy motoring ahead of you, taking two full days to explore the main EN 1 road that encircles the island, and a third day up on the heights. With three days, you should have one day of good weather for the mountains! A half-day tour is detailed, a full-day tour is hinted at, and the mountains have limited roads and you simply follow your instinct and enjoy the supreme tranquillity.

CAR HIRE
Ilha Verde Av Dr Machado Serpa, Madalena; ✎ 292 623 183, and at the airport; ✎ 292 622 002; e reserve@ilhaverde.com; www.ilhaverde.com **Rent-a-Car Colombis** Av Machado Serpa, 9950 Madalena; ✎ 292 622 661; Pico airport ✎ 292 622

002; central reservations ✎ 296 304 891; e reserve@ilhaverde.com; www.ilhaverde.com **Rent-A-Car Oásis** Estrada Regional, 9940-344 São Roque do Pico; ✎ 292 642 516; e racoasis@racoasis.mail.pt

TRAVEL AGENTS
Aerohorta Rua João Bento Lima, 9940 São Roque do Pico; ✎ 292 642 450; e hcosta@aerohorta.pt; www.areohorta.pt **Picotur** Av Padre Nunes Rosa, 9500 Madalena; ✎ 292 622 499; e picotur@mail.telepac.pt. All

services for visitors to the island inc rural lodging. **Teles** Rua Carlos Dabney, 9950 Madalena; ✎ 292 622 258; e tta.angra@telestravel.com; www.telestravel.com

🏠 WHERE TO STAY

There are two hotels in or close to Madalena, and near Lajes is a delightful complex of cottages and rooms, with restaurant, all set in a woodland garden by the sea. Around the island there are several small *pensão* and rural houses – see page 45. Many of the private homes offering lodging have a meeting point to pick up guests for the first time, or will meet the ferry.

MADALENA

🏠 **Hotel Caravelas***** (69 rooms) Rua Cons Terra Pinheiro, 9950 Madalena; ✆ 292 622 500; e geral@hotelcaravelas.net; www.hotelcaravelas.net. Modern city hotel near the harbour. *Dbl €67–95, sgl €57–83.*

🏠 **Pico Hotel**** (46 rooms, 23 apts) Rua dos Biscoitos, 9950 Madalena; ✆ 292 628 400; e picohotel@mail.telepac.pt; www.picohotel.com. About 20 mins' walk out of town along the main road. 2 restaurants, 2 bars, sauna, Turkish bath, hydro-massage and open-air swimming pool. May close sometime 2006 for much-needed refurbishment. *Dbl €80–100, sgl €63–85.*

LAJES

🏠 **Hotel Aldeia da Fonte****** Silveira 9930 Lajes; ✆ 292 679 500; e info@aldeiadafonte.com; http://aldeiadafonte.com. 5 mins by car from Lajes. A series of basalt-built self-catering cottages and bedrooms with a central restaurant and lounge bar in a charming garden/woodland setting on cliffs a few metres above the sea. A great effort has been made to integrate the buildings with the landscape. Also offers bicycle hire, guided tours of the island in Portuguese, English and German, guided climbs of Pico, dolphin and whale watching from the hotel's private tower, sailing in a whaling boat – 3hrs at sea with a crew of 3 ex-whalers to enjoy the sea and coastline – traditional fishing with local fisherman and his boat, a day with a traditional Azorean family doing bread making, feeding pigs and chickens, milking cows and having lunch, and a series of self-guided walks from the hotel. Also available is 24hr private medical and nurse care for the elderly who want to escape crowds and northern winters. Excellent restaurant. *Dbl €64–93, sgl €56–78, also 2- and 4-person self-catering studios and suites from €70.*

CAMPING

⛺ **Santo António** São Roque; ✆ 292 642 135; e cms@mail.telepac.pt. Excellent 24hr supervised sheltered site amid pine trees with all amenities, barbecue, tennis court, children's playpark, deer enclosure. Within 200m are restaurants, a disco and the sea. Close by are the Furna pools and access to the sea.

⛺ **Lajes** At the far end of town within easy walking distance of all amenities.

✖ WHERE TO EAT

There is quite a number of eateries, as well as the hotels with restaurants. Note that there are very few places in the eastern sector of the island, east of Lajes and São Roque.

MADALENA Most of the restaurants offer a self-service buffet at lunchtime, with a set price of around €6–7 for soup, bread and main course. Dessert, drinks and coffee are extras.

✖ **Mascote** Rua do Colegio; ✆ 292 622 264. Pizzas cooked in wood-burning ovens; barbecued chicken a speciality.

✖ **A Parisiana** Rua Alexandre Herculano; ✆ 292 623 771. Located by the Madalena swimming pool. Menu includes shellfish; caters for weddings and parties, and has good views of the night-time lights of Horta.

✖ **Restaurante O Marisqueira** Av Padre Nunes da Rosa, next to the wine co-operative; ✆ 292 623 901. Seafood, traditional dishes such as black pudding with pineapple. Nice busy atmosphere.

✖ **Café Restaurante Geladaria Golfinho** Rua Carlos Dabney; ✆ 292 622 116

SÃO JOÃO

Restaurante Marisqueira de Manuel Maciel Rua da Igreja; ☎ 292 673 116. Nice ambience, with some tables having view over the harbour, and fresh fish. Good, though the proprietor may be over confident.

SANTO ANTÓNIO

Restaurante Furna ☎ 292 642 666. Excellent fish. *Open every day.*

SÃO ROQUE

Aguas Cristalinas Rua das Poças; ☎ 292 648 230

LAJES

Restaurante Lagoa Largo São Pedro; ☎ 292 672 272. Menu includes shellfish. *Open every day.*

Restaurante Hocus-Pocus Silveira; ☎ 292 679 504. Belongs to the Aldeia da Fonte Hotel and offers traditional menu, international and Chinese specialities. Nice ambience, good surroundings; definitely trying to do things differently. Recommended.

NIGHTLIFE

MADALENA

Bar Pub Biscoitos Rua dos Biscoitos; ☎ 292 623 723

Bar Porta (Clube Naval–Bar Pub) Rua do Ouvidor Medeiros; ☎ 292 622 264

Registo Nocturno Via Rápida da Madalena; ☎ 292 623 926. Discotheque.

LAJES

☆ **O Farol (disco)** Santa Cruz das Ribeiras; ☎ 292 678 369

Restaurante Lagoa (sometimes uses the café as a pub) Largo de São Pedro; ☎ 292 672 272

SÃO ROQUE DO PICO

Snack Bar do Clube Naval de São Roque do Pico ☎ 292 642 150

Pub Sun7 m 914 635 099

☆ **Discoteca Skipper** ☎ 292 642 185

FESTIVALS

In July Madalena celebrates its patron saint, Santa Maria Madalena, with several days of cultural and musical events. Coinciding with the Festival of Our Lady of Lourdes is the week-long Semana dos Baleeiros or Week of the Whalers. This is celebrated every August in Lajes by a whaling boat regatta and with *fado* and other traditional music as well as modern concerts, an arts and crafts fair and other cultural events. São Roque celebrates Cais de Agosto at the end of July with music and guest bands, guided excursions on Pico Mountain, other guided walks, and exhibitions. Especially popular are the boat trips in restored whaleboats belonging to the São Roque yacht club. In the first or second week of September the Pico Wine Co-operative holds a grape festival with folk dancing and other events to celebrate the harvest.

Espírito Santo (Lajes)	second week of June
Domingo do Espírito Santo (Madalena)	second week of June
Espírito Santo (Criação Velha)	second week of June
Terça-Feira do Espírito Santo (Madalena)	second week of June
Festa de Santa Maria Madalena (Madalena)	last week of July
Cais de Agosto (São Roque do Pico)	last week of July
Festa do Sr Bom Jesus Milagroso (São Mateus)	first week of August
Festa de São João Pequenino	middle of August
Semana dos Baleeiros (Lajes)	fourth week of August

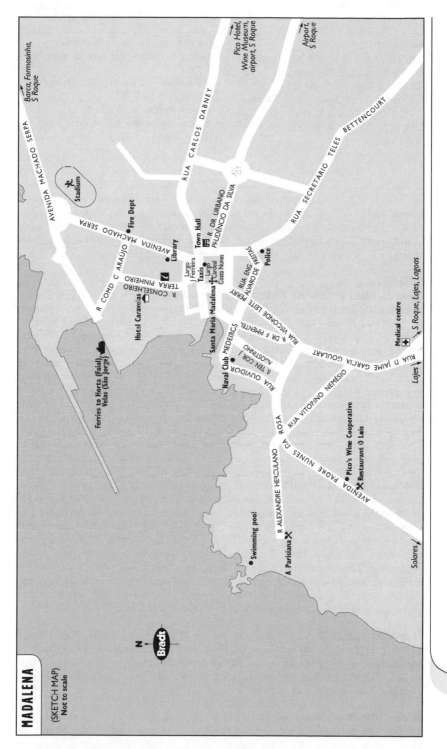

MADALENA

(SKETCH MAP)
Not to scale

N
Bradt

Barca Formosinha,
S Roque

Pico Hotel,
Wine Museum,
airport, S Roque

Airport,
S Roque

AVENIDA MACHADO SERPA

Stadium

Fire Dept

RUA CARLOS DABNEY

R. DR URBANO
PRUDÊNCIO DA SILVA

RUA SECRETÁRIO TELES BETTENCOURT

AVENIDA MACHADO SERPA

Library

Town Hall

R COMD C ARAÚJO

R CONSELHEIRO TERRA PINHEIRO

Largo
J Ferreira

Taxis

Largo
Cardeal
Costa Nunes

Police

Hotel Caravelas

RUA RNG

RUA ÁLVARO DE FREITAS

Santa María Madalena

RUA VISCONDE LEITE FERRY

RUA D JAIME GARCIA GOULART

Medical centre

S Roque, Lajes, Lagoas

Ferries to Horta (Faial),
Velas (São Jorge)

Naval Club MEDEIRCS

R TEN COR J
AGOSTINHO

RUA OUVIDOR

RUA DR F PIMENTEL

Lajes

AVENIDA PADRE NUNES DA ROSA

RUA VITORINO NEMÉSIO

R ALEXANDRE HERCULANO

Pico's Wine Cooperative

Restaurant O Luís

Swimming pool

A Parisiana

Solares

USEFUL NUMBERS

Emergency ℡ 112
Police Lajes, Estrada Regional; ℡ 292 672 410;
Madalena, Rua Secretário Teles Battencourt; ℡ 292
622 860; São Roque; ℡ 292 642 115
Health centres Lajes, Lg Vigário Gonçalo G Lemos,
℡ 292 679 400; Madalena, PÁ Dr Caetano
Mendonça; ℡ 292 628 800; São Roque, Rua do Cais;
℡ 292 648 070.

Post office Lajes, Rua Gen Lacerda Machado.
Madalena, Rua Visconde Leite Perry. São Roque, Rua
do Cais.
SATA Air Açores Rua Dra Maria Glória Duarte,
Madalena; ℡ 292 622 411
Airport information ℡ 292 622 414
Tourist information office Rua Conselheiro Terra
Pinheiro, Madalena; ℡ 292 623 524

WHAT TO SEE AND DO

Essential to Pico's past, and very much the present because of the tourism that is
keeping the island's history in the forefront of consciousness, are wine and whales.
This means the extensive vineyards around the coast near Madalena and the wine
museum and three very different whale museums. Then there is the landscape and
of course all the little villages that can be visited on a car tour.

MUSEUMS

Museu dos Baleeiros (Whalers' Museum) *(Rua dos Baleeiros, Lajes;* ℡ *292 672 276; Open 1
May–30 Sep, Tue–Fri 09.30–12.30 and 14.00–17.30, weekends 14.00–17.30; 1 Oct–30
Apr, 10.00–12.30 and 14.00–17.00, weekends 14.00–17.30; closed Mon and bank holidays)*
This is a fascinating exhibition about whaling as it was in the Azores until 1985. The
exhibits are appropriately displayed in three original 19th-century boathouses plus
ancillary areas. They include boats, tools and other artefacts, photographs, many good
examples of scrimshaw, a blacksmith's workshop and much else, as well as a library
well stocked with titles about whaling and cetaceans. Twenty years ago it was a tiny
museum where you often had to get the key from a nearby house to gain admission.
Long-held ambitions for a museum to truly reflect the bravery and lifestyle of the
Azores' whalers have now been realised and the displays are constantly being
improved. The museum provides an essential experience for any visitor wishing to
understand the role of whaling in the social and economic history of the islands.

Museu da Indústria Baleeira *(Rua do Poço, São Roque;* ℡ *292 622 147; open 1 May –30
Sep, Tue–Fri 09.00–19.00, and Sat, Sun and holidays 09.00–17.00; 1 Oct–30 Apr, Tue–Fri
09.00–18.00)* Housed in the old whale factory that was built in 1946 and closed in
1984 to become a museum ten years later. The original USA-manufactured
machinery is well oiled as though it had only just finished working. You can begin to
see what it must have been like when a huge sperm whale was brought in for
processing; definitely missing is the smell, not even a lingering whiff, which would
really have brought it to life. Hopefully in time there will be some explanation of the
machinery and how it was all done, but the curator is enthusiastic and may be free to
give you a guided tour. It is located near the harbour and Clube Naval.

Cachalotes e Lulas *(*℡ *292 673 267; open 1 May–30 Sep weekdays 10.00–17.30 and Sun
14.00–17.30)* In the small village of São João, on the south coast west of Lajes, this
remarkable museum concentrates on the sperm whale and its prey of squid *(cachelotes
e lulas)*. There are life-sized models, photographs and video, with notes in both
Portuguese and English.

Wine Museum *(Open Tue–Fri 09.00–12.20 and 13.30–17.00, Sat and Sun
09.00–12.30; closed Mon; admission free)* About a 30-minute walk on the main road

(Rua Carlos Dabney) to the airport and close to the Hotel Pico. Take the road off left just before you get to the hotel and you will come to the museum housed in an old Carmelite convent enclosed by a high stone wall and doors painted orange. Look out for the conspicuous tall araucaria and large metrosideros tree by the entrance. There are fascinating old photographs and early equipment. You can also taste and purchase Pico wines. A real bonus in the garden is a small grove of dragon trees and their seedlings, totalling around 70 stems. The largest individual tree has a canopy spread of about 16m and a stem diameter of 1m.

WINE

Cooperativa Vitivinicola winery (*A short walk past the municipal swimming pool in the Av Padre Nunes da Rosa;* ✆ *292 622 262; www.picowines.net; open Mon–Fri 08.00–17.00*) Here you can see the production and bottling plants, and taste their Angelica and Lajido. Guided tours should be booked 24 hours in advance.

Moinho do Frade (*Open Jun–Sep every day 09.00–17.00 except Mon; Apr, May, Oct, Sat 16.00–17.00, Sun 09.00–10.30; Nov–Mar, Sun 09.00–10.00 and 14.00–15.00*) The historically important UNESCO World Heritage wine growing area just south of Madalena starting at Criação Velha captures an important economic and social period of the Azores. This recently restored windmill provides a splendid elevated view over an extraordinary landscape.

Cachorro Adega Near the airport, a small traditional *adega* (wine cellar) with local wine and liqueurs for tasting and purchase along with some handicrafts is open in summer.

CAVES

Gruta das Torres (*Further information from Direção de Serviços da Conservação da natureza;* ✆ *292 666 990; e grutadastorres@sapo.pt. Maximum tour group size is 12, €3.50 pp, seniors free. Open May–Oct weekends 14.30–17.30; Jun–Sep every day 14.30–17.30; Jul and Aug 10.00–12.00 and 14.30–17.30*) A ten-minute drive from Madalena, it is signposted near Criação Velha. This lava cave is a fascinating volcanic phenomenon arising from lava flowing from the eruptions of Cabeço Brava and appears as a tunnel running through and emerging from an old lava flow. The principal tunnel is 4,480m long and mostly around 15m high. There are much smaller lateral secondary tunnels that show greater geological diversity. There is good public access and explanation and the entrance has been built of basalt rocks cleverly designed to blend into the landscape.

The surfaces of lava flows often develop into two types which have been given the Hawaiian names of aa and pahoehoe. The aa is formed from the more viscous lava which soon congeals and does not travel far and the surface is a jumbled mass of angular and rugged rocks. A pahoehoe surface is formed from more fluid lava and frequently resemble huge coils of rope; as the lava cools it often produces a skin-like surface beneath which the lava is still liquid and as this continues to flow the smooth skin gets wrinkled and ropey. The image comes to mind of a dollop of hot jam on a plate to test the setting point from the wrinkles when pushed by the cook's finger. Occasionally this skin-like solidified crust gets attached to the sides of the channel and when the molten lava beneath drains away the crust is left suspended, thus forming an empty tunnel. Liquid lava dripping from the roof congeals into stalactites and other curious shapes and the tunnel may present numerous different manifestations of the lava flow. With time they can also develop secondary features such as stalagmites and stalactites of limonite, an iron mineral, or silica. This tunnel shows good examples of both lava types and is rich *with Chris Beer*

Traditional Azorean shore-based whaling was a punishing way of life. The whalers used open boats, hand harpoons and lances and never adopted the rocket harpoons of the large whaling fleets. Before the introduction of motor launches, the men had to sail and row their boats out to where the whale had been sighted; then, after killing a whale, they had to tow it as far as 50km back to land. They possessed great courage and had a great respect for the whales.

From vantage points above the coast men known as *vigias* would spend their days looking for whales, using nothing more than a telescope or binoculars. Mornings were the most productive times and on a good day the blow of a sperm whale could be seen from 35km away. Once a whale had been sighted the *vigia* would send a message, often by firing a small rocket, to the village where the whaleboats were kept. The boats, known as *canoas*, were similar to but slightly longer than the whaleboats used by Yankee whalers, with a crew comprising a helmsman, harpooner, and five oarsmen (one more than the Americans). Latterly, the boats would set out under the tow of a motor launch, letting go of the tow when about a mile from the whales to avoid the engine noise scaring the whales. The boats were originally directed by the *vigias* using a system of large sheets laid out on the hills, but some time around World War II VHF radios were introduced.

After releasing the towline the crew would either sail or row very close to the whale, and a 2.5m harpoon was thrown. This was done within 2–3m of the animal, although sometimes the *canoa* was sailed right onto the whale. The harpoon had to be thrown with such force that it penetrated deep into the flesh, allowing the iron head to go into the muscle beneath the blubber or snag behind a rib. The harpoon did little damage. The whale would immediately dive and take out line at a very fast rate, with water being poured onto the line to stop the friction setting it on fire. The men would quickly have to lower the sails and mast while at the same time avoiding the fast-running line down the middle of the boat, between each man's rowing position. Once several hundred metres of line had been taken out, the line would be fixed to the loggerhead – a post at the back of the canoe. Once the line was fixed, the *canoa* would then be towed along by the whale at speeds of up to 25–30km/h until it grew tired and surfaced. This tow was often called the 'Nantucket sleigh ride' and could be a very dangerous time for the whalers because, if the whale veered or doubled back, the boat could capsize and the crew be crushed or drowned. The crew made the final kill using hand lances, to pierce a lung or other major organ. The complete action usually lasted between one and three hours, but if it was a strong and healthy male it could sometimes take a day or even longer.

---

in geological forms. The temperature inside the tunnel is a constant 15°C throughout the year, and a high humidity is maintained by water filtering through the roof.

The guided tour takes about 45 minutes and you will be loaned a hard hat with a lamp. Good sensible shoes are essential. Before the tour you will be shown a ten-minute film in English or Portuguese about the volcanic caves of the Azores.

WALKING Pico Island is really failing on its services for visitors by not investing in its huge potential for walking trails. There is some glorious countryside with a lot of hidden history and of course landscapes unique to Pico, especially among the forested land and on higher ground. What should be avoided is walking on bare, dusty volcanic cinders in blazing sunshine, even if within close proximity to the sea. Apart from the ascent of Pico (see page 191) the best way to enjoy the island is

If other whales were close by, the killed animal would be left marked with a flag while these were hunted. The number caught in a day was limited by the number of harpoons carried (six was common). The motor launch stood by in support during the killing, to supply extra line and help with the lancing. If it was a solitary kill, a hole would be cut in the whale's flukes and the launch would tow it and the *canoa* to the whaling factory.

At the factory, steam winches would pull the carcasses up a slipway out of the sea. Local people would then often scrape the thin outer layer of skin off the whale for fishing bait. First the head was removed, to extract the more valuable spermaceti oil used in beauty products, then the blubber was cut into pieces and placed in giant steam-powered pressure cookers. After the oil was drained off, the remains were hydraulically pressed to remove the last of the oil, and what was left made into bonemeal. The guts were often towed out to sea and dumped.

Whalers received very little regular wages and relied almost entirely on their share of the catch. The factory took 25% of the oil together with all meat and bone, while the remaining 75% was divided equally, half going to the shareholders of the whaling company that owned the *canoas* and tow launch, the other half to the boat crews and *vigias*.

In 1949 there were still men whaling from all nine islands of the Azores with 484 whales caught using 125 *canoas*, but the industry was in decline and by 1979 these figures had dropped to 125 whales from just three islands using nine *canoas*. Substitutes for sperm-whale products, the serious decline in the planet's whale populations through over-hunting by other nations and consequent conservation legislation were important factors leading to the end of whale hunting in the Azores in 1984.

However, whales still have an important role in the culture and festivals of the islanders. There is a Whaler's Festival in Lajes do Pico each summer and sometimes one gets a chance to see an effigy of a sperm whale being paraded through the streets. Many of the old whaling villages still have one or more *canoas* and each summer sees challenges for rowing or sailing races between villages. The men lavish great care and attention on their remaining *canoas* and sometimes even commission new ones to be built especially for the races. Competition for a place in the crew is fierce. There is no more impressive sight in the Azores today than a dozen gleaming *canoas* coming at top speed into a small harbour while the whole town in festive mood cheers them on.

Chris Beer runs Whale Watch Azores; for more information see the website: www.whalewatchazores.com.

with a hire car and stop in the high country wherever you see the temptation to walk. There are many farm tracks to follow, and do remember not to walk off beaten trails because it is easy for the inexperienced to fall into holes well concealed beneath the moss, ferns and other vegetation.

BIRDS AND FLOWERS Pico offers the easiest access to remnant laurisilva forest and provided there is no thick fog, the EN 3 road passing **Lagoa do Capitão** will reveal a good number of the typical Azorean species including superb specimens of the handsome *Euphorbia stygiana*. The various lakes in this highland area can attract ducks and waders. The harbours offer good opportunities for birding, especially Madalena; the recommended place is **Ponto do Areia**, just to the south, which also gives sight of two small islands. **Lajes** has a number of habitats beyond the harbour thanks to a large eroded lava flow that offers intertidal pools and marshland. Vitally, it helps protects the town from winter storms, but has suffered

Not surprisingly, the extraordinary appearance of this tree has ensured it a place in parks and large gardens wherever there is a suitable Mediterranean climate. However, in its native state it is classified as endangered. The tree is endemic to the Canary and Cape Verde islands where already it is extinct on some individual islands, and there are just two surviving wild trees on Madeira, where it was once widespread in the arid lowland areas, especially on adjacent Porto Santo where it is incorporated into the town's coat of arms. So abundant was it on this island it seems that when the first settlers arrived they felled trees in large numbers without learning how to propagate them, and flooded the market with resin until the price dropped so low they ceased harvesting, thus inadvertently saving whatever trees remained. The fruits became famous for fattening pigs, but here, too, the tree is now extinct.

Bound to mythology, it would seem Hercules might have been the first plant hunter associated with it. His 11th and last labour was to seek and bring back three golden apples from the Garden of the Hespérides, and after searching all the known world he is thought to have located the garden on an island beyond the Atlas Mountains. The garden was guarded by Landon, the hundred-headed dragon, and when Landon was killed his blood flowed out across the land and from it trees sprung up which we now know as dragon trees.

With the scientific name of *Dracaena draco*, this very slow-growing umbrella-shaped tree grows to a height of 15m or more, develops a hugely wide crown, and produces numerous branched inflorescences of small greenish-white sweetly scented flowers followed by 1cm-wide fleshy orange fruits. After each flowering, the tree then branches. Their trunks do not have annular rings like most other trees so to determine their age one has to know roughly how often they flower, once every ten to 15 years (maybe more frequently in the Azores), and count the number of branches. Once thought to live for very many hundreds of years, this has been revised downwards to 600 or so. It would be fun to determine the oldest specimen in the Azores, since they have been cultivated here for at least 500 years.

From the dragon tree comes dragon's blood, the sap of the tree that upon drying becomes a reddish resin, and in the Canary Islands this was used by the aboriginal Guanche to embalm their dead. Dragon's blood was widely known in ancient times, used as a dye and medicine, but this probably came from *Dracaena cinnabarini* on the island of Socotra, and from Somalia. Other plants produce resins also known as dragon's blood and *Daemonorops*, a palm, from Sumatra, is the main source of the dragon's blood varnish for violins.

That *Dracaena draco* is now an endangered species is probably due to habitat loss and other human influences, but before the Spanish invaded and colonised the Canary Islands, we are told a flightless bird related to the pigeon and about the size of a turkey used to feed upon the fruits of the dragon tree. It soon became extinct, and one theory is that the dragon trees there declined because the seeds had to pass through the bird's digestive system before they would germinate. If this is true, it would be interesting to know if anything eats the seeds in the Azores, because they certainly seem to germinate well in the garden of Pico's wine museum!

badly in recent years. It is rated one of Pico's best sites for shorebirds, herons, terns and rarities.

WHALE WATCHING Pico is one of the main islands associated with whale watching because Lajes is where it all began, and company shops and offices are to be found in both Madalena and Lajes. Approved boat operators are listed on noticeboards by the quay. Similar services are also readily available across the channel in Horta on Faial, from where most of the larger more comfortable boats operate.

SWIMMING

Madalena Right in town, by the harbour, is one of the best swimming pools that looks really inviting, with space, sea views and Faial across the channel. There is also a good natural rock pool, where even with a good swell the surface is stable. Changing facilities, showers, etc and all for no charge. In summer there is a snack bar, but there is also a restaurant nearby. In midwinter, the locals were swimming in the harbour because the water there was warmer than the pool.

GARDENS

Quinta das Rosas (*Open 09.00–18.00*) This was a private garden and evidently once beautiful and filled with plants, especially roses. It was bequeathed by its owner to the government and some interesting exotic plants remain, while efforts are being made to restore it. A visit will pass an hour or so if you have time to fill; it is about ten minutes by taxi from Madalena.

CAR TOURS

Car tour 1 Madalena–São Roque–Lajes–Madalena Madalena years ago was a little sleepy sort of place and because it had not been touched for ages had a pleasing air. With the new harbour, new hotel and a huge amount of empty adjacent space left around for no obvious use except for car parking the whole place has become a visual shambles. No doubt in time it will be transformed, but at present the ferry terminus for Horta is the only attraction, aside from the swimming pool. Viewed from the sea at a distance with Pico Mountain in the background it looks very picturesque.

Depart from **Madalena** and first take the main road to the airport at Bandeiras and from near the airport follow the road signs to **Porto do Cachorro** on the northern coast. The tiny harbour, really just a slipway, is set among a tumble of black lava. This is contorted into many weird shapes and arches where the sea rushes in; in fact the sea has been rushing in rather effectively and the little cement pathway that once led the visitor safely through is being destroyed and you are now advised to keep your distance. The flat concrete building at the edge of the sea is for generating electricity from wave power. The black lava buildings are mostly *adegas*, places where village wine, the *vinho de cheiro*, is made and stored and in September it can be very jolly here. One of them is now a small museum and shop. You will find a sunken, grassy area and a larger stone house with a well in front that at one time served the nearby communities of both Santa Luzia and Bandeiras. Such wells, known as tide wells, were dug near the sea so that seawater entering it would be filtered and at least made brackish for general use and, in times of severe drought, drinking. Note also the typical stone and cement cisterns with their roofs sloping down to the centre to catch and store rainwater.

Continue parallel with the coast, coming first to **Lajido** where there is another communal well, this time in the middle of the road. An old distillery, *adega* and manor house are being restored. You have been passing through an area of *mistério*, a tumble of lava from the 1718 eruption emanating some 900m up the side of Pico. The lava took two years to cool and prevented travel between São Roque and Madalena so that people were obliged to go by sea. Right by the roadside just before you get to **Arcos** you should be able to make out the wheel tracks of oxcarts in the lava flow. You will come to **Santa Luzia**, a traditional wine-producing area, and then **Santana**. Some of the large, pretentious, and totally out of scale new houses intruding upon the landscape are summer holiday homes, some of their owners still working in North America.

Just past **Santo António** you come to an area called **Furnas**. Here the lava solidified as it flowed down and met the sea, and the smooth swirls of rock resemble congealed chocolate sauce. Continue to **São Roque** where there is a café in the centre of the village. If you want to visit the whale factory museum, before you get to São Roque look out for a house with green-painted shutters on your left; take the road off past it to go down to the harbour where you will find the museum near the Clube Naval. The club, incidentally, provides very good-value meals. If you miss this turn-off and get to the post office, you will need to go back about 200m.

From **São Roque** take the EN 2 signposted to Lajes and head for the mountains. There are glorious views behind you back to the coast as you climb. When the road stops climbing at around 700m the landscape is of rounded hills, pastures and remnants of the original forest that once covered much of the island. You will come to a junction with the EN 3 heading back to Madalena. Turn right, taking the EN 3 for about 2.5km to come to a small road off at 90° on your right leading to **Lagoa do Capitão**. This is just a small lake with a few isolated endemic junipers still withstanding the winds; walk anticlockwise round and follow the path leading off right uphill. Go behind the hill to be rewarded with a magnificent view of the whole length of São Jorge and, below, the coast of Pico around São Roque, something most visitors miss.

Retrace the way you came to rejoin the previous road, turning right in the direction of Lajes. Continue until you come to a narrow side road off to your left, signposted to **Lagoa do Caiado**. Drive down this road for a few hundred metres and here you will see some of the important native plant species, many of which are endemic, found only in the Azores. While botanically fascinating, do be very careful if you wander from the road because there are many deep hollows between the rocks under the covering of mosses for the unwary to fall into and possibly disappear!

Return to the main EN 2 road and descend to **Lajes**. It is a pretty drive; do allow time to take it slowly. Images that come to mind are of tall, stately cryptomeria trees, green meadows, hills, rounded hills, conical hills and glimpses through trees of hills going on higher up. Sunshine and shadow on the road; shining bright leaves; leaves of large-leaved gingers give a subtropical effect; and occasional camellia trees 5m tall are in full red bloom in January.

Lajes was the first settlement on the island and is well worth an hour's exploration. The 17th- and 18th-century houses offer interesting architectural details and the little chapel of São Pedro at the far end is a delight inside, built around 1460 by the first settlers. Regrettably it has been rendered with cement so that it could easily be mistaken for somebody's outbuilding; for centuries it had a thatched roof. Next to the Church of Our Lady of the Conception is the town hall, formerly a Franciscan convent. From the harbour there are fine views of Pico Mountain; the whaling museum is also just by the harbour – see page 184.

As you drive back to Madalena following the coast, you will see in the woodlands around **Misterio de São João** inviting picnic areas built by the forest services. At São João is the Cachalotes and Lulas Museum and then before you reach Madalena turn off the main road towards the coast to the village of **Criaçao Velha**. (If you have time, turn off before this and explore some of the coast and its settlements.) Criaçao Velha begins the wine-producing area along to the small port of **Areia Larga**, formerly used whenever bad weather closed nearby Madalena. This UNESCO-recognised heritage area captures something of former times when Pico wine was in full production and would have been swarming with hundreds of workers. You will see clearly above all the stone walls the **Moinho do Frade**, a restored mill which provided an elevated view over the vineyards – see page 185. Continue round the coast coming to the wine co-operative on the outskirts of Madalena near the municipal swimming pool.

Car tour 2 Around the coast of the eastern part

With a whole day stretching ahead of you a tour of the eastern sector is really a journey of gentle exploration following the main EN 1 road that encircles the island and dropping down to explore little places on the coast that appeal as and when you get to them. Guidance would spoil the fun, but there is just a couple of areas that you might not notice.

Calheta de Nesquim and Ponta da Ilha at the eastern tip

Coming from Lajes along the southern coast, drop down from the main EN 1 road to Calheta de Nesquim following the steep winding cobbled road (very slippery when wet) and stop at the Church of São Sebastião. This is a typical Roman Catholic village church immediately overlooking the harbour, dated 1856; note the old whalebone door latch and handle. Return to the EN 1 by the road you came down and when you come to conspicuous blue tourist signs take the first right to **Ponta da Ilha** and the immaculately kept lighthouse at the eastern tip of Pico. From here there is a fine view of the eastern sector of São Jorge and in the distance Terceira looking almost circular with a central plateau. Return to the EN 1 and immediately take the tourist sign to **Parque Matos Souto** and the **Desenvolvimento Agrario**. Awaiting you at the end of the winding road is a delightful garden with shade trees and ornamental flowers, lily pond and picnic tables maintained by the forestry service. Even if you are not ready for your picnic, it is charming to visit.

Once more return to the EN 1 and shortly you will come to **Piedade** where there is a bank and some shops. Along the very straight stretch of road following look out for a small viewing point of **Terra Alta**, a narrow concrete belvedere 330m atop the steep sea cliff; it provides a fine view across the channel of São Jorge while directly below you is a forest of pittosporum and a few native laurels trying to compete with the invader.

Take the turning down to **Santo Amaro** and stop in the square by the Church of Nossa Senhora do Carmo. About 100m along the road following the sea wall is the most charming crafts museum in a traditional house. Very original corn dollies, straw hats, embroidery, fish-scale flower pictures, weaving and other crafts are displayed, together with three rooms furnished in traditional manner. Another house is a craft workshop while a third is a small shop selling many crafts plus angelica liqueur and delicious fig jam. Near the slipway is the boatbuilding yard, the main centre for the whole of the Azores. Access to the sea at this point is very gentle, something so rare in the islands that this may be the reason boatbuilding began here.

Stay on the lower road and continue to **Prainha** and the square and its cafés at the side of the church with its little garden. From the main door of the church is a good view of São Jorge. Take the road that continues on behind the church which quickly turns steeply uphill to rejoin the EN 1 and continue to São Roque. You will pass by the **Prainha Forest Park**, a splendidly laid-out picnic and recreation area beneath the trees, with good washroom facilities.

WALK

THE ASCENT OF PICO (*Time: the ascent can take between 2 and 5 hours, depending upon how fit you are and weather conditions, but generally it takes between 2½ and 3½ hours. Allow half as long again for the descent.*) However many mountains you might have

WALK: ASCENT OF PICO

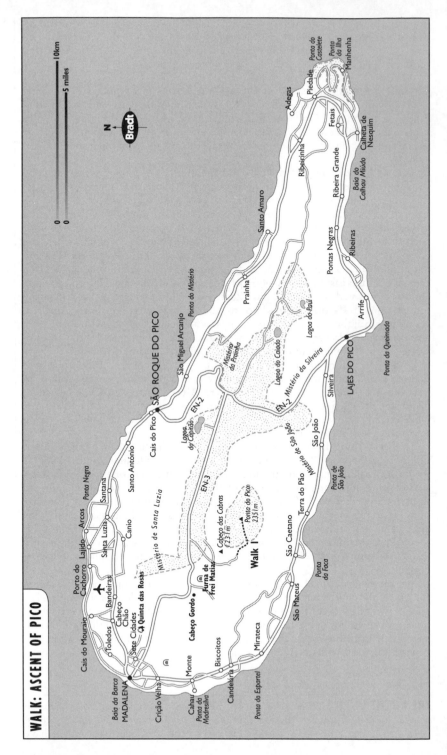

climbed, to be on the top of Pico is to be over 2,000m high in mid Atlantic, and that is an experience to stay with you for life if there are clear views. In June and July the two native species of thyme and heath, *Thymus caespititius* and *Daboecia azorica*, are in full flower and the higher slopes are a spectacular pink and wine, a veritable rock garden of massed colour.

You are strongly recommended not to attempt this on your own, and everyone must first register with the fire department. From June to the end of September this can be done at the start of the climb at Cabeço das Cabras; alternatively, and at other times of the year, registration is at the fire station in Madalena, on the Avenida Machado Serpa behind the Hotel Caravelas (\ *292 628 300*). There is a professional guide service. A list of *Guias de Montanho* is kept by the tourist office in Rua Conselheiro Terra Pinheiro, Madalena (\ *292 623 524*). The fire department also has the list of experienced trained guides qualified in first aid. The fee is from € 100, depending on the services required and if it is a night climb.

The above precautions are imposed because walkers do get into trouble as the ground can be dangerous off the small footpath and the weather changes very quickly. Incautious visitors have had to be rescued by the Civil Protection Service and a cavalier attitude to the mountain is irresponsible. The climb is not technically difficult, but it should be attempted only by strong walkers. There are some steep slopes; the path, such as it is, is very uneven. Part of the way is on slippery vegetation and in places over loose stones and cinders, and the ascent of the little peak at the summit is a 70m scramble. Also note the descent can be more difficult because of steep and uneven surfaces. Good strong walking shoes with a well-profiled sole are essential.

Before setting off it is wise to see what the day's weather is likely to be, for to make the ascent without the views would be terribly disappointing and very possibly dangerous. Therefore make your decision by 08.00. Alternatively be bold and arrange to be taken up to the start of the climb, by 04.00 at the very latest, so you can be high on the mountain, if not at the summit, for sunrise. The early-morning light has a special quality and as the sun catches the lower daughter volcanic cones and slowly spreads up the mountainside to strike you, banishing the cold of dawn, it vindicates the decision to make the effort. The ultimate, of course, is to watch the sunset, then bivouac and wait for the sunrise. Remember, though, that however hot it is at sea level, it can get cold at night near the summit, so be prepared. When I made the climb in June, Pico was surrounded by clouds and looked very unpromising. The next day dawned clear and was almost perfect, and the following day it rained torrents. As with all mountains, it is a mix of luck and timing.

The trail begins from the road at Cabeço das Cabras, and is clearly defined by the passage of many feet. The route is marked by 100m-interval posts. Beginning at around 1,200m, you are already more than halfway up. When you reach the rim of the crater, you drop down and cross to Pico Pequeno for the final 70m pitch to the summit. If the clouds are kind you should be able to see Faial, São Jorge, Graciosa and Terceira.

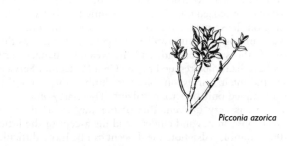
Picconia azorica

Part Four

WESTERN GROUP

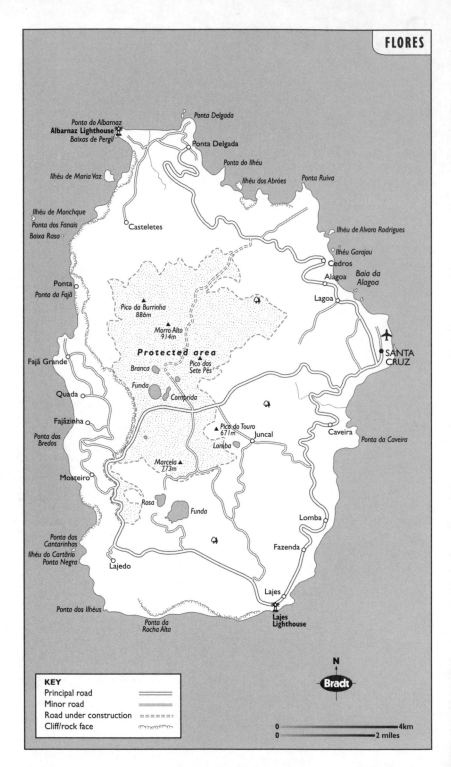

FLORES

Ponta Delgada

Ponta do Albarnaz
Albarnaz Lighthouse
Baixas de Pergil

Ponta Delgada

Ponta do Ilhéu

Ilhéu de Maria Vaz

Ilhéu dos Abróes

Ponta Ruiva

Ilhéu de Monchque
Ponta dos Fanais

Baixa Rasa

Casteletes

Ilhéu de Alvaro Rodrigues

Ilhéu Garajau

Cedros

Ponta
Ponta da Fajã

Alagoa

Baía da
Alagoa

Lagoa

Pico da Burrinha
886m

Morro Alto
914m

Protected area

Branca

Pico dos
Sete Pés

SANTA
CRUZ

Fajã Grande

Quada

Funda

Comprida

Fajãzinha

Ponta das
Bredos

Pico do Touro
671m

Lomba

Juncal

Caveira

Ponta da Caveira

Marcela
773m

Mosteiro

Rosa

Funda

Lomba

Ponta das
Cantarinhas
Ilhéu do Cartário
Ponta Negra

Lajedo

Fazenda

Ponta dos Ilhéus

Lajes

Ponta da
Rocha Alta

**Lajes
Lighthouse**

N

Bradt

KEY
Principal road
Minor road
Road under construction ======
Cliff/rock face

0   4km
0   2 miles

10

Flores

> At night, in the silence of this small sanctuary, you can almost hear the sound of the sun falling against the horizon ... afterwards, everything seems even more serene, but at the same time more intense, fragrant, inexplicably captivating, as if part of a poem.
> Quoted from the Aldeia da Cuada's brochure.

Not only have you now reached the westernmost island of the archipelago, you are also at the western extremity of Europe. Europe ends at Flores, the Isle of Flowers, on longitude 31° 15' W, and 1,380 miles from Lisbon. Given the island's small area, only 17km long and 12.5km wide, it is probably the most intensively rugged of the archipelago, with peaks, valleys, crater lakes and precipitous cliffs. Small pastures and arable fields all surrounded with hydrangea hedges or lichen-encrusted stone walls tie these together.

Although it is a long way from anywhere, Flores is an island of quite spectacular natural beauty and well worth the effort to reach. July and August are the peak times, June and September are busy, then tourism fades away. Come in winter, see no other tourists, enjoy sharp lighting, cloud effects, rainbows, storms, brilliant sunshine, wonderful conditions for photography – for in winter there is tremendous clarity – and simply escape from the madding crowds. Today, however, all too often the tourist is in a hurry to see everything and move on. Having invested travel time and fares to reach Flores, do stay at least three nights, even if you are not a walker; if you are, then think of five nights. If you want to visit nearby Corvo, you should allow an extra day. Ideally, you would spend a whole week. In winter, be tempted to rent an old restored comfortable cottage with wood-burning stove, bring books and CDs, and retreat for a month or three.

Whatever you do, make sure you have spare days in your itinerary to allow for cancelled flights due to bad weather. It is bad luck when flights are cancelled, but it does happen. There is a lovely story about a consul in Flores who had never left the island and, in the mid 1800s, boarded a ship that had called to take on fresh provisions. The weather became too rough for the ship to remain at the anchorage and stood out to sea for safety; the wind became stronger and it was impossible for a small boat to go ashore. Being short of provisions, the ship sailed away with the consul to its intended destination, arriving a few days later in England!

HIGHLIGHTS

These are mostly landscape and geological; the peaks of Sete Pes, Burrinha, Marcela and from Flores's highest point at 914m, Morro Alto, all best seen from the viewpoint overlooking the Fazenda da Santa Cruz Valley; the Rocha dos Bordões basalt pipes; the seven different lakes in the centre of the island; several waterfalls; sea cliffs 600m high; and, for navigators, the islet of Monchique used as one of the main reference points to check navigational aids when sailors relied upon astronomy. Everywhere the countryside is beautiful, and there is constant temptation to stop the car and quietly take in the atmosphere. For walkers, there is the ultimate in conversation stoppers: walking the length of Europe's westernmost coastline. In summer when the weather is settled, one of the finest ways to appreciate the island is to take a boat trip along the coast, part of which you will see anyway if you go to Corvo by boat.

GENERAL BACKGROUND

GEOGRAPHY This rugged island defiantly stands proud of the ocean, with many lengths of precipitous cliff challenging the sea to do its worst. In a few places the land descends less abruptly to meet the sea, resulting in ravines and narrow river mouths, and just occasionally the descent could almost be described as sharply gradual, for example in the northeast and the odd point of flat land in the east, convenient for the airport and main town of Santa Cruz. All the villages lie around the island's circumference, either close by the sea or perched upon the clifftops. Unique among the Azores for being without a large caldera or dominated by long fissures, the younger central zone is made from several eruptive centres while the exposed rocks around the coast are the oldest at over 600,000 years. Within historic times there have been no eruptions, and evidence suggests the volcanoes may now be extinct. The chance of history made Flores the frontier post of Europe rather than of the USA.

HISTORY The name Flores, meaning 'flowers', is thought to derive from the many yellow flowers of *Cubres* that adorned the sea cliffs at the time of Portuguese discovery. This is the local name for *Solidago sempervirens*, a North American species that might have been introduced, but has certainly been in the Azores for a very long time.

Diogo de Teive and his son João discovered the island around 1452, much later than the other two island groups. The first settlement was attempted by a Flemish nobleman at the bottom of the Ribeira da Cruz, a deep and dramatic valley with a small rocky beach giving access from the sea. They tried to grow woad for export but because of the island's isolation and lack of a good natural harbour this failed after a few years, and permanent settlement began only in 1504 with people mainly from Terceira and Madeira. Possibly by 1515 Lajes was already a small town, and 30 years later so was Santa Cruz, and by the end of that century the parish of Ponta Delgada on the north coast was also well established. Contemporary accounts tell us the population of Flores was around 1,300 people, and conditions primitive. The houses were straw-thatched huts, the paths were muddy and so bad they could not be used by wheeled carts. Seldom did they get a boat visit from Terceira, and then only between March and September because of the winds.

However, the Azores were good hunting grounds for pirates and corsairs and in June 1587 five English vessels destroyed Lajes. The Spanish organised each year two major convoys called the *Flota* and the *Galeones* to protect ships bringing back bullion from South America. In 1591 a British squadron waited to intercept the *Flota* on its way back from Mexico. The British crews had suffered greatly from illness and were largely ashore when a Spanish fleet sent to the Azores to meet and protect the *Flota* hove into sight. The British rapidly embarked but one ship, the *Revenge*, was slow to escape and was cut off. Single-handed the ship, under the command of Sir Richard Grenville, a wealthy landowner and cousin of Sir Walter Raleigh, fought the entire Spanish fleet for 15 hours, sinking two enemy ships before surrendering; an action immortalised by Tennyson's poem, *The Revenge*, beginning 'At Flores in the Azores Sir Richard Grenville...'. Sir Richard was mortally wounded and buried ashore but, being Protestant, not in consecrated ground. About the end of World War II a storm exposed near the shore the buried remains of a man much taller than the islanders, together with a big sword. Could this have been the long-lost grave of Sir Richard? If it was, the remains are again lost.

By 1770 the island was no more peaceful, for in that year two American privateers badly bombarded Lajes, but were eventually fought off with a cannon firing broken crockery, bottles and stones and finally a cannonball.

The early economic activity was survival; yams were the mainstay, plus potatoes and other vegetables together with fish and bread, with the export of woad and minor products such as archil (lichen), while sheep produced wool. By the middle of the 18th century supplying whalers and other shipping provided an income to the island, which peaked around the middle of the 19th century with meat, fruit and vegetables being exchanged or sold for export to the other islands, Madeira and beyond. Reflecting the economy the population also peaked at this time, and since then over the last 150 years has gradually declined, largely through emigration, from over 10,000 to the present total of around 4,500. Open-boat land based whaling began in 1860 and reached its peak in the late 1930s; there followed construction early in the next decade of the whale factory in Santa Cruz and a second one in Lajes, but these were always handicapped by the lack of a good harbour. Whales killed by Corvo men were towed to Flores for processing, and the last whale killed in the Western Group was off Corvo in 1981.

Roads within the island were bad or non-existent for a very long time, and only in the 1950s did this begin to change. What really ended the isolation of the island was the building of an airport, port improvements and the opening of a French meteorological observatory and satellite-tracking station in the 1960s. The French have gone, made redundant through new technology, and the economy depends upon meat and tourism. Fishing is small and enough for the island, although in the peak of summer visitors it can barely meet demand.

GETTING THERE AND AWAY

BY PLANE SATA Air Açores flies to Flores either from Ponta Delgada, Terceira or Faial (Horta) every day except Sunday. Return flights are again to either Terceira or Faial (Horta). There are also limited connections from Corvo.

BY FERRY Until recently there has been in summer a very occasional sailing from the central islands to Flores. Now, with a different operator, this may change and any summer service should be posted on the company's website (*www.transmacor.pt*).

BY YACHT Increasingly those crossing the Atlantic are making Flores their first landfall in the Azores. There are moorings in the port of Lajes das Flores. Some services are planned for the future (*Clube Naval;* ☎ *292 593 145*).

GETTING AROUND

There are public buses, but they are infrequent and do not always operate every day so it is better to ignore them. If you get stuck, you will find local drivers amenable to hitchhikers.

Taxi hire for a day's sightseeing tour costs around €100, €60 for half-day from Santa Cruz. Most likely your driver will follow the route described under *What to see and do* on page 203. The high-level tour described in *Itineraries* (see page 205) takes about four hours and the tour to Ponta Delgada on the north coast takes around two hours.

CAR HIRE

IUR Rent-a-Car Rua da Esperança, 9970-320 Santa Cruz das Flores; ☎ 292 590 110; e iur@ virtualazores.com; www.virtualazores.com/iur/
Auto Turísitica das Flores Tv São José 3, 9970-341

Santa Cruz das Flores; ☎ 292 592 990
Rent-a-Car Braga & Braga Zona Industrial Boqueirão, 9970-390 Santa Cruz; ☎ 292 592 685

TRAVEL AGENTS

Agência Viagens Hortatur Rua da Conceição 12, 9970-447 Santa Cruz das Flores; ☎ 292 542 006;

e hortatur@mail.telepac.pt; www.ciberacores.pt/hortatur

WHERE TO STAY

In Santa Cruz das Flores there are two conventional hotels and a small one that is part of a bar/restaurant. All are adequate, but lack comfort. There is rural accommodation in Fajã Grande. In the peak summer months demand is such that you will definitely have to book in advance.

Hotel Ocidental** (36 rooms) Av dos Baleeiros, 9970-306 Santa Cruz das Flores; ☎ 292 590 100; e hotelocidental@hotmail.com; www.hotelocidental.com. Good location, next to the sea. Many rooms have balconies and a splendid sea view. The hotel is tiled throughout and although spotlessly clean, it looks cheerless. Has a restaurant open Apr–Oct. Also offers diving and boat tours. *Dbl € 40–90, sgl € 29–68.*

Hotel Servi-Flor** (34 rooms) Bairro Francês, 9970-305 Santa Cruz das Flores; ☎ 292 592 453. Converted from the old accommodation and restaurant building that once belonged to the French-operated communications relay station, and known as the 'French Hotel'. Rather dark and gloomy, but well heated in winter. Bar, swimming pool, gym and mini golf. *Has a restaurant open throughout the year 12.00–14.00 and 19.00–21.00. Dbl € 59–74, sgl € 49–59.*

Pensão (Res) Vila Flores (18 rooms) (3a) Travessa de São José, 9970-341 Santa Cruz das Flores; ☎ 292 592 190. In the centre of town, with integrated public bar and restaurant.

Adeia da Cuada (14 cottages) (TA) Cuada, 9960-070 Fajã Grande; ☎ 292 590 040/856; e aldeiacuada@,ail.telepac.pt; www.aldeiacuada.com. On the west coast, 2km from Fajã Grande. This is

rental accommodation without catering. Through emigration Cuada village became deserted. Now, 14 of the abandoned houses have been refurbished to a high standard, with fully equipped kitchen, TV, stereo, telephone and heated by wood-burning stoves. Each has a small simple garden, pasture really, and access is by narrow paths between walls. It is charming, in a delightful pastoral setting near the sea. *Per night for a minumum of 2 nights' stay: 1-bedroomed cottage € 45–60; 2-bedroomed € 68–85; 6 bedroomed € 160–210.*

Casa de Hóspedes Argonauta (5 rooms) Rua Senador José de Freitas, Fajã Grande, 9960-030 Lajes das Flores; ☎ 292 552 219; www.argonauta-flores.com. In Europe's westernmost village, this recently refurbished traditional and characterful house has retained many early features. Rooms are all en suite, inc 2 suites which are claimed to have the largest bedrooms on Flores. Later in 2006 a second house with a garden and en-suite rooms will be available. Its Italian owner, Pierluigi Bragaglia, can provide optional Italian cuisine, and as the author of a now out-of-print guidebook to the walks on Flores, offers advice on the walking routes and a guide service; offers other guest services inc sea kayaking. *Dbl € 65–108, sgl € 57–93.*

CAMPING

Ä Fajã Grande A grazing field is prepared by the town hall each year for tents and is the only official campsite on Flores. This shares the facilities

provided for the beach and in summer there is a restaurant. *Nominal charge.*

✖ WHERE TO EAT

The options are very limited, and best in summer. All offer the basic Azorean fare without much variation in presentation. There are too many new snack bars opening and insufficient restaurants. They are mostly found in Santa Cruz.

SANTA CRUZ

✖ **Restaurante Lita** Travess da Alfandega, near the harbour; ↘ 292 592 245. Fairly cosy on a miserable wet night, in summer tables outside on roof terrace with ocean view.

✖ **Restaurante Sereia** Rua Dr Amas da Silveira (leading down to the harbour); ↘ 292 592 220. Nice working atmosphere, not smoky, and serves a truly memorable *linguiça*. Reliably open every day for lunch and dinner (*from 18.00*), and excellent value for money.

✖ **Restaurante Mares Vivas** Opposite Restaurante Sereia; ↘ 292 592 343

✖ **Restaurante Baleia** Lugar do Boqueirao, by the old whale factory; ↘ 292 592 462. Interesting area to stroll around before or after eating.

✖ **Servi-Flor Restaurant** In the old French hotel; ↘ 292 592 454

✖ **Café Rosa** Rua da Conceição; ↘ 292 592 162. Offers the cheapest all-in winter lunch.

There are also several snack bars. The **Snack Bar Golfino** in the Rua Travessa São José is breaking the mould by not selling alcohol, and as a consequence is not a smoky bar. Excellent coffee, cakes, snacks and sandwiches, pizzas, croissants and hamburgers.

LAJES

✖ **A Pousada** On the hill opposite the old lighthouse; ↘ 292 593 547. Very small and homely.

✖ **Café Flores** (previously known as O Alberto) On

the south road between Lomba and Lajes; ↘ 292 593 153. Offers pizza and similar fare.

FAJÃ GRANDE

✖ **Restaurante Balneario** By the beach; ↘ 292 552 170. With seating outside it is a good place to

watch the sunset. *Open only during the summer.*

PONTA DELGADA

✖ **O Pescador** A new small family-run restaurant and a welcome addition that should encourage

visitors to this rather distant northern village and the attractive hinterland.

NIGHTLIFE

A discotheque on the **Rocks at Fazenda** at Santa Cruz is open every evening during summer and at weekends in winter. Dancing girls sometimes present. Also two pubs **Gare do Oriente** (live music at weekends) and **Lucino's Bar** serving light meals and burgers, both in the centre of Santa Cruz.

Toste's Café, inside the Hotel Ocidentale, opens to non-residents in the evenings as a music pub where people can dance, mainly at the weekends.

FESTIVALS

In July the Emigrants Festival is Flores's biggest celebration, with music and folklore groups coming from other islands as well as Flores; there are exhibitions and various cultural events and a Carnival Ball.

Festa de N Sra Lourdes (Santa Cruz)   second week of February
Festa do Espírito Santo (throughout the island)   end of May

Festa de São Joáo (Santa Cruz)	fourth week of June
Festa de São Pedro (Santa Cruz)	end of June
Festas do Emigrante (Lajes)	middle of July
Festa do Sr Santo Cristo (Lajes)	first week of August
Festa de N Sra Guia (Santa Cruz)	first week of August
Festa de N Sra Milagres (Lajes)	middle of August
Festa da Santíssima Trindade (Lajes)	middle of August
Festa de N Sra Remédios (Lajes)	third week of August
Festa do Espírito Santo da Praça (Santa Cruz)	fourth week of August
Festa de N Sra Saúde (Lajes)	first week of September
Festa do Bom Jesus (Santa Cruz)	third week of September
Festa de N Sra Rosário (Lajes)	fourth week of September
Festa de N Sra Conceição (Santa Cruz)	second week of December

USEFUL NUMBERS

Emergency ☎ 112
Police Santa Cruz das Flores; ☎ 292 592 115; Lajes; ☎ 292 553 186
Post office Rua São Andre Freitas. *Open weekdays 09.00–12.30 and 14.00–17.45.*
Resident doctor At the Health Centre in Santa Cruz; ☎ 292 592 316 *(24 hours)*. There is no hospital on Flores and any serious emergency cases are flown to Terceira.

SATA Air Açores Rua Senator André Freitas, Santa Cruz das Flores; ☎ 292 592 425; airport ☎ 292 592 411
Tourist information Rua Dr Armas da Silveira, Santa Cruz; ☎ 292 592 369. *Open Mon–Fri 09.00–12.30 and 14.00–17.30, also at the airport Jun–Aug.*

WHAT TO SEE AND DO

MUSEUMS See below under *Santa Cruz das Flores.*

WALKING Described on page 208 are two excellent long-established coastal walks following old trails, plus some shorter walks, although these could all be better maintained and waymarked. It would be so nice if more routes could be opened up which would then provide several days of magnificent walking and make the journey to Flores doubly rewarding. As it is, any stroll into the countryside within sight of the sea carries the added frisson of excitement on account of the distance from anywhere else – half the Atlantic before major landfall. Meanwhile, really keen walkers should consider staying at Casa de Hóspedes Argonauta where guidance is available (see *Where to stay*, page 200).

BIRDS AND FLOWERS There are three protected zones: the extensive central area of lakes; the south coast from Lajes and along the west coast up as far as near Mosteiros; the northeast coast from Santa Cruz to the Albarnaz lighthouse and down to include the Ilhèu de Maria Vaz. These include the islets where the largest European colonies of roseate tern nest. However, it is thought their potential for Nearctic land birds and storm-tossed American vagrants that the westernmost islands offer the greatest birding excitement. A noted area for the land birds with its small fields and woodlands is around **Fajã Grande**. The central area has considerable and complicated geological interest while its humid Atlantic climate of fogs, strong winds and high rainfall has created boggy habitats dominated by juniper and sphagnum moss and other parts good for laurisilva species. Resident birds include canary, goldcrest, chaffinch, blackcap and grey wagtail and the whole wetland complex is regarded as an important area for regular migratory birds and also for the common tern.

SWIMMING

Santa Cruz das Flores A natural rock pool – see town map for location.

Fajã Grande Black-pebble beach and a quay for access with facilities and a restaurant open in summer.

BOAT TRIPS On a small and remote island what is available is inevitably going to vary each year, but trips in summer around the Flores coastline make a fascinating excursion to see the rock formations and seabirds; you can also see islets and various caves including the intriguing Gruta dos Incharéus below Caveira, 50m long and 25m wide. Boat owners might also arrange fishing trips. Check with the island's tourist information office in Santa Cruz (\ *292 592 369*).

DAY TRIPS TO CORVO In May, June, July, August and into September there are daily crossings from Santa Cruz, first departure 09.00, providing there are sufficient passengers. Price €25 per person with a minimum of six passengers. From October to April there are no passenger boats but there is a cargo/passenger service several times a week when sea conditions allow.

ITINERARIES Santa Cruz das Flores is the town of main interest, and the other villages are mentioned under the car tours below.

Santa Cruz das Flores This is the island's principal town and includes the airport, and an enjoyable exploration will take around three hours. The most striking building is certainly the 19th-century **Nossa Senhora da Conceição Church**, of substantial, solid architecture made more imposing by two towers framing the front elevation. Equally substantial is the charming Baroque **Convento de São Boaventure**, now the Flores Museum (*open Mon–Fri 09.00–12.30 and 14.00–15.30*). Begun in 1642 for the Franciscan Order, in 1734 it became a hospital and then later a school. Set around an internal cloister, the rooms display items to do with whaling including scrimshaw, old hand-tools of various trades, linen and wool production and weaving, agricultiural implements, and other ethnographic items. They have, too, a collection of religious statues plus jewellery and other objects concerned with the cult of the Holy Spirit. See also the **Church of São Boaventura** which is integral to the convent. Look to the Hispanic-Mexican influence in the chancel, the plant motifs and allegorical figures painted on the cedarwood ceiling, and a 16th-century Portuguese School *Annunciation*. Two British visitors, Joseph and Henry Bullar, described Santa Cruz in 1839 thus:

> the streets are long and narrow, and fields intervene between the houses. There are no large private dwellings, the great majority being cottages of the poor. Above them all rises the church, which is one of the largest in the Azores ... The Franciscan monastery, an extensive building, has been sold, and is shut up.

Traditionally, visiting strangers were accommodated in the convents in rooms set aside for guests. The garden opposite the monastery contains a handsome well. Nearby is Pimental Mesquita's house, built in the 17th century for the then governor of Flores and Corvo, and part of the Flores Museum. This is thought to be the oldest home on Flores and the first to have a tiled roof and glazed windows.

Car tours I suggest you do the lakes area in the high country and the south and west coast in one day; in fact this is about a four-hour tour. Then another day drive up to the northeast corner, to Ponta Delgada, about a two-hour tour. If you have enough days on Flores, then time your journey to the lakes and high country when

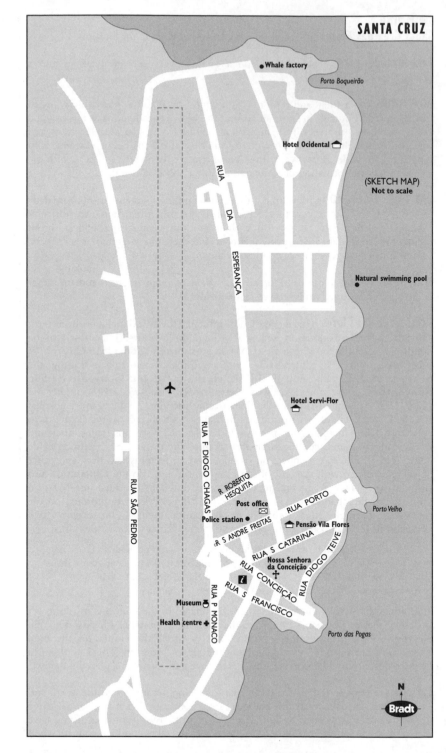

SANTA CRUZ

• Whale factory

Porto Boqueirão

Hotel Ocidental

(SKETCH MAP)
Not to scale

RUA DA ESPERANÇA

• Natural swimming pool

Hotel Servi-Flor

RUA F DIOGO CHAGAS

R ROBERTO HESQUITA

Post office

Police station •

RUA PORTO

R S ANDRE FREITAS

Porto Velho

Pensão Vila Flores

RUA S CATARINA

RUA DIOGO TEIVE

Nossa Senhora da Conceição

RUA CONCEIÇÃO

RUA S PEDRO

RUA P MONACO

RUA S FRANCISCO

Museum

Health centre

Porto das Pogas

N

Bradt

there is no fog. If the day is not clear but very windy this could be a good time, for often low clouds will be travelling quickly and you will get windows of clarity, often in spectacular light. Discuss this with your driver before you set off and go by his years of experience. There are plans to hard-surface the rough track that runs from near Comprida to join the main road between Cedros and Ponta Delgada in the far north, which if it happens would offer further route options.

Touring the high country together with the south and west Leave Santa Cruz by the Lajes road and take the first major turning off to your right, signposted to **Fajãzinha** and **Fajã Grande**. At the junction turn right to head into the mountainous lake area (if you went straight on you would reach Lajes). You will soon get marvellous views on your left of the Ribeira da Cruz as you ascend followed by a view to your right of Fazenda Valley. Then the landscape becomes open wet grassland and trees and you pass through an area called Castanheiro. Continue to the next asphalt road intersection and after passing a little chapel (Our Lady of Flores) turn left. At the next junction turn right, following the sign to **Lagoa da Lomba**. Continue on, and ignore the turning left down to Caveira and quickly on your right is the first of the seven lakes in the **Caldeira da Lomba**. It is surrounded by a large landscape of rounded, weathered cones looking like a series of headless shoulders. In winter the boggy tufted grasses and mosses reflect an emerald shimmer in the low light, darkened in places by the almost black-green of the rushes. Like all of these lakes, it is formed by a volcano cone collapsing upon itself, creating a crater. Most of the lake waters, however, come from springs and only a small proportion from rainfall. This lake is 15m deep. From the lake you can look across hydrangea hedges to the south coast.

Follow the road on, ignoring a left turning down to Fazenda and come to a junction. Ahead is a grand view of the **Boca da Baleia** – mouth of the whale. At the bottom of this huge valley is a group of forestry buildings and blocks of cryptomeria trees. Turn right, and as the road climbs you will see two lakes, one above the other. The top one is **Caldeira Rasa**, meaning 'flat', because, as you will see shortly, the lake is level with the road; it is 16m deep. The lower lake is **Caldeira Funda** of Lajes which means 'behind', named because it is at the back of Lajes. When you reach the next road junction, turn left and drive up to get a closer view of the two lakes. You will see Funda on your left and then Rasa on your right. At Lake Rasa you will find a turning place and two signs naming the lakes and giving their depths.

Turn round and retrace your route; pass the intersection you came from and continue straight on. You will cross a cement bridge and a sign identifying the **Ribeira Grande**, and come to the main road. Cross this main road and take the unsurfaced road opposite to go to Seca on your right and to Água Branca on your left further up the hill. At the point where the unsurfaced road changes to asphalt is the **Caldeira Seca** on your right. Opposite you can see **Caldeira Comprida**, but a better view can be had from the opposite side. Continue on up the hill and shortly you'll come to **Água Branca**, with a depth of a mere 2m. Follow on until you come to a turning place and retrace your route to the junction. At the junction turn right and continue until the yellow sign where you turn right to Lagoas. Now you get a better view of **Caldeira Comprida**, 17m deep.

Continue on to the top of the road where there is a turning place. Here you see **Caldeira Funda**, at 108m the deepest lake. Often the water appears black, and in the tourist literature you will increasingly see it called Caldeira Negra. However, in a certain light it also often appears in various shades of green and there is opposition to this name change! The highest mountain ahead of you with a radio/TV mast is Morro Alto, at 914m. Take the grassy steps up to a fine view of both **Caldeira Comprida** and **Caldeira Seca**. Take care, there are no safety rails. Return to the junction at the bottom and turn right. Soon you reach a junction with an unsurfaced road on your right going up Morro Alto. Ignore this, continuing down and cross another bridge over the Ribeira Grande and on until you find the crossing to Fajãzinha and Fajã Grande off to your right. After the bridge and before the crossing look out on your right for a very narrow opening in the 'walls' with a cobbled pathway. There really should be a *miradouro* sign here, because this is the **Miradouro of Craveiro Lopes**, the most spectacular view over Fajãzinha and Ribeira Grande. Facing west, it is also a wonderful place to view the setting sun.

Take the next turning right to go down to Fajãzinha and Fajã Grande. Ignore the turning almost immediately on your left up to the radio masts; it is better to see this view on your way back up. Continue down, ignoring the road off to your left to Fajãzinha, and at the beginning of the bridge and on your right you will see a white-painted watermill, the **Moinho da Alagoa**. If you are lucky, the miller may be there and the mill working. You can also take a short walk here – see *Four short walks for motorists*, page 208.

After passing two bridges the road gently descends. Look out for a wide asphalt road off to your right – it is not signposted. Take this; it is an upper road around Fajã Grande. You will pass a rock-crushing enclosure on your left and the road descends through dense pittosporum and acacia trees, and then past many white stone walls enclosing small fields. These have now gone to pasture, but presumably in earlier times they grew vegetables and other crops. Continue down until you find a road going off sharply back to the right. Take this turning and at the bottom reach a junction where you will find a small bridge. Turn right to go to the village of **Ponta da Fajã**, but it is a cul-de-sac so you will have to return. You can also make a short walk to the **Codfish Pool** – see *Walks* below. It is also the start of the last stage of the west coast walk to Ponta Delgada. Turn left to go to the bathing place and **Fajã Grande**. You will soon see the restaurant (open May to September) with its welcoming tables set out near the sea.

Looking north along the coast there is a good view of Ponta da Fajã with its high cliff backdrop and, out to sea, the Ilhéu de Monchique. When you leave the restaurant area and if there is not too much visitor traffic (it is a very popular area with the islanders so there could be many cars), drive on through the very narrow village main street to leave Fajã Grande and regain the road you came down on.

Turn right and climb the hill, this time taking the turn-off to the right, and stop at the viewpoint **Miradouro da Fajãzinha** beneath the radio/TV mast to enjoy the superb aerial view of Fajãzinha and Fajã Grande. Continue on this road, descending parallel with the coast, and you will soon see the deserted village of **Caldeira**. Shortly afterwards you come to the village of **Mosteiro**, the white-painted houses and church running down the side of a ridge with its background of 'organ pipes', the Rocha dos Bordoes. It is a charming scene, with the village surrounded by small fields enclosed by stone walls. The population numbers about 70.

Once you have passed the village you come to a T-junction where you turn right. Soon you get a good close view of the **Rocha dos Bordões**, and you can stop the car to better study the formation. The road continues on curving round beneath the rocks and soon the hillside above the road is covered in dense vegetation. There were once fields and pastures, all hedged with hydrangeas and you can still make out these boundary hedges in amongst all the aggressive invading growth of pittosporum, tree heather and myrica. The next village to come into view on your right is **Lajedo**; the road then curves away and you follow a straight stretch into **Lajes**.

Lajes has no real focus but you will see the church on your right surrounded by a cluster of buildings, so turn into the village and park near the church. From the front of the church is a good view down to the harbour. There is also a very clean public WC at the side of the belvedere. To explore the harbour, go back to the main road and turn left soon to find a road off left signposted to the port. Park on the spare ground opposite the Beira Mar café, and take the narrow road in front of the café. In a minute or two you will be at the beach, where there are picnic tables. There is also a tiny whaling museum that may be open. There are several snack bars but the only restaurant is the tiny **O Pousada**, on the hill opposite the lighthouse. Alternatively after you have left Lajes in the direction of Santa Cruz, there is **Café Flores** which offers pizzas and similar food.

Tackling the last, short sector of this island tour, note as the road climbs beneath dense evergreen trees on the road between Fazenda and Lomba two privately owned watermills by the side of the road. The first on the right is the **Moinho do Rei** and the second, on the left in a bend, **Moinho do Brisita**. Then you pass the village of **Lomba**. Just after that is the small village of **Caveira** and you come into the **Ribeira das Cruz** and get a view to Santa Cruz. This ribeira you are crossing is dramatic with its broken topography and dense evergreen vegetation. Look down to the coast and see the small and sheltered **Fajã do Conde**, the site of the very first settlement on Flores. Minutes later you pass the first houses of **Santa Cruz**.

Touring Ponta Delgada and the northeast Leave Santa Cruz from the northwest corner of the airstrip and quickly climb, getting views of the rugged coastline. Soon you are crossing ravines filled with evergreen pittosporum and myrica trees, and all is cool and humid. The pretty little village of **Fazenda de Santa Cruz** is unmistakable by its conspicuously sited church. On the clifftop high above you will see the rooftops of Cedros village. Below, in the bay, are many rocks including the largest, Ilhéu Alagoa. Drive round the **Ribeira do Cascalho** passing the tiny settlement of **Alagoa** and ascend to **Cedros**; just before the top of the climb there is a viewpoint marked by a low stone wall giving a fine view to Alagoa and Santa Cruz. As you continue you will get constant views of Corvo to your right. Leaving Cedros the road travels inland, but gives you a fine view of Ponta Ruiva way below on its exposed *fajã*. After about 8km you will see **Ponta Delgada** village below you; this is the largest village on Flores. From above, the land looks flat but this is deceptive for when you descend to explore the village you will find there are plenty of steep hills. The road forks towards the bottom of the descent and by following the left fork you will get a good view of the tiny harbour.

Head back on the same road: turn right (it is signposted), to go to the **Farol do Albarnaz**. This is a narrow asphalt track going to the lighthouse which was built in 1911 and is the most westerly navigational aid in Europe. There is a good view of the precipitous coast, and the large rock just off the boulder-strewn beach is the **Ilhéu de Maria Vaz**, while out to sea is the **Ilhéu de Monchique**, which can also be seen from Fajã Grande. Come back on the same road and this time continue going on straight into the village until you reach the **Casa do Povo**. I suggest you will find it easier to park here, since the streets are very narrow, and exploration is better on foot. You will discover there are two cafés close by. Return to Santa Cruz by the same main road.

WALKS

FOUR SHORT WALKS FOR MOTORISTS All can be done as part of the car tour as they are very short, but the fourth can be done as a separate expedition from Santa Cruz and fill a very pleasant couple of hours.

Short walk I Alagoa (*Time: about 20 minutes*) From Santa Cruz take the road to the north towards Ponta Delgada and at Alagoa, between Lagoa and Cedros, leave your car by the main road where you see a large rock-crushing depot, and walk down the unsurfaced road starting by the notice declaring the area has special protection for wild birds. This leads you between the scattered houses and down to the beach where you can swim if the sea is calm.

Short walk 2 Moinho do Alagoa (*Time: 10–15 minutes*) Not to be confused with the Alagoa above. You will see a stone-paved path starting 50m beyond the watermill. Follow this into the trees keeping left and going uphill. The path ends at a place called Grota da Prainha, which is really just a watery glade beneath the trees, but on the way you will get closer views of the Ribeira Grande waterfall.

Short walk 3 Poço de Bacalhau (the Codfish Pool) (*Time: about 10 minutes*) After you turn right to take the cul-de-sac to the village of Ponta da Fajã you will soon come to a small bridge over the pretty little Ribeira das Casas and its gurgling stream. There is a signposted footpath nearby; simply follow the stream past two old watermills. Finally you have to scramble over a stone wall to reach the pool and its waterfall.

Short walk 4 Parque Florestal, Fazenda de Santa Cruz Driving there, on leaving Santa Cruz take the north road passing Monte, and in Fazenda turn left in front of the bus shelter, just below the church. Go uphill past houses and ignore the right-hand turning to the church. Soon you come to a fork; go right for the park, and the dam. For a full description see page 213.

LONGER WALKS

Walk I Flores west coast walk (*Time: about 6¹/₂ hours*) By far the grandest walk to achieve is the west coast walk. If you are fit this can be done in one day, but to really enjoy the experience it is better done at the speed of the Azores and spread over two days. It is not so strenuous walking but there are steep ascents and, more importantly, steep descents which can be slippery in wet conditions or when smooth cobbles are buried by soft juicy foliage. There is also some boulder-hopping to do and at least one stream to cross. After rain it will be muddy in places, and sometimes the path may be running with water. You should avoid this walk on very windy days, especially in winter. Otherwise it is straightforward and you will be rewarded by wonderful ever-changing views of coast and countryside, and experience walking a route that has been in use for 500 years.

Stage I Lajedo–Mosteiro–Fajãzinha–Fajã Grande (*Distance: 8.5km; time: about 3¹/₂ hours*) For a shorter walk arrange to meet your taxi in either of the villages en route. This first sector crosses a series of hills and river valleys and passes within sight of the 'Rocha dos Bordões', the famous basalt rock formation, as well as giving some excellent coastal views. It includes a long and steep descent into Fajãzinha and a 'wet' river crossing of the Ribeira Grande (could be difficult after heavy rain).

Taxi to the Church of Nossa Senhora dos Milagres in the centre of Lajedo, from Santa Cruz. Opposite the church is an *império* with brown-painted doors. Follow the road that goes steeply up on the right of this building, and then left. The road levels off and you continue to where it ends and a cement path comes up the hill and joins it. Continue straight and you are on the footpath. There is, or maybe was, a tourist notice marking the start of the walk, but it faces flat-on the full force of the Atlantic winds without interruption all the way from the Statue of Liberty, and when I last saw it, was about to go into orbit.

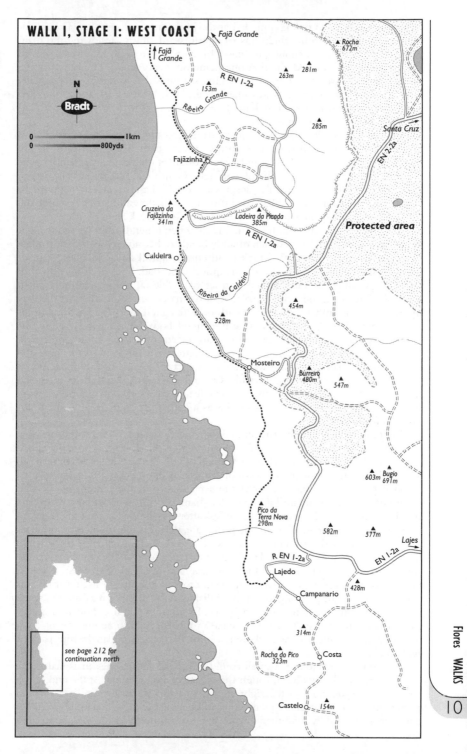

WALK I, STAGE I: WEST COAST

Fajã Grande

↑ Fajã Grande

▲ Rocha 672m

N

Bradt

R EN I-2a

▲ 281m

▲ 263m

▲ 153m

Ribeira Grande

0 ————— 1km
0 ————— 800yds

▲ 285m

Santa Cruz

EN 2-2a

Fajãzinha

Cruzeiro da Fajãzinha 341m

▲ Ladeira da Picada 385m

R EN I-2a

Protected area

Caldeira

Ribeira da Caldeira

▲ 454m

▲ 328m

Mosteiro

▲ Burreiro 480m

▲ 547m

▲ Bugio 603m 691m

Pico da Terra Nova 298m

▲ 582m

▲ 577m

Lajes

R EN I-2a

EN I-2a

Lajedo

Campanario

▲ 428m

see page 212 for continuation north

▲ 314m

Rocha do Pico 323m

Costa

Castelo ▲ 154m

Flores WALKS

10

209

Follow the cobbled trail keeping left at the junction you come to in a couple of minutes. From here route finding is straightforward, always following the main trail which varies from cobbles to grass. In approximately 30 minutes a second stream crossing is reached, the first one being only very small. The water can be heard but the dense vegetation makes it almost impossible to see. You are actually crossing an old stone bridge said to have been built by the Castillians some 500 years ago. Try to peer back through the trees and undergrowth, where the path has been left, to see the two stone arches.

In about another 30 minutes the next stream crossing comes as a surprise; it is flowing down your trail with no obvious onward path. Walk upstream on the boulders, keeping to the left side, and after a couple of metres the vegetation opens to reveal your onward path sharply off left. Climb up and out of the valley. Continue climbing, soon with a closer view of the basalt rock, and onward to Mosteiro. On reaching the asphalt road turn left, walk downhill, soon reaching the church and a tiny square with seats, a good spot for a break after 1½ hours.

Continue on downhill on the asphalt road; when it bends right you go straight ahead on a wide paved path which quickly bends right and crosses a river bridge. Continue on the grassy path which soon climbs uphill and rejoins the asphalt road. Turn left and continue along this quiet coast road. Soon it drops downhill and goes around the uninhabited hamlet of Caldeira, before climbing again towards another hilltop, with a mast. Approximately three-quarters of the way uphill watch carefully for the grassy path off left signed to Fajãzinha. Sometimes the sign has fallen down or is simply not there! Look for the path! Follow this path all the way. At its highest point there are spectacular views ahead of the next deep valley, the Ribeira Grande and the latter part of your walk; also the mountainous inland cliffs and waterfalls. The path down is mostly in trees and vegetation; it is steep but not difficult. Once in Fajãzinha you will soon reach a tiny square with a tree, and in summer a table and chairs. As you enter the square there is a shop on the right that doubles as a coffee bar. You are now about 2½ hours into the walk.

Continue on out of the square and take the narrow road down towards the sea; a second shop/coffee bar is on the corner. A new black asphalt road has been constructed down to the sea where before there was a simple unsurfaced track. To avoid this new road look out for a cobbled grassy path on your left, marked with a wooden post and red band; it joins the asphalt road at the bottom of the hill. Continue along the road until the sharp left-hand bend. You now have to cross the Ribeira Grande, which is not difficult unless after very heavy rain, but the situation is dynamic. When the Ribeira Grande is in spate, it moves the boulders around and the bank gets eroded. Last time the best route was to take the narrow path off right from the asphalt in the bend and go a short distance upriver. Then pick your way across the boulders and between the cane grass and find a place to cross. There is no way to avoid getting your feet wet when crossing the stream itself. On the far side you will see the path angling up the hillside. A 2m climb is necessary to reach it and again, you have to find the best place. In summer you may find all this very easy, because the tourism policy is to make a route through sometime during May. This obviously changes, because there is a confusion of accumulated white-painted blobs and arrows!

The path cuts inland of the small round hill ahead and reaches an asphalt road. Turn left and walk downhill through the village of Fajã Grande. At the end of the road, past the junction on the right signed to Ponta da Fajã, there is a bar and restaurant on the right, also a picnic area and pebble beach, while ahead there is a concrete quay used by swimmers. From here in summer you can telephone for a taxi.

Stage 2 Fajã Grande–Ponta de Fajã–Ponta Delgada (*Distance 11km; time: about 4 hours*) This walk begins with a cliff ascent of 350m. It is never very steep or difficult nor has it any vertiginous drops. It continues across high moorland often surrounded by a sea of blue hydrangeas in June–July and finally descends through pastures to Ponta Delgada. Throughout the walk there are many stream crossings, occasionally running along the path, creating short wet/muddy sections. There are directional signs, but the walk should not be attempted in mist or cloud as good visibility is essential to find your way across the middle section of high moorlands.

Either take a taxi to the *balneario* (bathing area) in Fajã Grande, and begin your walk with a coffee at the restaurant (in summer) and then walk round the beach to pick up the road into Ponta de Fajã, or take a taxi to the church at the far end of Ponta village.

From the church start the walk where the vehicle road ends and take the rocky track between stone walls. In a few minutes you are climbing up a wide grassy cliff path. Apart from a few wet areas as mentioned in the introduction, the path is fairly easy to follow. Observe the cloud level and if visibility is poor, when you reach the top of the cliff think seriously about postponing the walk and returning to Fajã Grande.

After approximately 35 minutes a junction is reached, the walk bends right and uphill into woodland; look out for goldcrests here in June. A wooden marker post confirms the way.

After a further 35 minutes a gate is reached which is the end of the cliff path. The views from here are excellent across the northwest corner, to Maria Vaz Island, the lighthouse at Ponta do Albarnaz and Corvo Island beyond.

From the gate, follow the grassy path which has turned inland. After approximately five minutes you meet the first of many stream-bed crossings. Scramble upstream for a few metres to find the ongoing path which veers left from the stream bed.

Ten minutes later, you reach a wet stream bed which can be easily crossed on small boulders. The ongoing path remains clear throughout the walk except after a grassy section where the ground drops down ahead – this is another stream crossing, approximately one hour 50 minutes from the start – the path goes down right, crosses the stream and bends back left and continues. Much of the time you can see Corvo directly ahead; the path runs parallel with the coast but slightly inland. There are many stone walls, hydrangea hedges and heather bushes, plus a number of rustic gates to pass through. Occasionally you will see a blob of red paint on a rock that confirms the way.

Further on, the grass path continues between two walls, the path becomes more stony and there is a very short steep descent. The path soon drops down through pastures. Some 2½ hours from the start there is a short wet muddy section with a stream running along your trail (this cannot be bypassed and is not quite as bad as it first appears) and soon after a clear stream is crossed.

Approximately three hours from the start the path emerges onto a new cement road. From here you have about 4km to walk to a café and the end of the walk. Turn left and follow this cement road. After 1.4km you will see a tourist sign on your left marking a path to Ponta do Albarnaz and Quebrada Nova dos Furnais. DO NOT take this! It can be a very difficult walk, and all it does is take you to the sea at the bottom of some forbidding cliffs. Continue straight and very quickly you come to an asphalt road, better described as an asphalt track. If you turn left, it is a 0.5km walk to the Albarnaz lighthouse, where you get a good close view of the large Ilhéu de Maria Vaz just offshore, and, beyond, the Ilhéu de Monchique. You will have to return to the junction. Alternatively, simply turn right and follow the asphalt track contouring past pastures and hedgerows with Corvo getting ever

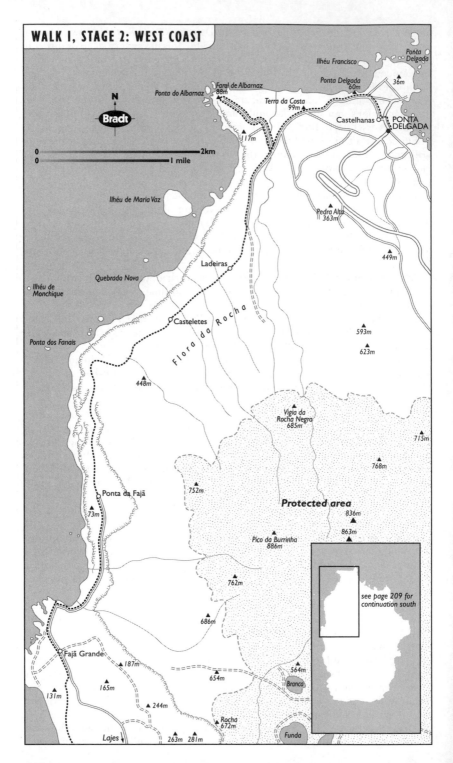

WALK I, STAGE 2: WEST COAST

Bradt

N

0 ——————— 2km
0 ——————— I mile

Ponta Delgada
Ilhéu Francisco
Ponta do Albarnaz
Farol de Albarnaz 88m
Ponta Delgada 60m
Terra da Costa 99m
36m
Castelhanas
PONTA DELGADA

117m

Ilhéu de Maria Vaz

Pedra Alta 363m

449m

Ladeiras

Quebrada Nova

Ilhéu de Monchique

Casteletes

Flora da Rocha

593m
623m

Ponta dos Fanais

448m

Vigia da Rocha Negra 685m

715m

768m

752m

Ponta da Fajã

Protected area

836m
863m

73m

Pico da Burrinha 886m

762m

686m

Fajã Grande
187m

see page 209 for continuation south

131m

165m

654m

564m
Branca

244m

Rocha 672m

Funda

Lajes
263m 281m

212

closer, and after about 1km begin descending. Ignore an asphalt track coming in from the right and continue straight down between stone walls. Turn left downhill to the village of Ponta Delgada and reach a crossroads. If you turn left in 100m you have a view of the tiny harbour and the village. Return to the crossroads and go straight across uphill. Continue on until you come to the *império* building and then a water fountain, followed by a small general shop and the new Casa do Povo, all on your right. Turn left at the junction and in 100m come to a blue-and-white café, Café do Sr José Adao, from where you can telephone for a taxi.

Walk 2 Down to Fajã de Lopo Vaz and return to Lajes (*Time: 45 minutes each way from the cliff top; 2¹/₂ hours to Lajes*) This walk descends from a small attractive picnic park to the largest beach on Flores (pebbles and sand) some 300m below. It claims to be the hottest area with a 'microclimate tropical' and bananas are grown.

The most pleasant way is to take a taxi the short distance from Lajes up to the picnic site above the *fajã*, the Parque das Merendas. This is a very pleasant spot, with lovely views over the countryside and out to sea, with picnic tables, barbecue and toilets beneath myricaria trees.

The walk down the cliff to the beach takes approximately 45 minutes each way as the descent needs care. The path down has more than 300 uneven stone steps; there are also well-formed sections of path on grass or earth. At times the drop off to the left is sheer but it is mostly well protected by vegetation, though not recommended after rain. There is no onward path from the beach and no road access and also no facilities. There is an occasional house and parts of the beach may be suitable for swimming when very calm – there is a strong undertow. It was one of the sites adopted by the early settlers, and gives a good feel of how hard life must have been in such an isolated place.

For the return to Lajes, simply walk back to the main road, and choose any route down – you will see the town laid out before you.

Walk 3 Parque Florestal, Fazenda de Santa Cruz (*Time: 1¹/₂ hours*) This is a charming park set in a valley surrounded by evergreen forest and dates from the time when the then extensive common lands were cleared and converted to more productive pastures and timber in the early 1960s. In addition to a small formal garden with azaleas, there are picnic tables and barbecue area, a children's play area and toilets. Maybe less to your liking are the caged birds (pheasants) and a deer enclosure. A short walk leads up to a viewpoint overlooking a small dam. By taxi it takes eight to ten minutes. You could also go slightly further on and ask to be put down at the dam. This is a peaceful spot with picturesque views, good for a picnic, and you can easily walk back to the park. If you cross the dam you will see a cobbled path leading steeply uphill beneath the trees. Should you follow this it goes between stone walls and hydrangeas and comes out after about 30 minutes into pastures where you get a fine view of the Ribeira da Badanela. Return the way you came.

Walk 4 Fazendas walk (*Time: about 2 hours*) This is a glorious, easy, rural walk in magnificent pastoral country surrounded by high valley sides and largely sheltered from wind. Magnificent on a sunny day if you want to be idle and take a long time over an easy walk, splendid on a windy or cloudy day, and absolutely perfect in winter.

Although the distance can be covered in a couple of hours, try to allow all day because it is so tranquil and you could extend the walk by combining it first by visiting the Parque Florestal (see above) and then walking back to the road fork to the start of the walk.

Flores WALKS

10

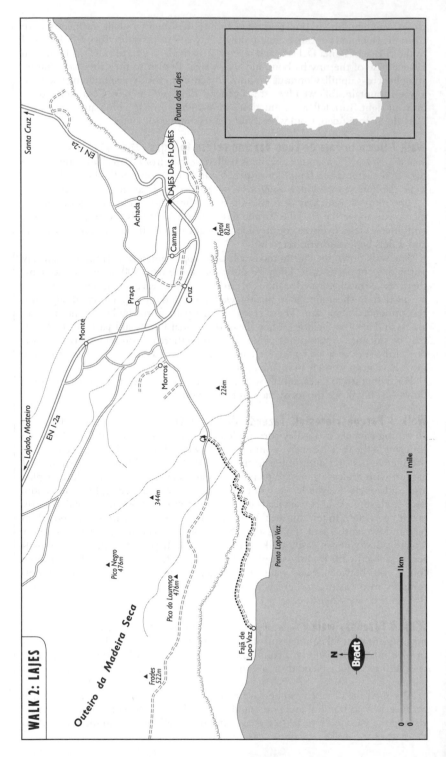

WALK 2: LAJES

Santa Cruz

EN 1-2a

LAJES DAS FLORES

Ponta das Lajes

Achada

Camara

Farol
82m

Praça

Cruz

Monte

Morros

226m

Lajado, Mosteiro

EN 1-2a

344m

Pico Negro
476m

Pico do Lourenço
476m

Ponta Lopo Vaz

Fajã de
Lopo Vaz

Frades
522m

Outeiro da Madeira Seca

N

Bradt

0 — 1km

0 — 1 mile

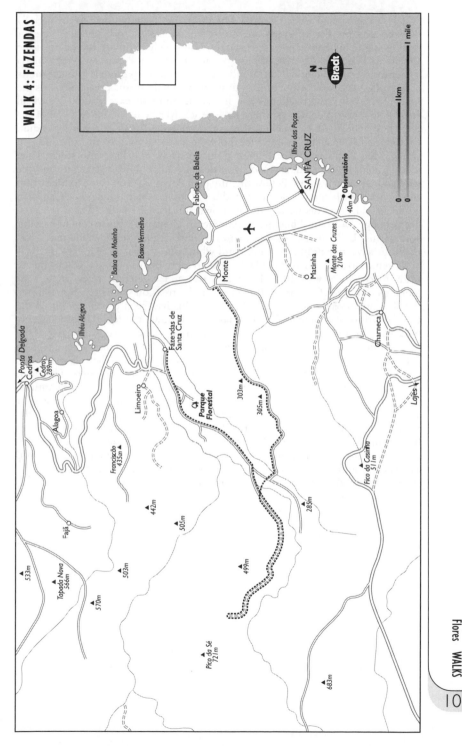

N ← **Bradt**

0 _____ 1km
0 _____ 1 mile

Ponta Delgada
Cedros
Cedros ▲ 289m
Alagoa
Fajã
533m ▲
Tapada Nova ▲ 566m
570m ▲
503m ▲
505m ▲
442m ▲
Francisção ▲ 435m
Limoeiro
Pico da Sé ▲ 721m
499m ▲
285m ▲
683m ▲
Pico da Casinha ▲ 511m
Parque Florestal
Fazendas de Santa Cruz
305m ▲
303m ▲
Monte
Charneca
Lajes
Matinha
Monte das Cruzes ▲ 210m
40m ▲ **Observatório**
SANTA CRUZ
Ilhéu das Poças
Fábrica da Baleia
Baixa Vermelha
Baixa do Moinho
Ilhéu Alagoa

Take a taxi to the Parque Florestal, but at the fork leading down to the park by the wooden carved signpost pay off your taxi. Take the left fork, which is a cinder road, going uphill between evergreen trees. You slowly climb up the valley of the Ribeira da Fazendas, the trees of pittosporum, acacia, eucalyptus and cryptomeria sometimes totally enclosing you, at other times opening to present intimate views of the valley. Look back from time to time and you will see the ocean. Towards the head of the valley the road ends and levels off, and you have glorious views all around you, except eastwards where lies the sea. Maybe it will remind you of the French Pyrenees. At a double green gate you see a *levada*, or water conduit, contouring off up a small side valley. Look up and slightly to your right and you will see the Pico da Ser, the highest point, in view. You have also reached the highest point of the road, and soon you descend for a short distance to find the road ending by some trees. Follow the tiny path down and you come to the stream and a most enchanting place where the sparkling water gurgles over smooth boulders and then cuts its way deeply down through the rocks. There is a pool deep enough for a refreshing splash and to leave a bottle of wine to cool in time for your picnic. Endemic plant species you can find around here include juniperus, rhamnus, faya, tree heath, vaccinium and viburnum.

To return to Santa Cruz should take you no more than 1½ hours. When you are ready to continue, walk back down the road and where the trees begin, start looking out *very carefully* for the first break in the trees on your right. You will see the start of a broken cobblestone path. Once this had been cemented, but at the time of writing it is now broken and has washed down the trail. Descend steeply below low stone walls under the pittosporum trees and soon you will arrive at the valley bottom. Cross the stream, the Ribeiro do Caneiro, and then ascend along a path between two walls which more or less goes diagonally up the valley side. On your left the view of the Fazendas Valley gets better at every step. This path eventually becomes cemented and you simply follow it to the top and continue when it changes to a cinder road at a place known as Beija Mão. In just over another kilometre you will be in the centre of Monte, where you drop down to the road junction and turn left. Santa Cruz Town looks like a children's model laid out below you. Shortly take the right turn steeply down at a small green-and-white-painted water tower and come to a T-junction. Turn right to join the main road again and soon you will see a mirror on the bend. At the side of the mirror take the steps down to São Pedro, to come out near the whale factory.

11

Corvo

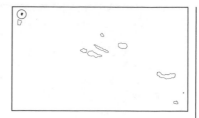

Corvo is by far the remotest island of the archipelago and must surely rate as one of the most isolated places in all Europe. This ancient volcanic remnant, so old that the time of its creation is uncertain, is surrounded by an often cruel and savage ocean, and inaccessible for months at a time from its nearest neighbour until the very recent advent of the aeroplane. It is the tiny elusive gem at the apex of the Azores crown. Day visitors from Flores making the boat crossing in settled summer weather are increasing, but for the true traveller intent upon getting a feel for this island there are seven rooms in a small residencial or a simple camping site available.

HIGHLIGHTS

Whether you arrive by plane or boat, you land in the island's only settlement, Vila Nova do Corvo. It is the only suitable place at sea level. Little has changed in the eastern segment of the town, the narrow cobbled streets between dark basalt walls of the houses all huddle tightly together in mutual protection against winter storms and to save valuable arable land much as they have always done. The only road snakes steeply up the hill to the cow pastures, and continues ever upwards to the caldera, a distance of 6km.

On a day visit there should be time enough to walk to the road's end to enjoy the view down into the crater which, at 300m deep and 2km across, is amongst the largest in the Azores. However, be warned: it is often shrouded in cloud. For those with more time, there are three walks to do, plus sea activities, but the greatest delight must surely come from simply being on Corvo and freeing your senses to absorb its atmosphere.

To make my first visit I had to charter a boat, and I gave a lift to an emigrant who had returned from California to Flores for the first time in 26 years. He was desperate to get to Corvo to see his 84-year-old aunt. Arriving at the little jetty, a small drama ensued with much embracing and tears between him and about a dozen islanders, and it was equally emotional when we departed four hours later. The boat's captain was given bunches of onions, and as we drew away from the harbour we were all sadly watching the tiny town grow smaller and smaller and the mists come down lower and lower.

GENERAL BACKGROUND

GEOGRAPHY As well as being the remotest island in the Azores, Corvo is also by far the smallest, at just 17.13km². It is also the smallest parish in Portugal. The island consists of a volcano summit with a caldera, at the bottom of which are small lakes. The highest point is Morro dos Homens at 718m. Given its size and isolation it is perhaps just as well that today there is no noticeable seismic activity and it is

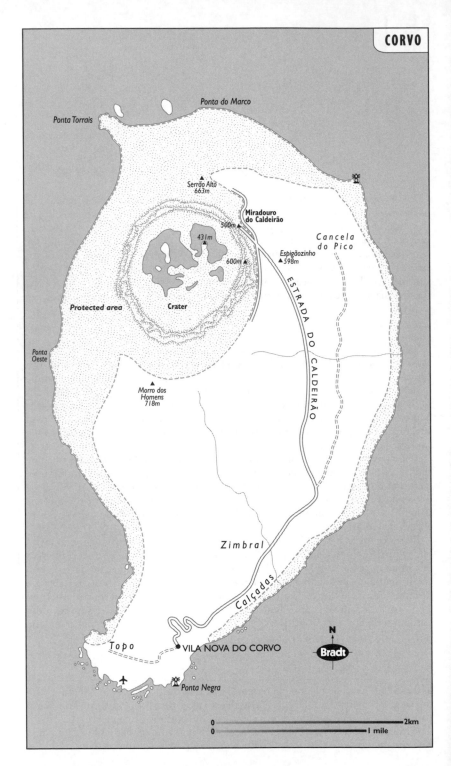

CORVO

Ponta do Marco

Ponta Torrais

Serrão Altō
663m

Miradouro
do Caldeirão

500m

*Cancela
do Pico*

431m

Espigãozinho
▲598m

600m

Protected area

Crater

Ponta
Oeste

E S T R A D A   D O   C A L D E I R Ã O

Morro dos
Homens
718m

Z i m b r a l

C a l ç a d a s

N

T o p o

VILA NOVA DO CORVO

Bradt

Ponta Negra

0 ————————————————————— 2km
0 ————————————————————— 1 mile

considered to be inactive. Since the western islands are the first obstacle that the Atlantic Ocean meets for over 1,000 miles, Corvo has been substantially eroded, especially along its western coast, so that the island now confronts the ocean with precipitous cliffs.

HISTORY Corvo means 'crow' or 'raven', but probably the name derives from a pre-Portuguese designation of Corvimarini or similar. Along with Flores it was the last of the islands to be discovered by the navigators, sometime around 1450. Permanent settlement began 100 years later and, because of its size, no safe harbour and isolation, it has remained an agricultural-based society. Early communication with Flores was by fire, the number lit coded for a doctor, priest or other urgent need. Money entering the island's economy had to come from outside and in the time of the pirates and corsairs it seems an unofficial relationship was established with them to everyone's mutual advantage. In exchange for water, food supplies and ship repairs, the islanders gained protection and luxury items.

The advent of the American whalers in the 18th and 19th centuries attracted able men to help crew the ships, and later land-based open-boat whaling generated some cash income. In 1830 there were some 3,000 sheep grazing the island. The first boys' school opened in 1845, followed by one for girls in 1874 thanks to a bylaw passed in Lisbon. Around the turn of the century imports included sugar, flour, coffee, wine, vinegar, *aguardente*, port wine, cheese from São Jorge, figs, candles, soap and leather. Important exports were cows and hides, but it was also a time of yet more emigration, to Brazil, the other islands, but mostly to North America. In 1864 the population was 1,095; now it is almost 400 after a recent modest increase, and occupies just one page in the Azores telephone directory. Beef cattle are winched from the quay into a boat during the summer months for transfer to Flores, where a larger ship takes them onwards. With an excellent new school, easily identified by its windows and doors most attractively framed in traditional blue and yellow, the new generation maintains contact with the outside world via the very latest technology, and has far better internet access than I have in rural England. At age 14, the pupils go to Terceira or São Miguel, boarding with families for which the parents have to pay.

GETTING THERE AND AWAY

This is not a straightforward process. Weather conditions are all-important, and the visitor should always allow for delays when planning a holiday itinerary. However, just because it is too windy for a plane to fly or the sea is too rough for a ship to come into port does not imply bad conditions on land.

I had some magnificent weather, changeable and exhilarating, for ten days one December. Exactly according to schedule SATA Air Açores flew me from Ponta Delgada via Terceira to Flores and a week later from Flores to Corvo. This time it was just me and a policeman as passengers. An hour later a storm blew in, and the next day I watched fascinated as 12m waves crashed over the end of the runway and I began to see myself on Corvo for Christmas. Twenty-four hours later and so typical of the Azores, the wind dropped long enough for the plane to land, fly to Flores and back, and take me to Faial exactly as printed in the timetable and displayed on the airline's website. At the same time high seas had prevented the usual supply-ship crossing from Flores for over three weeks, and the island was very short of fresh fruit and vegetables though I was assured there was still three months' supply of beer in stock. It was great, but a visit in summer should be easier!

BY PLANE SATA Air Açores fly regular but not daily flights connecting Corvo with Flores, Horta and Terceira.

BY FERRY There are small cargo boats linking Corvo with Flores that also take passengers. In summer there are the excursion boats which would probably provide a one-way journey.

BY YACHT There are moorings in the tiny harbour, but no services although there is a crane for emergencies.

GETTING AROUND

Walk!

WHERE TO STAY

⌂ **Guesthouse Comodoro** (7 rooms) Carminho do Areiro, 9980 Corvo; ☏ 292 596 128; e corvoazores@yahoo.com. About 5 mins' walk from the airport, everyone can tell you the way, but the guesthouse offers a free transfer. Rooms come with private bathroom. *Dbl € 50–55, sgl € 40–45.*

CAMPING
⚑ There is a good, flat, grass field at the end of and just above the airstrip, and by Corvo's tiny boulder-and-sand beach. There are simple facilities inc a barbecue, all free of charge.

WHERE TO EAT

✗ **Restaurante Traineira** Rua da Matriz, by the harbour; ☏ 292 596 207. With fish soup a speciality and always fresh grilled fish. In December to my considerable dismay the proprietor left for Flores on the plane I arrived on, and so the restaurant was closed and I have no first-hand experience. One of the hazards of winter travel! *Advertises as open every day 08.00–20.00.*
✗ **Snack Bar Irmãos Metralha**
✗ **Bar dos Bombeiros** Rua da Matriz and opposite the church.

NIGHTLIFE

🍺 **Convent Pub** (but no sign outside) This tall, old building, located next to the police station just above the airstrip, is a pub. In summer there are chairs outside. It was once long ago a priest's house. Great atmosphere. *Open every night.*
🍺 **Restaurante Formidavel** 2km from town, up the hill along the only road. Occupying three or four small pastures enclosed by stone walls, a tiny kitchen and larger barbecue area cooks for customers seated on chairs at tables on the grass. In another pasture is a circle of concrete for a dance floor, and a timber shed provides the bar. Dreamy views all around of pastures and the sea beyond, I cannot think of a happier place to spend an evening. *Open only during the summer months.*

FESTIVALS

Corvo is so small and with so few people that celebrations here seem like a big house party. The most important festival is that of Our Lady of Miracles. The dates of festivals may vary each year, so please check with the tourist information office.

Festa de Santo Antão   last weekend of May
Festa de São Pedro   last weekend of June
Festa do Dovino Espírito Santo   second weekend of July

Festa da Sagrada Família	last weekend of July
Festa de Nossa Senhora dos Milagres	14 and 15 August
Festival dos Moinhos, celebrated with the	
Festa de Nossa Senhora dos Milagres	
Festa da Senhora do Bom Caminho	second weekend of September

WHAT TO SEE AND DO

WALKING The best way to explore the island is to walk. Three walks are described below.

BIRDS AND FLOWERS More than half of the island is protected and this includes most of the coast. Marine areas also have protected status as they are especially rich in many species and a proposal to combine these and make a national regional park is under consideration. It seems you should never relax but keep alert for birds all the time; what little tree cover there is is on the eastern side – passerines, and the caldera lakes for ducks and waders. Peter Alfrey has written a most vivid and exciting (even for a botanist!) description of his visit in October 2005 that puts birdwatching on a totally different plane (see *Appendix 4*).

THE SEA For anything to do with the sea, boat trips, fishing, diving, contact **Nauticorvo** (*Rua da Matriz, 9980 Corvo;* ↘ *292 596 287;* e *nauticorvo@ mail.telepac.pt; www.nauticorvo.pt*).

VILA NOVA DO CORVO There is only one town, **Vila Nova do Corvo**, and no villages or other settlements. If you have come just for the day, as do most visitors, then Vila Nova certainly justifies an hour or two. Wander around the old part of town enjoying the details: from the harbour, the narrow streets called *canadas*, the play of sun and shadow on the cobbles, and the Church of Nossa Senhora dos Milagres – Our Lady of Miracles – with origins dating back to the 16th century. The present church was built between 1789 and 1795 and paid for by the Corvo population together with remittances from emigrants; the first priest was appointed in 1796, who came from Urzelina on São Jorge. Corvo was the first island to publish and have approved in 1984 a strategic development plan and all the old part of Vila Nova is a conservation area. The new half is not without interest, and reflects the enterprise of the islanders. If you explore the south coast below the airport you soon come to an old slipway by the windmills; this was where whales were brought up before the factory was built on Flores, and the blubber was reduced on the shore in the open. If the clouds are high, then the other thing to do is to ascend the only road to the high ground to see the caldera, the crater with its lake and small islands; see *Walk 1* for details.

WALKS

Corvo offers three very easy and very satisfying walks. Most visitors will want to go to the highest accessible point and see the caldera. Certainly if you are a day visitor crossing by boat from Flores this is the easiest to do for it follows an asphalt road all the way up so that if the clouds come down you can easily find your way. The summit often is in clouds, but do not be put off as these often clear for short moments, enough to give you a window to see down into the caldera, and on the way up or down there are views across pastures, the sea, and even as far as Flores. The second walk is again very easy, and must rank among the loveliest in all the Azores. It is both picturesque with all the pastures and at the same time dramatic because of the steep

Corvo WALKS

11

slopes above and below the path, the views of the sea and across to Flores, and the fact that you can be in such a glorious place and yet in the middle of the Atlantic Ocean. The third walk contours along on the east coast below the road to the caldera, and is a peaceful, easy walk, again surrounded by more pastures but this time you will also discover Corvo's few trees and patches of forest.

WALK 1 VILA NOVA TO THE CALDERA (*Time: 4 hours; distance: 12km*) Leave the harbour and turn right past the Restaurante Traineira and follow the narrow black-cobbled Rua da Matriz all the way up until you join the main road, also cobbled. Turn right for the caldera, and ascend. You rapidly get a fine view of Vila Nova, especially of the old, original part of town easily distinguished by the houses of natural stone, weathered pantiles, and the tiny *canadas* or lanes between them. Note the rear walls of the houses are virtually windowless, to protect them from the harsh winter winds. Soon the road changes from a cobbled surface to black asphalt, which continues all the way to the edge of the caldera. Walking along a road is a bore but it is little used and the scenery more than compensates, for you are in a land of pastures, stone walls, hedgerows and views to the sea.

After almost 2km you will see a temporary restaurant, the Restaurante Formidavel, among the pastures up on your left – the post and rope fence leads the way. Opposite is a wooden signpost to Fonte Doce. If the clouds have come down and visibility is poor, continue along the asphalt road. To avoid walking all the way along the main road you can take the cement road going up left between two houses and a prominent cement-rendered wall on the corner, just beyond the restaurant. Soon you pass the old butter factory and at the end of the cement road turn right (*for walk 2, turn left*).

This cinder road goes between walled fields and comes out again onto the asphalt road; turn left to continue to the caldera. You will come to a wide cinder road leading straight on where the asphalt road bends left (*this is walk 3*). Continue on the asphalt road and look out for another small road off on your left. You should be able to see where this goes, for it is another short cut, relieving you of the asphalt road. Rejoin the main road and continue up to the caldera. If mist and cloud are absent, the caldera is rather beautiful with its two lakes and their irregular margins and islets, and the inner slopes covered with pastures clearly divided by immaculate stone walls and hydrangea hedges. The lakes drain to a waterfall into the sea on the west coast.

To return to Vila Nova, retrace your steps.

WALK 2 VILA NOVA TO THE PASTURES BELOW MORRO DOS HOMENS (*Time: 3¹/₂ hours; distance: 4km from the asphalt road leading to the caldera, 6km from Vila Nova, 12km there and back*) This is magnificent. As for walk 1 as far as the Restaurante Fomidavel. Just beyond the restaurant take the cement road going up left between two houses and a prominent cement-rendered wall on the corner. Soon you pass the old butter factory and at the end of the cement road turn left. Continue until you come to two stone posts and a cattle grid. Do not turn right, since this leads to the new reservoir providing drinking water to Vila Nova and is a closed area. Turn left, and follow the cinder road. Soon you get wonderful views to Flores. As the road bends round you can discern Corvo's second volcano crater, or part of it since the west side has been eroded away. Almost at the end of the road you will see a small watercourse running down below on the left – it is partly lined with hydrangeas and gingers. There will also be, passing beneath the road at this point, a large grey plastic drainage pipe. From this point, if you look carefully about 60m down towards the watercourse, you should see a natural spring. Here you can either drink the water or better still, cool your wine to accompany a picnic.

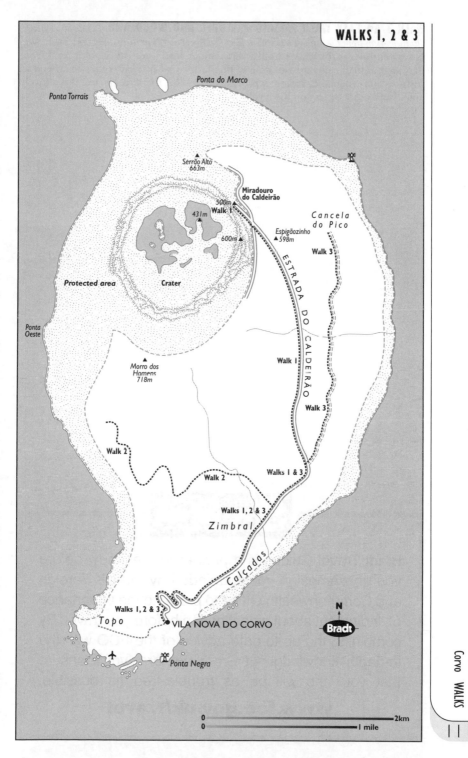

WALKS 1, 2 & 3

Ponta do Marco

Ponta Torrais

Serrão Altó
663m

500m
Walk 1

Miradouro
do Caldeirão

431m ▲

Cancela
do Pico

Espigãozinho
▲ 598m

600m ▲

Walk 3

Protected area   Crater

ESTRADA DO CALDEIRÃO

Ponta
Oeste

Morro dos
Homens
718m

Walk 1

Walk 3

Walk 2

Walk 2   Walk 2

Walks 1 & 3

Walks 1, 2 & 3

Zimbral

Calçadas

Walks 1, 2 & 3

Topo   VILA NOVA DO CORVO

N

Bradt

✈   Ponta Negra

0   2km
0   1 mile

WALK 3 AN EASY WALK PASSING PASTURES AND WOODLAND (*Time: 3¹/₂ hours; distance: 4km from the asphalt road, 6km from Vila Nova, 12km there and back*) From Vila Nova continue as for Walk 1 until a wide cinder road leads off on your right from the main asphalt caldera road. Follow this farm road until it comes to an end in pastures and woodland. It simply provides access for the farmers, but it is a lovely quiet walk more or less on the level.

Appendix I

LANGUAGE

Portuguese is notoriously difficult to pronounce, takes much practice, and ought to be mastered before trying to use any vocabulary. Fortunately, you will meet plenty of friendly Azoreans happy to coach you to say a phrase to the point where they can recognise it!

Many words can be guessed from English or Spanish and some Spanish speakers get along quite well with a mixture of *português* and *espanhol*. Examples include many words ending with -ion or -on in English and Spanish respectively which are similar in Portuguese but end in -ão (plural usually -ões) – *televisão, razão* (reason), *verão* (summer).

Take care, though, for some similar Spanish and Portuguese words have completely different meanings: *niño* (Spanish = child) versus *ninho* (Portuguese = nest); and it is best not to describe an ordinary man as *ordinário* as this implies he is common or vulgar.

PRONUNCIATION

ã + a followed by m	nasal (similar to 'ang').	o or ó	o when stressed (as in hot)
c	ss before i or e; k elsewhere	ou	o sound (as in both or window)
ç	ss	õ + o followed by m	nasal (similar to 'ong').
cc	ks	qu	k before i or e; kw elsewhere
ch	sh		
g	soft j before i or e; hard g elsewhere	s	z or sh (at end of syllable)
j	soft j (as in French)		
lh	ly (as in Spanish ll)	x	sh or s
nh	ny (as Spanish ñ)	z	soft j
o or ô	oo when unstressed		

ESSENTIALS

I have found these few phrases invaluable.

Hello	*Olá*
Good morning	*Bom dia*
Good afternoon	*Boa tarde*
Good evening	*Boa tarde*
Goodnight	*Boa noite*
Goodbye	*Adeus*
What is your name?	*Como sé chama?*
My name is …	*Chamou me* [shamow mu]
You're welcome	*de nada* (ie: 'it's nothing' – reply to thank you)
Please	*Por favor*
Thank you (masculine)	*Obrigado*

225

Thank you (feminine)	*Obrigada*		
Thank you very much (masculine)	*Muito obrigado*		
Thank you very much (feminine)	*Muito obrigada*		
It is very kind of you	*É muito amável*		
Yes	*Sim*		
Yes please	*Sim, por favor*		
No	*Não*		
No thank you (masculine)	*Não obrigado*		
I am sorry	*Desculpe*		
That is all right	*Está bem*		
Excuse me (to pass someone)	*Com licença*		
good	*bom*		
excellent	*óptimo*		

QUESTIONS

How?	*Como?*	How much (cost)?	*Quanto custa/é isso?*
How much?	*Quanto?*	What?	*(O) Que?*

NUMBERS

0	*zero*	16	*dezasseis*
1	*um*	17	*dezassete*
2	*dois*	18	*dezoito*
3	*três*	19	*dezanove*
4	*quatro*	20	*vinte*
5	*cinco*	21	*vinte e um*
6	*seis*	30	*trinta*
7	*sete*	40	*quarenta*
8	*oito*	50	*cinquenta*
9	*nove*	60	*sessenta*
10	*dez*	70	*setenta*
11	*onze*	80	*oitenta*
12	*doze*	90	*noventa*
13	*treze*	100	*cem*
14	*quatorze*	1,000	*mil*
15	*quinze*		

DAYS, MONTHS AND TIME

Sunday	*Domingo*	Thursday	*Quinta-feira*
Monday	*Segunda-feira*	Friday	*Sexta-feira*
Tuesday	*Terça-feira*	Saturday	*Sábado*
Wednesday	*Quarta-feira*		

January	*Janeiro*	July	*Julho*
February	*Fevereiro*	August	*Agosto*
March	*Março*	September	*Setembro*
April	*Abril*	October	*Outubro*
May	*Maio*	November	*Novembro*
June	*Junho*	December	*Dezembro*

after	*depois (de)*	now	*agora* [agwara]
before	*antes (de)*	today	*hoje*
day	*dia*	tomorrow	*amanhã*
never	*nunca*	yesterday	*ontem*

GETTING AROUND

aeroplane	*avião*	right	*à direita*
bus	*machimbombo* (★)	road	*estrada* [shtrada]
	autocarro (Portuguese)	Stop here, please	*Pare aqui, por favor*
car	*carro*	straight on	*em frente*
closed	*fechado*	street, road, highway	*rua*
here	*aqui*	there	*ali*
left	*à esquerda*	train	*comboio*
lorry, truck	*camião*	Where is it please?	*Onde é que é, por favor?*
open	*aberto*	Which way?	*Para onde?*

ACCOMMODATION

bathroom, toilet	*casa de banho*	cold/hot water	*água fria/quente*
bed	*cama*	hotel	*hotel*
guesthouse	*pensão*	toilet paper	*papel higiênico*

FOOD This includes sufficient restaurant Portuguese to help you through the usual menu.

In a bar/café

I would like ...	*Queria ...*
a beer, please	*uma cerveja, por favor* (for types of beer, see *Drinks* below)
a sandwich, please	*uma sanduíche, por favor* (these almost always come as rolls filled with ham, cheese or mixed: *fiambre, queijo* or *mixta*)
mineral water, please	*uma água mineral, por favor* (*com gas* − carbonated; *sem gas* = still)
two coffees, please	*dois cafés, por favor*
some more coffee, please	*Mais café, por favor*
the bill, please	*A conta, por favor*

In a restaurant

For two, please	*Para dois, por favor*	dinner	*jantar*
The menu, please	*O menu, por favor*	dish of the day	*prato do dia*
Enough, thank you	*Chega, obrigado*	the wine list	*lista de vinhos*
lunch	*almoço*		

Drinks Coffee comes in many forms: *café com leite* = white coffee; *café bica* = small strong black coffee; *café galão* = white coffee served in a long glass; *café garoto* = strong, black coffee, served in a small glass)

tea	*chá* (*chá da India* = India tea; *chá de camomile* = chamomile tea)
fruit drink	*um sumo de frutas*
iced	*fresco*
house wine	*vinho da casa* (*tinto*, red; *branco*, white)
bottled beer	*cerveja de garrafa*
draught beer	*cerveja de pressão*

Fish (Peixe) see also *Appendix 3*, page 240

clams	*ameijoas*	salmon	*salmão*
common sea bream	*pargo*	salted cod	*bacalhau*
forkbeard	*abrótea*	sardine	*sardinha*

horse mackerel	*chicharro*	shellfish	*mariscos*
lobster	*lagosta*	shrimps	*camarão*
mussels	*mexilhões*	squid	*lula*
octopus	*polvo*	swordfish	*espadarte*
prawns	*gambas*	tunny fish	*atum*
red fish	*boca negra*	wreck fish	*cherne*
red mullet	*salmonete*		

Meat (Carne)

beef	*carne de vaca*	rabbit	*coelho*
chicken	*frango*	sausage	*salsicha*
chop	*costoleta*	smoked pork sausage	*linguiça*
kid	*carne de cabrito*	spiced sausage	*chouriço*
liver	*fígado*	tongue	*lingua*
loin	*lombo*	veal	*carne de vitela*
pork	*carne de porco*		

Cooking methods

baked/roasted	*no forno*	smoked	*fumado*
boiled or pot-au-feu	*cozido*	steamed	*suada*
fried	*frito*	stewed	*estufado*
grilled	*grelhado*	tinned	*conserva*
roast/roasted	*assado*	with a sauce	*com molho*

Azorean/Portuguese foods

apple	*maça*	cake	*bolo*
beans with mixed		caramel custard	*flan*
meats	*feijoada*	chicken	*galinha*
beans	*feijão*	egg	*ovo*
beef	*bife*	fruit	*frutas*
biscuits	*biscoitos*	fruit salad	*salada de frutas*
bread	*pão*	garlic	*alho*
bread soup	*açorda*	honey	*mel*
butter	*manteiga*	ice cream	*gelado*
cabbage soup	*caldo verde*	lemon	*limão*
lettuce salad	*salada de alface*	peanuts	*amendoins*
lupin seeds	*tremoços* (usually in a	potatoes	*batatas*
	saucer on the bar counter)	rice	*arroz*
mixed salad	*salada mista*	sauce	*molho*
olive oil	*azeite*	soup	*sopa*
olives	*azeitonas*	sugar	*açúcar*
omelette	*omolete*	tomato salad	*salada de tomate*
orange	*laranja*	yoghurt	*iogurte*

HEALTH

casualty department	*banco de socorros*	hospital	*hospital*
diarrhoea	*diarréia*	to hurt (or ache)	*doer*
doctor	*médico*	ill	*doente*
fever	*febre*		

OTHER USEFUL WORDS

| battery | *pilha* | change | *câmbio* |
| book | *livro* | child | *criança* |

228

church	*igreja*	nothing	*nada*
currency	*devisas*	on the beach	*na praia*
enough	*bastante*	rain	*chuva*
hill	*colina*	sea	*mar*
house	*casa*	shop	*loja*
lake	*lago*	small	*pequenho/a*
large	*grande*	to swim	*nadar*
a little (not much)	*pouco/a*	too much	*demais/demasiado/a*
a lot (very, much)	*muito/a*	town	*cidade*
market	*mercado*	travellers' cheques	*tcheques de viagem*
money	*dinheiro*	village	*aldeia*
mountain	*montanha*	you	*você* (polite, formal),
night	*noite* [noyty]		*tu* (familiar)

UNIVERSITY OF THE AZORES SUMMER SCHOOL (*University of the Azores, Rua da Mãe de Deus, 9500 Ponta Delgada;* ℩ *+351 296 650 000;* e *cursoverao@alf.uac.pt; www.uac.ptcursos/cursovera*) As part of the summer programme Portuguese-language courses are offered at beginner, intermediate and advanced levels on São Miguel. Also courses in Azorean culture, society and art, on São Miguel, Terceira, Faial and Pico. Courses run for two to five weeks between June and July. Accommodation in university hostels and fees include costs of field trips and social events.

Salmonete
(red mullet)

Appendix 2

FLORA

Given that there are some 850 flowering plants and ferns in the Azores, the following 60 have been selected as those most likely to strike the eye of the visitor. Books that describe European flowers will identify most of the Azorean flora apart from the endemics, and the well-illustrated *Mediterranean Wild Flowers* by Marjorie Blamey and Christopher Grey Wilson, published by Collins, London, is helpful. The most difficult plants to identify confidently are the evergreen trees and shrubs. As always, the one plant you really would like to name will not be included!

The Latin name is given in italics, followed in brackets by the Portuguese vernacular where known, and by the common English name if there is one, and then the family.

EVERGREEN TREES AND SHRUBS

Myrica faya (faia) **Myricaceae** Evergreen shrub or small tree up to 8m. Leaves lanceolate, leathery, dark green, margins often toothed towards the apex and frequently rolled backwards. Flowers are unisexual and borne on axillary catkin-like spikes, male and female on the same plant; overall colour olive-green, withering to brown. Fruit small, rounded and very hard. All Azores islands, Madeira, Canaries and Portugal. Often a coastal shrub, but found up to 700m. At higher altitudes a member of the laurisilva association. Can form pure stands, but is often out-competed by alien *Pittosporum undulatum* and you can frequently see the two species fighting for dominance. Makes a good shelter hedge and was once used around orange orchards. Isolated trees make good garden specimens.

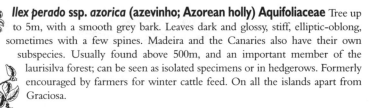

Ilex perado **ssp.** *azorica* (azevinho; Azorean holly) **Aquifoliaceae** Tree up to 5m, with a smooth grey bark. Leaves dark and glossy, stiff, elliptic-oblong, sometimes with a few spines. Madeira and the Canaries also have their own subspecies. Usually found above 500m, and an important member of the laurisilva forest; can be seen as isolated specimens or in hedgerows. Formerly encouraged by farmers for winter cattle feed. On all the islands apart from Graciosa.

Laurus azorica (louro; Canary laurel) **Lauraceae** Dark, glossy green, evergreen tree up to 10m, sometimes taller, with a dense crown. Young shoots clothed in dense brown downy hairs. Leaves alternate, varying between five and 15, 3–7cm, broadly lanceolate-elliptic, hairless above, softly hairy beneath at least when young, strongly aromatic when crushed; in the axils of the midrib and main veins are tiny, gland-like projections. Flowers creamy yellow, fruit ovoid, 1–2cm, broadly ellipsoid, green turning to black when ripe. Usually grows above 500m and a key member of the laurisilva forest.

Picconia azorica **(pau-branco) Oleaceae** Evergreen tree or shrub, leaves opposite, leathery, without hairs, two to three times as long as broad, with small white flowers on inflorescences from the leaf axils. Found mostly between 300–600m, once widespread and used for house building, its presence now rather scattered. Endemic to the Azores, but not found on Graciosa.

Frangula azorica **(sanguinho) Rhamnaceae** Large deciduous shrub or small tree with a wide spreading crown; branches little divided and leafy only towards the end. Leaves broadly elliptic, up to 15cm long with distinct parallel lateral veins. Flowers small, yellowish, in clusters from the leaf axils. Generally around 500m and up to about 1,000m altitude it is a member of the laurisilva forest, and also remnant hedgerows. On all islands except Graciosa and Corvo, now extinct on Madeira.

Prunus lusitanica **ssp.** ***azorica*** **(ginja; Azores cherry laurel) Rosaceae** Evergreen small tree to 4m, leaves somewhat leathery, to 10cm, oval and tapering at each end, dark green and shiny above, paler beneath, possibly finely toothed, leaf stalks red when young, the whole plant without hairs. Flowers rounded, white, in racemes of up to 20–30 from the leaf axils. Fruit cherry-like, oval to almost round, turning red at first, finally ripening purplish black. Above 500m in deep ravines or in dense laurisilva forest. Endemic and rare.

Myrsine africana **(tamujo; African boxwood) Myrsinaceae** Dense, low evergreen shrub to 1.5m, leaves 0.6–2cm, roughly egg-shaped with small teeth on margins. Flowers small, pale brown in clusters of three to six, followed by bluish-lilac 6mm-diameter fruits. Generally above 400m, it favours the shelter afforded by dense laurisilva forest where it can be abundant, but it also occurs in more open vegetation. Occurs from east and South Africa, and the Himalayas to China.

Persea indica **(vinhático) Lauraceae** Evergreen tree up to 15–20m tall, with a broad, rounded crown. Shoots finely hairy when young. Leaves without glands, 10–20 x 3–8cm, elliptic, leaf stalks up to 3cm, reddish; whole leaf becomes reddish when old. Inflorescence on stalks shorter than the leaves, flowers small, whitish. Fruit about 2cm. Ellipsoid, bluish-black when ripe. Found above 200m, introduced long ago (from the Canaries?), now naturalised. *Persea americana* is the avocado.

Clethra arborea **(lily of the valley tree) Ericaceae** Evergreen shrub or small tree to 8m with a bushy crown, twigs have obvious leaf-scars, and young twigs, leaf stalks and flower stems all densely covered in rusty hairs. Leaves about 12 x 5cm, somewhat crowded towards the shoot tips, leaf margins with forward pointed small teeth, with fine hairs on veins on underside, leafstalk often reddish. Flowers in simple or branched racemes up to 15cm long, erect, the flowers to 8mm, nodding, white, cup-shaped, scented. Endemic to Macaronesia (Madeira), probably introduced into São Miguel where it has rapidly naturalised on the hills above Furnas.

Pittosporum undulatum (incenso; Victorian box, orange berry) Pittosporaceae Vigorous tree to 14m, leaves 10 x 3cm, narrowing to a point, shiny dark green above, pale beneath, young leaves yellow-green, margins wavy. Flowers bell-shaped, about 1cm diameter, creamy-white in clusters, sweetly scented, February. Fruit orange when ripe, the pale brown seeds very sticky. Native of southeast Australia, it was introduced as an ornamental and used as a hedging plant to shelter the orange orchards but is now widely naturalised throughout the archipelago and is a major and aggressive component of the tree cover, especially on Santa Maria and Pico.

Hedera helix ssp. canariensis (Canary ivy) Araliaceae The familiar plant with climbing or creeping woody stems and evergreen leaves with three to five short, broadly triangular lobes. Yellow-green flowers in many flowered umbels, fruit rounded ripening black. Widespread between 100m and 1,100m, most common at mid altitude, and most luxurious in laurisilva forest. Also found in Madeira, Canaries, Portugal and northwest Africa.

Viburnum tinus ssp. subcordatum (folhado; Azorean laurustinus) Caprifoliaceae Evergreen shrub with oval leaves and small white to pink flowers in large terminal convex clusters, spring. Fruits are at first a vivid deep metallic blue, turning black as they mature. Associates with laurisilva forest, but can be seen in remnant hedgerows on Pico; generally above 400m and up to 900m. *V. tinus* is native of southern Europe, with a closely related species in the Canaries, but absent from Madeira. The Azorean subspecies differs from the mainland species by its more vigorous habit, more glossy leaves and larger inflorescences.

Vaccinium cylindraceaum (uva da serra) Ericaceae Deciduous shrub generally less than 2m tall, with 20–50mm-long finely toothed, narrowly oblong leaves; when young these are attractively red-tinged. Flowers borne in clusters, yellow-green tinged red; just how red the flowers are varies, partly due to age, and the combination of young red leaves and good red flowers in June puts this among the most attractive of the Azorean endemic plants. Grows generally above 400m and is conspicuous among the laurisilva forest, and often may be seen in old hedgerows. Occurs on all the islands. Fruits locally harvested for preserves.

Euphorbia stygiana Euphorbiaceae Many stemmed soft wooded shrub up to 2m tall with conspicuous narrow leaves 10–15cm long, apple-green and waxy with prominent pale midrib. Flowers terminal, yellow-green. Most easily seen in association with laurisilva, where it is moist and the surrounding vegetation provides shelter. A very noticeable plant of attractive form. Endemic.

Daboecia azorica Ericaceae Dwarf, heath-like evergreen shrub less than 15cm tall with alternate leaves to 8mm long. Flowers in terminal loose racemes, nodding, bell-shaped, ruby-red. Mostly above 500m, can be found in grassland but is most spectacular on the upper slopes of Pico where it forms magnificent carpets with *Thymus caespititius* in midsummer. Endemic.

Erica scoparia ssp. _azorica_ (urze; besom heath) Ericaceae Stout, evergreen shrub or small tree with narrow 4–7mm-long leaves in whorls. Insignificant reddish-brown flowers in interrupted terminal groups. Grows from sea level up to about 2,000m on Pico, at its best above 500m when part of the humid laurel forest. Long used for fuelwood, fencing poles, and woven shelter screens and brooms. Endemic, on all the islands, but large old specimens now rare.

Juniperus brevifolia (cedro-do-mato) Cupressaceae This endemic conifer was once a major tree in the laurisilva forests, producing a superb timber from trunks 40–60cm in diameter; these may still be seen as roof beams in old buildings. Today they are small trees or mostly shrubs with crooked stems affected by exposure and are to be found in remnant cut-over forest associated with other laurisilva species or sometimes surviving in hedgerows or as forlornly isolated specimens. The branches are short and numerous, densely foliate with needle-like leaves in whorls of three with two white stomatal (breathing pore) bands on the upper surface. Found usually above 500m, but also lower and on Pico they reach up to 1,500m. On all the islands except Santa Maria and Graciosa.

Arceuthobium azoricum (espigos-de-cedro; dwarf mistletoe) Viscaceae A genus of partly parasitic mistletoe found on conifers. The whole plant is yellowish-green with scale-like leaves and grows upon _Juniperus brevifolia_. At first difficult to find, the rather sickly colour of the small bunches of tangled stems become apparent from amongst the dense green leaves of its host. Above 600m altitude, it is found scattered in large laurisilva stands and is most easily discovered on Pico. An intriguing curiosity, it can be cultivated by taking cuttings of infected juniper when, after three years or so, the parasite will develop from the host tissue.

Lantana camara (cambará; shrub verbena) Verbenaceae Evergreen shrub to 2m, leaves oval, shortly pointed at apex, up to 6cm long, margins toothed, surface wrinkled, rough to the feel with a strong, pungent, lemony smell. Flower in hemispherical heads to 3cm across, yellow to orange or red often with a brighter 'eye'. Native to tropical America, this attractive flowering shrub has escaped from gardens and is naturalising and becoming a pest as it has in so many other places worldwide; poisonous to cattle.

Solanum mauritianum Solanaceae Large shrub or small tree up to 4m tall with foetid, softly hairy leaves ovate-elliptical, pointed at apex, up to 30cm long. Flowers up to 2cm across, violet-blue with yellow anthers, in many-flowered heads. Fruits round, 1.5cm across, deep yellow. Native of central America, it is frequently found near habitation and on waste ground.

HERBACEOUS PLANTS
Rocky coastal areas, formed by variously aged lava flows or volcanic ash
Crithmum maritimum (perreexil-do-mar; rock samphire) Umbelliferae A short, bushy plant with fleshy, hairless, once- to twice-divided greyish leaves. Flowers yellowish-green in umbels 3–6cm across. Usually seen growing alone or with few other species in lava close to the sea and tolerant of sea spray. Britain and western Europe.

Appendix 2 **FLORA**

A2

233

Gnaphalium luteo-album (**perpétua-silvestre; Jersey cudweed**) **Compositae** Shortish, white-woolly annual. Clustered yellow-reddish flowers. In sandy soils and lava cliffs. Rare in Britain, occasional in Europe, and in warm temperate regions worldwide.

Solidago sempervirens (**cubres**) **Compositae** Fleshy with leaves ending in small broad points at the tip. Flowers yellow in a closely branched panicle. Found as a coastal plant and occasionally elsewhere, particularly noted on the sea cliffs of Flores. Native of northeast America, and spread to the Azores in prehistory times.

Tolpis succulenta (**visgo**) **Compositae** Perennial herb with a woody base and becoming shrubby with age. Up to 30cm but can be as much as 100cm. Leaves narrow to broadly elliptic, often toothed, somewhat succulent. Flowers yellow, late summer/autumn. Grows near the coast on sea cliffs and gravelly places, as scattered individuals. To be found on all the islands, but in few localities, and in Madeira.

Azorina vidalii (**vidalia; azorina**) **Campanulaceae** Soft-wooded shrubby perennial with a main stem and branches to 50cm. Young plants form ground-hugging rosettes. Leaves dark green, often shiny, narrow, edged with forward-pointing rounded teeth, the whole plant somewhat sticky. Flowers nodding, bell-shaped, waxy, greenish-white to white to pink in an elongated raceme. Coastal plant in rock crevices and sandy places – even grit on the edge of asphalt roads. Most abundant among the rocks and sand below the airstrip on Corvo where it gets frequent sea spray. On all islands except Graciosa and Faial, but is often difficult to find. One of the loveliest endemic Azorean species, it is becoming increasingly popular in Britain as a tender garden plant.

Silene uniflora (**bermin; sea campion**) **Caryophyllaceae** Hairless, prostrate, much-branched perennial herb up to 30cm. Leaves without a stalk and often covered with a waxy bloom. Flowers with a bladder-like calyx, petals white, from March to late summer. Widespread coastal plant, also in Madeira, west and northwest Europe. Also found around the summit of Pico, but this may be a subspecies.

Plantago coronopus (**dia-belha; buck's-horn plantain**) **Plantaginaceae** Small herbaceous annual, biennial or perennial plant with rosettes pressed closely to the ground. Leaves somewhat fleshy, usually 2–6cm, linear-oblong, not lobed or with a few teeth or often twice-lobed. Flowers yellowish-brown, 3mm, borne in long, dense spikes on curved stems that are longer than the leaves. Very common in coastal habitats and an early coloniser. Can also be found inland on dry, waste ground.

Juncus acutus (**sharp rush**) **Juncaceae** Tall, up to 150cm, robust grassy perennial making dense prickly tussocks with stiffly pointed stems and reddish-brown flowers in a compact inflorescence. Although a widespread species – Madeira, Mediterranean, Britain, North America – it is included here because it is a typical plant of the coast.

Festuca petraea (**bracel-da-rocha**) **Graminae** Grass with narrow, stiff leaves 30–50cm tall, flowers in whitish-green panicles. Coastal plant on cliffs, on lava and in sandy places often exposed to sea spray. Forms pure colonies but these are now rare because of human interference along the coast and this species is found commonly mixed with other species. Endemic to the Azores and found on all the islands.

In laurisilva forest and at habitats generally above 400m

Leontodon filii (petalugo-menor) **Compositae** Perennial herb with up to five 20cm conspicuous, more or less elliptical leaves, toothed and hairy, bearing one to five yellow flowers on a branched stalk. Associated with the laurel forest, it likes wet, open places, often in grassland, usually above 600m, lower on Flores. Endemic, but not found on Santa Maria or Graciosa.

Senecio malvifoliius (cabaceira, figueira-brava) **Compositae** Perennial herb up to 120cm with rounded, lobed leaves 10–15cm, often found growing among shrubs which provide support. Flower colour varies from pale purple, bluish to white all on the same inflorescence, summer. An attractive plant usually growing in wet shady places, but I have seen it in a sunny hedgerow on São Miguel. Endemic, but not on Graciosa or Flores and Corvo.

Tolpis azorica **Compositae** Perennial herb up to 70cm, leaves crisp-looking, hairless, oblong, up to 15cm, margins deeply toothed. Flowers yellow on a branched inflorescence. To be seen in laurel forest and on constantly moist grassy slopes where it is conspicuous, generally above 600m. Endemic, not on Graciosa.

Erigeron karvinskianus **Compositae** Perennial, stems slender, flat on the ground with erect tips. Leaves to 3cm, flowers varying from white through pink to red-purple. A pretty little daisy from Mexico that has escaped from gardens in numerous temperate places worldwide; in the Azores it is adaptable to different habitats.

Cardamine caldeirarum **Cruciferae** Included here because it is endemic and widespread in the Azores above 400m (but not on Graciosa). In northern Europe it has bittercress relatives that are the weeds and curse of garden centres. Herb up to 50cm tall, basal leaves with five to six pairs of leaflets, flowers white. Likes wet places.

Centaurium scilloides (perennial centaury) **Gentianaceae** Low, spreading perennial with non-flowering decumbent (flat, tips turning up) shoots, found usually above 400m. Upper leaves lanceolate, about 1cm long. Flowers white, solitary or just a few together in

summer. Likes moist habitat, often with grasses. Could once easily be seen at several viewpoints, but seems to be disappearing, maybe due to visitor trampling. *C. scilloides* occurs in western Europe, generally with pink flowers, but some authorities classify the Azores plants as subspecies *massonii*, in which case they would be endemic. Francis Masson, Kew Gardens' first professional plant hunter, collected in the Azores in 1776 and this became one of the first plants from the Azores cultivated in England.

Hypericum foliosum **Guttiferae** Deciduous shrub to 0.5m with crowded narrowly ovate leaves and conspicuous yellow flowers 2–5cm diameter in terminal inflorescences. Normally above 400m, a member of the laurisilva forest but survives where this has been destroyed, and can also be found on steep grassy slopes. Endemic, on all the islands.

Thymus caespititius (erva-úrsula) **Labiatae** Dwarf, mat-forming plant with woody growth and upright flowering shoots to 5cm. Leaves to 6mm, narrow, spoon-shaped. Flowers in lax, small heads varying in colour from white through rose to almost lilac. Grows from low altitude to high on Pico, often in crevices on lava flows and on sandy banks. On the upper slopes of Pico it makes a spectacular summer display with *Daboecia azorica*.

Anagallis tenella (bog pimpernel) Primulaceae If you are looking at this in detail you will either be bored or very keen. Mat-forming, slender perennial with mostly opposite rounded to elliptical leaves. Flowers pink to whitish pink, somewhat bell-like on slender stalks, opening fully only in sunshine. Around 500m in wet or moist places, often near lakes. Western Europe.

Lysimachia nemorum ssp. azorica (palinha; yellow pimpernel) Primulaceae Evergreen herb with procumbent stems, quickly creeping and rooting at the leaf joints. Leaves opposite, more or less egg-shaped. Flowers solitary on slender stalks. A pretty, modest plant most often found in moist grassland and happiest above and around 500m. *L. nemorum* is found from Britain through to the Caucasus, the endemic subspecies *azorica* is found throughout the archipelago.

Ranunculus cortusifolius (bafo-de-boi) Ranunculaceae A handsome buttercup being an erect, up to 1m-tall herbaceous perennial, with slightly leathery basal leaves, lobed, rounded and heart-shaped up to 21 x 30cm. Flowers shining yellow up to 50mm diameter in a branched inflorescence. Usually above 500m but lower on Flores in permanently moist areas especially in the shelter of laurisilva forest in ravines, and occasionally in roadside gullies. Also found on Madeira and Canaries.

Polygonum capitatum Polygonaceae Prostrate perennial with rooting stems, often forming large ground-covering carpets. Leaves 2–5cm oval, green with purple V-shaped band, often covered with glandular hairs. Flowers pink in dense, stalked, more or less globular heads. Native to the Himalayas, it was introduced and has escaped on many of the islands, happily colonising young lava flows, stone walls and waste places.

Rubia peregrina (rapa-língua; wild madder) Rubiaceae Distinctive, trailing or scrambling, hairless, rampant evergreen perennial. Stems square and rough with downturned prickles, leaves in whorls of four to six. Flowers yellowish-green, 4–5mm, forming a leafy inflorescnce. Fruit rounded, ripening black and fleshy. Widespread, also in west and south Europe, north Africa.

Luzula purpureo-splendens Juncaceae This charming woodrush is a perennial, leaves grass-like, wide and up to 60cm long with fine hairs along the margins; flowers brown-purplish in clusters. Found usually between 500m and 1,100m altitude, preferring a moist grassland habitat, often on slopes, and amongst moss carpets around remnants of laurisilva forest, but also can withstand drought. Endemic, on all islands except Santa Maria and Graciosa.

Platanthera micrantha (Azores butterfly orchid) Orchidaceae Basal leaves two, about 10 x 4cm, erect to spreading. Stem leaves two to six, much smaller. Flowers in a rather dense narrowly cylindrical inflorescence, 8–13cm high and about 1cm across. Individual flowers numerous, small, yellow-green. Found between 200m and 1,000m but mostly above 600m in moist places in full sun to semi-shade; I have most often seen it in grass on roadside verges. The plant's characteristics are variable and some authorities recognise a second, similar species *Platanthera azorica* that is more stocky with larger leaves and a more lax inflorescence of whitish-green flowers. Of the orchids recorded for the Azores *P. micrantha* is the species most likely to be encountered; the other is a Tongue orchid.

Trachelium caeruleum (throatwort) Campanulceae Perennial herbs up to about 50cm tall with numerous small slender blue or lilac flowers in much-branched, leafless, broad flat inflorescences. In walls, roadside verges, etc, São Miguel, Terceira and Faial, west and central Mediterranean.

Arundo donax (cana; giant reed) Graminae A tall (to 5m) perennial rhizomatous grass, leaves 60 x 6cm, grey-green. Flowers in large terminal, feathery inflorescences, autumn. Introduced long ago, it thrives in volcanic sands around the coast and is used widely for shelter hedging. Strongly invasive, it quickly spreads if not strictly controlled. When grown in ideal conditions in the south of France the canes are supplied to make the reeds for musical wind instruments.

FERNS
Asplenium marinum (feto maritime; sea spleenwort) Aspleniaceae
A coastal, tufted, plant with a short, thick rhizome with dense blackish-brown scales, the whole growing tightly in amongst the rocks. Leaves 20–30cm long, pinnate, mid green and glossy above, dull and paler below, thickened and rather stiff; tolerant of salt spray. Madeira, Britain to western Mediterranean.

Blechnum spicant (hard fern) Blechnaceae Evergreen fern forming attractive crowns of long, sterile, pinnate leaves with a herring-bone appearance lying close to the ground; the young leaves are flushed red. The fertile fronds have a longer stalk, are much narrower, and are erect. Widespread in northern temperate lands, it is one of the commonest and most distinctive ferns in the Azores, usually above 300m.

Woodwardia radicans (chain fern) Blechnacea Found from the Azores to Java, this fern is one of the most attractive of the archipelago's fern flora. The fronds are from 1–2m long and up to 0.5m wide and often hang down over gullies and banks. The fronds produce bulbils towards the apex and these form new plants, hence the common English name. Usually found above 400m in moist places.

Culcita macrocarpa (feto-do-cabelinho) Dicksoniaceae Conspicuous large fern with strong erect stems up to 100cm tall. The frond is triangular in outline, often shiny and frequently of a yellow-green colour. Found mostly above 500m but also down to 150m. It is

associated with laurel forest and can be readily seen between the tree stems on the lava flows of Pico, but it also survives the loss of forest cover and can be found beyond the laurisilva. It has a prostrate rhizome covered with hairs, which were once collected and used for stuffing cushions etc. Found on all the islands except Santa Maria and Graciosa, it is native to Macronesia and the Iberian Peninsula.

Lycopodium cernuum (clubmoss) Lycopodiaceae A distinctive curiosity of a plant and a fern ally, its long creeping, looping stems rooting at intervals often spread over several square metres. Overall colour is yellowish-green and the tiny leaves are spirally arranged along the stems. The fertile leaves (sporphylls) are arranged in terminal cones (strobili). Generally found above 400m, frequently associated with laurel forest, but often also on steeply sloping banks where it can be a pioneer species on recently exposed surfaces. Also occurs by hot water springs. On all islands, except Santa Maria and Graciosa. In central Europe the strobili of clubmosses used to be collected, dried, and the fine yellow spores kept for use as a medicated talcum powder; sensitive to pollution, they are now rare and strictly protected there.

Osmunda regalis (feto-real; royal fern) Osmundaceae Large tufted fern with upright fronds up to 1m tall and 30cm broad, pinnate. Sporangia produced on some of the terminal pinnae of the fertile fronds. It has a distinctive, short, massive, erect rhizome and a tangle of wiry roots, once popular in mainland Europe until mid last century as compost for growing orchids. Growing in wet places, often in water, and found on all islands except Graciosa.

CULTIVATED PLANTS

Agapanthus praecox Liliaceae Perennial herb forming dense clumps from strong fleshy rootstocks with long strap-like leaves and large heads of blue flowers on leafless unbranched stems up to 60cm tall. Seeds black when ripe, borne in pendulous capsules. Native to South Africa, widely planted in towns and along roads, often naturalising.

Amaryllis belladonna (beladona; belladonna lily) Amaryllidaceae South African bulbous perennial with strap-shaped leaves in two ranks. Large funnel-shaped pink flowers produced in late summer before the leaves appear, six or more together on stout 60m stems. Frequently planted in public gardens and along roadsides, also naturalised.

Abelia x grandiflora Caprifoliaceae Attractive semi-evergreen shrub to 2m with long arching branches, the young leaves at first markedly bronze-pink; flowers tubular, five-lobed, in clusters, pink to white, flowering over an extended period from summer. Frequently planted on road verges.

Aloe arborescens Liliaceae Perennial succulent from South and east Africa with 60mm long grey-green leaves having sharp forward-pointing teeth. Inflorescence unbranched to 80cm, flowers tubular, 4cm, scarlet tipped greenish-white. A good ornamental thriving in hot dry places in private gardens and public places.

Acacia melanoxylon (blackwood) Mimosoideae Fast-growing Australian tree with leaves modified to reduced simple, flattened leaf stalks up to 14 x 2.5cm. Flowers in nearly spherical heads in branched racemes, very pale yellow, late winter. A much desired timber tree for high-value products. Seedlings are abundant on disturbed land, mature trees in gardens and woodland.

Metrosideros excelsa Myrtaceae Dense evergreen tree that in maturity develops massively heavy branches and trunk with many aerial roots swinging from its branches. The dark leathery leaves are silvery on their undersides, and in summer terminal flowers burst into a spectacular show of scarlet-stamened pin cushions, seldom all over the tree but in large patches. Called *pohutukawa* by the Maoris, in its native New Zealand it often begins life as an epiphyte and is commonly found on sea cliffs. Very tolerant of salt spray, this tree is often to be seen in public gardens and squares on most of the islands.

***Melia azedarach* (Persian lilac) Meliaceae** This tree has many local common names around the world where it has been widely planted, but originally it came from northern India and China. Deciduous, spreading tree with an open crown and handsome twice-pinnate leaves to 80cm somewhat like the European ash. Flowers violet-blue in loose sprays 10–20cm long, often with the new foliage, followed by 1–5cm-diameter round fruits ripening yellow, wrinkling and turning brown with age remaining on the tree long after the leaves have fallen. Planted as a street tree and in public gardens.

***Araucaria heterophylla* (Norfolk Island pine) Araucariaceae** A stately conifer endemic to Norfolk Island attaining 20m or more, with spreading branches in whorls. Leaves scale-like to 1cm, somewhat triangular, overlapping like roof tiles. Planted widely throughout the islands, they are all protected and special permission is necessary before they can be felled. Captain Cook on his second round-the-world voyage in the 1770s discovered them and enthused about their potential use for ships' masts but sadly the wood proved too spongy and heavy. In their natural state they grow to 60m with a trunk circumference of over 8m on dry but fertile shallow volcanic soils. This drought tolerance the Victorians soon realised made it an ideal house plant when young, and it is again coming back into fashion. Dating back to the Jurassic period 225 million years ago, they were browsed by dinosaurs, but in the Azores they are vulnerable to lightning strikes.

Appendix 3

FISH ON THE MENU

There are some 50 species of fish found in the waters around the Azores that can be eaten. Those more likely to be found in the islands' restaurants are detailed below in alphabetical order according to their Azorean common name. Resilience is an indication of how much exploitation a species can tolerate and how long a minimum population takes to double in time. Very low = more than 14 years; Low = 4.5–14 years; Medium = 1.4–4.4 years.

Abrótea Greater forkbeard *Phycis blennoides*. Commonly up to 45cm, max 110cm long, max weight 3.5kg. Found over sand and mud bottoms, a deep-water fish 10–800m, usually seen in caves, very shy, gentle fish; young more coastal. Feeds on crustaceans and fish. Eastern Atlantic, Iceland down to west Africa, and the Mediterranean. Resilience medium. Served as transverse steaks or filleted.

Atum Tuna or tunny. Three different ones are commonly eaten in the Azores: *Thunnus obesus* is mostly squeezed into tins while albacora, yellowfin tuna, *Thunnus albacares*, and Bonito, skipjack tuna, *Katsuwonus pelamis,* are served under Atum in restaurants. The yellowfin tuna reaches a max size of around 230cm and weight of about 180kg, and the skipjack 90cm and 23kg.

Badejo Island grouper *Mycteroperca fusca*. Max size 80cm, max weight 3kg. Subtropical, found above rocky areas, depth down to 200m. Azores, Madeira, Canaries and Cape Verde Islands. Resilience low. Served stewed, maybe grilled or baked in the oven.

Bicuda Yellowmouth barracuda *Sphyraena viridensis*. Max size 128cm, max weight 8.2kg. Depth 0–100m. Tropical, eastern central Atlantic. Feeds on fish, cephalopods and crustaceans. Resilence low. Eaten best as a transverse steak, also whole baked in the oven.

Boca Negra Blackbelly rosefish *Helicolenus dactylopterus*. Max size 47cm, max weight 1.5kg, reportedly living for around 40 years. Depth 50–1,100m. Deep-water fish found in soft bottomed areas of continental shelf and upper slope, feeds on crustaceans, fish, cephalopods. Venomous. Eastern Atlantic Iceland to South Africa, western Atlantic. Resilience very low. Served whole, good grilled or fried.

Bodião vermelho Ballan wrasse *Labrus bergylta*. Max size 65cm, max weight just over 4kg. Found around rocks and offshore reefs to a depth of 50m. Feeds on crustaceans and molluscs. Eastern Atlantic. Born first as female, then change sex after 4-plus years old. Resilience low. Served grilled.

Cherne Wreckfish *Polyprion americanus*. Max size 210cm, max weight 100kg. Deep water (40–600m), solitary, likes caves and shipwrecks. Feeds on large crustaceans, cephalopods and fish. Wide distribution, eastern and western Atlantic, southwest Pacific. Resilience low. Best served as transverse steaks, when thick and simply grilled a gastronomic highlight.

Chicharro Blue jack mackerel *Trachurus picturatus*. Max size 60cm. Depth to 270m, a schooling species favouring shallow coastal waters of islands, banks and sea mounts, feeds on crustaceans. Eastern Atlantic, Bay of Biscay down to Tristan da Cunha. Resilience medium. Eaten small, about 10cm, fried really crispy they are quite yummy.

Espada Silver scabbardfish *Lepidopus caudatus*. Max size 2m, max weight 8kg. Depth 100–600m. A deep-water school-forming fish found usually over muddy or sandy bottoms and migrates into midwater at night, when it is most often caught. Eastern Atlantic France to South Africa, southern Indian Ocean, southwest and southeast Pacific. Feeds on crustaceans, squid and fish. Resilience medium. Eaten as fillets.

Espadarte Swordfish *Xiphias gladius*. Max size 4.5m, max weight 650kg. Depth 0–800m. Oceanic, occasionally in coastal waters. Migrate to temperate or cold waters in summer, return to warmer waters in autumn. Feed on fish, also crustaceans and squid, using their sword to kill prey. Atlantic, Indian and Pacific oceans. Resilience low. Usually served as a transverse steak, too often cut measly thin; like a good beefsteak, it should be thick.

Garoupa Blacktail comber *Serranus atricauda*. Max size 43cm. Depth 1–90m, found over hard bottom; carnivorous, distributed eastern Atlantic. Resilience low. Served whole, usually grilled.

Goraz Garapau or Peixão Blackspot seabream *Pagellus bogaraveo*. Maximum size 70cm, max weight 4kg. Inshore waters to a depth of 700m, feeds on crustaceans, molluscs, worms and fish. Eastern Atlantic. Resilience low. Served grilled or baked in the oven. Locally regarded by some as 'horrible'.

Mero Dusky grouper *Epinephelus marginatus*. Max size 150cm, max weight 60kg. Depth 8–300m, subtropical, likes reefs and rocky bottoms, solitary and territorial, feeds on crabs, octopus and fish. Eastern Atlantic and western Indian Ocean, and western Atlantic. Resilience low, endangered. Served as fillets rather than steaks but also good poached or cooked in the oven.

Pargo Common seabream *Pagrus pagrus*. Max size 91cm, max weight 7.7kg. Depth down to 250m. Subtropical, found over rock or sandy bottoms, feeds on crustaceans, fish and molluscs. Eastern Atlantic north to the British Isles, western Atlantic, down to Argentina. Resilience medium, endangered. Served whole or as transverse steaks. Excellent covered with sea salt and oven baked.

Rocaz Large-scaled scorpion fish *Scorpaena scrofa*. Max size 50cm, max weight 2.9kg. Depth 20–500m. Subtropical, solitary, sedentary over rocky, sandy or muddy bottoms, feeds on fish, crustaceans and molluscs. Venomous. Eastern Atlantic. Resilience low. Very expensive but very nice! Served whole, grilled or poached.

Salmonete Striped red mullet *Mullus surmuletus*. Max size 40cm, max weight 1kg. Depth less than 100m. Found over rocky places and also sand and soft bottoms, feeds on shrimps, molluscs and fish. Eastern Atlantic. Resilience medium. Eaten whole.

Serra Atlantic bonito *Sarda sarda*. Max size 90cm, max weight 11kg. Depth range 80–200m, subtropical schooling species, cannibalistic, feeds on squid, shrimps and fish. Widespread Atlantic. Resilience medium. Served as fillets or transverse steaks.

Appendix 4

MAPS

Azores Road Map – AK9302, published by Freytag & Brendt. Folded map, scale 1:75,000. ISBN 3850843157. A topographical double-sided road map; £5.99.

Azores, published by Turinta in their regional series. Folded map, scale 1.75,000. ISBN 9895560435. A topographical map of the islands with tourist information; £6.95.

Portuguese Military Topographical Maps, scale 1:25,000. 36 unfolded maps covering all the islands, £12.95 each, available from Maps Worldwide Ltd, Datum House, Lancaster Rd, Melksham, Wilts SN12 6TL; ℡ 01225 707004; www.mapsworldwide.com.

BOOKS There are publications on selected technical topics about the Azores, but they are almost all in Portuguese. In English there is virtually nothing specific to the Azores, but there are several coffee-table books for sale in the local shops; possibly the best one because it has excellent photos and an informative text is:

de Frias Martins, António M *The Azores, Isles of Blue and Green* Ribeiro and Caravana, 2000; ISBN 971 97803 5 8.

For much more than a century there have been narrative accounts of authors' travels through the islands, but they, of course, are long out of print and very hard to locate.

Nemésio, Vitorino *Mau tempo no Canal* (1944), translated as *Stormy Isles: An Azorean Tale* (1998), ISBN 0 943722 24 1. Nemésio's novel provides intriguing windows into early 20th-century Azorean life and society, with coastal whaling at times a prominent feature. It is a story of unrequited love and two warring families in locations on Pico, Faial and São Jorge, and the intervening channels, and may still be available in Ponta Delgada bookshops.

Nature and conservation

São Viallelle *Dolphins and Whales from the Azores* Espaço Talasso, Azores, 1997. ISBN 972 8412 02 9. A small field guide with summary descriptions and photos of 21 species found in the Azores.

Schäfer, Hanno *Flora of the Azores*. Margraf Verlag, Weikersheim, 2002. ISBN 3 8236 1368 5. In English. 380 colour photographs and brief description of 650 native and introduced species.

Soares de Albergaria, Isabel *Azores Parks and Gardens* Argumentum, Lisbon, 2005. ISBN 9728489387. Pbk, available from Azores bookshops. In the format of a travel guide the 66 descriptions are liberally illustrated by excellent small photographs, old postcards and engravings, together with location maps and opening times. Most interesting and informative is the introduction in which the historical and social background sets the scene for most intriguing snippets appearing in the individual garden descriptions.

ARTICLE

Alfrey, P 'American vagrants on the island of Corvo, Azores', 2005, Birding World 18(11): 465–74.

WEBSITES

www.drtacores.pt Official Department of Tourism site offers history, geography and information on climate, travel, sporting holidays, museums and culture in English, German, French and Portuguese.

www.visitazores.org Site in English and Portuguese giving travel agents, accommodation, etc, run by the Azores Tourist Association.

www.destinazores.com Simple 'guidebook' in English, German and Portuguese giving very limited background information plus some accommodation and eating places.

www.transmacor.pt For details of inter-island ferry services.

www.sata.pt For inter-island flight schedules.

www.bbc.co.uk/weather/world/country_guides Select Portugal and follow links for a five-day forecast for the Azores.

www.weatheronline.co.uk For a seven-day wind and sunshine weather forecast (good before climbing Pico). From the homepage select 'sailing', then 'Europe', then 'Atlantic route' and finally 'Azores'.

www.montanheiros.com Site of the Sociedade de Exploração Espeleoligica whose headquarters are in Terceira, see page 114.

www.teatromicaelense.pt For programme details of the theatre in Ponta Delgada.

www.wdcs.org Whale and Dolphin Conservation Society, the world's most active charity dedicated to the conservation and welfare of all whales, dolphins and porpoises.

http://whale.wheelock.edu/whalenet-stuff/Azores Shows satellite tagging observation maps for sperm whales in the Azores, part of a programme to monitor migration of selected species.

www.horta.uac.pt University of the Azores, Department of Oceanography and Fisheries.

www.azores-ecocentre.org Website of the Azores Ecocentre. This page is not currently available.

www.cineclube.org For information on films being shown in the Horta theatre; see page 166 for details.

www.flytap.com For flights throughout the year via Lisbon to the Azores.

Bradt Travel Guides

www.bradtguides.com

Africa

Africa Overland	£15.99
Benin	£14.99
Botswana: Okavango, Chobe, Northern Kalahari	£15.99
Burkina Faso	£14.99
Cape Verde Islands	£13.99
Canary Islands	£13.95
Cameroon	£13.95
Eritrea	£12.95
Ethiopia	£15.99
Gabon, São Tomé, Príncipe	£13.95
Gambia, The	£13.99
Ghana	£13.95
Johannesburg	£6.99
Kenya	£14.95
Madagascar	£14.95
Malawi	£13.99
Mali	£13.95
Mauritius, Rodrigues & Réunion	£13.99
Mozambique	£12.95
Namibia	£14.95
Niger	£14.99
Nigeria	£15.99
Rwanda	£14.99
Seychelles	£14.99
Sudan	£13.95
Tanzania, Northern	£13.99
Tanzania	£16.99
Uganda	£13.95
Zambia	£15.95
Zanzibar	£12.99

Britain and Europe

Albania	£13.99
Armenia, Nagorno Karabagh	£13.99
Azores	£13.99
Baltic Capitals: Tallinn, Riga, Vilnius, Kaliningrad	£12.99
Belgrade	£6.99
Bosnia & Herzegovina	£13.99
Bratislava	£6.99
Budapest	£7.95
Cork	£6.95
Croatia	£12.95
Cyprus see North Cyprus	
Czech Republic	£13.99
Dubrovnik	£6.95
Eccentric Britain	£13.99
Eccentric Cambridge	£6.99
Eccentric Edinburgh	£5.95
Eccentric France	£12.95
Eccentric London	£12.95
Eccentric Oxford	£5.95
Estonia	£12.95
Faroe Islands	£13.95
Hungary	£14.99
Kiev	£7.95
Latvia	£13.99
Lille	£6.99

Lithuania	£13.99
Ljubljana	£6.99
Macedonia	£13.95
Montenegro	£13.99
North Cyprus	£12.99
Paris, Lille & Brussels	£11.95
Riga	£6.95
River Thames, In the Footsteps of the Famous	£10.95
Serbia	£13.99
Slovenia	£12.99
Spitsbergen	£14.99
Switzerland: Rail, Road, Lake	£13.99
Tallinn	£6.99
Ukraine	£13.95
Vilnius	£6.99

Middle East, Asia and Australasia

Georgia	£13.95
Great Wall of China	£13.99
Iran	£14.99
Iraq	£14.95
Kabul	£9.95
Maldives	£13.99
Mongolia	£14.95
North Korea	£13.95
Oman	£13.99
Palestine, Jerusalem	£12.95
Sri Lanka	£13.99
Syria	£13.99
Tasmania	£12.95
Tibet	£13.99
Turkmenistan	£14.99

The Americas and the Caribbean

Amazon, The	£14.95
Argentina	£15.99
Bolivia	£14.99
Cayman Islands	£12.95
Costa Rica	£13.99
Chile	£16.95
Chile & Argentina: Trekking	£12.95
Eccentric America	£13.95
Eccentric California	£13.99
Falkland Islands	£13.95
Peru & Bolivia: Backpacking and Trekking	£12.95
Panama	£13.95
St Helena, Ascension, Tristan da Cunha	£14.95
USA by Rail	£13.99

Wildlife

Antarctica: Guide to the Wildlife	£14.95
Arctic: Guide to the Wildlife	£15.99
British Isles: Wildlife of Coastal Waters	£14.95
Galápagos Wildlife	£15.99
Madagascar Wildlife	£14.95
Southern African Wildlife	£18.95
Sri Lankan Wildlife	£15.99

Health

Your Child Abroad: A Travel Health Guide	£10.95

Index